Churchill's Eagles

Churchill's Eagles

The RAF's Leading Air Marshals of the Second World War

Richard Mead

Pen & Sword
AVIATION

First published in Great Britain in 2024 by
Pen & Sword Aviation
An imprint of Pen & Sword Books Limited
Yorkshire – Philadelphia

Copyright © Richard Mead 2024

ISBN 978 1 03610 413 9

The right of Richard Mead to be identified as
Author of this Work has been asserted by him in accordance
with the Copyright, Designs and Patents Act 1988.

A CIP catalogue record for this book is
available from the British Library

All rights reserved. No part of this book may be reproduced or
transmitted in any form or by any means, electronic or mechanical
including photocopying, recording or by any information storage and
retrieval system, without permission from the Publisher in writing.

Typeset by Mac Style
Printed in the UK by CPI Group (UK) Ltd, Croydon, CR0 4YY.

Pen & Sword Books Limited incorporates the imprints of After
the Battle, Atlas, Archaeology, Aviation, Discovery, Family History,
Fiction, History, Maritime, Military, Military Classics, Politics,
Select, Transport, True Crime, Air World, Frontline Publishing, Leo
Cooper, Remember When, Seaforth Publishing, The Praetorian Press,
Wharncliffe Local History, Wharncliffe Transport, Wharncliffe True
Crime and White Owl.

For a complete list of Pen & Sword titles please contact

PEN & SWORD BOOKS LIMITED
47 Church Street, Barnsley, South Yorkshire, S70 2AS, England
E-mail: enquiries@pen-and-sword.co.uk
Website: www.pen-and-sword.co.uk
or
PEN AND SWORD BOOKS
1950 Lawrence Rd, Havertown, PA 19083, USA
E-mail: uspen-and-sword@casematepublishers.com
Website: www.penandswordbooks.com

Contents

Acknowledgements	vii

Introduction	1
The origins of the RFC and the RNAS	5
The RNAS 1914–18	6
The RFC Western Front 1914–18	8
The RFC elsewhere 1914–18	11
The Trenchard Years 1918–29	12
The Locust Years 1930–33	15
The Expansion Years 1933–39	17
The Home Commands 1939–45	21
The Overseas Commands and Air Forces 1939–45	28

The Air Marshals	34
Arthur Barratt	34
Donald Bennett	42
Norman Bottomley	51
Frederick Bowhill	59
Harry Broadhurst	65
Ralph Cochrane	73
Arthur Coningham	84
William Dickson	95
Sholto Douglas	103
Hugh Dowding	114
William Elliott	126
Basil Embry	135
Douglas Evill	145
Wilfrid Freeman	153
Guy Garrod	162
Arthur Harris	171
Roderick Hill	182
Leslie Hollinghurst	190
Philip Joubert	198
Trafford Leigh-Mallory	207

vi   Churchill's Eagles

Hugh Lloyd	214
Arthur Longmore	221
Edgar Ludlow-Hewitt	226
Cyril Newall	232
Keith Park	236
Richard Peirse	245
Charles Portal	251
John Robb	260
Jack Slessor	266
Arthur Tedder	276
Appendix – Other Leading Air Marshals	284
Abbreviations	292
Bibliography	295

Acknowledgements

I would like to thank Charles Hewitt, the Managing Director of Pen & Sword, for agreeing to publish yet another of my books, and Matt Jones, the Production Manager, for handling the process of publication so smoothly. George Chamier has once again been my editor and I am most grateful to him for his pleasingly light touch.

Introduction

My first book, published in 2007, was the result of very many years of research. *Churchill's Lions* described the Second World War careers of 125 British generals, including nineteen who were officers of the Indian Army and two who were Royal Marines. Between them they covered all the land campaigns undertaken by the British Empire against Germany, Italy and Japan, with the exception of those in the South-West Pacific which were carried out by Australian and New Zealand ground and air forces.

Many of the generals covered in *Churchill's Lions* had either written an autobiography themselves or attracted a biographer, but the majority had not. I therefore followed it up by writing the first full-scale biographies of three of them, all of whom I regarded as particularly important, but none of whom had put pen to paper themselves or had others do it for them. Although the large majority of the remainder were still theoretically available for the same treatment, I doubted that any of them would arouse sufficient interest amongst readers or, perhaps more pertinently, amongst publishers.

I therefore decided to focus elsewhere. My knowledge of the exploits of the leading flag officers of the Royal Navy during the Second World War was enough to tell me that all the most important or interesting ones had already found biographers or, in some cases, had written their own stories. I thus turned my attention to the RAF, about which I knew at that time much less than I did about either of the two older services, but which seemed to offer more promise. My first choice as a biographical subject, Marshal of the Royal Air Force the Lord Elworthy, was actually four years younger than the youngest general in *Churchill's Lions* and, although he rose to the rank of acting air commodore and did important work during the War, he was only to achieve prominence twenty or so years later.

The officer whom Elworthy most admired during his long service career was Air Chief Marshal the Hon. Sir Ralph Cochrane, under whom he had served on three occasions during the War, becoming in due course his Senior Air Staff Officer at 5 Group Bomber Command, and it was Cochrane who became the fifth of my full-scale biographical subjects. I learnt a very great

2 Churchill's Eagles

deal about the RAF as a result of my research into the careers of both these two men, although, as both Cochrane and Elworthy spent the entire war in the UK, the former mostly and the latter exclusively in Bomber Command, they were not by themselves representative of the very wide range of the third service's operations between 1939 and 1945.

From research for my other books, which in addition to the biographies included a study of Field Marshal Montgomery's wartime staff, I already knew how vital, indeed at times decisive, the RAF's contribution had been to the campaigns undertaken by British armed forces as a whole, over both land and sea. It seemed to me that this wide diversity could be illustrated by looking at the careers of the service's wartime leaders, in much the same way as I had done many years previously with *Churchill's Lions*. As in that book, the subjects would have to include the Great Men of the War – Portal, Tedder, Dowding, Harris and a few others who were household names at the time – but the majority would be relatively unknown to all except those with a deep interest in the subject. There would not be anything like the number covered in my earlier book. In terms of personnel, the RAF at its height was just over third of the size of the British Army and less than a quarter of that of the British and Indian Armies combined: in the light of this, thirty senior airmen seemed to be about the right number.

Why, once again, include Churchill in the title, other than for purely commercial reasons? It must be said that, with the exception of the Battle of Britain and the Battle of the Atlantic, the bulk of the Prime Minister's attention throughout the war was devoted to the land campaigns, as he recognized that it was only by occupying the territories of the Axis powers that victory could be achieved. His exasperation with the leadership of the armies in the field up to the summer of 1942 caused him to sack many of his senior generals, until he found those who were going to deliver victory. Churchill had himself campaigned as a soldier in the last decade of the nineteenth century and had also served as First Lord of the Admiralty in both world wars and as Secretary of State for War and Air in the aftermath of the Great War: he thus believed, often incorrectly and to the despair of the General and Naval Staffs and senior commanders, that he understood how armies and navies operated, but he seldom made the same assumption about air operations.

Churchill did, however, recognize the importance of air warfare from its very early days. During his time at the Admiralty in the run-up to the Great War, he was largely responsible for the formation of the Royal Naval Air Service. Moreover, whilst the War Office insisted in the early days on procuring all its aircraft from the Royal Aircraft Factory, Churchill was keen to utilize the skills of the private sector in design and manufacturing. This meant that the RNAS was equipped with technically advanced machines from Sopwith and other companies well ahead of the RFC. At the end of the Great War he was instrumental, as Secretary of State for War and Air, in the preservation of the independence of the newly founded RAF, whilst, as Secretary of State for the Colonies shortly afterwards, he found a role for the young service as a cost-effective policeman in troublesome parts of the Empire. On the back benches in the 1930s he was vociferous in his calls for air defence to be significantly expanded in the light of German re-armament.

In spite of his giving priority to land and sea operations, Churchill was far from uninterested in the RAF, for which he entertained a considerable regard, although this was tempered to some extent by political expediency, as demonstrated by his attempt to distance himself from the destruction caused by the bombing campaign in the last year of the War and particularly the raid on Dresden in mid-February 1945. He certainly knew most of the subjects of this book and some of them very well. As an indication of his identification with the service he frequently appeared throughout the War in RAF uniform, having been appointed Honorary Air Commodore of 615 (County of Surrey) Squadron, Auxiliary Air Force in 1939. On 1 April 1943, the twenty-fifth anniversary of the establishment of the RAF as an independent service, the Air Council very astutely awarded him honorary wings – the badge being otherwise reserved exclusively for those who had qualified as pilots – which he greatly appreciated.

My choice of the thirty air officers to write about has been entirely personal. Many of them chose themselves by virtue of the high appointments which they held during the War. On the other hand, a few men who held very senior jobs were excluded, notably some members of the Air Council. In particular, I left out three who were unquestionably important, two serving successively as Air Member for Personnel, Philip Babington and Bertine Sutton, and one as Air Member for Supply and Organisation, Christopher Courtney. Courtney actually held the appointment for the entire period of hostilities except the first four months. He would have relieved Hugh Dowding as AOC-in-C of Fighter Command in 1939 had it not been for the injuries he suffered when the aircraft in which he was returning from Northern Ireland crashed into a mountain in Cumbria. These three men all did excellent work, as did Ralph Sorley, who sat as an additional member of the Air Council from March 1943 to October 1945 as Controller of Research and Development at the Ministry of Aircraft Production. Sorley's most important contribution

4 Churchill's Eagles

to victory, however, had actually occurred many years earlier when he was largely responsible for the new generation of fighters in the late 1930s being equipped with eight machine guns instead of the two which had hitherto been regarded by the RAF hierarchy as sufficient. However, it is difficult to write very much about any of them, and the same applies to some of those who led Training Command, later divided into Flying and Technical Training Commands, and Maintenance Command.

The substantial majority of my subjects were born in the 1890s. The oldest, Frederick Bowhill, was born in 1880 and retired in 1942, only to be brought back to run the new Transport Command. Dowding, born in 1882, should have retired before the War, but was kept on, firstly because of Courtney's injury and then because he was seen to be essential to Fighter Command. At the other end of the age scale are three men who, unlike all the others, were born in the twentieth century and were thus too young to have served in the Royal Flying Corps, the Royal Naval Air Service or the new Royal Air Force during the Great War. Donald Bennett, Harry Broadhurst and Basil Embry nevertheless all represent important facets of the RAF's wartime operations.

The section on each officer is substantially devoted to his career during the Second World War, but I have also provided a description of his service during the Great War, the inter-war years and the post-war years. I have shown both the highest rank achieved up to 2 September 1945 and the ultimate rank achieved during his career, where it is different, together with the orders and decorations awarded during the officer's lifetime.

In addition to the thirty officers whose careers are described in the main part of the book, many others are mentioned, and the wartime careers of a number of those who attained the rank of air vice-marshal and above are set out in tabular form in an Appendix. In such cases, on the first occasion that they are mentioned in each section, their names are shown in italics.

In order to set the scene for the reader, I have begun by describing briefly the formation and operations of the RFC and the RNAS up to the time of their merger into the RAF, and of the RAF itself for the brief remainder of the Great War, then the long and difficult period between the two world wars when it was both fighting for its independence and preparing for the next conflict at a time of huge budgetary pressure. I have also written a brief description of each fighting command and of each major superior overseas command or other formation in which the RAF participated.

As I had found with *Churchill's Lions*, my admiration for my biographical subjects grew significantly with the telling of their stories. Like the British and Indian Armies, the RAF began the War ill-equipped relative to their two most professional foes, the Germans and the Japanese, although there was one merciful exception, the decision to equip the squadrons of Fighter Command with two outstanding aircraft, the Spitfire and the Hurricane, in numbers sufficient to lead to victory in the Battle of Britain. Other deficiencies were largely remedied by late 1943, not only by the introduction of much better British aircraft, notably the Lancaster and the Mosquito, but also with the decision to buy American aircraft when these were suitable. Churchill's appeal to Roosevelt before the United States entered the War – 'Give us the tools and we will finish the job' – was particularly relevant to the 'Eagles' of the RAF.

Although it encountered many setbacks during the course of the Second World War, the RAF developed into an outstandingly effective organization, which played an immense role in the defeat of the Axis Powers. That its success relied to a very considerable extent on the high quality of its senior officers is, I hope, clearly demonstrated in this book.

The origins of the Royal Flying Corps and the Royal Naval Air Service

The history of heavier-than-air flight began at Kitty Hawk, North Carolina on the bitterly cold morning of 17 December 1903, when Orville Wright flew a powered bi-plane, *The Flyer*, for the modest distance of 120 feet. By the end of that day, he and his brother Wilbur had made three further flights, each longer than its predecessor and the last one of 852 feet. Whilst the fragile aircraft was too damaged to continue any further, the principle had been established, and the brothers went on to design and construct other aircraft, each one more sophisticated and practicable than its predecessor.

A few far-sighted individuals recognized the military applications of powered fixed-wing aircraft at an early date, but it took governments, not least the British Government, a great deal longer. It was not until 1908 that British Army Aeroplane No. 1 was acquired, designed by Samuel F. Cody, the son of 'Buffalo Bill' Cody. This aircraft crashed on its first outing, and official interest waned again. In the following year, however, Louis Blériot made the first crossing of the English Channel by air, an event with serious implications for the defence of Great Britain. Blériot's own country, France, already took the possibilities of employing aeroplanes in a military context more seriously than the British. Major Frederick Sykes, a qualified pilot who was the British observer at the 1911 annual manoeuvres of the French Army,

6   Churchill's Eagles

reported back on the advances which had been made, and this, together with growing concerns about German aggression in the aftermath of the Agadir incident in the same year, caused the War Office to take notice at last. The Royal Flying Corps, consisting of a Military Wing and a Naval Wing, was created by royal warrant on 13 April 1912,

The British Army already had another interest in aviation. As far back as in 1878 the Royal Engineers had established the Army Balloon Equipment Store at Woolwich, and this expanded over the next few decades from tethered and free-flying balloons into powered airships. Cody himself was involved with the first of these, *Nulli Secundus*, which had its maiden flight in September 1907. Spurred on by the evident success of the German Zeppelin programme, a number of other airships were also designed and tested, although these were not rigid airships with a frame like the Zeppelins, but either non-rigid, with a self-supporting envelope, or semi-rigid, with a keel but no other frame. They were largely unsuccessful and, at the beginning of 1914, the four that remained were transferred to the Royal Navy, which thereafter took over responsibility for all lighter-than-air aviation.

The Navy's involvement with airships had, in fact, only post-dated the Army's by two years. Its first attempt at a design of its own was a rigid airship, the *Mayfly*, which seemed satisfactory at first, but which broke up disastrously in the air in September 1911. Thereafter, the service relied initially on imports from France and Germany and, in due course, on the four airships transferred from the Army.

In 1911 the Royal Navy had also made a very modest commitment to heavier-than-air aviation by selecting four of its officers for a flying course, which was delivered by instructors provided by the Royal Aero Club. These officers, together with a number of others who followed them, became in due course the core of the Naval Wing of the RFC when it was established in 1912; an Air Department was formed at the Admiralty at the same time. From the earliest days the Naval Wing styled itself as the Royal Naval Air Service, with the full encouragement of Winston Churchill as the First Lord of the Admiralty, and on 1 July 1914 it was formally placed under Admiralty control.

The RNAS 1914–18

The prime roles of the RNAS on the outbreak of war were to carry out maritime reconnaissance over the English Channel and the North Sea from bases in both England and France, and to attack and destroy German warships, including submarines. It must be said that they were more successful in the former role, but they did provide a very useful appendage to the ships of the Royal Navy, engaged in particular in combatting the U–Boat menace. Moreover, RNAS aircraft also attacked naval bases, not only those in relatively close proximity to the fighting taking place in France, but also further afield on the coast of Germany, by deploying seaplanes and later primitive aircraft carriers.

The RNAS was particularly fortunate to have established temporarily the rights to aircraft manufactured by Sopwith. This meant that it had first call on some of the most advanced fighting planes of their time, notably the 1½ Strutter, Pup, Triplane and Camel, at times when these would have been most useful to the RFC.

The RNAS was formed into wings from the beginning of the War, the first of which were deployed to France, where they established themselves in airfields close to the Channel coast. Its aircraft were active in bombing German naval bases as well as in defending against enemy intruders, and they did valuable work in the early days by covering the Allied retreat from Antwerp and Ostend, in which RNAS Rolls-Royce armoured cars were also prominent. The aircraft were also employed in attacking both Zeppelins (indeed, they scored the first ever success against the airships) and aircraft engaged in bombing targets in England.

Two wings of the RNAS were also sent to the Mediterranean, where they were engaged in the Gallipoli campaign and subsequently in Macedonia and Palestine. One wing based in Southern Italy and Malta was also employed in searching for enemy submarines in the Adriatic and the Mediterranean.

The RNAS had assumed all responsibility for airship development and employment in early 1914, using not only its own collection of airships, but also the four transferred from the RFC. The German U-boats began to pose a serious threat to cross-Channel shipping and, in early 1915, the Admiralty called for designs of new models of airship which could be manufactured relatively cheaply and in quantity. The first of these, the Submarine Scout, was a non-rigid airship with a 60,000 cu. ft. envelope, below which was slung the fuselage of a BE.2. The size of the envelope was gradually increased in subsequent models, whilst new larger classes, the Coastal and the North Sea, were also built using trilobe envelopes. The North Sea had an envelope of 360,000 cu. ft. and an enclosed car holding a crew of ten, who were provided with sleeping accommodation, a necessary amenity for flights which could last up to 48 hours.

8   Churchill's Eagles

The expansion of the airship service called for a great increase in aircrew, but volunteers from the Royal Navy were quick to apply. The results in terms of German U-boats and other ships destroyed were very modest, but the mere presence of an airship over a convoy was often sufficient to keep the submarines at bay, and as a deterrent they made a valuable contribution to the war at sea around the British Isles

Further work also began on rigid airships, production of which had been halted after the loss of the *Mayfly* in 1911. Vickers submitted plans for the 23 Class, which was designed in the company's Barrow works, much of the work being carried out by a talented young engineer named Barnes Wallis. The airships were built both there by Vickers itself and elsewhere by sub-contractors. The capture of a downed Zeppelin nearly intact in September 1916, however, provided proof that the 23 Class was outdated, and work began on new and larger classes, although none of these were ready in time to see action before the Armistice. Neither was the sole semi-rigid airship, acquired from the Italians, which arrived in the UK just in time for the Armistice in November 1918.

The RFC on the Western Front 1914–18

At the time of the declaration of war by Great Britain on Germany on 4 August 1914, the RFC comprised the former Military Wing, the Royal Aircraft Factory at Farnborough and the Central Flying School at Upavon. The first of these consisted of four fully-equipped squadrons, Nos 2, 3, 4 and 5, each of thirteen aircraft, whilst another two were forming and No. 1 Squadron, which had been originally equipped with balloons, was converting to aircraft. Several types were in use, including BE2s manufactured by the Royal Aircraft Factory, Sopwith Tabloids, Avro 504s, Farman bi-planes and Blériot monoplanes. All of these were dispatched to France under the command of Brigadier General Sir David Henderson, with Frederick Sykes initially as his Chief of Staff and then as second-in-command.

Initially, the RFC was engaged almost entirely in reconnaissance for the British Expeditionary Force and proved its value almost immediately when it reported that the BEF was about to be trapped by two German armies, a fate avoided only by an immediate retreat from Mons in the last week of August. The small force demonstrated its worth yet again when it identified a German thrust to the east of Paris, allowing the French to avoid being enveloped themselves and instead to deliver a strong counter-attack on the River Marne.

After the First Battle of Ypres, when the opposing armies fought themselves to a standstill at the end of 'the race to the sea', the RFC, now fully recognized as a valuable resource, was able both to reorganize – spare parts in particular had posed a real problem and the squadrons had often only been able to keep going by using French equipment – and to redefine its role. There was a significant change in structure when wings of between two and four squadrons were created, each of which was allocated to a corps within the BEF, or sometimes to two neighbouring corps. It was by this time clearly recognized that every unit must be composed of aircraft of the same type, although this was to take some time to achieve.

In the meantime, as the 'New Army' was being formed to replace the 'Old BEF', which had been decimated at Ypres, the RFC was significantly enlarged. For the squadrons in the field, observation continued to be their primary purpose, together with specific artillery spotting. Instead of reporting on enemy movements, of which there were few, as the front had settled down to a static line, the focus was on mapping the enemy trenches, helped by the early use of aerial photography. Contact with enemy aircraft was infrequent, and the earliest aircraft were essentially unarmed, although pilots and observers carried rifles and pistols. Some early attempts were made to bomb the enemy, but these were primitive and ineffective.

In August 1915 Henderson was posted back to the War Office, where he ably represented the RFC on the Army Council. His relief was Brigadier General Hugh Trenchard, who was now on his way to becoming the towering figure of British military aviation in its first decade-and-a-half. Trenchard had spent much of his army career in Africa, but had learnt to fly on his return to the UK and had been appointed first as Deputy Commander of the Central Flying School and then as Commander of the Military Wing of the RFC. He was subsequently posted to France in command of No. 1 Wing prior to taking over from Henderson. He was already on good terms with General Sir Douglas Haig, who was to succeed Field Marshal Sir John French in command of all the British forces in France in December 1915.

During the summer of 1915 a new German aircraft made an appearance, the Fokker *Eindecker* (monoplane). This was equipped with a forward-facing machine gun, synchronized to fire through its propeller, a considerable advance on handheld weapons. The 'Fokker Scourge' as the aerial offensive mounted by these aircraft was called, initially wreaked havoc on the inadequately armed British planes. These were rapidly fitted with Lewis guns to be fired by the observer, which limited the German ascendancy, but it was not until the arrival of the Sopwith 1½ Strutter in May 1916, armed

10   Churchill's Eagles

not only with a machine gun for the observer, but also with one geared to fire through the propeller, that the fighters were on level terms, at least temporarily.

As the numbers of squadrons grew, so did the organization. The wings were now placed under brigades, two wings to each. In addition to the wings, each brigade incorporated an aircraft park, whose stores were sufficient to supply all the squadrons' requirements for a month, whilst depots were established in rear areas to cater for additional reserves of engines, armament and other equipment.

Trenchard was nothing if not offensively minded, and during the Battle of the Somme in the summer of 1916 the fight was carried vigorously to the enemy. In the autumn, however, the Germans not only introduced two excellent new bi-plane fighters, the Albatros and Halberstadt D-type, but also tactics devised for its *Jagdstaffeln* (fighter squadrons) which were specifically designed to destroy Allied fighters. This enabled them to begin to establish air superiority during the winter, a result substantially achieved by the spring of the following year in time for the German strategic withdrawal to the Hindenburg Line, which was carried out with a minimum of interference from the air by either the British or the French. In order to consolidate their superiority, the Germans then grouped their *Jagdgestaffeln* into much larger *Jagdgeschwader*, the first of which was commanded by Manfred von Richthofen.

This was a difficult time for the RFC, which incurred substantial losses of men and aircraft. These were made up, albeit with some difficulty, and by the time of the Battle of Passchendaele in the late summer of 1917 the RFC squadrons were numerically superior to their German opposite numbers. Moreover, much better aircraft were being introduced, notably the Sopwith Camel and the SE5a, both fighter interceptors which, in the right hands, were a match for any of the contemporary German aircraft, together with the Bristol Fighter, a two-man fighter reconnaissance aircraft which was to prove so good that it remained in service into the early 1930s. Until the end of the War the British fighters remained on better than even terms with the Germans.

Although the air war on the Western Front was dominated by fighters and reconnaissance aircraft, bombers were also introduced. Single-engined De Havilland 4s carried out tactical bombing raids, whilst Handley Page 0/400 heavy bombers attacked more strategic targets such as railway marshalling yards, ammunition dumps and communications centres. There was an important development in the summer of 1918, when the Independent Force was established to carry out bombing raids from France against German cities, in response to the continuing German raids on the United Kingdom.

The Independent Force was commanded by Trenchard, who in January of that year had become the first Chief of the Air Staff following the amalgamation of the RFC and the RNAS into the Royal Air Force, separate from both the Royal Navy and the British Army. Trenchard, however, had a very poor relationship with Lord Rothermere, the Secretary of State for Air, and resigned three months later, to be replaced by Frederick Sykes, by this time a major general. The Independent Force was a relatively small one, eventually comprising nine squadrons of Handley Page 0/400s and De Havilland DH 10 medium bombers, based at the Chateau d'Autigny-la-Tour in Lorraine in the French sector of operations. In its brief history it carried out many bombing raids on the Saar and as far afield as Frankfurt and Bonn, but it lost a large number of aircraft. It cannot be called a great success, but it demonstrated to Trenchard the possibilities of this type of warfare.

The RFC elsewhere 1914–18

Although hostilities on the Western Front required the deployment there of a substantial majority of the RFC's squadrons, it was engaged elsewhere as well.

The most significant operations took place over the UK itself, as the result of a bombing campaign by the Germans, which began in January 1915. This campaign was carried out initially by airships, Zeppelins for the most part, although the first one to be shot down over the UK was a Schütte-Lanz. The airships were much more important for their effect on British morale than for the damage they caused, which was modest. They first appeared over Norfolk in January 1915, with the first raid on London taking place later that year on the night of 31 May/1 June. Further raids followed, mostly on London and the East Coast, but some also on the Midlands.

Although the weight of bombs dropped was very small by later standards, there were many fatalities, the majority of whom were civilians. There was thus, inevitably, a clamour for effective defences to be put in place, comprising anti-aircraft guns, searchlights and fighters. The last of these found it difficult to get up to the altitude required for an attack and next to impossible to see the airships in the hours of darkness. Moreover, their guns did little damage initially and it was not until a satisfactory mix of explosive and incendiary rounds was devised that successes began to mount.

Although Zeppelin raids continued intermittently into 1918, it was recognized by the Germans that these craft had become highly vulnerable

12 Churchill's Eagles

and, from the summer of 1917 onwards, they were substantially replaced by heavy bombers, for the most part the highly effective Gotha G.IV and G.V, but also the giant Zeppelin-Staaken R.VI. Much faster moving and more manoeuvrable than the airships, these posed new challenges for the defences. However, successes by the defenders increased, as a result of which the Germans switched from daylight to night-time bombing in the autumn of 1917. During 1918, however, a more sophisticated defensive system was devised, consisting of belts of AA guns, interspersed with areas patrolled by aircraft, substantially Sopwith Camels and Bristol Fighters, together with a line of barrage balloons placed around the eastern side of London. Moreover, the use of blackouts and shelters in underground stations helped to limit the casualties.

By the standards of 1940–45, the damage done and casualties incurred by these raids were very modest, but the effect on civilian morale had been significant. Nevertheless, some lessons were learnt which would have an impact on the next major conflict.

The other European theatre in which the RFC found itself involved was Italy. The Battle of Caporetto in October and November 1917, for which the Austro-Hungarians were significantly reinforced by experienced German formations, was a major defeat for the Italian Army, which had to be bolstered by the transfer of both British and French divisions in order to stem any further advance into Northern Italy beyond the line of the River Piave. Air force elements accompanied the ground troops to the extent, in the case of the British, of three squadrons of Sopwith Camels, two of R.E.8s and, in the following summer, one of Bristol Fighters, which together gave a good account of themselves.

Other RFC elements were based in Southern Italy to counter the threat of German and Austrian submarines based at Cattaro (now Kotor in Montenegro). Still further afield, the Middle East Brigade of the RFC was formed to supervise air operations against Turkish forces in the Near East, where its aircraft provided support for General Allenby's campaign in Palestine and Syria, as well as those in Mesopotamia and Macedonia, but the numbers of aircraft involved were relatively small and their impact, other than on the morale of the enemy, was only modest.

The Trenchard Years 1918–29

It would be impossible to exaggerate the importance of Hugh Trenchard to the youngest of Great Britain's armed forces. He played an immense role during the Great War as the commander of the RFC on the Western Front from August 1915 to January 1918, when he became Chief of the Air Staff for the first time. His differences with Lord Rothermere caused his resignation, but within months he was back in France at the head of the Independent Force, engaged on bombing industrial targets in Germany. He was brought back to London to lead the RAF in early 1919, shortly after the appointment of Winston Churchill as Secretary of State for War and Air.

The RAF, formed by amalgamating the RFC and RNAS on 1 April 1918, was resented by both of the two senior services, which wanted to bring the appropriate elements back under their control, and it was the Royal Navy which was to prove the more hostile, taking strong exception to the loss of its naval air arm. On a number of occasions in the early 1920s committees were set up or reports commissioned to consider the future of British military aviation, and all of these came down on the side of an independent air force, very substantially due to Trenchard's powers of persuasion. He had one particularly strong argument on his side and it was one which appealed to the Treasury, which held a strong hand in such deliberations at a time of economic retrenchment, following the enormous financial sacrifices of the war years. Trenchard was able to demonstrate that the RAF provided a highly cost-effective solution to the problems of policing certain distant parts of the British Empire. He was strongly supported by Churchill, at the time the Secretary of State for the Colonies.

Trenchard's first success came in the remote territory of British Somaliland, in which a religious leader, Mohammed Abdullah Hassan, nicknamed the 'Mad Mullah', threatened a serious revolt. The War Office proposed sending two divisions to put down the insurgency, but Trenchard promised that the same result could be obtained by colonial troops and a squadron of light bombers. A brief bombing campaign against insurgent villages soon put an end to the uprising, and the Mad Mullah fled the country. Trenchard then repeated the trick on a much larger scale in Iraq, until 1918 a part of the Ottoman Empire, but now a new country under the rule of one of the sons of the Sharif of Mecca, an ally of Great Britain during the Great War. Iraq was threatened by both Kurdish revolt and Turkish incursion, and although ground forces were also employed in some strength, it was the RAF which led a successful campaign, at a fraction of the cost of relying entirely on troops. Trenchard, however, was markedly less successful in India, where the politically powerful Indian Army accorded a low priority to the RAF in its frequent campaigns against the Pathans on the North–West Frontier.

14   Churchill's Eagles

Any hope of more general expansion by the RAF, particularly in the UK itself, was stymied by the 'Ten Year Rule', proposed by none other than Churchill to the then Prime Minister, Lloyd George, in 1919, under which an assumption was made that the United Kingdom would not be obliged to participate in a major war for the next ten years. The Rule was renewed every year and was not finally abandoned until 1932.

Cost thus remained a big issue, and this was partly catered for by a decision to standardize on very few types of aircraft. The excellent Bristol Fighter became the main fighter aircraft, both in the UK and overseas, remaining in service into the early 1930s, although the Sopwith Snipe was also retained for a few years after the Great War, largely for home-based squadrons, and other types were to emerge in the mid-1920s, notably the Armstrong Whitworth Siskin. The light bomber role was given to the DH9a, itself a descendant of the wartime DH4, and it proved to be nearly as long-lived in service as the Bristol Fighter. The standard heavy bomber was the Vickers Vimy and its later derivative, the Vickers Virginia, whilst yet another derivative, the Vickers Vernon, became the RAF's first dedicated transport aircraft. Other types began to see service from the mid-1920s onwards, but the 'Brisfit' (Bristol Fighter), the 'Ninak' (DH9a) and the Vimy family remained at the core of the RAF's establishment of aircraft for the first decade of its existence.

Trenchard realized that it was not only aircraft that were essential to an independent air force, but also the education and training of the men who were to fly them and look after them on the ground. The Central Flying School had been the very first institution to address this, its formation just predating Trenchard's own involvement with it when he became the deputy to the first Commandant, Captain Godfrey Paine RN, in 1912. Trenchard had no connection with the formation of the RNAS Training Establishment, the predecessor of the RAF College at Cranwell, but it was he who established the latter as the primary training institution for RAF officers seeking permanent commissions. He also quickly recognized that the service would require a large number of highly qualified engineers and mechanics and set up the No. 1 School of Technical Training at Halton to teach apprentices everything they would need to know about the repair and maintenance of aircraft.

The other major institution founded by Trenchard was the RAF Staff College, which he considered to be vital to the development of the most promising officers of the rank of flight lieutenant and squadron leader, who would not only learn how to undertake staff duties, but also gain a wider understanding of the service and the other two services as part of their preparation for higher command. The college was opened in Andover in 1922 under the command of one of Trenchard's closest colleagues, Robert Brooke-Popham, who designed the initial syllabus and remained in post for the first four years.

One of Trenchard's most important innovations was the short-service commission, whereby those who were keen to fly, but did not wish to commit themselves to a full-time career, were able to serve in a regular unit for five years, after which they would remain in the Reserve of Air Force Officers. This produced a good source of trained pilots who could be recalled at need. Subsequently, it was decided to recruit directly into the RAFO, whereby those who wanted to learn to fly were trained at schools run by aircraft manufacturers, at the conclusion of which they were awarded commissions and were available for call-up. Trenchard also saw to the creation of the Auxiliary Air Force (later 'Royal'), in which those who were keen on flying or maintaining aircraft in their spare time could be trained and then join an AuxAF squadron, commanded by one of their own but with a regular adjutant, at which they would spend most of their weekends as well as attending an annual summer camp. Finally, there was also direct recruitment into the Special Reserve, in whose squadrons there was a cadre of regular officers and airmen, including the CO, but which did not require the time commitment of the AuxAF.

Trenchard stepped down as CAS on 1 January 1930, having put the RAF on a firm footing, albeit that it remained of modest size. It had earned the admiration of the British public, not only because of its achievements in the Great War, in which the leading air aces had become popular heroes, but also through adroit publicity, achieved to some extent by mounting events such as the annual Hendon Air Pageant, later called the RAF Display. Trenchard had, most importantly of all, managed to fend off the combined opposition of the Royal Navy and the British Army, arguing successfully for the young service's retention as a single independent force, notably by employing the argument that 'the air is one and indivisible'. More difficult times, however, lay ahead.

The Locust Years 1930–33

Trenchard was relieved as CAS by his closest protégé, Air Chief Marshal Sir John Salmond, who was highly regarded throughout the service. Some eight years younger than Trenchard, he had commanded a squadron on

16   Churchill's Eagles

the Western Front in late 1914 and early 1915, before going on to lead a wing and then a brigade, returning to the UK in mid-1917 to reorganize the whole system of flying training. He was then appointed Director General of Military Aeronautics, with a seat on the Army Council, before succeeding Trenchard in command of the RFC, later the RAF, in France. In 1922 he was appointed as the overall commander of the British forces in Iraq, carrying out Trenchard's policy of air control with considerable success. In 1925 he became the AOC-in-C of the RAF's key home command, Air Defence of Great Britain ('ADGB'), before joining Trenchard on the Air Council on 1 January 1929 as Air Member for Personnel.

Salmond's appointment as CAS could not have come at a worse time, coinciding as it did with the start of the Great Depression, following the stock market crash a few months earlier. A minority Labour Government, headed by Ramsay MacDonald and sustained by Liberal support, was in no mood to spend money on the armed forces, whilst the World Disarmament Conference, which opened in 1932, acted as a further disincentive. Throughout the term of Salmond's appointment, the armed services saw no growth in personnel; indeed, it was not until close to the end of the decade that this changed significantly, although much else had improved for the RAF by then in terms of the numbers and quality of its aircraft and ground establishments.

In the meantime, Salmond had to do the best he could with the resources available to him. ADGB was the core of the Metropolitan Air Force, consisting as it did of the Wessex Bombing Area, with its bomber squadrons in the South of England, Norfolk and Lincolnshire, and the Fighting Area with fighter squadrons concentrated around London. Together with the Auxiliary Air Force and the Special Reserve, about forty squadrons were in ADGB at any one time. Also under ADGB's overall command were the AA guns of the Royal Artillery and the part-time volunteer Observer Corps. In addition, there were the Inland Area, with a small number of army cooperation squadrons, and the Coastal Area, with a similar number of flying boat squadrons.

The RAF overseas consisted of Middle East Command (Cairo), Transjordan and Palestine Command (Jerusalem), British Forces in Iraq (Hinaidi, near Baghdad), RAF India (New Delhi), RAF Mediterranean (Malta) and Aden Command, which between them disposed of some thirty squadrons of all types.

By the turn of the decade both the DH9a and the Bristol Fighter had had their day, although some of the former could still be found in service.

The light day-bomber role had been assumed by the Hawker Horsley in the UK and the Fairey IIIF in Egypt, the Sudan and Aden, whilst the general purpose Westland Wapiti equipped most of the squadrons in Iraq and India. All of these were to be overshadowed by the Hawker Hart, an elegant multi-purpose aircraft which was to spawn a number of variants. The heavy bomber role was still filled by the Vickers Virginia, and its replacement in 1933 was yet another heavy bi-plane bomber with an open cockpit, the Handley Page Heyford.

As far as fighters were concerned, the Bristol Bulldog began to replace the 'Brisfit' and the Siskin in 1929. Rugged though it was, it was actually slower than the Hart, leading Hawkers to produce the Demon as a fighter variant of the latter. Not long afterwards the sleek Hawker Fury entered squadron service, the first RAF aircraft to be able to exceed 200 mph in level flight.

Vickers continued to dominate in the transport role. The Valentia followed its predecessors, the Vernon and the Victoria, looking much the same as, but being significantly more capacious than its predecessors.

Salmond's years as CAS proved to be the most difficult ones for the RAF since the Great War, but this was certainly not due to him. It was his misfortune that he reached the top of his profession at a time of significant financial retrenchment by the British Government, accompanied by the constant threat of disarmament. Inevitably, the British Army and the Royal Navy continued their campaigns to gain control of elements of the RAF and, whilst they were unsuccessful, their combined weight meant that the RAF was denied the funds it required to keep up with many foreign air forces, not only the French, the Italian and the American, but also, as would become apparent later, the German.

Salmond was due to be succeeded by his brother Geoffrey, another highly talented officer, but the latter fell seriously ill and died a month later. He therefore remained in post as a caretaker for nearly a month after his official retirement date, pending the appointment as CAS of Air Chief Marshal Sir Edward Ellington.

The Expansion Years 1933–39

In more ways than one Edward Ellington was an unlikely choice to replace Geoffrey Salmond as CAS in March 1933. He had, for a start, no experience of flying operations in the Great War, unlike all his predecessors and his next five successors, although he had learnt to fly in 1912 and was on a course at the Central Flying School when war broke out. Instead, he spent the next

18   Churchill's Eagles

three years as a staff officer in the BEF and at the War Office on duties unrelated to the RFC. In November 1917, however, he was appointed Deputy Director General of Military Aeronautics, before succeeding John Salmond as Director General in January 1918 and, early in the next year, becoming Controller General of Equipment, later renamed Director General of Supply and Research, with a seat on the Air Council. His subsequent career was more conventional for a future CAS, as he was appointed AOC successively in the Middle East, Iraq and then India, before becoming AOC Air Defence of Great Britain in February 1929. When Geoffrey Salmond died, Ellington was back on the Air Council serving as Air Member for Personnel.

Ellington was also quite different in character to either Trenchard or John Salmond; both were strong personalities, whereas Ellington was inclined to be rather withdrawn and even, on occasion, inarticulate, particularly when in conference. Nevertheless, it was under his leadership that the RAF made huge strides towards modernization, leaving it, if not on a par with its future major enemy, then at least the beneficiary of a number of decisions and actions which would sustain it through the difficult early years of the forthcoming war and provide a sound platform for the future.

When Ellington took up his appointment, the Disarmament Conference was still in session in Geneva. However, Germany, with Adolf Hitler recently appointed as Chancellor, withdrew from both the Conference and the League of Nations in October 1933, following attempts by France in particular to deny it equality. Unbeknownst to Great Britain, France and the United States, the Luftwaffe had come into being earlier in the same year, following the training of substantial numbers of pilots in Russia.

The inevitable failure of the Disarmament Conference caused a shift in defence thinking in the UK. As far as the RAF was concerned, the emphasis was inevitably on both home defence and offensive operations mounted from the United Kingdom. In order to achieve this, the first of a series of expansion schemes was conceived, Scheme A being adopted in July 1934. This called for a front-line strength of 1,544 aircraft by March 1939, of which 1,252, in 84 squadrons, would be based in the UK. In addition, new airfields would be constructed at Marham, Feltwell and Stradishall.

There would in due course be twelve expansion schemes proposed (A to M, not including I), of which only five – A, C, F, L and M – were approved by the Cabinet. Of these only Scheme F, given the go-ahead in February 1936 and calling for 124 squadrons in the UK, 26 in the Fleet Air Arm and 37 overseas, with 2,516 aircraft in total, was actually completed, all the others being overtaken by events. The acceleration was provoked by

Introduction   19

the revelation, by Hitler himself during a visit in March 1935 to Germany by the Foreign Secretary, Sir John Simon, that the Luftwaffe had reached parity in numbers with the RAF.

As important as the bald numbers of aircraft and squadrons was the composition of the aircraft themselves. The bi-plane bombers such as the Hawker Hart and the Vickers Virginia began to be phased out, although this would take some time, to be replaced in the second half of the decade by the light and medium monoplane bombers, the Fairey Battle, Bristol Blenheim, Handley Page Hampden, Armstrong Whitworth Whitley and Vickers Wellington. Moreover, specifications were also drawn up for three heavy bombers, the Avro Manchester, the Handley Page Halifax and the Short Stirling, although none of these would enter squadron service until well into the forthcoming war.

Although the numbers of aircraft proposed for the UK were in favour of the bombers in the ratio of 5:2, it would be the fighters which bore the brunt of the action against the Luftwaffe in the first instance, and it was thus fortunate that, two years before the specifications were issued for heavy bombers, one appeared in 1934 for a completely new type of monoplane fighter. Ever since the days of the Fokker *Eindecker*, the standard mounting of one or two machine guns had been in the nose of the aircraft, firing through the propeller. Now a young squadron leader, Ralph Sorley, later to rise to the rank of air marshal but then serving in the Operational Requirements section of the Directorate of Operations & Intelligence at the Air Ministry, insisted that any new fighter should mount eight Browning machine guns, four in each wing. This was accepted by Sydney Camm of Hawker and R. J. Mitchell of Supermarine, and the Hurricane and Spitfire duly emerged in 1935 and 1936 respectively and were immediately ordered in large numbers, the Hurricane entering service in December 1937 and the Spitfire in August 1938.

Expansion also involved the building of new airfields, although relatively few of these were actually finished during Ellington's time as CAS. They were built to a very high standard, with solid offices, accommodation and infrastructure, including large hangars. They did, however, all have grass runways at this stage. In line with the large expansion of the bomber fleet, most of them were situated in the east of England, from Suffolk up to Yorkshire, facing Germany across the North Sea

It was clear by 1936 that Air Defence of Great Britain was too unwieldy a command for a future war and it was split into Bomber Command, Fighter Command, Coastal Command and Training Command, the last of these formed out of Inland Area. In order to create a much larger pool of aircrew, the RAF Volunteer Reserve was formed to supplement the Auxiliary Air Force.

There was one setback for the RAF under Ellington, when the Royal Navy, to Trenchard's horror, obtained administrative control of the Fleet Air Arm in July 1937; this was followed two years later by full control.

Ellington was succeeded in September 1937 by Air Chief Marshal Sir Cyril Newall, who had had experience of command at squadron and wing level in France in the Great War, substantially in bombers, and an orthodox career subsequently. Immediately prior to his appointment as CAS he had been Air Member for Supply and Organisation, in which role he had been intimately involved with the expansion schemes. With Lord Swinton, the Secretary of State for Air, he was now directly responsible for Scheme J, which was rejected by the Government on the grounds of expense and replaced by the cheaper Scheme K. The latter foundered on the news of Hitler's *Anschluss* in Austria in March 1938 and was replaced by the more ambitious Scheme L, itself overtaken by Scheme M at the time of the Munich crisis. The last of these, the final scheme as it turned out, called for 2,550 aircraft in the Metropolitan Air Force by 31 March 1942 but was itself overtaken by events.

The Munich Agreement in September 1938 was widely regarded as a shameful act of appeasement, but it was a blessing for the RAF, which would have been hopelessly unprepared to fight at the time. The eleven months that followed were vital both in building up the strength of Fighter Command and in ensuring that orders were ramped up for the three new heavy bombers, although the first of these, the Short Stirling, did not undertake its initial operation until February 1941. Moreover, the 'Phoney War', which lasted until the German invasion of Norway on 9 April 1940, provided yet more breathing space.

The overseas commands were placed on a low priority in terms both of the absolute number of aircraft and of the types of aircraft deployed. Whereas in the UK the fighter squadrons were almost all converted onto the new fast monoplane fighters, the Hawker Hurricane and the Supermarine Spitfire, by the spring of 1940, in the Middle East, where the Italian territories in Libya and Ethiopia constituted a serious threat, the most modern fighter was the bi-plane Gloster Gladiator, whilst further east other bi-planes such as the Westland Wapiti and the Hawker Hart remained in service.

The Home Commands 1939–45

Fighter Command

In spite of the scrapping of the 'Ten Year Rule' and the commitment to expand the RAF in the UK, by the middle of 1936, two years after the first scheme had been approved, there were still only thirteen fighter squadrons in the UK and all of them were twin-gun bi-planes.

New fighters were, however, about to emerge, the Hawker Hurricane in late 1937 and the Supermarine Spitfire in the summer of 1938: the bi-planes were phased out, with the exception of the Gloster Gladiator, which remained in squadron service until early 1941. The two new aircraft were monoplanes and, in the right hands, a match for the best German fighter of the day, the Messerschmitt Me 109E, their nimbleness making up for their lower speed and rate of climb. Most importantly, they were both armed with eight .303 machine guns, four in each wing, on the insistence of Ralph *Sorley* in the Operational Requirements section of the Air Ministry.

The new aircraft arrived just in time. Production was initially slow, but the Munich Agreement, deeply unpopular though it was amongst those who believed that the UK and France had effectively capitulated to Hitler, together with the German leader's own reluctance to strike towards the west for the first eight months of hostilities, gave Fighter Command's AOC-in-C Hugh **Dowding** just enough time to build up his force to a level at which it could compete with the Luftwaffe. He still had to fight, not always successfully, to preserve his squadrons from what he saw, quite correctly, as futile demands for reinforcing the RAF in France in June 1940 following the German invasion of that country.

The Battle of Britain itself was one of the defining conflicts of history, unquestionably saving the United Kingdom from invasion in the late summer and early autumn of 1940. The Germans themselves were handicapped by the short range of their own fighters and the relatively modest loads of their bombers, but it was still a very tough fight. Dowding worked in perfect harmony with his opposite number in AA Command, General Sir Frederick Pile, and with the commanders of three of his four groups, notably Keith **Park** at 11 Group, but there was tension with Trafford **Leigh-Mallory** at 12 Group. Leigh-Mallory was persuaded by Douglas Bader, one of his squadron commanders, that the Germans would be more effectively opposed by 'Big Wings' of two to three squadrons, rather than by single squadrons, which themselves frequently operated in flights rather than as a whole. The Big Wings were certainly effective once they managed to catch

22   Churchill's Eagles

the German bombers, but in the opinion of Park, and to some extent of Dowding, they were always too late to attack the Germans before the latter reached 11 Group's airfields.

Although victory was undoubted, the battle ended on a sour note which saw Dowding, who had admittedly been expecting to retire for a long time, and Park posted to new and relatively unimportant jobs and succeeded respectively by Sholto **Douglas** and Leigh-Mallory. The Germans turned to raiding by night, posing a problem for Fighter Command as its night fighters, initially Boulton-Paul Defiants and Bristol Blenheims, were handicapped both by their poor performance in the air and by the absence of effective airborne interception radar. It was the advent of a much better aircraft, the Bristol Beaufighter, and improved radar, which started to take a toll on German intruders.

With daylight raids hugely reduced, Fighter Command went on the offensive in 1941. Initially this took the form of 'Rhubarb' operations, effectively 'tip-and-run' raids on German airfields within the fighters' operating range, which comprised a fairly modest area of North-West France. There were also a large number of 'Circus' operations, in which the fighters were joined by Bristol Blenheims, attacking airfields, power stations, ports, coastal shipping and other suitable targets. Overall, however, the cost of these raids was greater than the rewards and they were largely responsible for delaying the supply of modern Spitfires to the RAF in North Africa and Malta, where they could have made a much more worthwhile contribution to the war effort. Moreover, the appearance of a new German fighter, the Focke-Wolf Fw 190, threatened air superiority, even after the arrival in service of the Mark V Spitfire.

Fighter Command retained its defensive role during the Baedeker Raids in the spring of 1942, the Baby Blitz in the first five months of 1944 and the V-1 attacks which succeeded the latter, but it also continued to take the battle to the Germans, notably in the Dieppe Raid of August 1942, during which it largely succeeded in protecting the landing troops from attacks from the air, albeit at the cost of serious losses of its own aircraft. Shortly afterwards, Douglas was succeeded as AOC-in-C by Leigh-Mallory.

In late 1943, with the Allied invasion of North-West Europe now set for the late spring or early summer of 1944, considerable changes were made. Leigh-Mallory left Fighter Command to become the AOC-in-C of the Allied Expeditionary Air Force (AEAF) and was succeeded by Roderic **Hill** at Fighter Command, which was now renamed Air Defence of Great Britain (ADGB). The majority of its squadrons, which numbered more than 100, were transferred to the Second Tactical Air Force, which had been formed out of Army Co-operation Command under Arthur **Coningham**.

ADGB, with its name restored to Fighter Command in late 1944, played a significant role in the initial stages of the invasion of Normandy and the ensuing battles. It was now equipped with more modern aircraft, not only improved marks of the Spitfire, but also the De Havilland Mosquito, which had become an outstanding night fighter in addition to its other capabilities, the North American Mustang, with a much greater range than the others, the Hawker Typhoon and later the Hawker Tempest. The Tempests were increasingly deployed on shooting down the V-1 flying bombs, whilst Fighter Command also provided escorts for Bomber Command over the North Sea and, in the case of the Mustangs, over Germany itself until the end of the war.

Bomber Command
Partly because of the overriding demands of protecting the country, the major offensive formation, Bomber Command, took even longer than Fighter Command to reach maturity, being equipped initially with aircraft which became obsolete very quickly and with little in the way of accurate navigational aids.

At the outbreak of war 1 Group, equipped with the hopelessly inadequate Fairey Battle, became the core of the Advanced Air Striking Force in France, where it was effectively destroyed in May 1940. The Group was reconstituted with the Vickers Wellington, by some way the best bomber of the early period of the war, which also initially equipped 3 Group.

2 Group's aircraft at the outset was the Bristol Blenheim, a medium bomber which carried out operations against German shipping and ports, incurring enormous losses in so doing, and later participated in 'Circus' raids alongside Fighter Command over France. It began to be phased out in late 1941 with the introduction of some highly capable American aircraft, the Douglas Boston and the North American Mitchell, whilst a number of squadrons were later converted to Mosquitoes. Divorced effectively from the rest of the command by its different types of activity, 2 Group was transferred to the Second Tactical Air Force in late 1943.

By the beginning of the War 4 and 5 Groups were also equipped with medium bombers, the former with the Armstrong Whitworth Whitley, the latter with the Handley Page Hampden. Unlike the Wellington, these aircraft were in truth already obsolete and were replaced in 1942 by four-engined bombers, respectively the Handley Page Halifax at 4 Group and the Avro

Lancaster, the outstanding heavy bomber of the war, at 5 Group. 3 Group exchanged its Wellingtons for the third British heavy bomber of the War, the Short Stirling, but this proved to be a poor performer in the bombing role and was replaced by the Lancaster. 6 (RCAF) Group became operational at the beginning of 1943, operating a mixture of Lancasters and Halifaxes, Bomber Command was commanded by Edgar **Ludlow-Hewitt** from 1937 to 1940, by Charles **Portal** briefly in 1940, prior to his appointment as CAS, and by Richard **Peirse** from 1940 to early 1942. After the brief temporary appointment of John *Baldwin*, Arthur **Harris** took up the baton as AOC-in-C and held it until after the end of the war. His appointment came in the aftermath of the Butt Report into the accuracy of the command's squadrons, the overall conclusion of which was that only one in four crews claiming to have hit a target in Germany actually bombed within five miles of it.

Harris was a completely single-minded commander, whose goal was to destroy the great cities of Germany and, by so doing, win the war. He quickly demonstrated his determination by mounting three 'Thousand Bomber Raids' in the summer of 1942, accepting that the technology available at that time could not deliver precision bombing, although new aids to navigation about to come into service, *Gee*, *Oboe* and *H2S*, were to improve accuracy considerably. Some cities were to suffer hugely, notably Hamburg and Lübeck, but others, including those in the main target area, the Ruhr, proved to be more resilient.

There was only one man who could control Harris and that was Portal. The CAS compelled the AOC-in-C to do a number of things to which he was opposed, the most important of which was the creation of 8 Group to act as Pathfinders to the main force. Harris was, however, permitted to select the commander and he appointed Donald **Bennett**, a difficult character but one who would always obey Harris and who turned his group into a vital component of the command.

Another decision of Portal's with which Harris disagreed was the raising of a new squadron, No. 617, within 5 Group to carry out the most famous raid of the war, in which the Möhne and Eder dams were destroyed. Harris, however, was so impressed by the result that he had the squadron used for special duties thereafter, which included the sinking of the battleship *Tirpitz*. In due course 5 Group was effectively detached from the Main Force of Bomber Command and, under the command of Ralph **Cochrane**, operated substantially on its own, becoming known to the rest of the command as the 'Independent Air Force'. Both Bennett and Cochrane were longstanding protégés of Harris, but they loathed each other!

Another important addition to Bomber Command in late 1943 was 100 (Bomber Support) Group, which deployed bombers packed with electronic equipment to deceive the German defences, and Mosquitoes to attack the German night fighters threatening the bomber streams.

Much to Harris's displeasure, Bomber Command, which had fought the Battle of the Ruhr in the spring and early summer of 1943 and the Battle of Berlin later that year and into 1944, was placed at the disposal of General Dwight D. Eisenhower, the Supreme Commander, Allied Expeditionary Force in 1944, in order to support the invasion of North-West Europe. In fact it made a significant contribution to the campaign on the ground before reverting to its main task later in the year.

Acting in concert with the United States Eighth Air Force, Harris stepped up his bombing campaign in the autumn of 1944 and the spring of 1945, causing tremendous damage to German cities, which culminated in the controversial raid on Dresden between 13 and 15 February 1945.

Coastal Command
Coastal Command was very much the Cinderella of the fighting commands in its early days, equipped as it was with obsolete or otherwise inadequate aircraft and not enough of them. The Battle of the Atlantic was said by Churchill to have caused him more anxiety than any other campaign, but it was to a significant extent his own neglect of the command which meant that it was not until mid-1943 that the situation began to improve, with the command by then employing new long-range aircraft equipped with state of the art air-to-sea radar and highly effective depth charges, torpedoes and rockets.

At the outbreak of war the lumbering Vickers Vildebeest was the command's only torpedo bomber, whilst its flying boats were antiques, with the sole exception of the Short Sunderland, of which there were too few. The Lockheed Hudson and the Avro Anson which were supplied to the command in the early years, whilst much more modern, were inadequately equipped with offensive weaponry, effectively small bombs rather than depth charges. In spite of all the efforts of the AOC-in-C, Frederick **Bowhill**, it was not until 1941 that the command scored its first confirmed 'kill', and U-boat sinkings remained very low relative to the loss of Allied merchant ships.

Bowhill's successor as AOC-in C in early 1941 was Philip **Joubert**, who had previously held the post for a year in 1936/7. Under him the command grew significantly and more modern aircraft arrived, the Bristol Beaufort, the Armstrong Whitworth Whitley and, best of all amongst the land based

26 Churchill's Eagles

aircraft, the Vickers Wellington, whilst new flying boats included more Sunderlands, as well as the American Consolidated Catalina.

There was also a reorganization of the command's groups in that year, with 15 Group based in Liverpool and responsible for the Western Approaches to the Mersey and the Clyde, 16 Group in Kent, focused on the southern North Sea and the English Channel, 17 Group in Edinburgh with responsibility for training, 18 Group in Rosyth looking after the Northern North Sea and 19 Group in Plymouth covering the South-Western Approaches and the all-important Bay of Biscay, across which all the U-boats based in Western France had to travel. In addition, bases were set up in Iceland and Gibraltar and, later in the war, in the Azores. It was 15 and 19 Group which were the most concerned with the protection of North Atlantic convoys, whilst 16 and 18 Groups went on the offensive against German coastal traffic.

Joubert's term of command of just over two years saw both new aircraft and much better technology being introduced. The latter included much improved Air to Surface Vessel Radar and the Leigh Light to illuminate targets. However, the early success by the codebreakers of Bletchley Park in cracking the German Navy's signal codes was completely undone in February 1942 by the Germans adding a fourth rotor to their Enigma machines, and it was only in early 1943 that the new code was cracked. By that time new very long-range Consolidated Liberators had arrived, equipped with the most modern ASV radar and effectively closing 'the Gap', the area of the Atlantic thitherto uncovered by Allied aircraft.

At much the same time Joubert was relieved by a strong and vigorous commander, Jack **Slessor**, who took full advantage of this situation. Moreover, the command's Beauforts had been replaced by modern Beaufighters, which carried out frequent raids against German coastal convoys from Norway to the Netherlands. Combined with much more effective and more numerous convoy escorts, this resulted in German U-boat losses mounting, whilst the tonnage of Allied shipping sunk was significantly reduced. Slessor was himself succeeded a year later by Sholto **Douglas**, another very able commander, who drove home his advantage, helped by Bomber Command's attacks on U-boat factories and the canals which conveyed new vessels to their ports. Moreover, Coastal Command was fully involved with the protection of Allied shipping on D-Day and thereafter.

In addition to its operations in the protection of Allied shipping and the destruction of German coastal traffic, Coastal Command was also responsible for the Air Sea Rescue service and the Photo Reconnaissance and Meteorological services, all of which carried out work vital to the war effort.

Training Command, Flying Training Command and Technical Training Command

Training Command was formed out of Inland Area in July 1936, making it actually the first of the new Home Commands. By May 1940 it was clear that the training demands of aircrew on the one hand and ground crew on the other were so different as to require two separate organizations.

Flying Training Command carried out the training of pilots, navigators, wireless operators and air gunners, but not of flight engineers. The first step was the Initial Training Wing, which instilled discipline through drill and carried out assessments of aptitude through a series of exercises and tests, largely carried out in the classroom. Those deemed suitable for flying training were then posted to Elementary Flying Training Schools, learning to fly in Tiger Moths or similar aircraft. On passing out from the EFTS, the would-be pilots were posted to Service Flying Training Schools, at the end of which the successful trainees were awarded their wings. Those who failed to qualify as pilots, either at the EFTS or the SFTS, were re-mustered as navigators, wireless operators, bomb aimers or air gunners at the appropriate schools. Those who passed out of the SFTS and those who graduated from the specialist schools in navigation, wireless telegraphy or gunnery would come together again at Operational Training Units, where, if they were in Bomber or Coastal Command, they would sort themselves out into crews. At this point the crews of the larger aircraft would also be joined by flight engineers who had passed out under the auspices of Technical Training Command.

The demands of Fighter, Bomber and Coastal Commands for airfields in the UK housing operational squadrons were such that those providing flying training were in short supply. However, this was overcome by the implementation of the Commonwealth Air Training Plan, which was established initially by Great Britain and the Dominions of Canada, Australia and New Zealand in December 1939, with South Africa and Rhodesia joining subsequently. This resulted in the training of tens of thousands of pilots and other aircrew in those countries, but most significantly in Canada, where a large proportion of the students were from the UK. Moreover, once the United Sates had entered the war, it became possible to train pilots in that country as well.

Technical Training Command covered most other forms of training, notably that of riggers, fitters, armourers and others directly concerned with the repair and maintenance of aircraft. Moreover, there were a large number of other specialist schools devoted to the training of men and women carrying out every function in the RAF.

28 Churchill's Eagles

Maintenance Command
Maintenance Command was formed in April 1938 to take control of all UK-based maintenance units, which numbered over two hundred by the end of the war. Such units overseas were administered locally.

Balloon Command
Balloon Command was set up in November 1938, in the certain knowledge that, in the event of war, Germany would carry out a bombing campaign. The Command in due course set up five groups, Nos. 30 to 34, deployed around the major population centres. The HQ was in Stanmore, close to the HQs of both Fighter Command and the Army's Anti-Aircraft Command.

Ferry Command and Transport Command
Ferry Command was formed in mid-1941, initially to handle the movement of new aircraft built in Canada and the USA across the Atlantic to the UK. It subsequently became responsible also for the movement of aircraft from the USA and the UK to North Africa using the 'Reinforcement Route' via West Africa, and later still the delivery of new aircraft to India. It changed its name to Transport Command in March 1943 and, with the advent of airborne operations in North-West Europe theatres, it subsequently took on the role of dropping troops into battle from aircraft or in gliders, as well as carrying materiel and providing casualty evacuation.

The Overseas Commands and Air Forces 1939–45

British Air Force in France
BAFF was a short-lived command under Arthur **Barratt** in France in 1939/40, comprising the Air Component of the British Expeditionary Force and the Advanced Air Striking Force. The latter was formed from 1 Group Bomber Command, which was equipped with the hopelessly inadequate Fairey Battle. Both formations were effectively destroyed in the brief campaign leading up to the evacuation of the BEF from Dunkirk.

Middle East Command
From a purely geographic perspective, the RAF in the Middle East covered by far the largest area in the whole service. It was not, strictly speaking, a functional command, but it had a sole commander-in-chief and was broadly controlled from his HQ in Cairo. At the beginning of the war it covered Egypt, the Sudan, British East Africa, Somaliland, Palestine, Transjordan,

Iraq, Cyprus and Malta and, as the war progressed, it extended to Italian East Africa, Greece (including Crete), Libya and the Reinforcement Route from West Africa.

The AOC-in-C Middle East at the beginning of the War was Air Chief Marshal Sir Arthur **Longmore**, upon whom fell the burden of operations against the Italians both in Egypt and Libya and in Ethiopia and Eritrea. The entry of Italy into the war had huge repercussions for the RAF, albeit that the Italian Air Force bore little resemblance to that of its Axis partner. Longmore's aircraft were largely obsolete: the Bristol Blenheim Mark 1 as a light bomber, supported by the Bristol Bombay, a transport aircraft converted to a bomber, with even older aircraft such as the Vickers Wellesley on the East African front. The most modern fighter was the bi-plane Gloster Gladiator, also supported by even older aircraft. It was three old Gladiators – Faith, Hope and Charity – which provided the sole fighter presence on Malta.

In order to get more modern aircraft to Egypt as quickly as possible, the Reinforcement Route was set up, running from West Africa to Khartoum and then up the Nile to Cairo. The first batch of Hurricanes arrived in Egypt in late September 1940 and all were committed to the Western Desert. In addition, the first Wellingtons arrived but, to the annoyance of Churchill, who could only see the numbers of aircraft in service and failed to understand both the need to tropicalize them and the incidence of wear and tear from desert conditions, Longmore kept asking for ever more aircraft with better capabilities. The RAF was working on several fronts at once: East Africa, the Western Desert and later Greece and Crete. Success in East Africa was followed by disaster in the Western Desert, although 202 Group did valiant work there, whilst the campaign in Greece was a total disaster, with the RAF element destroyed.

In the summer of 1941 Longmore, who had by then totally lost the confidence of Churchill, was replaced by his deputy, Arthur **Tedder**, who was to remain in the Mediterranean for the next two and a half years. Tedder's vital advantage was that he was supported to the hilt by Charles **Portal**, the CAS, who protected him from Churchill's interference. In late 1941 202 Group became AHQ Egypt and 204 Group became initially AHQ Western Desert and later the Desert Air Force, under the command of Arthur 'Maori' **Coningham**. The DAF was to provide support for the Eighth Army throughout the North African campaign and the subsequent campaigns in Sicily and mainland Italy, latterly as part of the Mediterranean Allied Air Forces.

30   Churchill's Eagles

RAF Malta was under Tedder's overall control, but it effectively fought its own war, under first Hugh **Lloyd** and then Keith **Park**. The island was subjected to continuous attack from both the Italian Regia Aeronautica and the German Luftwaffe from June 1940 until the spring of 1943. Not only was it heavily engaged in its own defence, but it also carried out offensive operations against Axis convoys to North Africa and attacks on enemy ports and airfields in Sicily and Southern Italy.

Following the creation of the Mediterranean Allied Air Forces, Middle East Command effectively reverted to the control of the Air Ministry in respect of the RAF's activities in the Eastern Mediterranean, Egypt, Libya, the Near and Middle East and East Africa.

Mediterranean Air Command and Mediterranean Allied Air Forces
The spring and early summer of 1943 saw the defeat of the Axis forces in North Africa. The Casablanca Conference in January had resulted in an agreement between the British and Americans on joint operations in the Mediterranean theatre, although for the time being these were confined to the taking of Sicily. A new Anglo-American command was established, Mediterranean Air Command, with Tedder as its commander. The new command included operations in North Africa and Malta, but operations in Sicily and later in mainland Italy became the province of its subordinate formation, Mediterranean Allied Air Forces, under Carl Spaatz. MAAF was itself divided into the Strategic Air Force, effectively the heavy bombers under Spaatz's fellow countryman, Jimmy Doolittle, the Tactical Air Force under Coningham and the Coastal Air Force under Lloyd.

The Strategic Air Force was almost exclusively American, the one British component being 205 Group with three squadrons of Wellingtons. Whilst it carried out attacks on targets in Italy's industrial heartland, it also undertook significant bombing operations in Southern Germany. The Coastal Air Force, on the other hand, comprising largely formations of fighters and light bombers, was dominated by the RAF, although in addition to the Americans it included units of the French Air Force. The Tactical Air Force was relatively equally divided between the British and the Americans, the former in the guise of the Desert Air Force, which retained its name until the end of the war. Although there were changes in composition, this structure was retained for the Italian campaign.

One formation which was broadly subject to oversight by MAAF, but which in practice operated substantially independently, was the Balkan Air Force. This was set up under AVM William **Elliot**, later succeeded by AVM

George *Mills*, to carry out operations in support of Marshal Tito's forces on the east side of the Adriatic Sea, primarily in Yugoslavia, but also in Albania and Greece, whilst it also had some involvement in the defence of Warsaw. This was possibly the most polyglot air force of the war, comprising units not only from the RAF, but also from the Yugoslav, Italian, Greek and South African Air Forces, with intermittent involvement also by the USAAF and, for a brief period, the Soviet Union's Red Air Force.

Allied Expeditionary Air Force
Allied Expeditionary Air Force ('AEAF') was formed as the result of decisions on the proposed invasion of North-West Europe taken at the Quebec Conference in August 1943. The appointed commander was Trafford **Leigh-Mallory**, then AOC-in-C Fighter Command, who held both positions pending the appointment in November 1943 of Roderic **Hill** to Fighter Command, which was renamed Air Defence of Great Britain.

The British Component of AEAF was the Second Tactical Air Force ('2TAF'), which supported the British and Canadian elements of Twenty-First Army Group on operations in France, Belgium, the Netherlands and Germany from the invasion of Normandy until the end of hostilities.

The American component of AEAF was Ninth Air Force, which had come into being in North Africa and seen active service there, before being transferred to the UK. Thereafter it carried out operations in support of US forces in North-West Europe.

Second Allied Tactical Air Force
2TAF was formed on 1 June 1943, just over a year before it fully assumed the purpose for which it was designed, namely to support the British element of the invasion of North-West Europe and the subsequent campaign. It was commanded initially by John *D'Abliac*, who was relieved by Coningham on his return from the Mediterranean. It consisted initially of 2 Group, which had been transferred from Bomber Command, and 83 (Composite) Group, which had been part of Fighter Command.

2 Group, unlike any other in Bomber Command, had been entirely equipped from the outset with medium bombers, initially exclusively the Bristol Blenheim, but by mid-1944 the group comprised six squadrons of De Havilland Mosquitoes, four of North American Mitchells and two of Douglas Bostons. It was commanded by AVM Basil **Embry**, who been shot down early in the war, but managed to escape back to the UK and was one of only two officers in the RAF to be awarded three bars to his DSO.

32   Churchill's Eagles

83 Group was commanded by AVM Harry **Broadhurst,** who had led the Desert Air Force in North Africa from January 1943 and had, with the encouragement of Major-General Freddie de Guingand, Montgomery's chief of staff, invented a new highly effective system of air attack in support of ground troops at Mareth in Tunisia in March 1943. By D-Day his group included four squadrons of Spitfires, four of Hawker Typhoons employed in a ground attack role and one of rocket-firing North American Mustangs.

2TAF subsequently included 84 Group, with a similar mix of aircraft, whilst 85 Group provided maintenance facilities.

RAF Singapore & Malaya, RAF Burma and India Command

If the RAF had been kept short of modern aircraft in the Middle East, the situation in the Far East was much worse. At the beginning of December 1941 RAF Singapore & Malaya consisted of four squadrons of Brewster Buffaloes, which were effectively obsolete by the standards of modern fighters, two squadrons of antiquated bi-plane Vickers Vildebeest torpedo bombers, two squadrons of Lockheed Hudsons and one of Consolidated Catalinas. These were no match for the Mitsubishi Zeros flown by the Japanese, whose comrades began landing on the west coast of Malaya on 8 December, and had been effectively destroyed by the time the enemy was approaching Singapore. The same could be said of RAF Burma, although the Curtis Tomahawks operated by both the RAF and the American Volunteer Group put up a much better fight.

India Command was formed in the spring of 1942 under Richard **Peirse,** absorbing all the groups which had been formed in India and Ceylon. Facing the Japanese across the border with Burma were the two groups comprising AHQ Bengal, 221 Group to the north in the area around Imphal, where a number of airfields were built, and 225 Group on the east side of the Bay of Bengal covering the Arakan. 222 Group was set up to defend Ceylon, 223 Group was based in Peshawar, covering the North-West Frontier, whilst 225 Group in Bangalore was responsible for the rest of India. Two groups had functional rather than geographical responsibilities: 226 Group in Karachi dealt with supply and maintenance and also the preparation for operations of all aircraft arriving from the UK or the Middle East, whilst 227 Group took over all training.

Air Command South-East Asia and Eastern Air Command

The entry of the United States into the war caused some significant changes in the Far East, including the absorption of India Command into Air

Command South-East Asia. Peirse remained in overall command, succeeded by Guy **Garrod** in November 1944 and then Keith Park in February 1945. Further groups were created to carry out various functions in India, but the major change was the creation of Eastern Air Command under Major General George E Stratemeyer, which took responsibility for all operations against the enemy.

The Americans were focused on bolstering the Chinese against the Japanese invasion of their country, with the Strategic Air Force carrying out bombing raids in China as well as Burma, whilst Troop Carrier Command lifted materiel over 'the Hump', the mountainous area between India/Burma and China, whilst also supplying the Allied ground forces in action in India and Burma. 221 and 224 Groups, now equipped with modern fighters, fighter-bombers and dive bombers, provided support for ground operations in those countries under a new umbrella organization, Third Tactical Air Force, which was commanded by John **Baldwin** and then Alec *Coryton*. 3TAF also controlled, as far as was possible, the all-American Air Commando Force which provided air support for the Chindits.

The Air Marshals

Air Marshal (later Air Chief Marshal) Sir Arthur Barratt KCB, CMG, MC, DL (1891–1966)

The achievement of high rank and responsibility by a British officer immediately before or in the early stages of a major war has often proved to be a blight on his future progress. The British tend not to start their wars well for many reasons, of which government parsimony before the event, an under-estimation of the qualities of the enemy or enemies and a failure to develop in advance the means of waging war in terms of both the right equipment and the right strategy and tactics, rank amongst the most obvious. It was Arthur **Barratt's** misfortune to be appointed to command the British Air Forces in France ('BAFF') a mere four months before the opening of the German *Blitzkrieg* in the West, during which the RAF suffered one of the most serious defeats in its history. Whilst the responsibility for this lay substantially elsewhere, and whilst he went on to serve in senior appointments for the rest of the War and to make a significant contribution to the use of air power in conjunction with ground forces, Barratt's name is not one of those readily associated with eventual victory.

Barratt was commissioned out of the Royal Military Academy at Woolwich into the Royal Field Artillery in December 1910. He transferred to the Royal Flying Corps in the summer of 1914 and, after passing the course at the Central Flying School, was posted as a pilot to 3 Squadron early in 1915. The squadron, like most of those employed on the Western Front at the time, was substantially engaged in aerial reconnaissance for the British Expeditionary Force, providing Barratt with his first experience of army cooperation, in which he would in due course become known as a specialist. He was promoted to Flight Commander in the squadron in June 1915, serving in due course under one of its best-known commanding officers, Edgar **Ludlow-Hewitt**.

In September 1916, by now a temporary major with a Military Cross for gallantry in the air, Barratt was appointed to command 6 Squadron, flying BE2s and RE8s and undertaking much the same army cooperation duties as previously. He moved in April 1917 to the command of 49 Squadron, this time flying DH4s in a light bomber role. Further promotion to temporary lieutenant colonel came in June 1917, accompanied by his appointment to command 3 (Corps) Wing, whose several squadrons were responsible once again for supporting the Army. His final service in France came as commander of 2 (Corps) Wing right at the end of the Great War. By that time he had obtained a permanent commission in the newly formed RAF, with the rank of wing commander.

Two themes ran through Barratt's career: training and army cooperation, both in the inter-war years and during the Second World War. His first appointment in the former role came in 1921 at the RAF College at Cranwell as Assistant Commandant under Air Commodore Charles Longcroft, who had established the college two years earlier. Cranwell was by then the entry point for most of those seeking permanent commissions in the General Duties branch of the RAF. This was followed in April 1923 by his appointment as Senior Officer Administration at the newly re-formed 3 (Training) Group, based at RAF Spittlegate, near Grantham.

In January 1924 Barratt was selected to attend the Army Staff College at Camberley, providing him with highly valuable connections for the future. The college had closed during the Great War but had re-opened in 1919. The course ran for two years, its students being mostly British Army officers of the rank of captain and major, together with a small number from the Indian Army, Commonwealth armies, the Royal Navy and the RAF. It was designed not only to inculcate all aspects of staff duties into the students, but also to prepare them for higher command: indeed, without the all-important initials *psc* (passed Staff College) after their name on the Army List, army officers had little hope of progression beyond the rank of lieutenant colonel. In the second year, the course moved on not only to staff duties at corps and army level, but also to the wider aspects of international politics. The Commandant was Major General Sir Edmund Ironside, who was to be Chief of the Imperial General Staff at the time when Barratt was in command of the RAF in France in 1940.

Barratt's next appointment was a highly appropriate one, commandant of the newly formed School of Army Cooperation, based at Old Sarum, near Salisbury. One of the lesser-known RAF training establishments, the school taught the tactics adopted with some success during the Great War, focusing on reconnaissance, the mapping of enemy positions, artillery spotting and tactical bombing. Its task was not a particularly easy one, due to some continuing hostility towards an independent RAF at a senior level

36   Churchill's Eagles

within the British Army, which had tried but failed to retain its own air arm. There were, however, some recent successes to draw on in the RAF's favour, notably the suppression of unrest in British Somaliland and Iraq, supported by relatively modest army units.

A brief attachment to the Shanghai Defence Force as the Air Staff Officer to the GOC was followed in November 1927 by Barratt's selection for the staff of 22 Group, formed eighteen months earlier to include all the army cooperation squadrons. Just over a year later, he was appointed as Chief Instructor at the RAF Staff College in Andover. The Commandant was his former CO, Ludlow-Hewitt, succeeded in late 1930 by Philip **Joubert de la Ferté**, whilst the other members of the directing staff included Roderic **Hill**, Ralph **Cochrane** and Arthur **Tedder**. The last of these replaced Barratt as Chief Instructor in early 1931, when he left for a tour of nearly four years in India, initially in command of 1 (Indian) Group and then as Senior Air Staff Officer at Air HQ in New Delhi.

Barratt returned in early 1935 to become Director of Staff Duties at the Air Ministry, before being appointed Commandant of the RAF Staff College a year later. On the Directing Staff were men who would achieve high command in the forthcoming war and thereafter, such as Leslie **Hollinghurst** and William **Dickson**, whilst the students were those who would go on in the coming war to command squadrons, wings, stations and even groups and to hold important staff positions.

Barratt had been expected to take up the position of AOC-in-C India, but with the threat of war with Germany becoming ever more serious, in August 1939 he was appointed Principal RAF Liaison Officer to the French Air Force. In January 1940 he became AOC-in-C of a new command, British Air Forces in France ('BAFF'), which was composed of two separate components. The first of these was the Air Component of the British Expeditionary Force ('BEF'), commanded by AVM Charles *Blount*, like Barratt a former Commandant of the School of Army Co-operation. This component had been created in late 1939 to provide the BEF with its own dedicated support and comprised several types of aircraft. Four squadrons, increased later to five, were equipped with the Westland Lysander, a slow single-engined monoplane destined to be engaged in tactical photo-reconnaissance. Four more squadrons operated Bristol Blenheims, light twin-engined monoplane bombers, tasked with the role of strategic reconnaissance, whilst four squadrons operated Hawker Hurricanes and a further two Gloster Gladiators, as protection for both the reconnaissance aircraft and the BAFF's airfields.

The second component of the BAFF was the Advanced Air Striking Force ('AASF'), commanded by Air Vice-Marshal Patrick *Playfair*. Formed with the initial intention of carrying out short-range strikes against targets in Germany itself, the reluctance of the French to provoke retaliation meant that its purpose was changed to carrying out attacks on German ground forces. The core of the AASF was eight squadrons of Fairey Battles, two-seater single-engined light bombers which up to that time had equipped No. 1 Group of Bomber Command. They were accompanied by two squadrons of Blenheims and two of Hurricanes.

During the 'Phoney War' there were a number of encounters between the BAFF and the Luftwaffe, demonstrating immediately the inadequacy of the Battle, which proved itself to be disastrously vulnerable to both enemy fighters and anti-aircraft guns, with the result that daylight reconnaissance operations were abandoned. The Hurricanes of the Air Component and the AASF were successful against infrequent German bomber incursions, but they lost aircraft to the Messerschmitt 109s until they modified their own tactics, after which the engagements became more evenly balanced.

The Germans opened their offensive in the West on 10 May 1940. The invasions of the Netherlands and Belgium saw the effective destruction of their small air forces, whilst both the Battles and the Blenheims of the AASF suffered crippling losses, as did the Blenheim squadrons of Bomber Command, which were also flung into the fray. The Hurricanes, on the other hand, gave a good account of themselves against the German bombers, although the latter managed to destroy one complete Blenheim squadron on the ground in a devastating attack on its airfield. Although there were no good days, the nadir of the AASF's fortunes came on 14 May in an attack on German pontoon bridges over the Meuse near Sedan, when thirty-nine of sixty-three Battles and five of eight Blenheims were shot down. The following day, Barratt ordered that no more daylight raids were to take place.

The major demand of the BEF and, even more pressingly, of the French Government, was for fighters, strongly resisted by Air Chief Marshal Sir Hugh **Dowding**, AOC-in-C of Fighter Command. Dowding was determined not to allow his aircraft to be reduced in numbers below the level he believed to be essential to protect the United Kingdom. As a result, Barratt's own fighter pilots were carrying out four or five sorties every day and becoming exhausted. The situation changed when Churchill flew over to Paris on 16 May to be confronted with the news that the French had no strategic reserve. He immediately telegraphed a request for reinforcement, and six Hurricane squadrons were allocated to the campaign in France, albeit flying over every day to operate from French bases.

38   Churchill's Eagles

When the Germans reached the Channel coast north of the Somme on 20 May, the BEF found itself fighting on two fronts and, before long, falling back on Dunkirk. The last fighters of the Air Component returned to England on 20 May. The AASF was now down to three squadrons of Hurricanes and six of Battles, based south of the Somme in support of the 'Second' BEF, which was attempting unsuccessfully to hold the line of that river and later that of the Seine. The last remaining Battles left for England on 15 June and, although temporarily reinforced, the Hurricanes followed them three days later. During the course of the whole campaign the BAFF had lost over 200 Hurricanes, of which the majority were destroyed on the ground or abandoned as unfit for operations, whilst 78 Blenheims, 137 Battles and 35 Lysanders were also lost.

Other than writing his despatches, Barratt remained unemployed until November 1940, when he was appointed AOC-in-C of the newly established Army Co-operation Command. This was formed from 22 (Army Co-operation) Group, which had itself been re-formed only that June from the remnants of the Air Component and the AASF under the command of Charles Blount, who had subsequently been killed in a flying accident.

During its relatively short life, Army Co-operation Command comprised three groups. Two of these were formed in November 1940, 70 Group, which had hitherto formed part of Fighter Command, for training and 71 Group for operations. Rather less than a year later, 41 Operational Training Unit ('OTU') was formed within the group out of the training squadron of the School of Army Co-operation, specifically to train pilots in tactical air reconnaissance on Westland Lysanders and Curtis Tomahawks. In the spring of 1942 the Lysanders were replaced by North American Mustangs, the early versions of which, like the Tomahawks, were not suitable as fighter interceptors but had very good low-level characteristics for attacks in support of ground forces.

42 OTU was initially formed within 70 Group to convert Lysander pilots to Blenheims and also to a Blenheim derivative, the Bisley, later called the Blenheim V, which proved not to be a great success. With the creation of the Airborne Forces, the OTU switched to the training of glider pilots from the newly formed Glider Pilot Regiment, initially on the General Aircraft Hotspur and then on the Airspeed Horsa and General Aircraft Hamilcar. In November 1943 the OTU was transferred to 38 Group, whose gliders and tugs were thenceforward fully dedicated to the Airborne Forces.

In October 1942 43 OTU was formed to train army pilots in Air Observation Post ('AOP') duties, using the British Taylorcraft Auster to bring accurate fire onto artillery targets. AOP, although not known as such until some years later, had been one of the functions of the RFC/RAF during the Great War, but, following the experience of the BEF in 1940, it was decided that the Royal Artillery should itself provide the pilots, who became part of the Army Air Corps and wore its wings: however, it was also agreed that they should be trained by the RAF, which in addition provided the ground crews. On active service, initially in the Tunisian campaign and then in Sicily, Italy, North-West Europe and Burma/India, the Army had full operational control.

The second new formation of November 1940 was 71 Group, which was responsible for operations. In the summer of 1941 a reorganization took place, in which the squadrons were formed into wings under the direct control of HQ Army Co-operation Command and the group was disbanded. The wings were allocated to the Army's Home Commands – Scottish, North-Eastern, Eastern, South-Eastern, South-Western and Western – with a single squadron allocated to Northern Ireland. They thus became effectively the Air Component of Home Forces, with a senior air staff officer located at GHQ Home Forces to provide the necessary link. An additional wing (No 38) was subsequently formed to provide the aircraft and gliders for the Airborne Forces and this in due course was enlarged into 38 Group, by that time independent of any other command.

In September 1942 72 Group was formed to carry out the very specialized training of the six month-old RAF Regiment. Defence of the RAF's airfields had become a major issue in 1940, when it had proved totally inadequate during both the campaign in France and the Battle of Britain. The responsibility at this time lay with the Army and, although the Air Ministry had formed a Directorate of Ground Defence to provide co-ordination with the Army's Inspectorate of Aerodrome Defence, it now wanted full control of the regiment. Similar problems with airfield defence had emerged in the Middle East, where fast-moving campaigns had led to what the RAF considered were unnecessary losses. An independent committee was set up which recommended that the RAF should take over the role. Training of the recruits was initially undertaken by the Royal Marines and the Brigade of Guards, but the RAF soon brought this aspect under its wing as well.

One of the most important functions of Army Co-operation Command was to establish a reliable method of communication between the Army and the RAF during military operations. In late 1940 Group Captain A. H. Wann, who had commanded the luckless Battles in the AASF, and Colonel J. D. Woodall wrote a report on the use of RAF air liaison officers embedded

40   Churchill's Eagles

with army formations to call down support when it was required. This led to the creation of Army Air Support Controls ('AASC'), whose functions were to receive calls for air support and to then mount sorties against selected targets. They employed a system of 'tentacles', whereby two-way wireless networks were used to request support from Army HQ, which was either located alongside Air HQ or had a significant RAF presence. The response time between a request and a strike was progressively reduced to thirty minutes, a very significant improvement over what had been the case thitherto.

Although all the development work took place in the UK, this was all somewhat theoretical, but there was one theatre in which operations had been continuing without interruption since the summer of 1940, the Western Desert of North Africa. Barratt wanted to see the system in action, so in August 1942 he flew to Egypt, where the newly arrived Lieutenant General Bernard Montgomery, an enthusiast for the closest co-operation with the RAF, had very recently taken command of Eighth Army. During the Battle of Alam Halfa, Barratt was able to see the work of 2/5 AASC, which was co-located with the Operations Rooms of Eighth Army and Air HQ Western Desert (later the Western Desert Air Force and later still the Desert Air Force). This system was to be one of the great successes of the War, far better than anything conceived by the Germans.

In June 1943 Army Co-operation Command was reformed as 2nd Tactical Air Force, which would go on under Coningham to carry out the tactical operations of the RAF in North-West Europe from D-Day until the end of the War. Barratt moved on to become AOC-in-C of Technical Training Command. This command had been formed in May 1940, when Training Command was split into two, the other element becoming Flying Training Command, which focused exclusively on the training of aircrew. Technical Training was responsible for all other training, which was largely focused on aircraft repair and maintenance and all other aspects of engineering, but also included training on the handling of ordnance and on communications. Its components included 22 Group, which had itself been re-formed after spawning Army Co-operation Command, as well as 24, 26, 27 and 28 Groups.

Technical Training Command lacked the glamour of the operational home commands or the overseas air forces, but it did vitally important work, producing large numbers of both men and women who formed the backbone of the service behind the scenes during the last two years of the War.

In October 1945 Barratt was appointed Inspector-General of the RAF. This appointment dated back to August 1935, when Robert **Brooke-**

Popham became the first one, succeeded in due course by Marshal of the RAF Sir Edward Ellington, who had just stepped down as CAS. More often than not it was an end-of-career appointment, but it was nevertheless an important one. The Inspector-General was given a substantially free hand as to his programme of inspections, but typically he would visit a number of RAF stations or other establishments each week and write a report on each of them for the Air Ministry, with copies to other relevant recipients. Overseas visits were carried out as well, the Inspector-General's remit extending to the whole of the RAF.

Barratt took over from ACM Sir Edgar **Ludlow-Hewitt**, who had held the position for five and a half years, by far the longest term of any Inspector-General. Between May 1940 and November 1943 there had been in succession three additional Inspectors-General, AM Sir Thomas *Williams*, ACM Sir Arthur **Longmore** and ACM Sir **Philip Joubert de la Ferté**, but a second appointment was no longer considered necessary. The War had ended and the RAF was being rapidly run down, but it remained vital that high standards should be maintained in a much smaller force and the very existence of the Inspector-General helped to ensure this.

Demobilization was itself an issue, with 'hostilities only' officers and men desperate to get back to civilian life and impatient for their release. Particularly in the Far East, where the process seemed to many to be very slow, there was considerable feeling amongst those waiting to be demobbed that they were low on the list of priorities. In a number of RAF stations there were strikes, and there was a mutiny in the Royal Indian Navy. Barratt was visiting the country on an inspection tour in early 1946 when this unrest was at its peak and he experienced the anger of the men directly on a visit to RAF Drigh Road on the outskirts of Karachi. The men were gathered together for him to address them and, although he was given the opportunity to explain the circumstances and to ask for patience, his appeal to return to work was ignored and the strike continued for the next four days. He subsequently chaired a Court of Enquiry, and in due course, although repatriation was accelerated, a small number of the ringleaders were court-martialled.

Barratt retired in March 1947, taking on the largely ceremonial position of Gentleman Usher to the Sword of State. He is largely remembered by history for the most difficult period in his career, the command of BAFF in the dark days of 1940, but he went on to make a considerable, albeit low-profile, contribution to the success of the RAF during the War.

Air Vice-Marshal D. C. T. Bennett CB, CBE, DSO (1910–1986)

Wars, and particularly world wars, are great accelerators of progress. This can be seen most clearly in technological advances. By way of example, in 1939 the RAF was relying for its strategic bombers on a pre-war generation of medium-sized aircraft with payloads up to 7,000lbs. Six years later, its most capable heavy bomber could carry a normal load of twice that weight or, suitably modified, a single 22,000lb bomb. Even more remarkable was the ability of such bombers to find their targets, with the assistance of new aids to navigation. In 1941 only one in five bombers came within five miles of their target. By 1945 precise navigation and accurate marking enabled large formations to wipe out a whole city.

The enormous expansion of the RAF, as with the other services, also led to accelerated promotion. The use of acting, temporary and war substantive rank meant that younger men could be promoted far beyond what would have been their expectation in peacetime. These two phenomena, dramatic technological advances and fast track seniority, came together in the person of Donald **Bennett**, the leader of Bomber Command's Pathfinder Force throughout its existence and, at the age of thirty-three, the youngest man in the RAF's history to achieve the rank of air vice-marshal.

Like so many of the RAF's future senior officers, Bennett hailed from the Antipodes, having been born and educated in Queensland. He joined the Royal Australian Air Force in 1930, transferring to the RAF on a short-term commission in the following year. His first posting in the latter was to 29 Squadron, flying Armstrong Whitworth Siskin fighters, but in 1932 he attended a course on flying boats and this was followed by a posting to 210 Squadron at RAF Pembroke Dock. There he attracted the favourable attention of Arthur **Harris**, simultaneously the unit's commanding officer and the station commander, and a man who was to have an immense impact on Bennett's career many years later. Harris was particularly keen on giving his Supermarine Southampton crews exercises in night flying over the sea, and Bennett proved himself exceptionally adept at this and at navigation in general. It was thus no great surprise that his next posting was as an instructor at the School of Naval Co-operation and Air Navigation at RAF Calshot, where he also took and passed the Long Navigation Course and obtained a First Class Navigator's Licence.

Part of the incentive for obtaining such a qualification was the opportunity for Bennett to take part in an air race from the UK to Melbourne as part of that city's centenary celebrations. Having secured a position as the navigator in one of the entries, however, his participation came to an end when the aircraft's undercarriage collapsed on landing at Athens.

In August 1935 Bennett's short-term commission in the RAF came to an end, and although he was transferred back to the RAAF he was not to stay in that service. Instead, after a brief interlude in Australia and on the introduction of Harris, he joined Imperial Airways as a pilot, initially based in Egypt flying Short Calcutta flying boats between Alexandria and Brindisi. The Calcuttas were replaced in early 1937 by the new Short Empire flying boats, which offered the epitome of passenger comfort. The Empires were, however, incapable of crossing the Atlantic without a significant reduction in passenger numbers and freight to compensate for the increased fuel requirement. Imperial Airways decided to mount a smaller seaplane on the back of an Empire derivative, and at cruising altitude to detach the former, which would then fly on to North America with sufficient fuel. The testing took place in the UK, following which Bennett piloted *Mercury*, the name of the 'piggy-back' aircraft, from Foynes in Ireland to Montreal on the first ever non-stop east-to-west transatlantic crossing. He later flew *Mercury* down to Cape Town, establishing a long-distance record on the way.

Following the outbreak of war in 1939, Imperial Airways was merged with British Airways and the combined business was nationalized as the British Overseas Airways Corporation (BOAC). In the summer of 1940 Bennett was seconded from BOAC as Flying Superintendent to the Atlantic Ferry Organisation, which was charged with delivering to the UK aircraft which had been manufactured in the USA. In November of that year he led the first flight of factory-fresh Lockheed Hudsons across the Atlantic, followed by a number of other deliveries of both that type of aircraft and the Consolidated B24 Liberator. However, in October 1941 he was asked by the RAF to set up a new air navigation school, in which role he was re-commissioned into the RAFVR, initially as a temporary wing commander. Two months later, having completed his task, he was ordered to report to 4 Group in Bomber Command, where he was already known to the AOC, AVM Roderick *Carr*. Carr appointed him CO of 77 Squadron, flying Armstrong Whitworth Whitleys out of RAF Leeming against targets in both Germany and France.

In August 1941, some months before Bennett's posting to Bomber Command, the British Government, which had become increasingly concerned by what appeared to be very modest results from the strategic bombing campaign, had received a report into bombing accuracy.by a civil servant, Mr D. M. Butt. The overall conclusion was deeply disturbing. Of those aircraft which had claimed to attack the target, only one in three

44 Churchill's Eagles

had come within five miles of it. The figure dropped to one in five as a proportion of total sorties and to one in ten over the heavily defended Ruhr, whilst in the new moon period it dropped overall to one in fifteen. This revelation contributed to the transfer elsewhere of the AOC-in-C of Bomber Command, Air Marshal Sir Richard **Peirse**, in early 1942 and, after a brief interregnum, to the appointment as AOC-in-C of Harris, Bennett's former commander at Pembroke Dock. It may have been on Harris's initiative that Bennett was appointed CO of 10 Squadron in 15 April 1942, also at Leeming, but now equipped with Handley Page Halifax heavy bombers.

Less than a fortnight later, Bennett's aircraft was brought down during a raid on the battleship *Tirpitz*, which was moored in a Norwegian fjord near Trondheim. The crew all managed to parachute out safely and, once on the ground, Bennett met up with his wireless operator, the two of them succeeding in crossing the border to neutral Sweden, helped by friendly Norwegians. In the internment camp there they met two other members of the crew, and Bennett was subsequently to discover that the remaining three had been captured by the Germans. He himself was repatriated to the UK, arriving back there exactly a month after he had set off, to be informed that he had been awarded the DSO.

Bennett resumed operations with 10 Squadron, but, shortly before he was to set off on a bombing operation against the Italian fleet he was summoned to a meeting at Bomber Command HQ, where he was told by Harris that he was to take command of a new group devoted to target marking. The genesis of this lay with the Butt Report, which had continued to exercise minds at the Air Ministry. In particular, the Director and Deputy Director of Bombing Operations at the Air Ministry, respectively Air Commodore John *Baker* and Wing Commander Sidney *Bufton*, had argued strongly for a discrete target marking force. This was strongly resisted by both Harris, who thoroughly disliked the idea of a *corps d'élite*, and his group commanders, with the sole exception of Carr. The idea did, however, receive much more support at station and squadron commander level. Armed with evidence of this, Bufton was able to persuade the VCAS, Wilfred **Freeman**, who in turn convinced the CAS, Charles **Portal**, that such a force was essential to future success in the campaign.

Although Harris was initially unhappy with the decision, he decided to make the best of it. He had reserved to himself two important decisions, the name of the new formation and the identity of its commander. As far as the first was concerned, he disliked the Air Ministry suggestion of Target Finding Force and opted instead for Pathfinder Force (PFF). The name of

Basil **Embry**, a young and forceful leader, was put forward as its commander, but Harris preferred Bennett, who was duly appointed. Harris told him of his opposition to the whole concept and said that he would waste no effort on it, but also promised to support Bennett himself in every way he could.

The Pathfinder Force was formed on 15 August 1942, with its HQ at RAF Wyton. Each group in Bomber Command other than 2 Group, which operated only medium bombers, was ordered to supply one squadron, and these were 7 Squadron with Short Stirlings, 35 Squadron with Halifaxes, 83 Squadron with Avro Lancasters and 156 Squadron with Vickers Wellingtons. To these was added 109 Squadron, which had been engaged on the trials of electronic navigational aids, and which now joined the PFF with its De Havilland Mosquitoes. In due course the force was to standardize on the Lancasters and Mosquitoes. Initially, administrative services were provided by 3 Group, whilst the PFF concentrated on establishing itself operationally. The AOC of 3 Group was AVM Ralph **Cochrane**, who found Bennett difficult to work with on occasion, although the relationship between the two men at this time was perfectly civil.

It was decided at the outset that PFF aircrews would carry out more operations per tour than the rest of Bomber Command, initially set at sixty against thirty, but changed before long to forty-five. To compensate for what was a considerable extra risk, they were promoted to one rank above where they would otherwise have been and were also allowed to wear a special badge, a gold hovering eagle, on the flap of the left-hand breast pocket of their uniform. In spite of this, there were rarely enough volunteers, but Bennett employed in his HQ an experienced bomber pilot, Hamish Mahaddie, to act as his talent scout around the other groups, with considerable success.

There had been a number of advances in aids to navigation, the first of which, *Gee*, had appeared in early 1942. The navigator on a bomber would receive on his instruments a series of pulses, sent by a master and two slave stations. He would then measure the differences in their time of arrival, which would establish two co-ordinates, from which the aircraft's position could be accurately determined using a lattice framework overlaid on a map. Although, as it was a passive system, the aircraft's location could not be detected, there were two problems with it. The first was that, due to the curvature of the earth, the effective range was only 350 miles, which reached as far as the Ruhr Valley but no further. The second was that the Germans learnt how to jam the signal,

The second system was *Oboe*, which came into general use in December 1942, with much of the testing having been carried out by the Pathfinder

46   Churchill's Eagles

Force. This was also governed by ground stations, two in this case, which sent out pulses and received them back, enabling both the controllers and the aircraft's navigator to determine not only the position of the aircraft, but the point at which its bombs should be released. *Oboe* was inhibited by the inability of the stations to control more than one aircraft at a time, and this required large formations of aircraft to be accompanied by a small number of *Oboe* leaders. For the same reason as *Gee*, its range was limited, but it proved to be much more difficult for the Germans to jam and it became increasingly used in Mosquitoes, which had a much higher ceiling than the heavy bombers, thereby extending the effective range. Together with *Gee*, *Oboe* took the science of navigation well past the system of dead reckoning on which navigators had relied in the past.

Finally there was *H2S*, introduced in January 1943 and once again pioneered in its practical use by the PFF. This was a self-contained radar, mounted in the aircraft, which looked down on the ground over which it flew, displaying an impression on a screen in the navigator's compartment. It proved to be most useful when there was a feature which stood out, such as a coastline or a river. It had one serious drawback, however, that its transmission could be picked up by the *Naxos* radar warning receivers in German night fighters, enabling them to home in on their targets.

In addition to the navigational aids, a number of pyrotechnics were tested by the PFF. They included a range of flares used both as primary markers and to illuminate the target area. These were capable of being activated on the ground or at any given altitude by means of barometric fuses, and some were parachute flares which made a very slow descent to the ground. Target indicators were high-powered candles, produced in numerous colours, which were communicated in the briefing to the accompanying bomber crews and were difficult for the Germans to replicate as decoys at short notice.

The PFF employed three basic methods of target marking. The most straightforward was 'Newhaven', where the target was marked visually on the ground in clear conditions. The second was 'Paramatta', in which the target had to be located by *H2S* due to poor visibility and the target indicators were dropped blind, followed by a back-up of different coloured markers at which the following crews were instructed to aim. The last was 'Wanganui', sometimes known as 'sky marking' and used in conditions of zero visibility, when flares, fused to ignite at the estimated top of the cloud cover, were dropped blindly and the following crews were instructed to bomb through them.

A number of specific duties were allocated to the PFF crews. Of the most important, 'Route Markers' dropped flares at pre-established points on the route to guide the Main Force of bombers; 'Visual Markers' dropped their flares and markers in 'Newhaven' raids; 'Illuminators' used H2S for blind marking; 'Backers-up' dropped not only further target indicators, but also incendiary bombs; and 'Recenterers' arrived half-way though a raid to re-mark the target, in order in particular to compensate for any 'creep back', which became all too common as bombers sought to get away as quickly as possible.

The Pathfinders carried out their first operation against the town of Flensburg on the Baltic coast on the night of 17/18 August 1942, just three days after the force's formation. It was not a success; indeed, the town reported no hits at all, although two towns in nearby Denmark were bombed, albeit with very modest casualties. The second raid, a week later on Frankfurt, was little better, and it was not until the third raid, on Kassel on the night of 27/28 August, that significant damage was done to the target. Thereafter, Pathfinders participated in all major raids, for the most part with growing success, although there were frequently nights when the results turned out to be disappointing.

In January 1943 the Pathfinder Force was designated as a separate group within Bomber Command, 8 (PFF) Group, with Bennett promoted to acting air commodore. It was as such that it participated in the major campaign of the first half of 1943, the Battle of the Ruhr, in which Harris sought to destroy the largest industrial area in Germany. A number of specific cities and towns were attacked, of which the most important was Essen, home of Krupps, the country's largest armament company. The whole of the Ruhr lay within the range of *Oboe*, and Bennett built up his Mosquito squadrons to be able to provide a highly accurate approach to and marking of the target. Against more distant targets it was not nearly so effective at this time. In addition to more Mosquitoes, 8 Group now received two further Lancaster squadrons, one each from 5 Group and the new 6 (RCAF) Group.

When the Battle of the Ruhr, judged to have been a success, came to an end in July 1943, it was followed almost immediately by the much shorter Battle of Hamburg. Hamburg was the second city of Germany after Berlin and the largest port in Europe. It was also a highly suitable target, an old Hanseatic city, with narrow streets and buildings constructed with a high proportion of wood. Furthermore, it was close to the coast and on a large river, which made navigation by *H2S* that much more effective. Four raids were mounted against the city, on the nights of 24/25, 27/28, and 29/30 July

48   Churchill's Eagles

and 2/3 August. The first of these was notable for the introduction of another technological innovation. This was *Window*, strips of paper coated with aluminium foil, which were dumped in bundles from aircraft, creating an echo which completely confused the German ground-based and fighter interception radar. The result was to render the defence largely ineffective and to save many bombers from destruction at the hands of both anti-aircraft guns and night fighters.

It was the second raid, however, on the night of 27/28 July, which was one of the most devastating carried out. The initial marking by 8 Group was not as accurate as intended, concentrated as it was on the residential area. Conditions on the ground were very dry, with high temperatures and little rain having fallen for some weeks. The wooden buildings were thus extremely susceptible to incendiary bombs, and the result was a series of fires which eventually combined into an enormous firestorm, sucking up oxygen. Some 40,000 people were killed, and most of the rest of the population evacuated the city. Two further raids were carried out, one of which also largely hit the residential area, the other a failure due to a major thunderstorm, but by that time the city was a ruin.

A fortnight after the last raid on Hamburg, on the night of 17/18 August, a major raid was mounted by the combined bomber groups on Peenemünde, a location on the Baltic coast which intelligence had identified as the site of the development, manufacture and testing of the new V-1 flying bomb and V-2 rocket. This occasion marked the first time that a master bomber was used by 8 Group in order to guide in the bombers and correct inaccurate marking. This was not an entirely new concept. It had been invented for the Dams Raid in May 1943, during which Guy Gibson of 617 Squadron had directed his aircraft onto the Möhne and Eder Dams by the use of wireless intercoms. The squadron's parent formation, 5 Group, had subsequently used it on a successful raid on the Zeppelin works in Friedrichshafen, in which the aircraft had been accompanied by four Pathfinder aircraft from 8 Group, but the master bomber and his deputy had come from 5 Group squadrons. The raid had been substantially successful and, although 5 Group went its own way in 1944, the Main Force of Bomber Command would henceforward use 8 Group master bombers for all its raids, in which their aircraft circled over the target for the duration of the bombing giving directions as necessary to the attackers.

Neither the increasingly advanced navigational aids, nor the involvement of 8 Group with its navigational aids, marking techniques and master bombers, were to provide success for Harris's next offensive, the Battle of Berlin. Berlin was spread over a large area, with broad streets and concrete buildings, quite unlike Hamburg; moreover, it was beyond the range of *Oboe*. It was also very well defended. The sixteen raids between 18 November 1943 and 25 March 1944 caused much damage, but were overall a major failure, with huge losses to the bomber force, whilst a further sixteen raids on other cities during this period were, with a few exceptions, not notably more successful. They were followed two weeks after the last raid on Berlin by one on Nuremberg which produced Bomber Command's highest losses of the War.

There were no other Main Force raids on Berlin after this, but the city was not completely ignored. The Mosquitoes of 8 Group had been a great success, their altitude and speed allowing them to escape most of the defenders. The bomber version of the aircraft proved to be capable of carrying a single 4,000 lb 'Cookie', which even on its own caused considerable damage. Bennett put his bomber Mosquitoes together to form the Light Night Striking Force, which was employed initially to mount diversionary raids to distract attention from the Main Force, but later increasingly as a completely independent formation, with a major focus on Berlin. As well as causing damage, the raids ensured that significant numbers of guns and aircraft were allocated to the defence of the capital city, denying these to other fronts.

In the meantime, there had been significant developments at 5 Group, commanded by Cochrane since the end of February 1943. These were initiated by 617 Squadron, which had been retained as an independent special duties unit following the Dams Raid. The arrival of Leonard Cheshire as CO in November 1943 led to some new thinking on the squadron's tactics, using a new type of bomb sight. Cheshire persuaded Cochrane to let him carry out very low-level marking by Lancasters, the first such operation being carried out on a factory in Limoges in February 1944. Cheshire was eager to use the faster and more agile Mosquito and managed to borrow two of the aircraft, which he used for the first time two months later with great success. Harris, who had originally wanted to have a target-marking force in every single group, responded to the news by ordering Bennett to release two squadrons of Lancasters and one of Mosquitoes to 5 Group, which thereafter operated substantially independently of the Main Force. Bennett was furious, describing the move as 'a tremendous slap in the face to a Force which had turned Bert Harris' Bomber Command from a wasteful and ineffective force into a mighty and successful one.'* His relationship

---

* Bennett, *Pathfinder* First Edition p.214.

50   Churchill's Eagles

with Cochrane, never a particularly cordial one, plummeted and remained very poor for the rest of the War. He lobbied on a number of occasions to have his aircraft returned to him, but his attempts were unsuccessful. In the meantime, and for the rest of the War, he banned his own squadrons from carrying out low level marking, which he considered to be too dangerous, notwithstanding the results obtained by 5 Group.

Another blow came in October 1944 when 3 Group was also hived off from the Main Force in order to use the new *Gee-H* navigational and blind bombing system, which combined elements of both *Gee* and *Oboe*. The controllers were each able to handle more aircraft than was possible with *Gee*, so the device was carried by as many as a third of the group's aircraft, on which the others could take position.

Bennett was deeply unhappy with these developments, which marked the end of his monopoly on target marking, but 8 Group nevertheless went on to provide a vitally important service to 1, 4 and 6 Groups for the rest of the War, with increasingly good results as the Allies took more and more territory on the Continent and the German defences were worn down. Even without the units 'lent' to 5 Group, the group grew to number sixteen squadrons, six of Lancasters and ten of Mosquitoes, fully justifying Bennett's promotion to acting air vice-marshal in December 1943.

After the end of the War in Europe, Bennett resigned from the RAF and was elected unopposed as the Liberal Member of Parliament for Middlesbrough West in a by-election, although he lost his seat in the General Election just over two months later. He then became General Manager of British South American Airways, operating two derivatives of the Lancaster, first the Lancastrian and then the Tudor. The airline, hitherto privately owned, was nationalized in 1946, with Bennett remaining in charge as chief executive. It proved to be an unhappy time, as a number of aircraft came to grief. In January 1949 a Tudor was lost without trace over the Atlantic, and the Government grounded the remainder of the fleet. Bennett protested strongly, which led to his dismissal. He later went into a number of other commercial ventures and at one time owned Blackbushe Airport.

In 1958 Bennett published *Pathfinder*, a memoir of his flying career up to the end of the War. The book contained explicit criticisms of Cochrane's actions in both 3 and 5 Group, leading Cochrane to threaten legal action in respect of a number of inaccuracies, which he maintained, with considerable justification, threw doubt on his own fitness to run a bomber group. Bennett was forced to agree to a number of amendments for the subsequent paperback edition, although further reprints after Cochrane's death reverted to the original text.

It has sometimes been asserted that Bennett was the only Bomber Group AOC not to receive a knighthood. This was far from the truth. Twenty of the thirty-five wartime AOCs were never knighted, and of the fifteen who were, all but two, one of whom was Cochrane, were honoured some time after they had moved on from the post and thus recognized subsequent promotions and other achievements.

Bennett was undoubtedly a difficult and demanding man, but his leadership of the Pathfinders was a major factor in the growing success of Bomber Command in the last three years of the War. It was largely due to his efforts that bombing accuracy improved hugely, causing great concern in Germany, which itself led to both the country's Eastern and Western Fronts being denied adequate air support and the number of guns that they needed.

Air Marshal (later Air Chief Marshal) Sir Norman Bottomley KCB, CIE, DSO, AFC (1891–1970)

For the greater part of the War responsibility at the Air Ministry for the day-to-day conduct of all the RAF's activities, other than human resources, logistics and training, lay with the Deputy Chief of the Air Staff, under whom were a number of Assistant Chiefs, who between them covered operations, intelligence, policy, operational requirements and tactics. From May 1941 until May 1942 and from July 1943 to September 1945, this appointment was held by Air Vice-Marshal N. H. (later Air Marshal Sir Norman) **Bottomley**, providing valuable continuity.

Bottomley had applied to join the RFC from the East Yorkshire Regiment in December 1915 and was accepted for instruction as a pilot, passing out in April 1916 and joining 47 Squadron, which was just forming at Beverley in his home county and was subsequently engaged in home defence against airship attacks. The squadron departed for Salonika before the end of the year, but Bottomley did not accompany it, being posted instead to 50 Squadron in Kent as a flying instructor. He must have shown some particular aptitude for initial flying training as, in the spring of 1917, he was selected to become an instructor at the British Flying School in Vendôme, which was actually operated by the RNAS. He was to serve there until the end of the War and was awarded the Air Force Cross in November 1918. He was selected for a permanent commission in the RAF as a flight lieutenant in August 1919.

52   Churchill's Eagles

Bottomley spent most of the next decade on staff duties, serving initially in 1 Group in the UK and then in Egypt, although in the last eighteen months of his service there he was Chief Flying Instructor at 4 Flying Training School at Abu Sueir. In 1924 he attended the third course at the RAF Staff College at Andover, following which he was posted to the Air Ministry in the Directorate of Operations and Intelligence. In October 1928 he was appointed to his first and only squadron command at 4 Squadron, flying initially the long-lived Bristol Fighter and then the Armstrong Whitworth Atlas in an army co-operation role.

Bottomley was clearly well regarded for his intellect, as he was selected first to attend the Imperial Defence College for its 1930 course and then to join the Directing Staff at the Staff College, where Philip **Joubert** was the Commandant and Bottomley's fellow instructors included men of the calibre of Arthur **Tedder**, Ralph **Cochrane**, Charles *Medhurst* and George *Pirie*.

Thus far in his career, Bottomley had had no experience of operations since defending Hull and other UK cities against airship raids in the Great War. This was now to change, as in October 1934 he was appointed to the command of 1 (Indian) Group, with promotion to group captain.

In the face of constant threats to the RAF's independence after the Great War from both the Army and the Royal Navy, Lord Trenchard had cast it in the role of an inexpensive solution to peace-keeping in some of the Empire's more difficult territories. This had worked very well in British Somaliland, Iraq and Aden, in all of which the RAF became the dominant armed service. It did not, however, succeed to anything like the same extent in India, whose North-West Frontier remained troublesome throughout the inter-war period and occasionally burst into open revolt. To the Indian Army in peacetime the frontier represented the single largest reason for its very existence, and it was determined not to allow what many of its senior officers considered to be an upstart service to threaten this state of affairs.

This changed with the appointment in March 1935 of Air Marshal Sir Edgar **Ludlow-Hewitt** as AOC India. Ludlow-Hewitt was a highly intelligent and experienced officer who had for the two previous years served at the Air Ministry simultaneously as Deputy Chief of the Air Staff and Director of Operations and Intelligence, and he continued to enjoy the confidence of the then CAS, Sir Edward Ellington, and his successor in 1937, Sir Cyril **Newall**. More pertinently to his new appointment, he had been AOC Iraq from 1930 to 1932 and had a very good understanding of how to impose peace on rebellious peoples through air operations. He managed to establish a good working relationship with the C-in-C India, General Sir

Robert Cassels, although a great deal of suspicion, amounting at times to outright hostility, remained within the senior ranks of the Indian Army.

The RAF played only a small role on the Frontier in 1935, Bottomley's first full year in India, although the Army was engaged for much of that year in a campaign against the Mohmand tribe. From 1936 to 1939, however, thanks to Ludlow-Hewitt, it was much more fully employed in operations against Ghazi Mirzali Khan Wazir, better known as the Faqir of Ipi, who roused the tribes of Wazirstan, the Wazirs, Mahsuds and Bhitanni, in a long-running revolt against British rule. 1 (Indian) Group bore the brunt of the RAF's role, deploying nine squadrons, albeit never all at once, from their stations at Peshawar, Risalpur and Kohat. They were mostly equipped with Westland Wapitis, rugged aircraft well suited to army co-operation, although Hawker Harts and Audaxes were also operated. Punitive action against villages was less common than in Iraq and Aden; on the other hand, the aircraft were frequently used to protect columns of troops and also trains. The Faqir was allowed no respite and forced to remain constantly on the move, and as the campaign progressed, the RAF's offensive role became more important, whilst the Army was confined to road protection. Amongst other developments, Bottomley implemented a policy of dive bombing rather than medium level bombing, improving precision when villages were attacked, the inhabitants having been warned by leaflets in advance to evacuate them.

Having been appointed a Companion of the Order of the Indian Empire in the Coronation honours list and further rewarded for his leadership by a DSO, the citation for which mentioned his frequent low level reconnaissance flights over the battlefield, Bottomley arrived back in the UK in early 1938 to take up a new appointment as Senior Air Staff Officer at Bomber Command, the right-hand man to the AOC-in-C, who was Ludlow-Hewitt. It seems likely that the latter had asked for Bottomley specifically after their work together in India. Ludlow-Hewitt was not a particularly easy man to serve, an austere non-smoking, non-drinking Christian Scientist, but he demanded exceptionally high standards and to him is due the credit of bringing Bomber Command to the highest possible state of efficiency by the time that war was declared, although he could do nothing about the quality of its aircraft. There were already five groups, No.1 operating the Fairey Battle, No.2 the Bristol Blenheim, No.3 the Handley Page Harrow, replaced in 1939 by the Vickers Wellington, No.4 the Armstrong Whitworth Whitley and No.5 the Handley Page Hampden. Although these aircraft were an advance on the bi-plane light and medium bombers of the early to

54   Churchill's Eagles

mid-1930s, with the sole exception of the excellent Wellington they were deficient in most other respects and compared very unfavourably with the medium bombers starting to appear in Germany.

Just as concerning to Ludlow-Hewitt at the time of his appointment was the command's preparedness for war, which he considered seriously deficient, particularly as to both flying training, with night flying experience almost unknown, and the equipment aboard the aircraft, notably navigational aids. Furthermore, the increase in the number of men making up a crew, from the two who had manned the Hawker Hart of the mid-1930s to the six who were required for the Wellington, all of whom needed specialist training, threw up yet more problems. Ludlow-Hewitt was tireless in his travels around his command, giving station and squadron commanders a very hard time and gradually lifting standards. Whilst he was away from his HQ at High Wycombe, Bottomley held the fort.

Ludlow-Hewitt led Bomber Command through the early months of the War, when it was strictly limited to attacks on ports and shipping, whilst even industrial targets remained off-limits, due to concerns about killing or wounding civilians. Even this highly restricted warfare resulted in a number of disasters: RAF orthodoxy, espoused by Bottomley himself, held that, with tight formation flying, bombers could hold off fighter attacks with defensive fire, but this proved to be catastrophically wrong, especially in daylight. Ludlow-Hewitt had one unfortunate weakness, that he was severely distressed by casualties amongst his own men and, for this reason if no other, he would never have had the stomach for a full-throttle bombing campaign. In April 1940 he became instead an outstanding Inspector-General of the RAF, in which role his eye for detail was exactly what was needed.

Ludlow-Hewitt was followed at Bomber Command by Charles **Portal**, who would play a major part in the rest of Bottomley's wartime career, but Portal left the command in October 1940 to relieve Newall as CAS. He was succeeded by Air Marshal Sir Richard **Peirse**, who, in the light of the Blitz on Great Britain by the Germans, was authorized to extend Bomber Command's operations to German industrial cities. Bottomley did not remain at High Wycombe for long, however, succeeding Arthur **Harris** as AOC 5 Group in November 1940 and thereby continuing to be one of Peirse's immediate subordinates.

5 Group at this time was still substantially equipped with the Handley Page Hampden, a relatively fast and manoeuvrable aircraft, but not one suited to a sustained bombing campaign against German industry or, as the Battle of the Atlantic was gathering momentum in favour of the Germans in the

spring of 1941, against German and French ports. It remained in squadron service until early 1942, doing particularly valuable work in laying mines amongst the inshore shipping channels of the North Sea and the Baltic, but from the end of 1940 it began to be replaced by the Avro Manchester.

In June 1941 Bottomley was summoned by Portal to become Deputy Chief of the Air Staff at the Air Ministry, where he would remain for the rest of the War. From 1920 to 1940 the DCAS had been the right-hand man of the CAS, with direct responsibility for all the RAF's affairs except those presided over by the Air Member for Personnel and the Air Member for Supply and Equipment. Bottomley's predecessors in the appointment had included Newall, Ludlow-Hewitt and Peirse, and his immediate predecessor was Harris. In 1940, however, the new position of Vice-Chief of the Air Staff was created, held initially for a short time by Peirse and then by the immensely talented and influential Wilfrid **Freeman**, who became Portal's chief confidant. Thereafter the Vice-Chief was always considered to be senior to the Deputy Chief, although both sat on the Air Council. It was VCAS who acted for the CAS whenever the latter was away, a frequent occurrence during Portal's tenure. There was a Vice-Chiefs of Staff Committee, which sat regularly throughout the War, mostly to deal with the less important tri-service matters, but also to act for the Chiefs of Staff Committee when its members were at the frequent Allied conferences, but there was no Deputy Chiefs of Staff Committee.

As DCAS, however, Bottomley did chair the regular meetings of the Assistant Chiefs of the Air Staff and the directors of their departments; these sessions addressed all the important issues which were current and on which immediate decisions had to be taken. The Assistant Chiefs were responsible respectively for Operations, Intelligence, Operational Requirements and Policy. Beneath them were a number of directorates, notably Planning, Overseas Operations, Bomber Operations, Fighter Operations, Air Transport Operations, Maritime Operations, Operational Requirements, Tactics and Public Relations. Training was also initially included, but was split off in July 1940 under an additional Member of the Air Council.

Two of Bottomley's subordinate Assistant Chiefs took up little of his time. One was Richard *Peck*, who was responsible for Policy, which amongst other things meant looking into the future, and also for Public Relations, which included contacts with the Press in which he was, more often than not, the anonymous 'Air Ministry Spokesman'. The other was Ralph *Sorley*, the ACAS (Operational Requirements), who was the leading RAF expert on the development of new aircraft and had been substantially responsible

56   Churchill's Eagles

for the Spitfire and Hurricane being armed with eight machine guns in their wings rather than the traditional two in the nose. In 1943 he was to become the Controller of Research and Development at the Ministry of Aircraft Production with a seat on the Air Council and was succeeded by AVM John *Breakey*, who had been running the Directorate of Operational Requirements.

Between May 1941 and May 1942, Bottomley took direct responsibility within the Air Staff for Operations, but in the latter month the post of DCAS was abolished and he became instead the ACAS (Operations) alongside the other Assistant Chiefs. In July 1943, however, and until shortly after the end of the War, this move was reversed, with Bottomley once again becoming DCAS with a separate ACAS (Operations) reporting to him, initially AVM W. A. *Coryton*, followed by AVM T. M. *Williams* in August 1944,.

Inevitably, the oversight of operations undertaken by overseas commands was made much more difficult than that of home commands by geography and time. In practice a very high degree of control was accorded to their AOCs-in-C, acting in conjunction both with their naval and military counterparts and, after the United States entered the War, under the orders of their Supreme Commanders.

It was a different matter for the home commands, which were on the DCAS's doorstep. Coastal Command, however, took up a relatively small amount of Bottomley's time, since operational control had been ceded to the Royal Navy in February 1941, whilst Transport Command was only formed in March 1943 and was much smaller than the others until after the end of the War. This left Fighter and Bomber Command, the two formations which took up most of his time.

When Bottomley arrived at the Air Ministry in late 1940, the Battle of Britain was at an end, although the Blitz on London and other cities was at its height, and Hugh **Dowding** had been replaced as AOC-in-C by Sholto **Douglas**. Fighter Command had proved itself as a defensive formation, at least in daylight; effective night fighters were yet to emerge. Over the next two years it was to develop an offensive role by way of fighter sweeps over France, with a view to bringing to battle and defeating the German fighters. Codenamed 'Rhubarbs', and 'Circuses' when accompanied by bombers, these operations were in retrospect of doubtful value, with RAF casualties outnumbering those of the Luftwaffe.

Part of the problem was the excellence of the German fighters. The Messerschmitt Bf.109E of the Battle of Britain, once released from tightly escorting the slow-moving bombers, had proved itself a tough opponent to the Spitfire Mk 1, whilst the Bf.109F which replaced it turned out to be superior. The latter met its match in the Spitfire Mk V, which was then itself outclassed by the Focke-Wulf 190, which first appeared in late 1941. The Spitfire, however, proved capable of almost infinite upgrading and the Mk IX was produced to counter the Fw.190, but there was no such alternative for the Hurricane, which was relegated to service in the Middle East and later the Far East.

Just as important was the development of night fighters. The unimpressive Boulton Paul Defiant and Bristol Blenheim were replaced by the Bristol Beaufighter, equipped with the first effective Airborne Interception radar, and then by the excellent De Havilland Mosquito. By mid-1944 Fighter Command had very effective control over British airspace as far as enemy bombers were concerned, but the appearance of the German flying bombs produced yet another challenge, countered to some effect by the Hawker Tempest.

Douglas was followed in November 1942 by Trafford **Leigh-Mallory**, and, a year later and for the rest of the War, by Roderic **Hill**, at which time Fighter Command was re-named Air Defence of Great Britain for eleven months. Whatever the name, there were no major differences of policy between the AOC-in-Cs and Bottomley.

Not so Bomber Command! When Bottomley was appointed DCAS, Peirse was still AOC-in-C, but the perceived failures of the command, highlighted by the Butt Report in August 1941 which concluded that only one in four bombers were able to drop their bombs within five miles of their target and that the results were even worse over heavily defended areas such as the Ruhr Valley, resulted in his removal; he was sent out to India and succeeded on an acting basis by AVM John *Baldwin*, prior to the arrival of Harris in February 1942.

The division of responsibility between the Air Ministry and the commands was that the former determined the overall strategy, expressed in a succession of directives, and the latter delivered it. Directives could also be used for specific operations, the most famous of which, as far as Bomber Command was concerned, was Operation CHASTISE, the Dambusters Raid. Provided that they complied with the directives, the AOCs-in-C had considerable latitude on how they executed them.

Harris did not see the relationship in quite the same light. As far as he was concerned, Bomber Command was a war-winning formation, but only if it followed the path set by himself, which was not always the same as the one determined by the Directorate of Bomber Operations.. This led inevitably

58   Churchill's Eagles

to tension between the two parties. Whilst Harris and Bottomley had a tolerably good personal relationship, their professional differences were many. Bottomley was supported by the Director of Bombing Operations, Air Commodore John *Baker*, and the Deputy Director, Group Captain Sydney *Bufton*, who succeeded Baker from March 1943 until the end of the War in Europe. Harris saw the three men as a thorn in his side and was wont to refer to them as 'the three Bs'!

In most circumstances, the Air Ministry had the upper hand. Examples of this were the formation of the Pathfinder Force, the Dambuster Raid and the switch from bombing Germany to supporting Operation OVERLORD, the invasion of North-West Europe. In each case determined opposition from Harris was overridden ultimately by Portal, the CAS and a man whom Harris unequivocally admired.

The most serious division between the two sides was over the general conduct of the allied bombing campaign for the last two years of the War in Europe. In June 1943 a directive, which was based on decisions taken at the Casablanca Conference earlier in the year, was issued on the orders of the Combined Chiefs of Staff to both Bomber Command and the US Eighth Air Force in respect of Operation POINTBLANK. This called for focused attacks on Germany's submarine yards, aircraft industry, transportation networks and oil plants. The USAAF interpreted this literally, while Harris did not, instead persisting with area bombing. He was, however, forced to change direction when responsibility for the bombing campaign between March and August 1944 was switched from the Air Ministry and the US Strategic Air Forces in Europe to General Eisenhower, Supreme Commander Allied Expeditionary Force, acting through Tedder as his deputy. The priorities became instead, firstly, support for ground operations in the period leading up to and the initial months after D-Day, and secondly, attacks on the V-1 flying bomb sites.

When the strategic bombers were released back to the Air Ministry and the US Strategic Air Forces, it was Bottomley to whom Portal deputed control over Bomber Command. Once again Harris interpreted his directives liberally, preferring area bombing to attacking what he described as 'panacea' targets, primarily oil production and distribution facilities, but also roads, railways, canals and communication centres. Neither Bottomley nor, more importantly, Portal, was able to control him completely, whilst his profile was too high to allow him to be sacked.

It was only after the end of the War against Japan that Harris stepped down and there was no further role for him. He was succeeded as AOC-in-C by Bottomley, who had a very different task on his hands. His first priority was to reduce Bomber Command to a strength appropriate for peacetime. Only two operational groups, Nos 1 and 3, and one training group, No. 91, were retained, whilst the number of squadrons or training units in each was significantly reduced. Some new units emerged, notably the Central Bomber Establishment, set up to look into the future in the light of both the move towards the development of jet aircraft and the implications of the atomic bomb.

In January 1947 Bottomley took over from Arthur Barratt as Inspector-General of the RAF. It was important that the running down of the wartime establishment should not compromise the high standards of the service in terms of personnel and equipment, and the Inspector-General was there to ensure that this was the case. After a year in the role he retired, to become the director of administration at the BBC, effectively the deputy to the Director-General.

Although Wilfrid Freeman thought that Harris was the stronger of the two as DCAS, Portal valued Bottomley highly enough to keep him in that key position until the War was over, whilst Bottomley also enjoyed the confidence of Sir Archibald Sinclair, the Secretary of State for Air. There can be no doubt that, albeit in a low-profile way, he made a great contribution to the RAF's prosecution of the war in the air.

Air Chief Marshal Sir Frederick Bowhill GBE, KCB, CMG, DSO* (1880–1960)

By some way the oldest RAF officer in continuous employment for almost the entirety of the Second World War was Frederick **Bowhill**. Only seven years younger than Hugh Trenchard, the 'Father of the RAF', and exactly a year younger than Trenchard's immediate successor, John Salmond, the CAS from 1930 to 1933, Bowhill had reached air rank over a decade before the beginning of the War and was to lead two of the most important commands throughout all but the final months of the conflict

Known to his friends as 'Ginger' for his red hair, Bowhill began his working career in the Merchant Marine, in which he served for some sixteen years, qualifying as a Master Mariner. In 1898, however, he also joined the RNVR as a midshipman, being promoted to sub-lieutenant in 1904 and to lieutenant in 1911. In the following year, whilst on leave from his employer, Peninsula & Orient, he learnt to fly and, the year after that, applied to join the RNAS. He was posted initially to HMS *Hermes*, a light cruiser which

60   Churchill's Eagles

had become the first seaplane carrier in the Royal Navy, its three aircraft being launched from a platform constructed over the fo'c'sle.

Shortly after war was declared against Germany, Bowhill was appointed to command HMS *Empress*, a steam packet converted into a seaplane carrier for three aircraft. The ship participated in the Cuxhaven Raid on Christmas Day 1914, in which nine aircraft from the *Empress* and two other similar vessels attacked the Zeppelin sheds in the German port with only modest success, although the threat of further such raids caused the temporary relocation of the German High Seas Fleet.

In August 1916 Bowhill was appointed to command 8 Squadron RNAS in Zanzibar for operations against the Germans in East Africa, for which he was awarded the DSO. He returned to Europe to command 62 Wing in the Aegean, during which time his aircraft were diverted to supporting the White Russian forces of General Denikin against the Bolsheviks, for which he received a bar to his DSO.

On the formation of the RAF in 1918 Bowhill became a lieutenant colonel and in the following year he was awarded a permanent commission with the rank of wing commander. He returned to Africa in the autumn of 1919, this time to Somaliland, where he was prominent in Trenchard's first successful demonstration of peace-keeping in the British Empire through air control, flying in operations against Mohammed Abdullah Hassan, better known as the 'Mad Mahdi'. After a brief period in Palestine and Egypt, he returned to the UK in the summer of 1920, initially on the staff of Group Captain Robert Clark-Hall at 29 Group and then as the Chief Staff Officer at the group's parent formation, Coastal Area; this was the forerunner of Coastal Command, with which he would become intimately associated many years later. In 1924 he was posted back to the Middle East for four years, finishing his tour as SASO HQ Iraq Command, in which role he was able to use his earlier experience in air control against hostile insurgents.

In May 1929, by now highly regarded by his superiors, he returned to the UK for his first posting to the Air Ministry, as Director of Organisation and Staff Duties. Two years later he was appointed to command the Fighting Area of Air Defence of Great Britain with the rank of air vice-marshal. By that time the Bristol Fighter and the Armstrong Whitworth Siskin had been phased out of service, to be replaced by the rugged but rather slow Bristol Bulldog, which equipped the majority of the Fighting Area's squadrons, and the faster and more elegant Hawker Fury, the first RAF fighter to achieve a speed of more than 200 mph. The Fighting Area was concentrated in an arc around London through the Home Counties and East Anglia. Bowhill was deeply concerned about the effectiveness of his force, whose deficiencies were highlighted in the air defence exercises shortly after his arrival. This was, however, at a time of government parsimony, and it was not until the Ten Year Rule was abandoned in the year after he took command that things began to change; but even then the fighters were, at least for the time being, the poor relation of the bombers.

In July 1933 Bowhill returned to the Air Ministry, this time with a seat on the Air Council as Air Member for Personnel in succession to Edward **Ellington**, the new CAS. By this time the Expansion Period was under way, with Scheme A being given government approval in July 1934. With many more airfields and squadrons proposed, it was Bowhill's job to ensure that the growing service was properly manned. On the one hand it was by a long way the smallest of the three services, and more than doubling the numbers of personnel from the nearly 20,000 in 1933 to over 40,000 in 1937 was not necessarily a huge demand, especially at a time of high unemployment in the country. On the other hand, it was the most technical of the services and, both in aircrew and ground crew, training to a satisfactory level of ability required a great deal of time; this was one of the AMP's responsibilities. Bowhill also proposed the formation of the Women's Auxiliary Air Force, which was to make a major contribution to the manpower issue. His achievement as AMP was certainly appreciated; by the time he stepped down to become AOC-in-C Coastal Command in August 1937 he had been both knighted and promoted to air marshal.

Coastal Command was at the time by a long way the Cinderella of the three 'fighting' home commands. Its tasks were seen as maritime reconnaissance, trade protection and, more generally, co-operations with the Royal Navy. The Navy, having failed in its attempts since 1918 to have the RAF absorbed into the other two services, had focused in the 1930s primarily on gaining full control of carrier-borne aviation, and in this it proved successful in May 1939, when the Fleet Air Arm was returned to the control of the Admiralty. It had less interest in shore-based aircraft, whilst understanding that these had their own uses. In Bowhill the Navy found that it had a willing collaborator who, after long years of sea service himself, could understand their requirements and was eager to help.

Unfortunately, the tools at Bowhill's disposal were few and for the most part ineffective. Even when war was declared two years after Bowhill's appointment, his force was woefully deficient in both numbers and modern aircraft. Its backbone consisted of ten squadrons of Avro Ansons, a twin-engined aircraft which was designed for communications and training; with

62   Churchill's Eagles

a single forward-firing machine gun, another in a dorsal turret and a modest bomb load of 360 lbs, it was hardly capable of serious offensive action. There were also two squadrons of Vickers Vildebeest biplane torpedo bombers, which were effectively obsolete, six squadrons of twin-engined flying boats, three each of Saro Londons and Supermarine Stranraers, both of which had entered service as recently as in 1936 but which lacked both the weaponry needed for tackling surface vessels and submarines and the range for open ocean reconnaissance. The only modern aircraft came in the form of three squadrons of Short Sunderlands, which would prove to be outstanding and whose various marks equipped the command throughout the War and for long afterwards.

From his HQ at Northwood, Bowhill had to make do with what he had, but his lack of resources was such that he was even reduced to using De Havilland Tiger Moth light biplanes for short range sweeps, known as 'Scarecrow Patrols', over the English Channel and North Sea. As it happened, the 'Phoney War' did not stretch his modest forces as unduly as it might have, the German U-boats of the time lacking the range to threaten Atlantic trade to the extent which was to become quickly apparent after the fall of France, although from the start they proved to be a serious menace around British coasts. Bowhill, whose nautical roots went deep and who harboured no resentment towards the Royal Navy for its attacks on the RAF in the inter-war period, made a considerable effort to built strong links with his naval counterparts and encouraged the same from his subordinates at all levels. In particular, he built up a vital channel of communication between his HQ and the Submarine Tracking Room at the Admiralty, and in February 1941 he redeployed the HQ of 15 Group, which was responsible for operations over the Western Approaches and the Irish Sea, from Plymouth to Liverpool, where it was co-located with the Royal Navy's HQ Western Approaches.

In spite of this close inter-service co-operation, the results were modest. If the weaponry available was poor, the means of finding the enemy was even poorer. There were a few modest successes, one of which was the identification of the German ship *Altmark* in the Jøssingfjord in February 1940, which led to the liberation of British merchant seamen who had been taken prisoner by the *Graf Spee*.

In the summer of 1940 there had been a move by Lord Beaverbrook, in alliance with A. V. Alexander, the First Lord of the Admiralty, and Admiral of the Fleet Sir Roger Keyes, the Chief of Combined Operations, to hand over Coastal Command to the Royal Navy. Wilfrid **Freeman**, the highly regarded VCAS, threatened to resign if this happened, and the Sea Lords at the Admiralty were less than enthusiastic. Coastal Command did come nominally under the Royal Navy's operational control, largely in terms of establishing its priorities, although effectively it was always directed by the AOC-in-C.

By early 1941 Coastal Command had improved on a number of fronts. The Vildebeests were long gone, to be succeeded by Bristol Beauforts, whilst longer-range aircraft, the Armstrong Whitworth Whitley, whose service in the command was relatively short-lived, and the very effective Vickers Wellington were both released from Bomber Command as the latter began its conversion to four-engined bombers. The Ansons were replaced by the first American aircraft to be deployed by the RAF, the Lockheed Hudson. These initially arrived by ship in parts, which were then assembled in the UK, but from November 1940 they began to be flown over. Consolidated Catalina flying boats were also added. Coverage of the Atlantic was greatly improved by the dispatch of squadrons to Iceland in October 1940, whilst important developments were taking shape on ASV radar to locate U-boats on the surface and the Leigh Light to illuminate U-boats on the surface at night; the latter was promoted by Bowhill, but subsequently rejected by his successor, only to be reinstated when the alternative failed to work satisfactorily.

Arguably Bowhill's greatest individual contribution to the war at sea came in May 1941, shortly before he left Coastal Command. The German battleship *Bismarck* had broken out into the Atlantic and sunk the pride of the Royal Navy, the battlecruiser HMS *Hood*. Substantial naval forces were deployed to destroy the ship, but contact was lost. The naval commanders believed that Captain Lütjens would steer directly for Brest, but Bowhill, drawing on all his knowledge and experience of the sea, thought that he would sail south first before turning east towards the French coast. He asked permission to send a Catalina to cover this particular course and it found the *Bismarck*, which allowed HMS *Ark Royal*, steaming up from Gibraltar, to send off the Fairey Swordfishes which crippled the ship sufficiently for the British pursuers to be able to sink it.

Bowhill had actually been due for retirement in 1939, but like Hugh **Dowding** he was asked by the then Secretary of State for Air, Kingsley Wood, to stay on. Now, a few months short of his sixtieth birthday, his service was extended yet again. This time it required him to cross the Atlantic to become AOC of the newly formed Ferry Command. The first flight of the Hudsons across the Atlantic in November 1940, which was led by Donald **Bennett**, was followed over the course of the war by thousands

64 Churchill's Eagles

more of many types of American and Canadian-built aircraft. The rapidly increasing volumes required a separate organization to control the flow, and the Atlantic Ferry Organisation ('ATFERO') was set up at Dorval Airport, near Montreal, by a Canadian businessman, Morris W. Wilson, employing civilian pilots, navigators and wireless operators, who were repatriated by sea after their flights. ATFERO operated initially under the auspices of the Ministry of Aircraft Production. By the summer of 1941 it was clear that it needed a much more substantial RAF presence, and Ferry Command was established, with its HQ at Dorval.. The movements on the other side of the Atlantic were handled by the Overseas Air Movements Control Unit ('OAMCU'), based in Gloucester. In July 1941, a month after Bowhill had arrived in Canada, the responsibility for ATFERO was transferred from the MAP to the Air Ministry and re-named Ferry Command, which also took control of OAMCU, re-named 44 Group, in the following month.

The growing activities of Ferry Command became too much for the civilian American and Canadian pilots and other aircrew, so Bowhill arranged for them to be supplemented by the best of the aircrew trained under the Commonwealth Air Training Plan in Canada and the United States. He himself was joined in Canada by his wife, an exceptionally popular WAAF officer who always saluted him punctiliously!

In the meantime, a number of transport operations had grown up in other major theatres of war. These included the Aircraft Delivery Unit, later 216 (Ferry) Group, which handled from its HQ in Egypt all movements on the West African Reinforcement Route, which ran from Takoradi on the coast of Ghana, across West Africa and the Southern Sahara to Khartoum in the Sudan and thence up the Nile to Egypt. Its equivalent in India, based initially outside Karachi to receive and refurbish aircraft arriving in India and dispatch them to the front line in Burma, was 179 (Ferry) Wing.

In March 1943 all these activities were brought together as Transport Command, with its HQ in Harrow. It now comprised four groups, 44, 45 (the former Ferry Command and still based in Dorval), 216 and 229, the last of these the successor to 179 Wing. Bowhill was appointed AOC-in-C. He had in fact technically retired from the RAF on 1 July 1942, but had been immediately re-employed in the rank of substantive air vice-marshal (air marshal on taking over Transport Command) and acting air chief marshal.

Transport Command was to grow significantly for the remainder of the war. Not only did it continue with its ferrying and purely transport functions, but it increasingly supported military operations on the ground. These included the invasion of Sicily, the unsuccessful attempts to seize the main islands of the Dodecanese and, most importantly, the operations of the British airborne divisions in North-West Europe, notably at Arnhem and the crossing of the Rhine. These divisions already enjoyed the dedicated services of 38 Group under Leslie **Hollinghurst** which was not part of Transport Command, but for these specific operations 38 Group was joined by the new 46 Group from Transport Command, whose duties otherwise were to supply the British and Canadian armies and evacuate their casualties.

Bowhill retired at last in March 1945, having handed Transport Command over to Ralph **Cochrane**. He then served as Chief Technical Adviser to the Ministry of Civil Aviation for many years, finally retiring in 1957. He had enjoyed a remarkably long career, which saw him remaining in high command in the RAF long after his contemporaries had retired. To him can be ascribed the beginnings of the transformation of Coastal Command from a very weak peacetime force, which had been largely ignored by both ministers and service chiefs, into a highly effective one, although it only achieved its full potential under his successors. He also created Transport Command, which made a very substantial impact on the closing stages of the war and was to become in peacetime one of the most important formations of the RAF.

Air Vice-Marshal (later Air Chief Marshal Sir) Harry Broadhurst
GCB, KBE, DSO*, DFC*, AFC (1905–1995)

Harry **Broadhurst**, 'Broady' to all those who knew him well, was not only one of the most charismatic RAF officers to achieve high rank during the Second World War, he was also one of the most successful. His specialization was in fighters and fighter-bombers, not only in the United Kingdom during the Battle of Britain and for the following year, but also in the Western Desert, Libya, Tunisia, Sicily and Italy, during which time he came to the favourable notice of General (later Field Marshal) Sir Bernard Montgomery. Montgomery insisted on his return to the UK in early 1944 that he should command the RAF group which would co-operate so well with Second Army during the campaign from Normandy to the Baltic and, although Broadhurst went on to high rank and command thereafter, it is as an RAF officer whom Monty regarded as a key member of his own team that he is probably best remembered.

Broadhurst always had a yen to join the RAF, but his father, who had himself served in the Army, insisted that he should enter his own old service and he was duly gazetted as a second lieutenant in the Territorial Army

66   Churchill's Eagles

shortly before his twentieth birthday. He did, however, persuade his CO to arrange for him to be seconded to the RAF in October 1926 in order to train as a pilot, which he did with 11 Squadron, flying the Vickers Horsley. Remaining with the squadron, he applied for and was awarded a short service commission in the RAF, resigning from the TA at the same time. Having taken courses in signals and electrical wiring, which would stand him in good stead subsequently, he was appointed 11 Squadron's signals officer.

In November 1928 11 Squadron left by sea for India, arriving at Risalpur in January 1929, where it was re-equipped with the general-purpose Westland Wapiti. Risalpur, close to Peshawar, was one of several RAF stations on the North-West Frontier, and the squadron became involved in tackling two rebellions which took place between April 1930 and March 1931, one by the Afridi tribe in the Khyber area, the other by the Nationalist Redshirt party in the country around Peshawar. In spite of Trenchard's successful policy elsewhere in the 1920s and 30s of suppressing revolt by vigorous air action, the Army in India preferred to handle any insurgency itself, usually by blockade and the building of fortified posts along the major roads. The RAF was effectively confined to supporting a few small actions and establishing communications with the outposts, and it would be several years before a more efficient practice of army/air co-operation was established in India.

Broadhurst returned to the UK after his two-year tour, which was recognized by a mention in despatches, and was posted to 41 Squadron, which operated the single-seat Bristol Bulldog fighter, a much more lively aircraft than the Wapiti. He took to it like a duck to water, becoming a highly proficient practitioner of both gunnery – he came top three years running in the air firing competitions held at Sutton Bridge – and aerobatics, leading aircraft from the squadron in the annual Hendon Air Display, which involved a combination of tight formation flying and breathtaking individual stunts. In the autumn of 1933 Broadhurst attended a flying boats pilots' course, but he was actually removed from it before its completion when he was appointed a flight commander of another fighter squadron, No.19, which also flew Bulldogs, although it converted in 1935 to the much faster Gloster Gauntlet.

In November 1936, shortly after being granted a permanent commission, Broadhurst was posted to 4 Flying Training School at Abu Sueir in Egypt as Chief Ground Instructor. He returned home in the summer of 1937, having in the meantime been both promoted to squadron leader and awarded the Air Force Cross. After a brief period on the staff of 2 Group, his only experience of bombers in his entire career until nearly twenty years later, he joined the

RAF Staff College course at the beginning of 1938, graduating at the end of that year and being appointed to command 111 Squadron at RAF Northolt.

A year before Broadhurst's arrival, 111 Squadron had been the first to equip with the Hawker Hurricane, the RAF's first monoplane fighter. At the end of October 1939 it was transferred to RAF Acklington for a six weeks' stay and it was whilst it was there that Broadhurst brought down a Heinkel 111 to score the squadron's first victory of the war. For this and his leadership generally, Broadhurst was awarded the Distinguished Flying Cross in the New Year's Honours of 1940. Shortly afterwards he was appointed Wing Commander Training at 11 Group at Uxbridge, but on 10 May, the day that the Germans invaded France, he became the station commander at RAF Coltishall in Norfolk. Such was the situation in France, however, that on 18 May he was seconded to command 60 (Fighter) Wing, part of the Air Component of the British Expeditionary Force; but nine days later, following the withdrawal of the RAF's squadrons from France, he was back in Coltishall. His first task thereafter, on the orders of the AOC-in-C of Fighter Command, Hugh **Dowding**, was to tour the command to lecture pilots on lessons learnt in France, after which he was appointed to command RAF Wittering under **Leigh-Mallory**, which was not on the front line during the Battle of Britain but, when the Germans began to bomb British cities, played a major role in defending the East and West Midlands, and Broadhurst himself flew on operations as often as he could. During the earlier part of the battle, moreover, the station did see a considerable turnover of squadrons arriving from 11 Group under **Park** to recuperate from their participation in the main battle. In December 1940 Broadhurst was posted to command RAF Hornchurch, a sector station covering the Thames Estuary, and apart from six weeks attached to the British Air Staff in Washington DC in October and November 1941 in order to brief the Americans on Fighter Command's activities, he continued to see action there and on fighter sweeps over France until May 1942. Broadhurst's own tally by the time he left Wittering was thirteen German aircraft destroyed, seven probables and ten damaged, and he had been awarded the DSO, a bar to the DSO and a bar to the DFC. He had had one very close call himself, when his Spitfire was hit, first by an enemy fighter and then by flak on his way back to England. He limped home and managed to execute a perfect belly landing.

In May 1942 Broadhurst became the Deputy Senior Air Staff Officer at 11 Group, which had been commanded by Leigh-Mallory since December 1940. He was there for only five months before he received a posting to Egypt,

68   Churchill's Eagles

with promotion to acting air commodore, as a supernumerary at Western Desert Air Force ('WDAF'), which the Air Ministry considered to be in need of a senior officer with experience of modern fighter tactics. Neither Sir Arthur **Tedder**, the AOC-in-C Middle East, nor Arthur **Coningham**, the AOC at WDAF, welcomed this, and Broadhurst was kept waiting in Cairo. After a long wait with no summons he went to Air HQ Middle East to ask to be returned to the UK, at which he was sent up to the desert, where he relieved George *Beamish* as SASO WDAF on 29 November 1942.

The WDAF had grown out of 204 Group, itself formed in April 1941 under Air Commodore Raymond *Collishaw*, who handed it over to Coningham three months later. It comprised the fighters and light bombers operating over the Western Desert of Egypt and Libya in support of what shortly became Eighth Army, notably during and in the aftermath of Operation CRUSADER, which saw the Army advance to the border of Cyrenaica and Tripolitania and subsequently withdraw again to the Gazala Line. Having been defeated there in June 1942 by Rommel, a further retreat was inevitable, this time to the Alamein Line. Under General Sir Claude Auchinleck, the C-in-C Middle East, the Eighth Army fought the indecisive First Battle of El Alamein, after which Auchinleck was succeeded by General Sir Harold Alexander, with Bernard Montgomery in command of Eighth Army. At the end of October and into November Montgomery fought the Second Battle of El Alamein, which pushed the Axis forces into headlong retreat.

One of Montgomery's first decisions on taking over Eighth Army had been to place his HQ alongside that of the WDAF. Operations and Intelligence were particularly closely co-located, and Broadhurst, who had met Monty in the UK earlier in the year and had got on very well with him, now developed close relationships with Eighth Army's staff officers and notably the Chief of Staff, Freddie de Guingand. He discovered that a system of co-operation had been developed using Army Air Support Controls, whereby signallers operating wireless tentacles in divisional and brigade HQs could call for air strikes to be carried out by the RAF. This system had worked well at both Alamein and at Alam Halfa nearly two months earlier, albeit that the response times before the RAF arrived were still only rarely less than thirty minutes and often much longer. Moreover, the RAF's priorities remained first air superiority, which Broadhurst himself believed had been substantially achieved over the Luftwaffe and the Regia Aeronautica by the time he arrived in the desert, and second high level bombing, not only of front lines, but also of rear areas and communications. This, so it transpired as Eighth Army followed up the retreating Germans, was not always very accurate against military traffic, as the bombers tended to release their payloads at a right angle to the enemy direction of travel, rather than along it, in order to avoid anti-aircraft fire.

On 18 February 1943 Coningham was appointed to command the North African Tactical Air Force ('NATAF'), incorporating both the now renamed Desert Air Force ('DAF') and the US XII Air Support Command, which provided a similar service to the Allied Armies in Tunisia, together with the Anglo–American Tactical Bomber Force: Broadhurst succeeded him as AOC Desert Air Force, with promotion to air vice-marshal, the youngest in the RAF at the time. By then Eighth Army was approaching the Mareth Line in Tunisia, where a frontal attack was initially repulsed, with heavy casualties. Montgomery then set in train an alternative strategy, a left hook through the mountains by the New Zealand Division, later reinforced by other formations. This, too, encountered substantial opposition at El Hamma, barring a breakout to the coast behind the Mareth defences.

De Guingand and Broadhurst now came up with a major innovation, on which they had been working for some time. This involved the use of fighter-bombers to pulverize the enemy positions continuously just ahead of the ground attack, effectively acting as mobile artillery. Broadhurst had carried out trials which he believed proved that this would work, but his proposal to use it in action was resisted by both Coningham, who considered it to be too dangerous, and by many of the pilots concerned. Broadhurst persisted, however, and Coningham grudgingly allowed it to go ahead. The main ingredient other than the aircraft consisted of RAF ground controllers up with the forward troops in armoured cars; these were able to call in and direct strikes as required ahead of the advance. In the mid-afternoon of 26 March, sixteen squadrons of 'Kittybombers' (Curtis P-40 Kittyhawks carrying bombs under their fuselages or wings) attacked out of the sun, protected against counter-attack by five Spitfire squadrons overhead and supported by a squadron of Hurricane 'tank-busters', all of which caused havoc amongst the defenders and played a material role in forcing their retreat. This was the first demonstration of what later became known as the 'cab rank' system of army/air co-operation. Coningham's fears were not realized, as losses of aircraft were acceptably low at less than 5 per cent.

The same tactics were employed by the DAF in the final thrust towards Tunis in May 1943, in conjunction with the other formations in NATAF. The next campaign was mounted to occupy Sicily, for the invasion of which both the planning and the initial control of Eighth Army's sector were carried out in an underground command centre in Malta. Montgomery wanted the

70   Churchill's Eagles

air operations during the invasion period to be controlled by Broadhurst and he was accordingly summoned to Malta. However, Tedder, by this time the Allied Air C-in-C in the Mediterranean, insisted that command should be vested in Keith **Park**, the AOC Malta, and this remained the case until the DAF established itself in Sicily. Thenceforward the DAF staff worked alongside that of Eighth Army as they had been accustomed to do in North Africa. At one point in the campaign Broadhurst's closeness to Montgomery and de Guingand nearly resulted in his demise. He was asked to accompany them in Monty's personal Flying Fortress to Palermo to meet Monty's fellow army commander, George Patton. The runway at their destination, however, proved to be far too short. It was only the quick reactions of the pilot which saved them as he braked into a sharp turn, thereby avoiding hitting a building with disastrous results. Even so, the undercarriage collapsed and the aircraft was a write-off!

The DAF continued to support Eighth Army in the next campaign, on the mainland of Italy in the autumn of 1943 and the ensuing winter. The terrain was difficult and, other than in the plain along the Adriatic coast, airfields were few and far between. Broadhurst, however, had managed to liberate a Fieseler Storch left behind by the Luftwaffe. This was a two-seater communications aircraft, much prized for its exceptionally short take-off and landing characteristics, which gave him access to the smallest airfields. It was so light that Broadhurst's first such aircraft was blown off a beach and into the sea, but he managed to procure another.

Montgomery left Italy on the last day of 1943 to take up his appointment as C-in-C 21st Army Group in preparation for the invasion of North-West Europe. Less than three months later, Broadhurst was summoned back to the UK to take over the command of 83 Group from AVM William **Dickson**, who in turn succeeded him at the DAF. 83 Group was the formation of the Second Tactical Air Force ('2 TAF') which was to support the British Second Army in much the same way that the DAF had supported Eighth Army. Broadhurst had been asked for specifically by Monty, whose request had been made via the Chief of the Imperial General Staff, Field Marshal Sir Alan Brooke, to the Chief of the Air Staff, MRAF Sir Charles **Portal**. The excellent relationship which Broadhurst had established with Monty's staff and his familiarity with Lieutenant General Miles Dempsey, who had been GOC XIII Corps under Montgomery in both Sicily and Italy and was now commanding Second Army, had provided a compelling argument for the move. Broadhurst's immediate superior was once again Coningham as AOC-in-C 2 TAF, who reported to Leigh-Mallory as C-in-C Allied

Expeditionary Air Forces. Tedder, as Deputy to the Supreme Commander, General Dwight D Eisenhower, was given the oversight of all Allied air operations, which included those of Bomber Command and the US Eighth Air Force, as well as 2 TAF's American equivalent, US Ninth Air Force.

On D-Day itself Broadhurst flew over the beaches in a Spitfire and reported back what he saw to De Guingand. 83 Group's task in the aftermath of the landings was to support Second Army in pushing back the Germans around the city of Caen. Montgomery's own strategy was to draw German formations, particularly armoured divisions, onto the British front, allowing the American First Army to overrun the Cherbourg Peninsula and then to break out into Brittany and Maine. This strategy was poorly understood by Tedder and Coningham, who expected to see advances all along the line, which would, inter alia, result in the capture of enemy airfields, notably the large one at Carpiquet, west of Caen.

When Carpiquet failed to be taken, Tedder and Coningham became increasingly critical of Montgomery. Monty, for his part, instead of communicating with Coningham, his RAF opposite number, preferred to deal directly with either Broadhurst or Leigh-Mallory. The criticisms of Tedder and Coningham, which began with the lack of airfields and continued with Montgomery's failures to advance as far as he had promised on either side of Caen, nearly cost Montgomery his job, but he was protected by Brooke, who managed to convince Churchill to keep him in place.

In the meantime Broadhurst and his American opposite number, Major General Pete Quesada, were managing very well and were able to base an increasing number of their aircraft in Normandy due to the excellent work of the airfield construction units, who were able to deliver ten airfields in the British sector during June and a further seven in July. Broadhurst moved his Advanced HQ to Normandy alongside Dempsey's and close to Montgomery's Tactical HQs on D-Day+1. 83 Group at this time comprised ten wings, which between them contained twenty-nine fighter, ground attack and reconnaissance squadrons and four artillery spotting squadrons. It was in the ground attack role that the group most distinguished itself. Instead of Kittyhawks, the ground attack squadrons were equipped with Hawker Typhoons, armed with both cannon and rockets. The climax of 83 Group's campaign in Normandy came on 7 August and the following days, when the group and Quesada's 9th Tactical Air Command destroyed the German armoured divisions which were attacking Mortain in an attempt to cut off the American advance out of Normandy. The Typhoons and the American

72 Churchill's Eagles

Republic P-47 Thunderbolts created carnage there and later in the Falaise pocket, in which much of the German Army in Normandy was trapped.

2 TAF now included two more formations, 84 Group supporting First Canadian Army and 85 Group controlling all ground units, notably repair and maintenance. The advance to Brussels was relatively straightforward, but thereafter resistance began to stiffen and Second Army failed to establish a bridgehead over the Lower Rhine in Operation MARKET GARDEN. Whilst 84 Group's Typhoons were able to soften up the enemy for XXX Corps driving up the narrow corridor from the Belgian border to Nijmegen, at Arnhem itself 1 Airborne Division's radio communications failed miserably, and it was not possible to provide the close support necessary for the paratroopers.

At the end of 1944 83 Group found itself heavily in demand once again, this time in the Ardennes during the Battle of the Bulge, when, as soon as the weather permitted, every possible aircraft was thrown into first stopping the Germans and then driving them back. On the first day of the New Year the Luftwaffe mounted its last great attack of the war against Allied airfields, particularly those around Brussels. Tremendous damage was done to the aircraft on the ground, but they were easily replaced, whilst the Germans had not only lost many aircraft but, more importantly, also their pilots, and both were in critically short supply.

83 Group continued to provide air support until the German surrender in May 1945, with Broadhurst particularly responsible for the detailed planning of air operations during the crossing of the Rhine. He had had one particular upset during the campaign when his Storch, which he had had crated up and shipped back from Italy and had used extensively after D-Day, came to grief. Flying back from Evere, near Brussels, to his HQ at Eindhoven, he forgot to adjust the fuel supply, the engine cut out and the Storch landed on a flat roof, which then collapsed. Broadhurst emerged unscathed, but the aircraft was a write-off.

Knighted for his wartime service shortly after the end of the war in Europe, Broadhurst went on to have a distinguished post-war career. A year as Air Officer Administration at Fighter Command was followed by his becoming AOC of 61 Group in the UK. He spent 1949 as a student at the Imperial Defence College, after which he was appointed SASO at HQ British Air Forces of Occupation in Germany. In April 1952 he became Assistant Chief of the Air Staff (Operations) under first John **Slessor** and then 'Dicky' Dickson as CAS, his only term of service at the Air Ministry. He then commanded the Second Tactical Air Force, formerly the British

The Air Marshals 73

Air Forces of Occupation, before being appointed AOC-in-C of Bomber Command.

It was whilst he was at Bomber Command that Broadhurst, who had walked away from near disaster in both a Spitfire and a Fieseler Storch, had his most serious accident. Returning from a world tour in 1956 to show off the RAF's newest V-Bomber, the Avro Vulcan, he was acting as co-pilot as the aircraft attempted to land in fog at Heathrow. The pilot totally misjudged his approach and made a very hard landing in a field a few hundred yards short of the runway, which destroyed the undercarriage. Broadhurst and the pilot were able to eject, but the other four members of the crew were killed.

Broadhurst's last appointment was as Commander, Allied Air Forces Central Europe. He retired in March 1961 to become managing director of A. V. Roe & Co, manufacturers of the Lancaster and Vulcan amongst many other fine aircraft, and when that company was taken over by Hawker Siddeley, he became its Deputy Managing Director.

Much admired throughout the RAF and by many in the British Army, Broadhurst's early career was as a fighter man through and through, but he became one of the leading exponents of tactical air power in support of land campaigns. A man of notably sunny disposition, he was always made very welcome at Montgomery's HQ, where he managed skilfully to avoid involvement in the inter-service politics which bedevilled the relationships further up the tree.

Air Marshal (later Air Chief Marshal) the Hon. Sir Ralph Cochrane GBE, KCB, AFC (1895–1977)

With the exception of the Battle of Britain, by some way the most famous episode in the history of the RAF during the Second World War was the Dambusters Raid. Unlike the Battle of Britain, which saved the United Kingdom from invasion at a time when it was militarily at its weakest and ensured the country's survival until it could be joined by powerful allies, the Dambusters Raid, whilst causing serious damage to Germany's industrial infrastructure for a short period, was inconsequential in the greater scheme of things. It was, however, a shining example of heroism and inventiveness, and both the raid's leader, Guy Gibson, and the scientist who created the weapon which did the damage, Barnes Wallis, became household names. The same could not be said of the RAF officer who was given the responsibility for both planning the raid and raising and training 617 Squadron to execute it. This was Ralph **Cochrane**, the AOC 5 Group Bomber Command, who

74   Churchill's Eagles

was, in the eyes of many, the most successful bomber group leader of the war.

Cochrane was born in 1895, the third son of the 1st Lord Cochrane of Cults and grandson of the 11th Earl of Dundonald, the Chief of the Cochrane clan. His great-grandfather, Thomas Cochrane, 10th Earl of Dundonald, was one of the outstanding naval officers of both the Napoleonic Wars and the Wars of Independence in South America and Greece, and there was a very strong naval tradition in the family. It was unsurprising, therefore, that he entered the Royal Naval College at Osborne shortly before his thirteenth birthday, his two years there followed by two more at the Royal Naval College at Dartmouth and his appointment thereafter as a midshipman in the Royal Navy.

The beginning of the Great War found Cochrane serving in the Grand Fleet on the battleship HMS *Colossus*, but, not least because he was subject to sea sickness, he volunteered for an unspecified transfer, which turned out to be to the airship branch of the Royal Naval Air Service. The airships were largely deployed against the threat of German U-boats, and although there were few outright victories, their very presence over a convoy did deter the submarines. Cochrane undertook patrols over the English Channel and North Sea, but became more involved as a test pilot, both of non-rigid and rigid airships, and it was whilst he was testing the latter that he first met Barnes Wallis, who was working as a designer at Vickers. For his work Cochrane was awarded the Air Force Cross at the end of the War.

In the summer of 1920 Cochrane was sent out to Egypt, both to set up what it was hoped would become a major staging post on the future airship route to India and Australia and to test airship fabrics in a hot climate. It was whilst he was there that he met MRAF Viscount Trenchard, the 'Father of the RAF', who told him not to waste his time but to learn to fly an aeroplane. This he did at 4 FTS and he was subsequently appointed a flight commander in 45 Squadron, flying Vickers Vernon transport aircraft based at Hinaidi, just outside Baghdad in Iraq. In November 1922 a new commanding officer was appointed to the squadron, Arthur **Harris**, who would much later play a significant role in Cochrane's career. Moreover, Cochrane's fellow flight commander was Robert *Saundby*, whose career path would cross both Cochrane's and Harris's at much the same time. Harris obtained permission to convert the Vernons into bombers, by cutting a hole in the nose of the aircraft for a bomb sight and carrying bombs under the wings, achieving more success against rebel Kurds than more conventional light bombers.

On Cochrane's return to the UK in January 1924 he was appointed as Officer Commanding No.3 Squadron of the Boys' Wing at RAF Cranwell, in which future ground crew for the RAF received their technical training. After just over a year, and having passed the necessary exam, he was selected for the RAF Staff College at Andover and, on passing out, was appointed as a staff officer at HQ Wessex Bombing Area, with particular responsibility for training. This took him to all the area's stations to ensure that the correct standards were being applied. Two of the squadrons with the highest standards were based at Worthy Down, not far from Andover, No.58 commanded by Harris and No.7 by another officer who would have a major impact on Cochrane's career, Charles **Portal**. Both were focusing heavily on night flying, which they believed bombers would have to carry out in any war.

In 1928 Cochrane was posted to Aden as the second most senior officer on the staff of Aden Command. A year later and in spite of an injury incurred in a crash landing, he was appointed CO of 8 Squadron, flying Fairey IIIFs over the Aden Protectorate. This gave him further experience of bombing operations against rebellious tribesmen. He returned to the UK towards the end of 1929 to join the directing staff at the RAF Staff College.

In January 1932 Cochrane was posted to the Air Ministry, working in the Plans section of the Directorate of Operations and Intelligence, first under Portal and then under Harris. Whilst he was there he was briefly seconded to join the AOC Middle East, Air Vice-Marshal Cyril **Newall**, as the Air Ministry representative on a tour of East Africa and Rhodesia to consider the defence needs of the British colonies there. His term at the ministry was followed by a year as a student at the Imperial Defence College in 1935, after which he was posted to HQ Inland Area, which subsequently became Training Command.

It was whilst Cochrane was serving at Training Command that he was asked by Harris, on behalf of the Air Ministry, if he would be prepared to go to New Zealand to advise the Government about the country's air defence, which had hitherto been effectively the responsibility of the army. Two previous visits to the country by senior RAF officers since the Great War had resulted in little action being taken, and the Ministry was now only prepared to send a middle-ranking officer – by then Cochrane had three years seniority as a wing commander – albeit one whose intellect was by that time widely recognized. He accepted the assignment and travelled by ship to New Zealand, where he rapidly produced his recommendations for the Labour Government, which was concerned about the rapidly changing

76   Churchill's Eagles

political climate both in Europe and in Asia. These were accepted in full, and Cochrane was asked to stay on as the first Chief of the Air Staff of the Royal New Zealand Air Force, a position which, with the agreement of the Air Ministry, he was delighted to accept. As the appointment was to be for at least two years, he arranged for his wife and children to join him in Wellington.

Promoted to group captain, Cochrane assembled an excellent team to form the new Air Board and immediately set about drafting the legislation to establish the RNZAF as an independent force. This was quickly enacted, and he set about implementing his own recommendations, which involved recruiting and training a large number of men for both air and ground crew, ordering modern aircraft, together with some older ones as a temporary expedient, and building new airfields, which were established at Whenuapei near Auckland and Ohakea near Palmerston North, both on the North Island. The existing base at Wigram, near Christchurch on the South Island, was devoted to training. Cochrane also went on a cruise around the Pacific Islands to mark out sites for new airfields there.

Cochrane's term as CAS of the RNZAF came to an end in March 1939 and he was posted back to the Air Ministry as a Deputy Director of Intelligence. This was not a job that suited him and he asked Portal, at the time the Air Member for Personnel, for a transfer and was appointed the station commander at RAF Abingdon. Early in 1940 he became Senior Staff Officer at 6 (Training) Group in Bomber Command and in July of that year AOC of 7 (Training) Group, with promotion to air commodore. The group consisted of four Operational Training Units, 13 and 16 OTUs providing the final stage of training on the Bristol Blenheim, whilst 14 and 15 OTUs did the same for Handley Page Hampdens.

Cochrane had been with 7 Group for less than four months when he received a visit from Portal, who was about to take up his appointment as CAS. Cochrane took the opportunity to point out what he regarded as a number of flaws in the flying training process. He was astonished when, at 06.00 on the following morning, he received a phone call from the Air Ministry instructing him to report immediately to the Ministry as Director of Flying Training. He arrived there at an important time, as the RAF was committed to substantial growth in all its home and overseas commands and was, at the same time, incurring significant losses. It was thus vital that the flying training process should turn out large numbers of pilots and other aircrew in as short a time as possible, although in practice, especially for Bomber and Coastal Command crews, this took at least a year. The students began at Initial Training Wings, with largely classroom instruction, and moved on to Elementary Flying Training Schools in which they learnt basic flying skills on aircraft such as the De Havilland Tiger Moth, and then to Service Flying Training Schools, where those destined for large aircraft converted to multi-engined types, and finally to the OTUs, which were the responsibility of the various front line commands.

Actual pre-OTU training came under the jurisdiction of the AOC-in-C Flying Training Command, but the Directorate of Flying Training was responsible for formulating policy and strategy and communicating them by way of directives. One major development had taken place by the time that Cochrane arrived. This was an agreement between the leading Commonwealth countries, most notably Canada, to provide training facilities in those countries not only to their own air forces, but also to the RAF, thereby freeing up airfields in the UK and allowing training to be carried out free of the threat of enemy attack. The British Commonwealth Joint Air Training Plan henceforward satisfied most of the demands for trained aircrew. It was later informally extended to the USA, in which country many British and Commonwealth pilots were trained.

Cochrane was responsible directly to the Air Member for Training, Air Marshal Guy **Garrod**, with whom he had a good relationship. His overall aim was to ensure that standards were met and that the syllabus and methods of training at each stage of the process met the demands of what were effectively his clients, the home and overseas commands. Uniformity was largely achieved by the production of official training manuals, written to be as simple and unambiguous as possible and backed up by a humorous magazine called *Tee Emm*, the abbreviation for 'Training Manual'.

After nearly two years as Director of Flying Training Cochrane was ready for a change, and it came in the form of his appointment as AOC 3 Group Bomber Command in September 1942. It was no coincidence that the AOC-in-C of Bomber Command since the previous February had been Harris, and that Harris's SASO was Saundby, thus reuniting those who had been the CO and flight commanders of 45 Squadron twenty years earlier. When Cochrane arrived at 3 Group, it was approaching the end of a long conversion of its squadrons from the excellent medium bomber, the Vickers Wellington, to the unsatisfactory Short Stirling, the first of the four-engined heavy bombers. The Stirling was bedevilled with technical problems, but most importantly, it was never able to achieve its planned altitude on operations, which left it especially vulnerably to both enemy flak and night fighters. On the other hand, it was now being equipped with the first of

78   Churchill's Eagles

a number of navigational devices, *Gee*, which allowed navigators to obtain accurate fixes of their position, and by early in 1943 would start to receive the *H2S* ground-scanning radar.

A third device, *Oboe*, which unlike *Gee* had the merit of being impervious to enemy jamming, was also becoming available, although it was largely confined to a new formation, the Pathfinder Force, later 8 (Pathfinder Force) Group, commanded by Donald **Bennett**. 3 Group provided administrative services and a link to Bomber Command HQ for the Pathfinder Force before it established its own HQ.

Cochrane had been largely out of touch with the many new developments at Bomber Command over the last two years and some of his initial proposals for the group's employment were not appropriate, but he soon recognized this. Moreover, he developed new ideas of his own during a busy period for Bomber Command, firstly over Germany and then, in early 1943, in raids against German naval bases in France from which U-boats were being deployed very effectively in the Battle of the Atlantic. These included 'time-and-distance' bombing, in which the bombers would release their loads at a precise time after passing over a particular landmark. He had little opportunity to refine such ideas in 3 Group, however, as at the end of February 1943 he was posted as AOC to 5 Group.

5 Group had not, by this time, achieved its later pre-eminence, but it was nevertheless highly regarded, in part because it had enjoyed an unbroken sequence of excellent commanders – Harris himself, Norman **Bottomley**, Jack **Slessor** and Alec *Coryton* – and in part because, having been allocated the relatively ineffective Handley Page Hampden at the beginning of the war, it had now been re-equipped with the Avro Lancaster, the outstanding British heavy bomber of the war.

Cochrane's squadrons were largely based in Lincolnshire, and it was from his HQ in Grantham, only two weeks after he had assumed command, that he was summoned to see Harris about a new and top secret operation, codenamed *Chastise*, whose objective was nothing less than the destruction of the great dams of the Ruhr and Weser valleys, notably the Möhne, the Eder and the Sorpe. Harris told Cochrane that a completely new weapon, codenamed *Upkeep* and known less formally as 'the bouncing bomb', had been designed by Cochrane's old friend from the airship days, Barnes Wallis, and that its delivery on target would require high proficiency in very low-level flying. He was ordered to form a new squadron to carry out the operation and to both supervise its training and plan the raid.

The one aspect of the operation for which Cochrane was not responsible was the selection of the CO of the new squadron, Guy Gibson, but he and Gibson got on well from the start. The new unit, soon to be designated as 617 Squadron, was based at RAF Scampton and it was there that Gibson, aided by Cochrane, began to assemble its crews, mostly highly experienced but also some relative novices. The two men devised a programme of low flying, including over some of the reservoirs and dams of Northern England and Wales. In the meantime trials of *Upkeep* were proceeding, initially at Chesil Beach in Dorset and later at Reculver on the north Kent coast. The plan for the raid was put together by a very small team of Cochrane himself, his SASO, Harry Satterley, the Station Commander at Scampton, Charles Whitworth, and Gibson. Flying large aircraft at a constant 60ft above water and launching *Upkeep* so that it bounced across the surface to the dams posed serious problems, but these were resolved by low technology solutions.

The raid was launched on the night of 16/17 May 1943. As far as its results were concerned it was a qualified success, with the destruction of the Möhne and Eder dams, causing loss of power and widespread flooding in the Ruhr industrial area and the Weser valley. However, the Sorpe Dam, of a different type of construction than the others, remained intact. Moreover, the cost to 617 Squadron was enormous, with eight out of the nineteen aircraft on the raid lost to accidents or enemy action. Nevertheless, the raid provided a welcome boost to British morale.

Harris decided to keep 617 Squadron in being for special operations, the intention being that the crews should be largely formed of those who had completed two bombing tours but wanted to keep flying. Unlike any of the other squadrons in Bomber Command, it was not subject to the normal planning process at the command's HQ, with Cochrane being given a significant amount of independence as to its employment. Gibson was called away to accompany Churchill to the Quadrant Conference, and the command devolved onto George Holden. He, however, was killed in a disastrous raid on the Dortmund–Ems Canal and, after a brief interregnum, was succeeded by Leonard Cheshire, who began the process of building the squadron up again, now concentrated on low level target marking and high level precision bombing, the latter using a new type of bomb sight.

In the meantime, Cochrane's attention was necessarily largely devoted to the rest of 5 Group, which since his arrival there had been engaged in the Battle of the Ruhr alongside the rest of Bomber Command. This involved attacks on every suitable night on the major cities of the Ruhr Valley, interspersed with others on industrial centres such as Munich, Stuttgart and

80   Churchill's Eagles

even Berlin. Cochrane was able to select one target of his own, the Zeppelin factory at Friedrichshafen, to demonstrate the effectiveness of time-and-distance bombing. This was successful, the bombers flying on to bases in North Africa, from which they all returned without loss. This raid also saw the first appearance of a 'Master Bomber', who controlled it from the air in much the same way that Gibson had done during the Dams Raid. The time-and-distance technique was employed again by 5 Group alone in a raid by all the Bomber Command groups on the V-weapons facility at Peenemünde.

The Battle of the Ruhr, widely considered to have been a success, was followed by the much shorter Battle of Hamburg, which saw the city effectively destroyed over ten days in July/August 1943. During that summer the targets were widely spread over Germany and Northern Italy, but towards the end of the year and into 1944 Harris attempted to do to Berlin what he had done to Hamburg. This was, however, a resounding failure, and he was reluctantly forced to give up towards the end of March 1944, that month concluding with a disastrous raid on Nuremberg, the costliest of the war. To the relief of many, Bomber Command now focused on bombing targets in France in preparation for the invasion of North-West Europe, for the initial period of which it became subject to the control of SHAEF.

In the meantime, Cheshire and 617 Squadron had been largely focused on the precision bombing of V-1 flying bomb sites in Northern France. Cheshire had developed a method of low-level marking, using selected pilots in Lancasters and achieving considerable success. For a raid on an industrial facility near Toulon, however, he managed to borrow two De Havilland Mosquitoes, one of which he flew himself, placing his markers with complete accuracy onto the target from 800ft. When Cochrane asked Harris for two more such aircraft, he was astonished to be given not only a whole squadron, but also two squadrons of Lancasters, all from 8 (Pathfinder Force) Group. Bennett, whose relationship with Cochrane had already become difficult, was furious and complained vigorously to Harris, who refused to let him have them back. Thenceforward, 5 Group was to operate substantially on its own, becoming known to the rest of Bomber Command as 'the Independent Air Force' and to 8 Group as the 'Lincolnshire Poachers'!

Cochrane was now able to develop more new ideas of his own. He had felt for some time that the marking methodology adopted by the Pathfinders led to targets being obscured by smoke. He now proposed to adopt 'offset' marking, whereby the markers were dropped 1,000 yards upwind of the target with a false wind communicated to all navigators, enabling them to calculate where the target was without it being covered by smoke: other variants of this improved accuracy even further. He also insisted on pilots carrying out what he believed to be a more effective way for their aircraft to 'corkscrew' to escape an attacking night fighter, implemented a new landing system to get returning aircraft onto the ground as quickly as possible and changed the aircraft maintenance regime with a beneficial effect on their availability for operations.

5 Group continued to focus on France in the aftermath of D-Day. Three nights after the initial landings 617 Squadron dropped for the first time Barnes Wallis's 12,000lb *Tallboy* bomb onto the Saumur railway tunnel, to deny the railway to German reinforcements. *Tallboy* was used increasingly thereafter on U-boat and E-boat pens and V-1 sites, but its spectacular success came on 8 November 1944, when 617 Squadron, with Cheshire's successor, 'Willie' Tait, in command, sank the German battleship *Tirpitz* in a Norwegian fjord.

Following Bomber Command's release from the control of SHAEF, 5 Group returned to Germany with increasing success. Unbeknownst to Cochrane, he had been asked for by Portal during the summer of 1944 to take up an appointment as ACAS (Policy) at the Air Ministry. However, Harris refused to release him and he continued as AOC 5 Group until January 1945, by which time the outcome of the war in Europe was certain. On New Year's Day he was awarded the KBE, a relatively rare event for an air vice-marshal and a very rare one for a serving group commander.

Cochrane's new appointment in February 1945 was as AOC-in-C Transport Command, with promotion to air marshal. Transport Command had been formed in March 1943, having initially grown out of the Atlantic Ferry Organisation, which was set up in late 1940 to control the supply of aircraft manufactured in the USA and Canada to the UK, prior to being taken over by the RAF and renamed Ferry Command in July 1941. Its first AOC-in-C was Frederick **Bowhill**, who now handed over to Cochrane. Portal was already thinking forward to the post-war requirements of the service and recognized that it would have to be significantly reduced overall, the exception being Transport Command, where he needed an extremely able organizer in the only part of the RAF expected to grow. At the time of Cochrane's appointment it comprised six groups, four in the UK and one each in the Middle and Far East. One of them was employed in airborne operations, most notably in the crossing of the Rhine by 21st Army Group, the others in ferry services, the transportation of supplies, trooping and the operation of trunk routes.

82   Churchill's Eagles

Transport Command did indeed grow in the aftermath of the end of the war in the Far East, initially because one of the most important tasks of the RAF was the repatriation of those serving abroad, most of whom would be discharged into civilian life. However, in early 1946 it hived off its groups in the Middle and Far East to local commanders, leaving it with the responsibility for all transport operations within the UK and Europe, trunk routes to all parts of the world, ferry services and airborne operations. Whilst based as Bushy Park, Cochrane did a great deal of travelling, flying as far afield as New Zealand, where he was able to rekindle old friendships. His duties also took him for the first time to the USA, where, amongst other things, he was invited to lecture at both the Air Command and Staff College and the National War College.

Cochrane had a number of concerns about Transport Command, notably a high accident rate, largely resolved by the decision that aircrew should be limited where possible to a single type of aircraft, and unserviceability, the solution for which was contrary to what might be expected, an increase in the hours which aircraft were allowed to fly before undergoing an inspection. He was later to say that Transport Command had been the toughest appointment in his RAF career, but he left it in September 1947 in good shape, as was evidenced by its performance in the Berlin Airlift the following year.

Cochrane's next appointment was as AOC-in-C Flying Training Command. There was not much that he did not know about flying training, having served as the training officer at Western Bombing Area and in Training Command, later commanding an operational training group before being appointed Director of Flying Training. The training programme had been significantly scaled down in peacetime, with the distinction between elementary and service flying training schools abolished and a reversion to the pre-war system of 'all-through' training. Although already much reduced, the RAF was still of considerable size, and some 3,500 aircrew, of whom 2,300 were pilots, passed out of flying training in 1948. Cochrane's major achievement, however, in collaboration with Basil **Embry**, the ACAS (Training), was to establish the RAF Flying College to teach the practical aspects of flying ever more complex aircraft, increasing numbers of which were now powered by jet engines.

Cochrane had an excellent relationship with Portal's successor as CAS, Arthur **Tedder**, by whom he was told that he would be recommending him as his successor. In the event, however, the Prime Minister, Clement Attlee, decided to appoint Jack Slessor. Slessor, however, invited Ralph to become VCAS, which he agreed to as he had always got on well with him. As well as acting as Slessor's right-hand man and sitting on the tri-service Vice-Chiefs of Staff Committee, he took responsibility within the Air Council for training, signals and operational requirements, the last of these the most important at a time when aircraft development was changing at a great pace, with modern jet fighters and the new V-bombers due to enter service and guided missiles being developed for both attack and defence.

Cochrane retired from the RAF in November 1952. He had been approached some years earlier by BOAC about joining the airline, probably as managing director, but with a lack of outstanding senior officers at the time he had been persuaded to remain in the RAF. The position in BOAC and its short-distance counterpart, British European Airways, had since been filled, so he looked elsewhere for a full-time job. He had a brief but unsuccessful time in a shipbuilding company, before joining Rolls-Royce to run its advanced research organisation, stepping down in 1961. He then spent some time helping his older brother in the lime works on the Crawford Priory estate and an associated brickworks, before setting up his own family business selling scientific modelling kits.

Throughout his post-war career and retirement Cochrane maintained close links with the veterans of 617 Squadron, attending all their reunions in the UK and one in Canada. He also helped authors, from Paul Brickhill onwards, who were writing on the Dambusters Raid and Bomber Command generally, and was much in demand as a lecturer and commentator on wider military matters. Rather less satisfactorily, he was appalled by the depiction of his actions in the memoirs of Donald Bennett, who had sparred with him frequently and deeply resented the removal by Harris of some of the Pathfinder squadrons. Only by threatening legal action did Cochrane succeed in having a number of corrections made in the first paperback edition.

For all his other achievements, Cochrane's reputation rests on his command of 5 Group from 1943 to 1945. Some who did not know him well regarded him as austere and humourless, and he certainly took war very seriously. He was, in fact, exceptionally highly regarded by both his superiors and his subordinates, not only for his organizational skills, but also for his ability to put aside conventional wisdom and come up with new ways of doing things far better than they had ever been done before.

84 Churchill's Eagles

Air Marshal Sir Arthur Coningham KCB, KBE, DSO, MC, DFC, AFC (1895–1948)

The Second World War differed from the First in that it was very much a war of movement on almost every front, giving rise to the development of tactics among the air forces of all the belligerents which had been completely unknown in the earlier conflict. This tactical innovation was seen first in Europe, where in Poland, the Low Countries and France the use of dive bombers became a highly potent ingredient of German success on the ground. The RAF took rather longer to work out how best to use air power in support of ground forces, but the constant to-ing and fro-ing of the campaign in North Africa from 1940 to 1943 demanded a high level of co-operation between the two services. One of the pioneers of tactical air power in the desert was Arthur **Coningham**, who went on to develop it to the very limits of its potential in North-West Europe.

Coningham was born in Australia but brought up and schooled in New Zealand. He was working as a farmhand when war broke out in Europe, but like many of his countrymen volunteered for active service, joining the Wellington Regiment as a private soldier, in which capacity he participated in the capture of the German Pacific Ocean colony of Samoa. Back in New Zealand he signed up once again, this time as a trooper in the Canterbury Mounted Rifles, and in June 1915 found himself at Gallipoli. His service there was completely undistinguished, as he developed typhoid and dysentery and was sent home. Once recovered, he sailed to England at his own expense, where he learnt to fly and was commissioned into the RFC Special Reserve. In the last month of 1916 he joined his first unit, 32 Squadron, on the Western Front.

32 Squadron was equipped with the Airco DH.2, a 'pusher' aircraft with a forward-firing gun which had seen off the Fokker 'Eindecker' but was no match for the Albatros D.1 now appearing on the German side. The squadron re-equipped with the DH.5, a robust aircraft which was well suited to ground attack but whose top wing, staggered back behind the pilot, made it very vulnerable to being hit from above and behind. Coningham had some success with the type but in July 1917 was wounded in the course of just such an attack and invalided back to England, albeit with both an MC and a DSO to his name. During his recovery he briefly commanded a Flying School before taking command of 92 Squadron, flying the excellent SE.5A, seeing a great deal of action and earning himself a DFC.

It was during the Great War that Coningham received his nickname of 'Mary', thought to be a corruption of 'Maori' in recognition of his New

Zealand roots and used thenceforward by everyone in preference to his given name.

Coningham was one of a relatively small number of officers to be granted a permanent commission in the new RAF in October 1919. He spent much of the next two years on training, first as an instructor at the School of Technical Training and then on a course prior to becoming an instructor at the Central Flying School, from where he participated in a display of aerial fighting at the Hendon Air Pageant. In early 1922 he was posted to Iraq as a flight commander in 55 Squadron, based in Mosul.

55 Squadron flew DH 9a light bombers, their purpose being to keep control of the local tribes, particularly the Kurds who were keen to establish their independence. This was achieved by bombing the villages of those who were causing trouble, albeit not without ample warning to evacuate them. In July 1923 Coningham was appointed to command the squadron until early in the following year, when he joined the staff first of HQ Egyptian Group and then of RAF Middle East. Whilst he was at the latter he led a pioneering flight of three DH 9a aircraft down the Nile to Khartoum and then across the Sahara to El Fasher in the Sudan, Fort Lamy in French Equatorial Africa and on to Kano in Nigeria. This would, in due course and in the opposite direction, become the West African Reinforcement Route, along which the RAF in Egypt and the Western Desert would, from the summer of 1940 onwards, receive its aircraft from the UK, shipped in crates to be assembled at Takoradi in Ghana. Coninham was awarded the AFC in recognition of his achievement.

On his return to the UK in 1926 Coningham was appointed to command B Squadron at the RAF College at Cranwell, giving him the opportunity to influence the development of a number of RAF officers who would in due course reach high rank. This was followed in 1930 by nineteen months as Chief Flying Instructor at the Central Flying School, following which he was posted back to Africa as Senior RAF Officer in the Sudan in succession to Sholto **Douglas**. This huge country was a backwater of the British Empire, but with his small command equipped with the multi-purpose Fairey 111F, which could be fitted with floats to enable it to land on the Nile, Coningham travelled extensively and was able to carry out army co-operation exercises with the troops based there, who were only too happy to be doing something different.

On his return to the UK in May 1935 Coningham was appointed to the staff of Coastal Area, renamed Coastal Command a year later and led first by Arthur **Longmore** and later Philip **Joubert**, before becoming SASO at

86 Churchill's Eagles

17 Group with promotion to group captain. 17 Group was responsible for all training within the command, but he had only been there six months before he was made station commander at RAF Calshot, the home of two flying boat squadrons.

In July 1939, with war imminent, Coningham was appointed AOC 4 Group Bomber Command, with promotion to air commodore. This was his first and, as it was to turn out, his only experience of strategic bombing, of which he was to remain a strong critic long after he had left. He got on well with his superiors as AOC-in-C, however, initially Edgar **Ludlow-Hewitt**, who rated him the best of his group commanders, and from April 1940 Charles **Portal**, who would later be a significant figure in his career. Portal served as AOC-in-C for only six months, however, before being replaced by Richard **Peirse**.

4 Group was located in Yorkshire, with its HQ first at Linton-on-Ouse and then at Heslington Hall near York, and it consisted initially of six squadrons flying the Armstrong Whitworth Whitley medium bomber. For the first nine months of the war its operations were limited to dropping leaflets by night over Germany, incurring very few losses from enemy action, and to attacks on shipping and naval and seaplane bases by day.

This changed, initially with the German invasion of Norway on 9 April 1940 and then with the attack on France, Belgium and the Netherlands on 9 May. The attempts to bomb German and Italian cities quickly showed up Bomber Command's weaknesses in target-finding and defensive capability and, whilst the Whitley proved to be a reliable workhorse, it was one which was already effectively obsolete as a strategic bomber. The group was just beginning to re-equip with the Handley Page Halifax four-engined bomber when Coningham received orders to proceed to the Middle East.

Coningham took up his new appointment as AOC 204 Group in the Western Desert at the end of July 1941. The group had been formed out of AHQ Cyrenaica and the units which comprised 202 Group, the latter having moved back to take command of all aircraft based around Cairo and the Nile Delta. Tommy *Elmhirst*, 202 Group's commander, was to become Coningham's AOA not long afterwards and remain as such through various appointments for the rest of the war, with the exception of a few months at the end of 1943 following his return to the UK on sick leave. Coningham's own immediate superior was Arthur **Tedder**, AOC-in-C Middle East, whom he did not know well at the time but with whom he was to build a friendly and ever closer working relationship in both North Africa and Europe.

The situation on the ground had changed frequently since the entry of the Italians into the war in June 1940. Their initial advance into Egypt had taken them to Sidi Barrani, following which a stunning campaign by Lieutenant General Richard O'Connor's Western Desert Force had destroyed most of the Italian Tenth Army and pushed what was left of it back to the border of Tripolitania. A new German-Italian Army under General Erwin Rommel had quickly struck back, forcing the British and Commonwealth forces out of Libya other than Tobruk, which was besieged, with some inconclusive actions then taking place on the frontier. In November 1941 the newly named Eighth Army under Lieutenant General Sir Alan Cunningham launched Operation CRUSADER to relieve Tobruk and force the Germans and Italians back again. After some serious setbacks, which saw Cunningham sacked and replaced by Lieutenant General Neil Ritchie, albeit under the supervision of the C-in-C Middle East, General Sir Claude Auchinleck, Tobruk was relieved and the Germans and Italians were once again forced out of Tripolitania.

Coningham had been at the heart of this campaign placing Air Headquarters Western Desert, as 204 Group had been renamed, alongside HQ Eighth Army. He had thirty-two squadrons available, flying many types of aircraft. Most of the fighters were Hawker Hurricanes, although there was a whole wing of American Curtis P-45 Tomahawks. The core of the bomber force was Mark IV Bristol Blenheims, supported by the Douglas Bostons and Martin Marylands of the South African Air Force. Three squadrons of the Fleet Air Arm equipped with outdated Fairey Swordfish and Albacores were tasked with attacking Axis shipping.

CRUSADER would have been a disaster but for Rommel's decision to withdraw from finishing off the British armoured formations and strike towards the Egyptian frontier, where he was turned back by British artillery. With his supplies exhausted, he was forced to withdraw into Tripolitania, harassed all the way by Coningham's aircraft. In January 1942, however, he struck again, his Afrika Korps forcing Eighth Army back to a line running south of Gazala. There the two sides confronted one another until 26 May, when Rommel launched his armoured divisions around the end of the Allied line. Notwithstanding the heroic defence of Bir Hacheim by the Free French, watched over by standing patrols of the RAF, Rommel pushed Eighth Army back again, retaking Tobruk and advancing as far as the Alamein Line, some 60 miles from Alexandria, where he came to a standstill.

The inconclusive First Battle of El Alamein caused Churchill to make major command changes during a key visit to Cairo in August 1942 with the

88 Churchill's Eagles

CIGS, General Sir Alan Brooke. Auchinleck was replaced by General Sir Harold Alexander, whilst following the death of Lieutenant General Gott, Churchill's first choice as Commander of Eighth Army, Lieutenant General Bernard Montgomery was summoned from the UK. Coningham was very favourably impressed at his first encounter with Montgomery, not least because the latter was wholly supportive of the closest cooperation between the two services, moving his HQ alongside Coningham's at Burg el Arab and integrating, as far as possible, Planning, Operations and Intelligence. This delivered good results very quickly, when Rommel tried to attempt once more a hook round the southern end of the British line. The Battle of Alam Halfa over the end of August and into September showed not only that Montgomery had outthought his opponent, placing his formations to counter just such a move, but also that the RAF could wreak serious damage, particularly during the retreat of the Axis forces back to their former positions. Montgomery and Coningham were both delighted.

The success at Alam Halfa was due not only to the close relationship between the two HQs, but also to the system of air support which had been developed. This had been in operation since the Army's stand on the Gazala Line and involved a new type of unit called an Army Air Support Control ('AASC'). The AASC at Army HQ dealt with target requests from its own signallers with the forward troops and also with changes in bomb lines, tactical reconnaissance reports, reports on enemy aircraft and reports from the RAF on the position of enemy tanks. When target requests were received, G (Operations) at Eighth Army was immediately consulted on potential conflicts with current operations and the priorities for air support. Whilst this was happening, a warning order was issued to the RAF wings, which were placed on stand-by and in which Army Liaison Officers were available to clarify the situation on the ground to their RAF colleagues. RAF (Operations) at Air HQ Western Desert would then accept or refuse the target and, if accepted, would receive the estimated time of arrival of the strike from the Wing concerned, which would be transmitted to the originator of the request. The urgency of the requests meant that the messages were often sent in clear rather than code, in spite of the fact that the Germans might be listening in.

In early September Coningham welcomed the arrival of six American squadrons, three of P-40 Kittyhawk fighters and three of North American B-25 Mitchell medium bombers, all of which had to be integrated into Air HQ Western Desert and trained prior to the next ground battle. He had also received his first Spitfire Vs, which were vitally necessary as both the

Hurricane and the Kittyhawk were by this time totally outclassed by the Messerschmitt 109G, which began to appear in the theatre in the summer of 1942.

Operation LIGHTFOOT, the first part of what became known as the Second Battle of El Alamein, was launched by Montgomery on the night of 23/24 October 1942. Heavy fighting took place on a relatively short section of the line closest to the coast. Although there were some local successes and the RAF did excellent work against both the Axis positions and their supply lines, no breakthrough was achieved and the fighting became a series of scrappy actions. Montgomery suspended the main offensive and then regrouped in the north for his second operation, SUPERCHARGE, directed at a weak point between German and Italian divisions. This was launched very early on 2 November, and forty-eight hours later, Rommel's army was in full retreat along the coast road, harassed all the way by Western Desert Air Force, as AHQ Western Desert had now been renamed.

It was during Eighth Army's pursuit of the German-Italian Panzer Army along the Mediterranean coast that Coningham's initial favourable opinion of Montgomery began to abate. For the RAF the overwhelming priority was the capture of Axis airfields, particularly those in the 'bulge' of Cyrenaica, which would allow a much greater coverage of convoys from Egypt to Malta, the latter still under siege and very short of supplies, the last of which had been received in mid-August. Coningham and Tedder both thought that Montgomery was excessively cautious. They were particularly disappointed that he failed to emulate O'Connor's successful dash across the desert south of the Jebel Akhdar to cut off the Italians retreating from Benghazi in early 1941. Instead, he methodically continued round the coast before pulling up on the frontier with Tripolitania near El Agheila, where Rommel had decided to make a stand. Both Coningham and Tedder believed that Montgomery was hoping that the Anglo-American forces which had landed in Algeria and Morocco in Operation TORCH in early November would be able to take Tripoli from the west, but, as it turned out, they got stuck in the mountains of Tunisia. Eighth Army eventually entered Tripoli on 23 January 1943.

The criticisms were not entirely one-sided. Many in the Army thought that the RAF had let the retreating Germans off lightly, preferring to offer ground support to the advancing troops, who only rarely needed it, rather than strafe the retreating German columns. Some surprise was expressed at the lack of damage to Axis transport from aerial attack; abandoned vehicles, of which there were many, were very much more likely to have run out of fuel than to have been destroyed from the air. This was ascribed by some

90   Churchill's Eagles

on the ground to the RAF's reluctance to bomb along the line of retreat, preferring to drop their loads at right angles to it to avoid AA fire.

At the beginning of March 1943, Coningham, promoted to acting air marshal, was appointed to command the North African Tactical Air Force ('NATAF'), which incorporated not only what was now to be called the Desert Air Force, but also 242 Group RAF, which had been supporting the British First Army in Tunisia, and the US 12th Air Support Command, which provided the same service to US II Corps. He was succeeded as AOC Desert Air Force by Harry **Broadhurst**, who since the end of the previous November had been his SASO.

The Allied command structure was somewhat complex. At the apex stood General Dwight D. Eisenhower, Supreme Commander in the Mediterranean. The Air C-in-C Mediterranean Air Command was Tedder, who set up his HQ close to Eisenhower in Algiers. One of Tedder's subordinates and Coningham's immediate superior was Lieutenant General Carl A. Spaatz at North-West African Air Forces, which included, in addition to NATAF, the North African Strategic Air Force (Major General James H. Doolittle) and the North African Coastal Air Force (Hugh **Lloyd**). Coningham was not overly impressed by Spaatz but was delighted to find that one of his closest friends in the RAF, James **Robb**, a flight commander in 32 Squadron on the Western Front and in another DH 9 squadron in Mosul and later a fellow bomber group commander in 1940/41, would be acting as Spaatz's deputy.

The early spring proved to be a dispiriting time for the Allies, now including the Free French, as the Germans conducted a vigorous defence of their positions in Tunisia and mounted a very nearly successful breakthrough at Kasserine. Montgomery, in particular, experienced a significant problem at the Mareth Line, where a head-on assault was defeated with heavy losses. He then dispatched the New Zealand Corps, later bolstered by other formations, in a wide left hook to outflank the Germans through the Tebaga Gap, but the defence proved too strong.

At this point Broadhurst and Montgomery's Chief of Staff, Freddie de Guingand, proposed to implement a tactic which they had been developing for some time, the use of Kittyhawk fighter bombers, controlled by officers on the front line, to act effectively as aerial artillery, attacking at very low level to break down defences. They had practised this on worn-out and captured vehicles for some time and were confident that it would work. Coningham was highly sceptical, sending his SASO, George *Beamish*, to try to persuade Broadhurst not to go ahead and warning him about what would be the severe personal consequences of failure. The idea was understandably also deeply unpopular with many of the pilots.

In the event, the operation was devastatingly successful. The attacking aircraft, controlled from the ground by RAF officers in armoured vehicles, came in out of the sun and met little effective opposition. Casualties were much fewer than even Broadhurst had expected. The Germans retreated in some confusion and the Mareth Line was breached. Thus was invented the 'cab rank' system of ground attack which would reach its pinnacle in the following year in Normandy. Similar attacks took place during the final assault on Tunis, whilst the Germans' attempts to reinforce their troops by air, due to command of the sea having passed to the Allies, led to the wholesale destruction of the transport aircraft concerned, the Junkers 52 and giant Messerschmitt 321.

With the surrender of the German–Italian Army on 9 May, Coningham was keen to relocate to a pleasant location, and he and his staff found one in a luxurious villa near Hammamet. There they worked hard and played hard, the latter category including entertaining King George VI and a number of visiting celebrities such as Vivien Leigh and Beatrice Lillie. A plan was emerging for the invasion of Sicily, not helped by Montgomery insisting on radical changes to what had previously been agreed. Coningham relocated to Malta three days prior to the invasion, which took place on 10 July. Control of operations in the first phase and until sufficient airfields had been captured or constructed was vested in Keith **Park**, the AOC Malta.

As usual, the capture of airfields had been a key priority, but although those in the US sector inland from Gela were speedily taken, the important group around Gerbini in the Plain of Catania remained tantalisingly out of reach, although their use was also denied to the Germans. Once again this created some tension between Coningham and Montgomery, exacerbated in mid-August when NATAF and the other formations under Tedder's command failed to prevent a very successful evacuation of Sicily by the Germans.

The DAF was on hand to provide air cover for the first landings on the mainland of Italy, in Operation BAYTOWN across the Straits of Messina on 3 September, but they were uncontested. On the other hand, the landings at Salerno by the Fifth US Army, with British X Corps under command, were vigorously opposed, and 12th Air Support Command was hard pushed to provide cover at an extreme distance from its bases in Sicily. The only German airfield, at Montecorvino, was partly occupied by British troops, but not sufficiently for it to be used until the Germans were eventually forced into a retreat.

The campaign in Italy saw a significant advance up the country, although the Germans contested Allied progress on a number of occasions before they were forced back to the Gustav Line, which they were to hold throughout the winter of 1943/44. On the Adriatic side of the peninsula, however, a major triumph was the capture of a group of airfields around Foggia, although these were of most benefit to the Mediterranean Allied Strategic Air Force, which was now able to strike not only at the industrial areas of Northern Italy, but also those of Southern Germany.

The first four months of the campaign in Italy marked Coningham's swansong as commander of what had now been renamed the Mediterranean Allied Tactical Air Force ('MATAF'), and he handed over to his highly capable American deputy, Major General John K. Cannon, in early January and flew back to the UK.

Coningham had long been earmarked for command of the 2nd Tactical Air Force ('2TAF'), which was designed to deliver to 21st Army Group the same level of air co-operation which NWATAF and MATAF had provided so ably for 18th Army Group in North Africa and 15th Army Group in Italy. He relieved Air Marshal John *D'Albiac*, who flew in the other direction to become Cannon's deputy. 2TAF was itself part of the Allied Expeditionary Air Force ('AEAF'), the other components being 9th US Air Force under Major General (later Lieutenant General) Lewis H. Brereton, with whom Coningham established a good working relationship, and Air Defence of Great Britain under Roderic **Hill**, as Fighter Command had been renamed. All of these formed part of the AEAF under Trafford **Leigh-Mallory**, for whom neither Coningham nor many of the other senior air force officers involved in the invasion had a great deal of time.

When Coningham arrived, 2TAF consisted of 2 Group and 83 Group. The former had originally been the light bomber group of Bomber Command, but had been transferred in June 1943. By early 1944 it comprised twelve squadrons, two of Douglas Bostons, four of North American Mitchells and six of De Havilland Mosquitoes. It was led by one of the younger and most colourful commanders, Basil **Embry**, who had had already had an eventful war, which had included a short period first as an adviser and then as SASO to Coningham at Air HQ Western Desert during Operation CRUSADER. Although he liked and admired Coningham, Embry had not enjoyed this appointment and eventually asked to be returned to the UK. However, he had no such difficulty serving under him as an operational commander.

83 Group controlled all 2TAF's twenty-nine fighter, fighter bomber, reconnaissance and artillery observation squadrons. When Coningham arrived back in the UK, it was commanded by AVM William **Dickson** and he would have been happy to retain him. However, Montgomery insisted on Broadhurst being brought back from Italy, on the grounds that his experience of working with the same personalities in 21st Army Group and Second Army as he had in Eighth Army would be invaluable.

Along with Bomber Command and its US equivalent, Eighth Air Force, 2TAF and Ninth Air Force were active in the skies over France in the spring of 1945 in line with the Transportation Plan, whereby German communications, especially bridges, tunnels and marshalling yards, became the priority targets. Coningham had been designated Commander Advanced AEAF, effectively managing the tactical air forces, whilst Tedder, not only Deputy Supreme Allied Commander but also effectively the leading Allied airman, dealt with the strategic air forces, whose commanders refused to take orders from Leigh-Mallory.

D-Day went well for the ground forces other than the Americans at Omaha Beach, with very little interruption by the Luftwaffe. The RAF and USAAF did, however, incur casualties from ground fire and from trigger-happy AA gunners in the Allied fleet. Broadhurst flew over the beaches and reported back to Coningham. The campaign, however, had only been under way for a short time when it became apparent that Montgomery was going to bypass Coningham, designated as his opposite number, and deal instead with either Leigh-Mallory, with whom he had a tolerably good relationship, and Broadhurst, whose opposite number was supposed to be Miles Dempsey, GOC Second Army.

Just as in North Africa, the focus of the air commanders was on the capture of airfields, and particularly the large base at Carpiquet, south-west of Caen. This city had actually been expected to fall on D-Day, but the Germans held out for just over a month, when its capture was preceded by an enormous raid by Bomber Command. In the meantime, however, airfield construction parties had been hard at work, and neither Broadhurst, who had been in Normandy since D-Day+1, nor his USAAF opposite number, Major General Pete Quesada, had major complaints about the lack of landing grounds. Coningham, supported by Tedder, continued with his criticisms, however, and Montgomery tried to have him replaced. However, Coningham retained the confidence of both Tedder and Portal and remained in position.

After failure to advance south-west of Caen in Operation EPSOM, Montgomery tried again to the south-east of the city in Operation

94 Churchill's Eagles

GOODWOOD. This failed to deliver what Montgomery had promised, giving more ammunition to his critics, but he and Coningham were destined to remain wedded together until the end of the campaign.

83 Group really came into its own during the German attempt to cut off the advance of General Omar Bradley's 12th Army Group into Brittany and Maine. Together with Quesada's aircraft, Broadhurst's rocket-firing Typhoons, using the 'cab rank' system, created havoc among the German armoured divisions, as they were to do subsequently at Falaise. In the meantime, 2 Group operating from UK airfields provided frequent support for 21st Army Group operations and attacked German communications and troop concentrations. The Allies broke out of Normandy completely, with Second Army liberating Brussels on 3 September and First Canadian Army moving up the Channel coast to liberate the ports.

HQ First Canadian Army had arrived in Normandy in mid-July, supported by a second army co-operation group in 2 TAF, No 84. The AOC was initially AVM Leslie *Brown*, who failed, however, to convince the Canadians that his aircraft were a support for ground operations rather than a substitute for them. He was relieved in early November by Teddy *Hudleston*, who had served as Coningham's SASO in Italy and, at the age of thirty-five, was one of the youngest air vice-marshals of the war.

83 Group continued to support Second Army although with little success in Operation MARKET GARDEN, the attempt by 1 Airborne Corps and XXX Corps to cross the Rhine at Arnhem. Support for the latter worked well, but that for the airborne troops at Arnhem was a failure, due to a prohibition on such activity until the landings had taken place and then a nearly complete failure of radio communication.

The Battle of the Bulge at the end of 1944 also started badly as weather closed down flying operations completely. On Christmas Eve the skies cleared and both 2 TAF and the USAAF hit back at the Germans with considerable effect. The Luftwaffe carried out its last great attack of the war on New Year's Day 1945, when it destroyed well over 400 aircraft on Allied airfields. However, it lost not many fewer planes itself, and whereas the Allies could replace aircraft very quickly and had not suffered in manpower, the Germans had a huge shortage of both, particularly experienced aircrew, for the rest of the war.

Following the Allied victory, 2 TAF became the British Air Forces of Occupation and, with Montgomery confirmed as Military Governor of the British Zone of Germany, Coningham was replaced by Sholto Douglas, with whom Montgomery had a good relationship. Coningham went on a three-week tour of the United States as a guest of the USAAF, with whom he had always been popular. In October 1945 he took up a new appointment as AOC-in-C Flying Training Command.

With no place for Coningham in the fast-contracting RAF, he retired on I August 1947. On 27 January 1948 he boarded an Avro Tudor of Donald **Bennett's** British South American Airways to fly to Bermuda on business. The passengers stayed overnight in Lisbon and flew on to the Azores on the following day. On the morning of 29 January, the aircraft left for Bermuda in bad weather. It was never heard of again.

Highly regarded by both his superiors and his subordinates, Coningham was an outstanding airman and a highly capable commander who transformed the once rather unfashionable business of army/air co-operation into a battle-winning machine. His difficult relationship with Montgomery could have been a handicap, but he stuck to his task and reaped the rewards in four campaigns.

Air Vice-Marshal W. F. (later Marshal of the Royal Air Force Sir William) Dickson GCB, KBE, DSO, AFC (1898–1987)

William **Dickson** was the last Chief of the Air Staff to have served in the Great War and the first officer of any of the armed services to become Chief of the Defence Staff. More than anyone else, he may thus be said to have been a bridge between, on the one hand, the infant RAF, fighting to protect its independence against both the Royal Navy and the British Army, and on the other, the greater central direction of the armed services which was to emerge in the second half of the twentieth century.

Dickson had begun his career in October 1916 not in the RFC, but in the RNAS as a direct entrant with the rank of midshipman. Having completed his flying training he was posted initially to the Naval Air Station on the Isle of Grain, before joining HMS *Furious*. This ship had been designed as a battlecruiser, but during the course of construction she had been redesignated as an aircraft carrier. The front turret was removed and the fo'c'sle was converted into a hangar, with a 160ft flight deck on top from which aircraft could take off. Subsequently, the rear turret was removed for a similar construction, this time with a 300ft flight deck for aircraft to land.

It was from this extraordinary vessel that one of the most spectacular raids of the War was mounted. Dickson and six other pilots, flying Sopwith Camels, were ordered to attack the Zeppelin yard at Tondern, now in Denmark but then in Germany. An initial attempt was called off because

96   Churchill's Eagles

of bad weather and another was successfully launched on 18 July 1918. The first wave of three aircraft, including Dickson's, destroyed two airships, and the second, also of three aircraft as one had been forced to return with engine problems, set on fire a captive balloon. Three aircraft landed in neutral Denmark, where the pilots were interned, whilst Dickson and the remaining two ditched near the *Furious*, although one of the pilots was drowned. Dickson was awarded a DSO.

After the Great War Dickson served successively as a pilot on two battleships, HMS *Revenge* and HMS *Queen Elizabeth*, both with flying-off platforms built on turrets. He was awarded a permanent commission in the RAF in August 1919 and in the following May was posted to 210 Squadron, which was equipped with the short-lived Sopwith Cuckoo torpedo bomber. As the RAF provided pilots to the Royal Navy, he then went back to sea for nine months in HMS *Argus*, a converted ocean liner and the first British aircraft carrier to come into service with a flight deck which ran the length of the ship.

His sea service at an end, Dickson spent just over a year as a test pilot at the Royal Aircraft Establishment at Farnborough, for which he was awarded the AFC, before taking up his first appointment at the Air Ministry, where he became the Personal Assistant to AVM (later Air Chief Marshal Sir) John Steele, the DCAS and also Director of Operations and Intelligence, himself a former RN and then RNAS officer.

Dickson returned to flying at Biggin Hill in the summer of 1926 as flight commander in 56 Squadron, which was equipped with the fast but not entirely reliable Gloster Grebe. In late 1927 he was selected for the RAF Staff College, where Edgar **Ludlow-Hewitt** was Commandant, and after passing out was posted to India. His initial appointment there was on the staff of No 1 (Indian Wing) Station at Kohat on the North-West Frontier, the home of 27 and 60 Squadrons. The frontier was relatively quiet during his stay there, although it burst into action just after he left Kohat in April 1930 to join the staff of AHQ India, initially as Personal Assistant to Air Marshal Sir Geoffrey Salmond. He was in India for nearly four years, which gave him the opportunity to see much of the sub-continent and to travel widely in the Far East. However, this was a frustrating time for the RAF in India, heavily subordinated as it was to the Army, and reduced to protecting columns of troops on punitive expeditions, rather than carrying out what was so successfully achieved in Iraq, Aden and British Somaliland, the control of tribesmen by bombing their villages.

Dickson returned to the UK in early 1934 and, after taking a refresher course at the Central Flying School and spending a few months on the staff of the short-lived Western Area, was appointed to command 25 Squadron at Hawkinge, flying the delightful, and for its time very fast, Hawker Fury. Just over a year later he joined the directing staff at the Staff College and in January 1939 went straight on to attend the Imperial Defence College on its last course before it was closed for the duration of the Second World War.

As a recent IDC graduate, Dickson found himself almost inevitably in a staff job again, in this case in the Directorate of Plans under John **Slessor**, beginning a relationship which would later prove to be very fruitful. The immediate task was to establish a strategic planning function, although there were diversions such as staff conversations with the French Air Force, which left most of the British dismayed by their ally's lack of preparedness. In the spring of 1940 detailed planning had to be carried out for the Narvik campaign, although this was overtaken by the demands of the Battle of France. After Dunkirk, the attention switched to prioritization and, other than the overwhelming necessity to build up Fighter Command for the immediate defence of the UK, the main priority advanced by the planners was a focus on strategic bombing.

Slessor was called away on special duty in the USA in October 1940 and was succeeded briefly by Charles *Medhurst*, before Dickson himself was appointed Director of Plans in March 1941. The year was dominated by the entry of both the Russians and the Americans into the war, and Dickson found himself having to explain to the Soviet Ambassador why the demands of his country for more and more aircraft could not be satisfied. There was a far more collaborative feel to the Arcadia Conference in Washington over the end of 1941 and into 1942, which Dickson and his fellow planners at the Admiralty and the War Office attended alongside Churchill and the British Chiefs of Staff.

Having spent nearly three years at the Air Ministry, it was probably with a sense of relief in June 1942 that Dickson was appointed to an operational role, briefly as SASO at 9 Group and then, just over a month later, as its AOC with promotion to acting air vice-marshal. 9 Group was the last to be formed in Fighter Command, in August 1940. Its area covered the industrial cities of the North-West and part of the West Midlands, including Liverpool, Manchester and Birmingham, together with North Wales and the Isle of Man. The defence of Liverpool, the destination for much of the eastbound North Atlantic convoy traffic, was its most vital concern. The need diminished subsequently, and by the time Dickson arrived there were only ten active squadrons. Dickson's term of command was short, however, as after a mere four months in the job he was posted as AOC 10 Group, responsible for the defence of South-West England and South Wales.

10 Group had given a good account of itself in the Battle of Britain, mostly in support of 11 Group, its eastern neighbour. It still had defensive responsibilities, mostly against night-time raids, for which it was equipped with Beaufighter night fighters. The 'Baedeker Raids', largely on cathedral cities, were by this time substantially over, but raids on Southampton, Portsmouth and Bristol continued. Moreover, Fighter Command had by this time also moved over to the offensive, with sweeps along the French coast, whilst air cover was provided to convoys approaching from the south-west in association with Coastal Command.

With some solid experience of fighter operations behind him, Dickson was appointed in March 1943 to form and command 83 (Composite) Group, the first of what were to be the two army co-operation formations of 2nd Tactical Air Force ('2TAF'), which was commanded at the time by Air Marshal John *D'Albiac*. Whilst still at 10 Group Dickson had visited North Africa in company with Air Marshal Sir Trafford **Leigh-Mallory**, then AOC-in-C Fighter Command, but later to be AOC-in-C Allied Expeditionary Air Force, in order to study the advances in army/air co-operation made by the Desert Air Force, and it was to be on this that 83 Group was modelled.

The group was composed of a large number of squadrons, deploying Spitfires as fighters for defence and reconnaissance and Hawker Typhoons as fighter-bombers for ground attack. Formed with the specific purpose of providing air support to Second Army, not only for the initial invasion of North-West Europe, but also for the duration of the subsequent campaign, it was based on airfields in the South of England and was expected to operate from them until airfields in France had been either captured or built. It was necessary to establish a very close relationship with the Army HQ and, for Dickson in particular, with the GOC, Lieutenant General Sir Kenneth Anderson.

Neither Dickson nor Anderson was able to reap the rewards of his work for a whole year on invasion planning, as in the spring of 1944 they were both replaced in their commands, respectively by Harry **Broadhurst** and Lieutenant General Sir Miles Dempsey. This was at the express wish of the newly appointed commander of 21st Army Group, General Sir Bernard Montgomery, who insisted on retaining those senior RAF officers with whom he had worked closely in North Africa and Italy.

Dickson effected a direct swap with Broadhurst, taking over the Desert Air Force in Italy in March 1944. The DAF was by this time a highly experienced formation and had fought its way from El Alamein to the Gustav Line, which ran across Italy from the mouth of the River Garigliano to a point on the Adriatic Coast north of the Sangro. The major German defensive position, which had already repulsed three assaults, was at Cassino.

The DAF had been a multinational formation in North Africa and this continued in Italy. It consisted of six wings: 244 and 324 RAF with Spitfire fighters, 7 SAAF with Spitfire fighter-bombers, 239 RAF with Kittyhawk and Mustang fighter bombers and 3 SAAF and 232 RAF with Martin Maryland, Martin Baltimore and Douglas Boston medium bombers, together with the 57th and 79th Groups of the USAAF, flying Republic Thunderbolt fighters and fighter-bombers and Mustang fighters. In addition, the independent 600 (City of London) Squadron was equipped with Beaufighter night fighters.

By this time the Luftwaffe in Italy had been depleted due to the demands of both the air defence of Germany and the inexorable advance of the Soviet armies on the Eastern Front, but it was still a real threat and losses were not inconsiderable. However, Dickson believed that operations in support of the ground forces justified tipping the balance even more from fighters to fighter-bombers. The focus was on the enemy's communications, road and rail traffic, bridges, tunnels and marshalling yards. In the run up to what was hoped would be the successful breaking of the Gustav Line after the failures of early 1944, Major General John K. ('Joe') Cannon, Dickson's immediate superior as the Commander of the Mediterranean Allied Tactical Air Force, launched Operation STRANGLE, the interdiction of all German movement, not only to the battle front, but also in and around Rome, the centre for all communications in Central Italy. This proved to have been outstandingly successful when the breakout from the Gustav Line was finally launched on 11 May 1944, leading in due course to a German retreat beyond Rome.

After Rome the Allied advance became much slower, partly because the country provided many defensive opportunities for the Germans, but also because a number of American and French divisions were diverted to Operation ANVIL, the invasion of southern France. Moreover, the formation of the new Balkan Air Force, to provide support to partisan and other activity in Yugoslavia and Albania, which had hitherto been the strict preserve of the DAF, took away three Baltimore squadrons and other potential reinforcements. The DAF continued to deliver much necessary support to the three British corps advancing up the peninsula to the next major German fortified position, the Gothic Line.

Just over eight months after he arrived, Dickson was summoned back to London to become the Assistant Chief of the Air Staff (Policy). With the result of the war in Europe no longer in doubt, Charles **Portal**, the CAS, had been looking for someone to take up what he considered to be a key role at the Air Ministry, looking forward towards the post-war RAF, which he knew would be very different and would need to be planned for well before the end of hostilities. His first choice was Ralph **Cochrane**, but Arthur **Harris** refused to let his best group commander go until the bombing campaign was within sight of being wound down. Dickson had impressed Portal whilst serving as Director of Plans, when they had been in close contact, particularly at the Arcadia Conference, and the CAS considered that he possessed the intellect to think forward to a new world.

Dickson clearly also impressed Arthur **Tedder**, Portal's successor at the beginning of 1946. The careers of the two men had never crossed previously, but only six months into Tedder's appointment, Dickson became Vice-Chief of the Air Staff, with promotion to air marshal. The Vice-Chief at this time was responsible on the Air Council for operations, intelligence and training, as well as standing in for the CAS whenever the latter was away. During the war the vice-chiefs of the three armed forces regularly held their own committee meetings to handle inter-service matters not considered essential for the chiefs and also to deputise for the chiefs when they were away.

After more than three years in Whitehall, Dickson was appointed AOC-in-C RAF Mediterranean and Middle East in March 1948. The area was still considered by the British Government to be of great strategic value, with the Suez Canal in particular of vital importance to the cohesion of the British Commonwealth and to the supply of oil from the Arabian Gulf.

Shortly after Dickson's arrival, the British Mandate for Palestine expired and the State of Israel declared its independence. This led to the First Arab-Israeli War, which lasted on and off for nearly a year until a United Nations-sponsored truce was declared. Great Britain remained strictly neutral, but its standing amongst a number of Arab states was diminished. Its relationship with the Government of Egypt was particularly fragile and was not helped by British forces remaining on the country's doorstep. As far as the RAF was concerned, Main HQ Mediterranean and Middle East had moved from Cairo to Ismailia in the Suez Canal Zone at the end of 1946, with a Rear HQ at Abu Sueir and the HQ of 205 Group at Fayid, both also in the Canal Zone

The last of these provided an important link in Transport Command's trunk route to the Far East and Australasia.

With the area for which he was responsible stretching from Gibraltar in the west to Aden in the East and from Iraq in the north to Kenya in the south, and covering the whole of the Mediterranean, the Red Sea and the Arabian Gulf, Dickson was responsible for the RAF's largest command in terms of geographical extent, and much of his time was spent travelling around it.

After two busy years Dickson returned to the UK and to the Air Council in March 1950 on his appointment as Air Member for Supply and Organisation. Tedder had left three months earlier to become the Chairman of the British Joint Services Mission in Washington, and the new CAS was Dickson's old friend Jack Slessor. Since they had worked together in the Plans Department of the Air Ministry they had been in close contact, firstly in Italy in 1944 when Slessor was simultaneously Deputy C-in-C of the Mediterranean Allied Air Forces and C-in-C RAF Mediterranean and Middle East, and then on the Air Council in 1946/7 when Slessor was Air Member for Personnel.

As AMSO Dickson was responsible for the overall organization of the RAF, for the provision of technical and warlike equipment, non-technical supplies and foodstuffs and for internal transportation and works services. He also took on the duties of the Air Member for Technical Services when that post was abolished in 1951. He was aided by five senior subordinates, the Directors-General respectively of Organisation, Equipment and Works and the two Directors-General of Technical Services. Even in a service which was already much reduced in size from the war years, this was a major responsibility.

By the time Dickson arrived back at the Air Ministry the Berlin Airlift was at an end, but the Korean War was about to begin. The RAF was unable to commit substantial forces to the United Nations, but it did dispatch three squadrons of Short Sunderland Flying Boats for reconnaissance and air-sea rescue duties and provide pilots for the USAF and RAAF, who became heavily engaged in active operations. It also transported the British troops engaged on the ground, but its ability to go much further was hampered by the outbreak of a Communist insurrection in Malaya, which required active engagement by way of air strikes. Much of the RAF's strength, however, was deployed in Germany to counter an increasingly aggressive Soviet Union, and Dickson had to ensure that the squadrons there were also well supplied.

102   Churchill's Eagles

At the same time he also had to carry out the planning for the deployment of the USAF on British bases.

On New Year's Day 1953 Dickson succeeded Slessor as CAS. By this time the RAF was moving fast to become a substantially jet-powered force. The first jet fighter, the Gloster Meteor, had entered squadron service in 1944 and was followed in 1946 by the De Havilland Vampire. Neither of these matched the performance of either the American or Russian jets of the period, and the RAF equipped two squadrons with the North American F-86 Sabre as a temporary measure pending the arrival of the superb Hawker Hunter in 1954. In 1951 the English Electric Canberra medium bomber was introduced. This versatile and long-serving aircraft had a tactical nuclear capability, but a strategic capability had to wait for the V-bombers, the Vickers Valiant entering service in 1955, followed by the Avro Vulcan in 1956 and the Handley Page Victor in 1957. Transport Command was not far behind Fighter and Bomber Commands, its first jet aircraft, the De Havilland Comet, appearing in 1956. Other developments included the first helicopter to enter RAF service, the Bristol Sycamore in 1953.

Dickson, promoted to marshal of the RAF on 1 June 1954, might have expected to retire at the end of a three-year term, but the then Prime Minister, Anthony Eden, had other ideas. He was determined to strengthen the position of the Ministry of Defence relative to the three service ministries, the Admiralty, the War Office and the Air Ministry, by the creation of a new role, the Chairman of the Chiefs of Staff Committee and Chief of Staff to the Minister of Defence. Dickson was duly chosen. As a representative of the smallest and most junior of the services, he may have been seen as more acceptable to the other two than either of them would have been to each other. He was, moreover, known as someone who was capable of seeing beyond the interests of his own service. His role was to represent the combined views of the three chiefs to the politicians, but he had a very small staff of his own and, as it turned out, very little influence on his political masters.

Dickson's term of office, which was to last three and a half years until July 1959, the last six months of which were as the newly styled Chief of the Defence Staff, was not a particularly happy one. It was blighted by disagreements among his colleagues, by his own relatively poor health, by the Suez Crisis, a military success but a political disaster, and by Duncan Sandys' Defence White Paper of 1957, which, amongst other things, saw the wholesale reorganization of the aircraft industry and the end of National Service, and was deeply unpopular with all three services. Through no fault of Dickson's, it was not a very satisfactory end to what had been an outstanding career. By any measure a first-rate officer, it was his lot to reach the pinnacle of his profession at the very beginning of the evolution of more central control of the armed services, which would prove to be far from easy.

Air Chief Marshal Sir Sholto Douglas (later MRAF The Lord Douglas of Kirtleside) GCB, MC, DFC (1893–1969)

Since the RAF was formed, only three of its officers have ever been promoted to the rank of marshal of the RAF without first becoming Chief of the Air Staff. One was Arthur **Tedder**, whose leadership in the Mediterranean and North-West Europe was recognised by his promotion and who went on to become CAS less than four months later. Another was Arthur **Harris**, subsequently a controversial figure but at the time of his promotion recognized for his outstanding contribution to the defeat of Germany. The third was Sholto **Douglas** who on the one hand had a highly distinguished wartime career, but on the other never led any of his various commands during their most important campaigns.

Douglas was at Oxford University when Great Britain declared war on Germany on 4 August 1914, but he immediately volunteered to join the Army and was commissioned into the Royal Field Artillery ten days later. In early 1915 he became an observer in 2 Squadron, engaged in reconnaissance and artillery plotting and, having enjoyed his experience in the air, applied to join the RFC as a pilot. He was accepted for flying training and in July 1915 joined 14 Squadron in the UK, before being posted to 8 Squadron on the Western Front, flying the BE2c in a reconnaissance role. He managed to survive the 'Fokker Scourge', becoming a flight commander and winning the Military Cross. After a brief period as a flight commander in 18 Squadron, he was appointed to form and command 43 Squadron in April 1916, taking it out to the Western Front, where it flew the Sopwith 1½ Strutter, the first British fighter to have a synchronized machine gun firing through the propeller.

Douglas was injured in May 1917 when his aircraft crashed on take-off and he spent the early summer of that year recuperating in Ireland. He was then appointed to lead 84 Squadron, which was equipped with the SE5, one of the best fighters of the day. Towards the end of the fighting he commanded 22 Wing and, following the Armistice, was appointed to command a training wing at Cranwell. In early 1919 he was awarded the Distinguished Flying Cross.

104   Churchill's Eagles

Not long afterwards Douglas decided to leave the RAF. He was employed in a number of jobs, the most notable of which was as a pilot in Handley Page's transport business, flying converted bombers. He was about to take up an office job in India when he had a chance meeting with Hugh Trenchard, 'Father of the RAF' and now its CAS. Douglas had known Trenchard well during the Great War and was attracted by his vision of the future, albeit that the RAF had by then shrunk very considerably from its wartime establishment. Trenchard persuaded him to reconsider, and in March 1920 he rejoined the service. His first appointment was to the staff of 1 Group, then commanded by Hugh **Dowding**, whom he persuaded to obtain three Handley Page V/100 bombers; he then led them at the RAF Flying Tournament at Hendon, terrifying the spectators, who included King George V, when he and his fellow pilots took off in formation over their heads. At the end of the year he was awarded a permanent commission and in the summer of 1921 he became Chief Flying Instructor at 6 FTS.

That Douglas was held in some regard by Trenchard was demonstrated by his selection for the first course at the new RAF Staff College, a fundamental building block in Trenchard's plan to create a fully independent service in the teeth of attempts by the Royal Navy and the Army to regain control of it. His fellow students included Keith **Park** and Richard **Peirse** and an officer who would be of the greatest importance to his career many years later, Charles **Portal**. The Directing Staff, led by the Commandant, Robert Brooke-Popham, formed a highly talented team which included Wilfred **Freeman**, Philip **Joubert** and Bertine *Sutton*.

It was, perhaps, inevitable that Douglas's first appointment after the end of the course would be to the Air Ministry, in the Directorate of Training and Staff Duties and substantially focused on the former. Nearly four years later he was looking forward to a posting in command of a RAF station, but instead found himself on the inaugural course of the Imperial Defence College in 1927. It is a measure of how highly he was already regarded that his fellow students included two future field marshals, Alan Brooke and Claude Auchinleck, who would go on to make great names for themselves in the next war but were both a decade or so older than Douglas. Both were lieutenant colonels, the equivalent rank to Douglas as a wing commander, to which he had been promoted in January 1925. Other RAF students included Richard Peirse once again, whilst Joubert was the RAF Instructor.

Douglas's first posting after leaving the IDC was the one he had hoped for earlier, station commander at RAF North Weald. This was, and would remain for many years, a fighter station. It housed 29 and 56 Squadrons which, together with 19 Squadron from nearby Duxford, all flying the stubby but versatile Armstrong Whitworth Siskin and led by Douglas, provided considerable entertainment in the Hendon Air Pageant of 1929.

In August 1929 Douglas was posted overseas for the first time since the Great War. He spent three months on the Air Staff of AHQ Middle East before being sent down to Khartoum as Senior RAF Officer in the Sudan. The only squadron there, No.47, was equipped with the general-purpose Fairey IIIF, whose wheels were converted to floats during the wet weather, allowing the aircraft to alight on the large flooded areas in the south of the country. One of the events which happened during Douglas's posting was the rescue of the former German air ace, Ernst Udet, who had been forced down in the swamps by engine failure.

On his return to the UK in the summer of 1932 Douglas was appointed as the RAF instructor at the IDC, a clear recognition of his intellect. Under the Commandant, Major General Robert Haining, the Army Instructor was his former fellow student at the college, Alan Brooke, whilst the Royal Navy Instructor was Bertram Ramsay, who would also make a considerable reputation for himself in the forthcoming war. During the summer vacation Douglas accompanied Haining to observe the summer manoeuvres of the Italian Army. Mussolini, by this time well established as the country's dictator, insisted on driving them around personally in his red Alfa Romeo and positioning them next to him as he harangued his troops.

At the beginning of 1936 Douglas returned to the Air Ministry, this time as Director of Staff Duties, a job which he understood well from his posting there a decade and more earlier and which was once again focused on training. His responsibilities for this continued when he was made Assistant Chief of the Air Staff in February 1938, but were also extended to cover operational requirements, working directly under the CAS, Cyril Newall. All types of aircraft were on order, but the emphasis was on getting into service as many as possible of the new fighters, both Hawker Hurricanes, which had already begun to equip Fighter Command squadrons, and Supermarine Spitfires, the first of which would arrive that August. Douglas was also particularly concerned with the development of various types of radar.

It was in June 1939, whilst he was serving as ACAS, that Douglas accompanied the Secretary of State for Air, Sir Kingsley Wood, and the AOC-in-C Reserve Command, ACM Sir Christopher Courtney, on a visit to Northern Ireland. As the aircraft approached the Irish coast, the weather deteriorated sharply and the pilot decided to return to England. Descending into dense fog he lost his bearings and eventually crash-landed

106 Churchill's Eagles

on a mountainside in Cumbria. Wood was knocked out, Courtney suffered a broken knee-cap and both the pilot and co-pilot were injured. Douglas crawled out of the wreckage and set off to find help, in which he was successful. Courtney's injury was serious enough for him to be unable to take over Fighter Command from Hugh Dowding later in the year.

On 23 April 1940, as the Battle of Norway was at its height and three weeks before the Germans invaded Belgium and the Netherlands, Douglas was appointed Deputy Chief of the Air Staff, with a seat on the Air Council. He was specifically responsible for all air operations of the RAF, at home and abroad, and for army and navy co-operation. The RAF commitment to the Norwegian campaign was necessarily modest, as fighter aircraft could only get to the country by aircraft carrier and these were at that time few and far between. When the campaign reached its inevitable conclusion, the remaining Gladiators and Hurricanes were flown off from near Narvik to land on HMS *Glorious*, the first time this had been attempted by Hurricanes. All landed safely, but the ship was sunk by German gunfire and all but two of the pilots were drowned.

The campaign in France and Flanders went little better, both the fighters in Air Component of the BEF and the light bombers in the Advanced Air Striking Force suffering huge casualties, whilst Dowding at Fighter Command, supported by Newall and Douglas, became increasingly reluctant to commit his own squadrons across the Channel. Douglas attended meetings in France with his opposite numbers, but these became increasingly defeatist on the French side, culminating in a decision to block RAF Wellington bombers based in southern France from taking off to bomb Italian cities.

Following the fall of France, it was thus actually with some relief that the RAF stood alone, and it was able to make up most of its losses in time for the Battle of Britain, which began on 10 July. Douglas was in close daily touch with Dowding throughout the battle. As it developed, however, serious differences emerged between Keith **Park**, AOC 11 Group, which was based on the front line in the Home Counties and was primarily responsible for the defence of London, and Trafford **Leigh-Mallory**, AOC 12 Group, which was based in East Anglia and the Midlands. 11 Group, lying closest to France and given relatively little warning of raids by radar stations and the Observer Corps, was compelled to scramble its squadrons at short notice, often very soon after they had landed to re-fuel, which gave them little time to assemble in any great numbers before committing themselves to attack. At 12 Group, however, Leigh-Mallory believed that the most important objective should be to destroy as many enemy planes as possible and that this could only be achieved by attacking them with three to six squadrons in a 'Big Wing'. His contention was that it was better to destroy a large number of aircraft on their way home than a few before they reached their targets. Park, on the other hand, believed that by the time these wings had formed up, the enemy would have turned for home and prove to be uncatchable. Moreover, he considered that a major part of 12 Group's role should be to protect 11 Group's airfields to the east and west of London.

This disagreement culminated in a meeting on 17 October at the Air Ministry, chaired by Douglas due to Newall's indisposition but attended by Charles Portal, soon to become CAS. Leigh-Mallory was accompanied by a squadron commander, Wing Commander Doulas Bader, the leading proponent of the Big Wing, and it has been questioned subsequently why such a relatively junior officer should have had any say in the matter. The minutes of the meeting record that it was agreed there was room for both methods, but although Park tried to have them amended to reflect his views more accurately, the Air Staff refused to do this.

Douglas was later to deny any partiality on the matter, but his name has subsequently been associated with the Leigh-Mallory camp. This was given more substance by what happened next: Douglas relieved Dowding as AOC-in-C Fighter Command on 25 November, whilst Leigh-Mallory succeeded Park as AOC 11 Group on 16 December. Instead of being feted for their very considerable victory, Dowding wrote his despatches and then retired from the service nine months later, whilst Park was posted to command 23 (Training) Group, an important job, but not one really worthy of his talents. Douglas was later to criticise both Park and Leigh-Mallory, the former for his lack of liaison with 12 Group, the latter for his reluctance to give 11 Group quick and effective support.

By the time that Douglas arrived at his HQ at Bentley Priory, the Germans had ceased daylight bombing raids, but the Blitz was at its height and would continue over the winter of 1940/1. The demand was thus for night fighters, but at first these were unable to achieve much success due to the unreliability of airborne interception radar. The Boulton Paul Defiants, which had proved to be highly vulnerable to fighter attack in France and in the Battle of Britain, had some successes as radar technology improved, but the majority of the victories were achieved by the Bristol Beaufighter, which replaced the Blenheim in Fighter Command as its primary night fighter. The first such victory was scored by Flight Lieutenant John Cunningham, who became so

108   Churchill's Eagles

adept that he was nicknamed 'Cats-Eyes', going on to score nineteen further victories, with an additional three probables and six damaged.

The Blitz on London petered out in the late spring of 1941, although attacks elsewhere continued, notably on ports. In the meantime, Fighter Command had turned to the offensive. Initially two types of operation were mounted. The first was codenamed *Rhubarb* and consisted entirely of fighters. These carried out raids on German airfields in North-West France, initially by relatively small numbers of fighters and later increasingly in wing strength, with the objective of destroying as many Luftwaffe aircraft as possible on the ground or in the air. The second type was *Circus*, which involved the fighters in accompanying Blenheims of 2 Group Bomber Command in targeted strikes, not only on airfields, but on ports, power stations and factories. In late 1941 the seriously outdated Blenheim began to be replaced by the Douglas Boston.

Neither type of operation delivered much value for money, the claims made being very much higher than the actual results achieved in terms of enemy losses, whilst Fighter Command's own losses were high; indeed, they were slightly higher in 1941 than they had been in the Battle of Britain. The operations could claim to have diverted enemy fighters, both from the Bomber Command routes across the Netherlands and Germany and from the Russian Front; however, the use of the best possible aircraft denied these to other theatres such as the Middle East and Malta, which had to continue relying on the Hurricane and the Curtis P-40 Tomahawk In any event, the Messerschmitt 109G was proving to be too much for the Spitfire V, whilst the Focke-Wulf 190 came as a big shock in the summer of 1941, although both aircraft were in due course effectively countered by the Spitfire Marks VIII and IX.

Cross-Channel operations continued into 1942, an early failure on behalf of the RAF in general being the escape of the battlecruisers *Scharnhorst* and *Gneisenau* from Brest to Bremen. The Dieppe Raid of 19 August 1942 was another failure, mostly for the ground and naval forces, but also for the RAF, to the extent that it lost 106 aircrafts to the Luftwaffe's 48; however, it could justifiably claim success in respect of keeping the enemy aircraft away from the landings.

Night fighter operations continued, particularly during the 'Baedeker' Raids on the cathedral cities of Exeter, Bath, Canterbury, Norwich and York, together with a number of others, in the spring and summer of 1942, in response to Bomber Command's destruction of the old Baltic cities of Lübeck and Rostock. This period also saw the introduction of the night fighter version of the De Havilland Mosquito, although Beaufighters remained in service until 1944.

In late 1942 Douglas was posted to Cairo to take over as AOC-in-C Middle East in succession to Tedder, who was due to become VCAS. Tedder, however, did not relish the idea of his new appointment and delayed the change until the Casablanca Conference in January, as a result of which he was appointed Air C-in-C, Mediterranean Air Command, with overall responsibility not only for the newly established North-West African Air Forces under Lieutenant General Carl Spaatz, but also for RAF Malta, now under Keith Park, and Middle East Command under Douglas. At the time the last of these was still responsible, among other things, for the activities of the Desert Air Force, commanded by Arthur Coningham, which by then was in Tripoli, supporting Eighth Army in its drive into Tunisia. It was not long afterwards, however, that the DAF came under the command of North-West African Tactical Air Forces, with Coningham promoted into command of the latter under Spaatz.

Since the entry of the Italians into the War on 10 June 1940, the AOC-in-C Middle East had been the RAF's most important operational commander outside the UK. With the focus of attention in the Mediterranean now being switched to finishing off the campaign in Tunisia and then to the invasion of Sicily, and with a growing commitment to supporting the land campaign in India and Burma, the Middle East had become a backwater. That is not to say that Douglas was other than fully occupied, but it was with sideshows. He was responsible for a vast area which covered Egypt, the Levant, Iraq, Iran, the Persian Gulf, Aden, the Sudan and East Africa. It also included Turkey, a neutral state in which there was no Allied military presence, but one which Churchill in particular hoped to persuade into the Allied fold. Not long after he had arrived in Cairo, Douglas was ordered by Churchill to travel to Ankara to hold discussions with the Turks on closer co-operation. After meetings not only with the most senior officers of the Turkish Air Force, but also with the President, Prime Minister and Foreign Minister, which he felt had gone well, he returned to Egypt; but in fact no real progress had been made, largely because the Turks were afraid that any attempt to join the Allies would be met with the destruction by bombing of Istanbul.

One of the most important formations under Douglas's command was 216 Group. This formation had grown out of the Aircraft Delivery Unit which, following the defeat of France and the entry into the war of the Italians, had been responsible for operating the Reinforcement Route. This vital operation saw aircraft delivered in parts by sea to Takoradi in Ghana, reassembled, flown across Africa to the Sudan and then up the Nile to Egypt, where they were refurbished for active service. With the escalation of the war in India and Burma and the opening up of a much shorter route from the UK to Egypt across North Africa, 216 Group now became an important component of a major communications network by providing staging posts and maintenance facilities for what was to become Transport Command, as well as for aircraft being delivered to the Russians and for others used to supply the Partisans in Yugoslavia.

RAF Middle East Command also provided bases for the Ninth US Air Force, commanded by Major General Lewis H. Brereton. This was actually a strategic formation, equipped with Consolidated B-24 Liberators engaged in bombing Axis territory from the south. Its most notorious engagement was Operation TIDAL WAVE, the raid on nine oil refineries around Ploesti in Rumania on 1 August 1943 which turned out to be a disaster. Of the 177 aircraft dispatched, only 88 returned, of which 55 were damaged. Whilst a great deal of damage was done to the refineries, oil production was quickly resumed.

Churchill continued to be obsessed with bringing Turkey into the war and, following the surrender of the Italians in September 1943, one of the ways in which he felt that this could be achieved was by expelling the Germans from the Aegean Sea, which, he believed, would also open the sea route to Russia through the Dardanelles. In this he had no support at all from the Americans, who saw it as an unnecessary sideshow, but he decided to proceed nonetheless.

In the aftermath of the Italian surrender, German forces had been rushed into the Eastern Aegean, which was occupied by its former allies. The first objective was the largest island, Rhodes, which was swiftly and ruthlessly seized by the Germans. Since Rhodes was the only island with substantial airfields, this was a blow to the British hopes. However, successful landings were made on Cos and Leros on 10 September and an airstrip was constructed on the former.

The Germans now moved a considerable force of aircraft into the Aegean and carried out air raids on the British-held islands. With this support, landings were made on Cos on 3 October and the British garrison was overwhelmed on the following day. Due to a successful interception by the Royal Navy of a similar force attacking Leros, the landings there from both sea and air were delayed to 12 November and the garrison was forced to surrender four days later. The other Italian-held islands were also quickly occupied. The RAF had given a great deal of support to the land forces, but unlike the Luftwaffe it was operating at the greatest extent of its range, and 115 aircraft were lost.

The failure of the Dodecanese campaign marked the nadir of Douglas's wartime career, compounded by the news that the post of Supreme Commander in South-East Asia, which he had hopes of occupying, had gone instead to Lord Louis Mountbatten. Having attended the Cairo Conference in November 1943, at which he was able to meet Churchill and Portal, he was hopeful of a move to a more active theatre of war, and this was, indeed, mooted shortly afterwards. However, it was not an appointment that he welcomed, Deputy C-in-C of the Mediterranean Allied Air Forces, in which he would be subordinated to an American, Lieutenant General Ira Eaker. Douglas liked Eaker personally but felt strongly that he was junior to himself, both in rank – Douglas had been promoted to acting air chief marshal, a rank equivalent to general in the USAAF, as long ago as in July 1942 – and in experience.

Churchill, who had been closely involved in senior Allied service appointments, was initially unsympathetic to Douglas's stance, but was eventually persuaded by Portal and the Secretary of State for Air, Sir Archibald Sinclair, to offer him the position of AOC-in-C Coastal Command. This Douglas accepted with alacrity, succeeding Jack Slessor, who was appointed to the position that Douglas had been so loath to accept.

Coastal Command had begun the war as the Cinderella of the home commands. It was woefully ill-prepared for the German U-boat campaign, despite the best efforts of its then AOC-in-C, Frederick **Bowhill**. However, by the time that Bowhill's successor, Philip **Joubert**, took over in June 1941, the situation had improved considerably. The original obsolete aircraft had gone, to be replaced by more modern types, not only for reconnaissance and the sinking of U-boats, but also for striking at German ships along the North Sea and Norwegian coasts. During Joubert's period of command, moreover, a number of major technical advances were made, and, by the time that he handed over to John Slessor in early 1943, Very Long Range ('VLR') aircraft had entered service, in particular the Consolidated B-24 Liberator, and these were equipped with both ASV (air to surface vessel) radar and the Leigh Light, the latter allowing an aircraft to attack a submarine on the surface at night.

Coastal Command's squadrons were by this time based in both the United Kingdom and Iceland, but there remained a large gap in its coverage in the mid-Atlantic. In spite of this, a combination of much improved convoy tactics, greater numbers of escort vessels, which included small aircraft

112   Churchill's Eagles

carriers, the breaking of the German naval Enigma code and increasing numbers of VLR aircraft led to a major defeat for the German U-boat fleet in May 1943 and its temporary recall by Admiral Dönitz to fit schnorkel breathing apparatus and equip with acoustic torpedoes.

Douglas was the beneficiary of what had gone before, but Coastal Command's war was far from over. It was now a much more substantial force than the one which Bowhill had commanded. It comprised five groups in the UK: 15 Group based in Liverpool, with primary responsibility for convoys arriving there and at other West Coast ports, 16 Group in Chatham looking after the southern part of the North Sea, 17 Group in Edinburgh, responsible for all training, 18 Group at Rosyth, responsible for dealing with the northern part of the North Sea and the coast of Norway and 19 Group at Plymouth covering the South-Western Approaches. In addition, there were major bases in Iceland and at Gibraltar, whilst 247 Group was established in the Azores after Portugal allowed bases to be used there from the summer of 1943.

Coastal Command was also responsible for two other organizations. The first of these was what had been 1 Photo Reconnaissance Unit, but now comprised five squadrons, based at Benson in Oxfordshire and flying unarmed high-altitude Spitfires and Mosquitoes on behalf of all the home commands. The second was the Air-Sea Rescue Service, deploying around the coasts of Great Britain a variety of aircraft from the bi-plane Supermarine Walrus to the lifeboat-carrying Vickers Warwick, together with a fleet of fast motor boats.

Douglas's arrival back in the UK coincided with a steadily increasing focus by all the UK operational commands on the forthcoming Operation OVERLORD, the invasion of North-West Europe, and, for Coastal Command in particular, on Operation NEPTUNE, the naval phase of the operation. The command was tasked in particular with protecting both flanks of the armada, one of which ran from Portland to Jersey and the other from North Foreland to Calais, from attacks by U-boats and E-boats. Douglas attended regular meetings held with all the senior airmen under the chairmanship of Leigh-Mallory, now the C-in-C Allied Expeditionary Air Force, and also with Admiral Sir Bertram Ramsay, the C-in-C Allied Naval Expeditionary Force, and his subordinate commanders. In the event, losses of ships to German submarines and surface vessels, particularly to the west, where no fewer than thirty squadrons were deployed in round-the-clock patrols under 19 Group's command, were very much lower than had been feared. Losses of Coastal Command aircraft, on the other hand, were not inconsiderable.

With the breakout of the Allied armies from Normandy in August 1944, and particularly because of the loss or blockade by land of all its bases in Brittany and South-West France, the U-boat fleet was compelled to operate from bases in the Baltic and Norway. A tight watch was thus kept upon the routes through the Kattegat and Skagerrak and into the Atlantic across the North and Norwegian Seas. The strike wings of Coastal Command were also kept very fully employed attacking coastal convoys and lone ships. Added to those still engaged in the Atlantic, the number of aircraft in the command grew to 793, its largest at any one time. Over the course of the war, 255 U-boats were sunk and a further 50 were shared with the Royal Navy, whilst 350 enemy surface vessels were also sunk. On the other side of the balance sheet, 1,777 aircraft and 5,866 aircrew were lost.

Following the defeat of Germany, Douglas was appointed C-in-C of the British Air Forces of Occupation in July 1945, taking over what had once been the Second Tactical Air Force. In addition to commanding all the RAF operational units in the British Sector, he was responsible for disbanding the Luftwaffe and destroying its remaining assets. In the New Year's Honours of 1946 he was promoted to marshal of the RAF along with Arthur Harris. He had hoped to succeed Portal as CAS, but that appointment went to Tedder.

When his term of appointment came to an end, Douglas had intended to retire. However, he was nominated to succeed Montgomery as Commander-in-Chief British Forces of Occupation and simultaneously as Military Governor of the British Zone of Germany and a member of the Allied Control Commission. This, once again, was not a job which he wanted, and it took the Prime Minister, by that time Clement Attlee, to persuade him to take it on, particularly as he had been the unanimous choice of the Cabinet.

Douglas did not enjoy his new role. He got on well with his American opposite number on the Allied Control Council, but found the French difficult and the Russians many times more so. The part of the job which he enjoyed the least, however, was sitting with his American, French and Russian colleagues as a Court of Appeal on the judgements and sentences handed down by the International Military Tribunal at Nuremberg. He took this responsibility with the utmost seriousness, but in the end concurred with the Tribunal, as did all the other Control Council members. He did, however, admit to a slight feeling of relief that Hermann Goering, one of his opponents on the Western Front in the Great War, had cheated the hangman by taking poison.

114   Churchill's Eagles

The winter of 1946/7 was the coldest for half a century and there was a high risk of famine, as food supplies in Europe were short. Much of Douglas's time was spent ensuring that both food and fuel were made available to the population, a considerable feat of administration. It was with some relief that he was eventually permitted to retire in November 1947, after eighteen months in a job which he regarded as the least enjoyable of his whole career.

Shortly afterwards, in the New Year's Honours of 1948, Douglas was ennobled as Baron Douglas of Kirtleside. He went on to become briefly a director of the British Overseas Airways Corporation and then, in 1949, Chairman of British European Airways, an appointment which he held for fifteen years.

It would be churlish not to place Douglas in the first rank of senior RAF officers of the war, yet somehow he assumed his most important appointments after the commands concerned had achieved their most glorious victories. The Battle of Britain was won two months before he was appointed AOC-in-C Fighter Command; the Desert Air Force, with El Alamein and the conquest of Libya to its credit, passed out of his control a short time after he arrived to be AOC-in-C Middle East; the crushing victory over the U-boats in May 1943 came during Slessor's and not Douglas's tenure as AOC-in-C Coastal Command; and the campaign in North-West Europe was over before he arrived in Germany. This is not to belittle his achievement which, both in command and on the staff, was considerable. He certainly enjoyed the respect and admiration of his superiors and his political masters, and he fully deserved both promotion to the highest rank in his service and elevation to a peerage.

Air Chief Marshal the Lord Dowding of Bentley Priory GCB, GCVO, CMG (1882–1970)

There are only two feats of arms of the RAF during the Second World War which remain high in the consciousness of the British public. One is the bombing raid by 617 Squadron which breached the Möhne and Eder Dams on the night of 16/17 May 1943; this certainly captured the imagination for its daring and heroism, but it had almost no impact on the war as a whole. The other was the Battle of Britain, and in this case the impact is acknowledged to have been immense. The result put paid to a German invasion of Great Britain, not only in the summer of 1940, but also for the rest of the war. Had the battle not been won, the future of Europe as a whole might have looked very different. As it was, Germany cast its eyes elsewhere, with ultimately disastrous results for its objective of European domination. Whilst both were RAF officers, the architect of victory in the Battle of Britain was as unlike the dashing and heroic Wing Commander Guy Gibson of 617 Squadron as it was possible to be. Although not entirely lacking in sense of humour, but never much inclined to socialize with his colleagues, let alone indulge in riotous behaviour, Hugh **Dowding** had picked up the nickname of 'Stuffy' whilst at the Army Staff College at Camberley before the Great War and it had stuck to him thereafter.

On leaving school in 1899 Dowding attended the Royal Military Academy at Woolwich, from which he was commissioned into the Royal Garrison Artillery. He served in Gibraltar, Ceylon and Hong Kong and then transferred to the Mountain Artillery in India for six years before being selected for the Staff College. Whilst at Camberley he learnt to fly in his spare time and then attended the Central Flying School, where Hugh Trenchard was the second-in-command and the future MRAF Sir John Salmond was one of his instructors. Initially, Dowding remained in the Royal Artillery but he became a reservist for the RFC and was accordingly called up when war was declared on Germany.

He was in due course posted to France, initially as an observer, but he then became a pilot, briefly in 7 Squadron in England and then in 6 Squadron in France, flying BE2s and BE8s over the First Battle of Ypres. In March 1915 he was posted to 4 Squadron as the officer in charge of the wireless flight. With this experience behind him he was then promoted to major and given command of the Wireless Experimental Establishment at Brooklands, which gave him a lasting interest in communications. Only three months later he received his first command appointment as CO of 16 Squadron in France, once again flying BE2s in a corps reconnaissance role as part of a wing commanded by Trenchard. Dowding was appointed to command a wing himself in February 1916, albeit one in the UK at Farnborough, before going back to France to take command of 9 Wing in time for the Battle of the Somme. However, he did not get on well with Trenchard, who was in overall command of the RFC in France by this time, and he was shuffled off into a series of administrative jobs in England. He was greatly relieved when he received a permanent commission as a group captain in the newly formed RAF in 1919.

In February 1920 Dowding was appointed to command 1 Group, based at Kenley and controlling stations also at Biggin Hill, Hawkinge and Manston, all of which would come under his command in the Battle of Britain many years later. With France seen at that time to represent more of a potential

116   Churchill's Eagles

threat to the security of Great Britain than the recently defeated Germany, this was a key appointment. Two years later Dowding moved to be Chief Staff Officer to AVM (later Air Marshal Sir) John Higgins at Inland Area, which at that time covered the whole country other than the Coastal Area.

In 1924 Dowding followed Higgins as his CSO when the latter was appointed AOC Iraq Command. The command had been established in 1921 following the Cairo Conference, at which Winston Churchill, then the Secretary of State for the Colonies, had proposed that all British forces in the country should come under the RAF. This came after Trenchard had proposed putting down a rebellion in British Somaliland by the use of air power, a strategy which had worked well and was then repeated in Iraq. Most of the RAF's operations in Iraq came as a result either of revolts against the newly imposed monarchy or threats by Turkey to recover territory lost after the Great War, but by the time Dowding arrived, the country was relatively quiet and remained so during his term of appointment.

In May 1926 Dowding was appointed Director of Training at the Air Ministry. He was there for over three years, which were uneventful but none the less valuable, partly because his relationship with Trenchard, which had been difficult since the latter part of the Great War, now improved considerably. One result of this was his next appointment in 1929, with promotion to air vice-marshal, as AOC in Transjordan and Palestine, where unrest was building between the Arabs and Jews and a general uprising was feared. Trenchard believed that this could be dealt with by the type of air control which had worked in Iraq. In the event, such trouble as there was turned out to be entirely political rather than military, but Dowding warned of serious problems ahead if it was decided to impose on Palestine the policies advocated by the Zionists.

He returned to the UK at the end of 1929 to become AOC Fighting Area within Air Defence of Great Britain, the command which controlled all the operational squadrons in the UK. The Fighting Area comprised substantially all the home-based fighter squadrons and was situated in the south-east of England: it would in due course become 11 Group. Dowding was only there for eight months, but they were valuable ones in the light of his future career. If anything, he was dismayed by the weakness of the country's air defences: although Germany was yet to become a threat, he and many others remained concerned about France.

In September 1930 Dowding joined the Air Council as Air Member for Supply and Research. Much of his attention in this appointment was devoted to the new aircraft being ordered for the RAF, particularly the fighters. He was determined to procure the most modern types of monoplane fighter and was prominent in the discussions held at Hawker in August 1933 on a new monoplane aircraft based upon the company's Fury bi-plane and powered by Roll-Royce's new Merlin engine. The prototype had its maiden flight on 6 November 1935 and the first production Hurricane entered squadron service in December 1937. Similar discussions took place with Supermarine with a view to capitalizing on the company's experience with its highly successful Schneider Cup-winning aircraft. Similarly equipped with the Merlin, the first flight of the Supermarine Type 300 took place on 3 March 1936 and the first Mark 1 Spitfire flew on 14 March 1938. Dowding was also instrumental in ensuring the acceptance of a proposal by Squadron Leader Ralph *Sorley*, of the Operational Requirements Section within the Department of Operations and Intelligence, that both the Hurricane and the Spitfire should mount four machine guns in each wing rather than the traditional two in the nose.

In January 1935 and by now an air marshal with a knighthood to his name, Dowding's job was split into two; he took on the position of Air Member for Research and Development, whilst Cyril **Newall** became Air Member for Supply and Organisation. Dowding's keen interest in technical developments in the field of wireless went back to his days in command of the Wireless Experimental Establishment in 1915, and to this was now added an interest in radar. In February 1935 a team led by Robert Watson-Watt carried out a test in Daventry which demonstrated clearly that it was possible to detect an aircraft in flight. Dowding immediately threw his weight and the Air Ministry's money behind further development, out of which emerged the Chain Home and Chain Home Low systems of respectively high- and low-level radar, operating from stations around the south and east coasts. One problem was that the system did not initially differentiate between friendly and hostile aircraft, but the fitting of an IFF (Identification Friend or Foe) transmitter on all aircraft solved this.

On 14 July 1936 Dowding arrived at Bentley Priory, a large mansion near Stanmore, north-west of London, to take up the position of AOC-in-C at the newly formed Fighter Command. He was not expecting his appointment to last for long, as he had been told earlier that year by both Edward Ellington, the incumbent CAS, and 'Ginger' **Bowhill**, the Air Member for Personnel, that he would be succeeding Ellington himself on the latter's retirement. A year later, however, Ellington wrote to say that the Secretary of State for Air had decided that the job would go instead to Newall. In spite of a natural disappointment that he would not get to the very top of his service, Dowding

118   Churchill's Eagles

soon realized that he was much better suited to where he was. He had now to oversee the introduction into squadron service of the two new fighters and the erection of radar stations and, at the same time, devise an entirely new system of control which would link all of them together.

The Filter Room at Bentley Priory, which received and processed information from the radar stations, and the Operations Room, which put this together with reports from all other sources, were together the nerve centre of the command. From the latter instructions went out to Group and Sector Controllers, all of them fighter pilots of considerable experience. Much of the 'manpower' was provided by women, and Dowding did not hesitate to recruit and train WAAFs, who were to become fundamental to the operation of what would in future be known as the 'Dowding System'.

There were three other organizations which had to be fitted into an increasingly complex structure. The first was Balloon Command, part of the RAF, which deployed all the country's barrage balloons, some near the coast, others around London and major cities. The second was the Observer Corps, manned by civilian volunteers. These were trained in aircraft recognition and occupied small posts, not only along the coast from Flamborough Head in Yorkshire to Poole Harbour in Dorset, but also inland where radar cover did not exist; from these they passed information on formations of enemy aircraft by phone links to group and sector HQs, which not only provoked an armed response by Fighter Command, but also air raid warnings along the projected route of the raiders.

The third organization to come under Fighter Command's operational control was AA Command, part of the British Army. From July 1938 this was led by Lieutenant General Alan Brooke (later Field Marshal Viscount Alanbrooke), who had as big a job as Dowding to get his command ready for the forthcoming war. Brooke established his HQ next to Dowding's at Bentley Priory and the two men saw each other almost every day, establishing a lasting mutual admiration. It was lucky for Dowding that, when Brooke moved on to become C-in-C of Southern Command in September 1939, he was succeeded by Lieutenant General (later General Sir) Frederick Pile, known to his friends as Tim. Pile and Dowding quickly established the same close relationship that the latter had enjoyed with Brooke as someone the AOC-in-C could readily turn to for advice. That the two men experienced similar problems in dealing with their respective political and military masters bound them close together. Remarkably, Pile was to continue in his appointment until March 1945.

The other man on whom Dowding could lean was his Senior Air Staff Officer from June 1938, Air Commodore Keith **Park**. Park had begun his military career as a gunner, albeit in the army of his native New Zealand, but he transferred to the RFC in 1916 and remained in the RAF after the Great War. He became intimately involved in the creation of the Dowding System and the training of all those involved in its application. He was thus just the man Dowding needed to become AOC of 11 Group, which would bear the brunt of any future attack from the Continent on London and the South-East. Park was to move to 11 Group in the late spring of 1940, his replacement as SASO being Douglas **Evill**, another capable and loyal subordinate who had been SASO to Arthur **Barratt** at British Air Forces in France.

In the summer of 1938, Fighter Command still looked very weak, with a mere twenty-nine squadrons operational, in which fewer than a hundred aircraft were Hurricanes, whilst Spitfires had yet to enter service. Dowding was one of many who welcomed the Munich Agreement between Germany, Great Britain, France and Italy as offering a breathing space to build up Fighter Command's strength. Two months earlier, however, he had received a letter from Newall to tell him that he would be required to retire from the RAF soon after the end of June 1939. His relief was to be Air Marshal (later Air Chief Marshal Sir) Christopher *Courtney*. Dowding himself was by then fifty-six years old and quite prepared to go. However, in March 1939 Newall wrote again to say that in the interests of the efficiency of the command, he hoped that Dowding would agree to defer his retirement until the end of March 1940. Three months later Courtney was injured in a plane crash and put out of action for several months. Whether or not this affected his ability to take over from Dowding in March 1940 is unclear, but in January of that year Courtney was in any event appointed Air Member for Supply and Organisation, a post he was to occupy with distinction until after the end of the war.

It had been agreed for some time that the minimum number of fully equipped squadrons needed for the air defence of the United Kingdom would be fifty-two, but Fighter Command began the war with the equivalent of thirty-four. Moreover, it was by now clear that fighters would have to be made available to both the Air Component of the British Expeditionary Force and the Advanced Air Striking Force in France, with the former including four squadrons of Hurricanes and two of the by now obsolete Gloster Gladiator and the latter employing two squadrons of Hurricanes.

120   Churchill's Eagles

Gladiators and a small number of Hurricanes were also sent to Norway after the German invasion, all of which were lost during the campaign.

When the Germans struck in the West on 10 May 1940, what Dowding had most feared came to pass. Losses of both aircraft and pilots in the Air Component and the AASF were very high, and replacements of the former could only come from Fighter Command once the direct output from the manufacturers had been exhausted. There were now only thirty-six squadrons in Fighter Command instead of the fifty-two believed by Dowding to be the minimum acceptable. By the end of 13 May over two hundred Hurricanes had been lost on the Continent and Dowding was compelled to send out thirty-two more. Two days later, he asked to put his case before the War Cabinet, at which he told Churchill and the other members that, at the current rate of attrition, he would not have a single Hurricane left in either France or the UK in two weeks time. Churchill was visibly furious.

On 16 May, Dowding wrote a letter to the Under Secretary of State for Air, which concluded:

I believe that, if an adequate fighter force is kept in this country, if the fleet remains in being, and if Home Forces are suitably organised to resist invasion, we should be able to carry on the war single handed for some time, if not indefinitely. But, if the Home Defence Force is drained away in desperate attempts to remedy the situation in France, defeat in France will involve the final, complete and irremediable defeat of this country.

This clearly made an impact on the War Cabinet, but a further six squadrons of Hurricanes were nevertheless diverted to France in response to the pleas of the French Government, to which eight half-squadrons were added later, albeit that they were there only in daylight hours, returning to airfields in England every evening.

During the evacuation of the BEF from Dunkirk, Fighter Command was heavily committed, operating from England. The relatively short range of the fighters meant that the time they were able to spend over the beaches was limited, but they were active in breaking up attacks by the Luftwaffe before these could reach the beaches. Because the soldiers and sailors could not see this, they believed that the RAF was not there at all and the reputation of the service suffered considerably, at least until Churchill told Parliament the real story on 4 June.

The Air Marshals   121

Most of the fighting to protect the evacuation was carried out by the squadrons of 11 Group, in which Park, with his HQ in Uxbridge, had been AOC since 20 April. The group's next-door neighbour to the west was 10 Group, led by AVM Sir Quintin *Brand*, with his HQ at Box, near Bath. To the north was 12 Group, led by AVM Trafford **Leigh-Mallory**, with his HQ at Watnall, near Nottingham, defending the industrial cities of the Midlands and North-West. 13 Group, under AVM Richard *Saul*, with his HQ near Newcastle, covered a huge territory in the North of England and Scotland. The last of these would only be involved in the forthcoming battle very briefly, but would provide an ideal area for exhausted squadrons to rest and re-equip.

The Battle of Britain is held to have begun on 10 July 1940, but this is a relatively arbitrary date, as fighting involving Fighter Command pilots had taken place before then. The first phase was the so-called *Kanalkampf* (Channel Fight) in which most of the German attacks took place on British convoys and coastal targets, drawing out the defenders. Messerschmitt 109s also carried out sweeps across the British countryside. In both types of operation losses in Fighter Command were high, and Dowding began to have deep concerns about his ability to re-equip, not necessarily with aircraft, which were coming off the production line in ever larger numbers, but with experienced pilots.

In the meantime, Dowding himself had had his mooted date of retirement extended twice. He had been expecting to go at the end of March 1940, but on the day before he had been asked to stay on until 14 July. On 5 July he was asked to defer the date yet again, this time to October.

The *Kanalkampf* was intended to draw out and destroy the defenders, but it was not an end in itself. Hitler had a much more ambitious campaign in preparation, one which would precede Operation *Seelöwe* (Sealion), the German invasion of Great Britain. Hitler's great fear was not of the RAF, but of the Royal Navy, which was far more powerful than its German counterpart. In spite of the relatively short distance across the English Channel, it was recognized that the invasion fleet would be highly vulnerable to British capital ships. These, however, were based at Scapa Flow, hundreds of miles away, and would not put to sea in the confined areas of the Channel and the North Sea without strong protection from the air. In order to provide the landing craft with a safe passage, therefore, it was essential that the RAF be wiped out.

The first phase was an attack on the British radar installations on the south coast of England, which began on 12 August in an attempt to blind the

122   Churchill's Eagles

British defences. Only one of these, at Ventnor in the Isle of Wight, was put completely out of action, and then only for three days; it went down again for longer subsequently, but was temporarily replaced by a small mobile unit. The most intensive phase of the battle, called *Adlertag* (Eagle Day) by the Germans, began on the next day, with the major concentration on Fighter Command's airfields. As would be the case throughout the battle, the claims by both sides were far ahead of reality, on this occasion the RAF with sixty-four victories, the Germans with eighty-four. The real numbers were thirty-four to thirteen.

The main attacks throughout the battle came from 2 and 3 *Luftlotten* (air fleets) based in France, but on 15 August *Luftflotte* 5, based in Norway, mounted an attack by some seventy Heinkel 111s and twenty-one Messerschmitt 110s on the North-East of England, from which it was believed that most of the RAF fighters had been diverted to the main battle in the south. The Germans were mistaken. Four squadrons of Spitfires and Hurricanes rose to meet them, causing serious losses with none to themselves A similar attack from Denmark on airfields near Hull met a similar fate. The Germans did not repeat the experiment.

18 August proved to be a very busy day for Fighter Command, after which there was something of a lull for the next few days, due largely to the poor weather. The Germans, however, had come to one significant conclusion, that the Junkers 87 Stuka dive bomber was far too vulnerable to fighter attack, and it was effectively withdrawn. Attacks were renewed with great intensity on 24 August, particularly on Park's airfields, and it was becoming clear that the help which he was requesting from 12 Group to defend them was not being adequately provided. This was because of the adoption of a new tactic by Leigh-Mallory, the 'Big Wing', which was to be a matter of great controversy, both for the remainder of the battle and thereafter.

Leigh-Mallory was not a great admirer of either Dowding or Park. He had chafed at the bit in the early stages of the battle, when his squadrons were kept on stand-by for attacks on the Midlands. Moreover, he had been seduced by a proposal from one of his squadron commanders, Douglas Bader. Bader, who had lost both legs in an accident before the War but managed not only to rejoin the RAF, but to fly as well as any able-bodied pilot, considered that 11 Group's tactics, essentially to scramble squadrons as soon as the German attacks developed, with a view to shooting down as many bombers as possible before they reached their targets, were wrong. He maintained that it would be far better to form 'Big Wings' of anything between two and four squadrons, which could then provide a sufficient force to shoot down many more bombers on their way back to France.

Dowding and Park were both dead set against this, believing firmly that it was their duty to destroy as many aircraft as possible before they reached their targets, particularly as these included both 11 Group's airfields and the priceless radar stations. The average time taken for an 11 Group squadron to scramble was three and a half minutes, which was expected to allow time to get up to a sufficient height to mount a successful attack on incoming German formations. The 'Big Wings' took very much longer, due to the number of aircraft congregating from several airfields, and often arrived after the Germans had gone. Bader, moreover, was dismissive of the role of the ground controllers and all too often used his own judgement as to where to fly and when. He resented being asked to protect 11 Group's airfields rather than taking the offensive.

By contrast, Park was getting full and timely support from Brand, his neighbour to the west. 10 Group was subject to attacks on its own airfields, but was also heavily committed to countering attacks on targets in 11 Group's area, notably Portsmouth and Southampton, and airfields such as Tangmere.

Going into September, Fighter Command's position was starting to look desperate. The problem was not so much a shortage of aircraft – the appointment of Lord Beaverbrook by Churchill to lead the Ministry of Aircraft Production had resulted in an adequate supply of new machines – as of trained pilots; many of those now being posted to front-line squadrons having had very few hours' experience on their aircraft. The need to defend the airfields meant that fewer aircraft could be provided for early interception before or just after the Germans had crossed the coast. The numbers of aircraft destroyed were broadly similar on each side, but whilst British pilots who baled out successfully would live to fight another day, the Germans were incarcerated. Although the Germans were still forecasting victory before very long, their pilots were constantly surprised at the number of defenders coming up to intercept them.

The priorities for the German attacks, however, were now changing. On the night of 24/25 August German bombs had fallen on the City of London. Incensed by this, Churchill ordered an immediate reprisal, and on the following night Bomber Command mounted its first raid on Berlin, to be followed by others. Although damage was minimal, the Germans were stunned and Hitler was furious, having been assured by Goering that such a thing was not possible. Having lost face amongst his own people, the Führer now ordered the attacks to be focused on London.

124   Churchill's Eagles

Notwithstanding the damage and heavy loss of civilian life, to Dowding this strategy came as manna from heaven. The new German policy manifested itself on 7 September, when a huge formation of enemy aircraft hit London. Losses on both sides were high, but Dowding's airfields were untouched. The change of tactics was confirmed by further raids on London two nights later and again two nights after that.

The climax of the Battle of Britain came on 15 September, the very day that Churchill chose to visit the Operations Room at 11 Group HQ with his wife Clementine. The first formation of attackers was broken up before even reaching the capital and the second incurred very heavy losses. Seeing from the boards that every single squadron was deployed, Churchill asked about reserves. Park's reply – 'There are none' – silenced the usually loquacious Prime Minister.

In fact the day represented a great victory for Fighter Command, with fifty-six enemy aircraft confirmed destroyed to twenty-six for the RAF, and it deserves its annual commemoration as Battle of Britain Day. Forty-eight hours later Hitler postponed Operation *Seelöwe* indefinitely. The battle was not yet at an end, however. Fighting continued at varying levels of intensity for the next month and a half, with 31 October chosen as a rather arbitrary date for the battle's end, although operations continued thereafter during the Blitz on London.

On 17 October, less than two weeks before the formal end of the battle, Dowding, Park, Brand and Leigh-Mallory were invited to attend a meeting at the Air Ministry. Newall was ill, and his chosen successor as CAS, Charles **Portal**, was present but took little part in the debate. The meeting was chaired by the DCAS, Sholto **Douglas**. Under discussion were the tactics employed by 11 Group on the one hand and 12 Group on the other. This meeting has come to be seen as controversial, partly because of the participation of Bader, at the time a mere squadron leader, who was there to advance the use of the 'Big Wing'. Bader's presence came as a surprise to Dowding and Park, who might, had they known about this, have brought one or more squadron commanders from 11 Group. The minutes of the meeting seem quite innocuous, recording that there was room for both types of tactic, recognizing that wings might be difficult to form when the enemy was already close, but acknowledging their value otherwise. Park, however, was unhappy with the tone and direction and subsequently asked for the minutes to be amended to include more precisely what he had said, but the Air Ministry refused his request. Brand, who had also submitted some corrections, was likewise denied.

The Air Marshals 125

Dowding was later to say that he was entirely on Park's side. He believed that Leigh-Mallory, unlike his other group commanders, had not run 11 Group in the way that he, Dowding, expected. However, it became clear that the Air Ministry, in the shape of both Douglas and the Under-Secretary of State for Air, Harold Balfour, himself a former RAF officer, inclined towards Leigh-Mallory, and what happened next confirmed this. On 13 November Dowding was informed in person by the Secretary of State for Air, Sir Archibald Sinclair, that he would be replaced eleven days later by Douglas himself. He was asked by the Prime Minister personally to go to the USA on a technical mission on behalf of the Air Ministry, a job for which he knew that he was unsuited and said so, only to have Churchill insist that he should do it. His time there, from 18 December 1940 to 5 May 1941, was not a success. On his return he wrote his despatches. He retired on 1 October 1941, only to be called back again by Churchill to undertake a review of potential economies in the RAF. Once again this was a task for which he was not suited and which he did not want. He eventually managed to retire on 15 July 1942.

In the meantime, Park had been succeeded at 12 Group by Leigh-Mallory, turning down a job at the Air Ministry in December 1940 and being appointed instead as AOC 23 (Training) Group. His reward for months of hard fighting and a momentous victory was to become a Companion of the Bath, an honour which his seniority alone justified and which Leigh-Mallory had received five months earlier.

Dowding had become a Knight Grand Cross in the same order during the battle and, more unusually, was elevated to a barony as Lord Dowding of Bentley Priory in 1943 in recognition of his achievements. There were many, not least King George VI, who thought that he should be promoted to marshal of the RAF, but this would have established a precedent at the time, as the rank had been reserved for those who were serving or had served as Chief of the Air Staff. This requirement, however, was set aside for Arthur **Harris** and for Douglas, both of whom were made up to MRAF on New Year's Day 1946. This would have been a highly appropriate occasion for Dowding to have joined them, but it was not to be.

The Battle of Britain is the only major engagement in which two nations have fought for air superiority without regard for operations taking place at the same time below them on land or at sea. It was remarkable that Dowding had thought through in great depth what was to be required for a campaign which had absolutely no precedent to lean upon, welding together not only his own organization, but many others as well, into a system which was to

126   Churchill's Eagles

function exceptionally smoothly when put to the test. He was without doubt one of the Great Men of the War, the victor of a momentous battle which had a decisive impact, not only on the outcome of the conflict, but on the history of the world.

Air Vice-Marshal W. (later Air Chief Marshal Sir William) Elliott GCVO, KCB, KBE, DFC* (1896–1971)

One of the most multi-national commands formed under the operational control of the RAF during the Second World War was the Balkan Air Force ('BAF'). Created specifically to support Partisan activity in Yugoslavia, but also closely involved with the liberation of both Albania and Greece, its units came not only from the RAF itself, in which two squadrons were manned by Yugoslavs and one flight by Poles, but also from the South African Air Force, the Royal Hellenic Air Force and the Italian Co-Belligerent Air Force. It even included from time to time units of the USAAF and, for a few months, the Soviet Air Force. It had a short life, from June 1944 to July 1945, but an extremely eventful one. The RAF officer who both formed the BAF and commanded it for the first eight months was William **Elliott**.

On leaving school Elliott joined the Army Service Corps, but he volunteered for the RFC in 1917. After qualifying as a pilot he was posted in the spring of 1918 to 142 Squadron at Ismailia in Egypt and then almost immediately to 14 Squadron as a flight commander. Both squadrons were operating in a corps reconnaissance role for the Egyptian Expeditionary Force as it pushed the Turks back out of Palestine and into Syria, with Damascus falling on 1 October and an armistice being signed at the end of that month.

Elliott was then posted to 47 Squadron, which was one of very few to see action in the immediate aftermath of the Great War, in this case in Southern Russia, supporting Denikin's White Russians against the Bolsheviks. Flying DH9a light bombers, he saw a great deal of action. In July 1919 he and his observer were shot down whilst attacking Red cavalry, but they managed to hold them off before being rescued by a fellow aircraft. Elliott was awarded the DFC in February 1919 and a bar to the decoration in April 1920. Having received a permanent commission during his service in Russia, he returned to 14 Squadron in Egypt in May 1921.

In October 1924 Elliott was appointed to his first job at the Air Ministry, in this case in the Directorate of Operations and Intelligence. In early 1928 he became a flight commander in 207 Squadron, flying the Fairey IIIF at Bircham Newton, but a year later he found himself back in the Middle

East, this time attached to Air HQ Palestine and Transjordan, but acting as a Liaison Officer to the French Air Force in Beirut. He returned to the UK in the autumn of 1931, in time to take up a place on the 1932 Staff College course.

At the end of 1932 Elliott took command of 501 (City of Bristol) Squadron at RAF Filton. This was one of five Special Reserve Squadrons, composed of both volunteer reservists and regulars, flying initially the Westland Wapiti general purpose aircraft, followed by its successor, the Westland Wallace. In 1936 the squadron's name was changed to 501 (County of Gloucester) Squadron, by way of signifying its enlarged recruitment area, and later in the same year it was absorbed into the Auxiliary Air Force.

On 1 April 1937, newly promoted to wing commander, Elliott found himself for the first time at the centre of Great Britain's military affairs when he was appointed as an assistant secretary to the Committee of Imperial Defence ('CID'). The CID had a long history, having been established in 1904 in the aftermath of the Boer War, which all recognized had not been adequately planned for. Its members were the Prime Minister, the Secretaries of State for Foreign Affairs, Home Affairs, the Colonies and War, the Chancellor of the Exchequer, the First Lord of the Admiralty, the First Sea Lord and the Chief of the Imperial General Staff. The Secretary from 1912 was the formidable Sir Maurice (later Lord) Hankey, who became simultaneously the Cabinet Secretary. The CID was replaced during the Great War by the War Council and later the War Cabinet, but emerged again after the Armistice, and shortly afterwards the original members were joined by the Secretary of State for Air and the CAS. In April 1936 a Deputy Secretary was appointed in the shape of Colonel Hasting (later General the Lord) Ismay of the Indian Army. When Hankey retired two years later, his appointments were split, with Sir Edward Bridges becoming Cabinet Secretary and Ismay Secretary of the CID.

In the early days of the CID it became responsible for a key document, known as the War Book. This contained references to all the relevant legislation, plans, minutes, orders, letters and telegrams which would be of critical importance on the outbreak of any war, including not only military matters, but also the arrangements for civil defence, the mobilization of manpower and the movement of industry onto a war footing. Elliott's specific role, as one of several assistant secretaries – the others including Major (later General Sir) Leslie Hollis and Major (later Lieutenant General Sir) Ian Jacob, both of whom would remain in position throughout the forthcoming war – was to keep the War Book up to date.

128   Churchill's Eagles

Following the declaration of war against Germany on 3 September 1939, the Prime Minister, Neville Chamberlain, decided to combine the Cabinet and CID Secretariats into a single War Cabinet Secretariat, with Bridges as the Secretary and Ismay as the Head of the Military Wing, of which Elliott remained one of the assistant secretaries. When Churchill succeeded Chamberlain as Prime Minister, the Military Wing became the Office of the Minister of Defence, who was Churchill himself.

As the assistant secretary involved specifically with RAF matters, Elliott found himself attending one of the most momentous meetings of the war. Within a few days of the German attack on France, Belgium and the Netherlands on 10 May 1940, the RAF squadrons attached to the Advanced Air Striking Force and the Air Component of the British Expeditionary Force had been decimated, and replacements for their Hurricanes could only come from Fighter Command. The AOC-in-C, Hugh **Dowding**, faced with increasing demands for his aircraft, asked to be allowed to present his case for retaining them to the War Cabinet. Somewhat to his surprise, he was invited to a meeting on 15 June. Elliott was later to say that Dowding had not been treated very courteously, consigned as he was to a chair at the edge of the room until summoned to the table. Once he was called upon to speak, however, he put his case very forcefully and at one point placed a graph in front of the Prime Minister which showed that, if the current rate of loss was maintained, he would not have a single Hurricane left in the UK after two weeks. In what Elliott later described as the most emotionally charged meeting he had ever attended, Dowding got his way. A few further squadrons were sent to France, but then the tap was turned off, in time for the losses to be made up before the Battle of Britain.

By early 1941 Elliott was keen to get back to operations. After the end of the Battle of Britain, the Germans had substantially ceased conducting daytime raids on England in favour of night bombing. The emphasis for the defence was thus focused primarily on night fighters. Sholto **Douglas**, Dowding's successor as AOC-in-C Fighter Command, knew that Elliott had shown great interest in this and requested that he be transferred to become Station Commander at Middle Wallop. Churchill was annoyed about losing Elliott but let him go.

Middle Wallop had been an important fighter station during the Battle of Britain. As the most easterly station in 10 Group, its squadrons had been frequently engaged in providing assistance to 11 Group next door, especially during raids on the latter's stations, notably Tangmere, and on Portsmouth and Southampton. It now housed 604 Squadron, equipped with Bristol

Beaufighters carrying the Mark IV Airborne Interceptor Radar in the night fighter role. The Squadron's star pilot was Squadron Leader John 'Cat's Eyes' Cunningham who, with his navigator Jimmy Rawnsley, had scored his first victory on the night of 19/20 November 1940 and had gone on to achieve many others. One of the most memorable came on the night of 7 May 1941, during a visit to the station by King George VI. The King met Cunningham and Rawnsley on the ground before they took off on their patrol and then, accompanied by Douglas and Elliott, went to the radar hut some miles away, where the controller explained what was happening on the screen. As he stood there, the controller identified a target for Cunningham and guided his aircraft onto it. The King was then invited to go outside and observe the luckless Heinkel 111 coming down in flames!

In late 1941 Douglas had Elliott transferred to HQ Fighter Command to focus on night defences, but at the end of April 1942 he was posted to the Air Ministry as Director of Plans. Here he found himself back within the central direction of the war. The Director of Plans of each of the three armed services in the pre-war period had been largely preoccupied with his own service, but in the run-up to the war it was recognized that more co-operation between them was essential. A Deputy Director, whose focus was on joint rather than single-service planning, was appointed for each one. By the time that Elliott was appointed, however, the structure had been further refined and the Joint Planning Staff ('JPS'), comprising the three Directors of Plans and their subordinates, had become one of two offshoots of the Chiefs of Staff Committee, the other being the Joint Intelligence Sub-Committee. The JPS had three offshoots itself, the Strategical Planning Section, the Executive Planning Section and the Future Operational Planning Section, and its staff included Liaison Officers from the Ministry of War Transport, the Ministry of Economic Warfare, the Political Warfare Executive and the Ministry of Home Security. The purpose of the JPS was now to look forward at the overall strategic situation.

Elliott was the RAF's Director of Plans from four months after the entry of the United States into the war until four months before the invasion of North-West Europe. This period saw the turnaround in Allied fortunes, from a low point in 1942 when they were on the back foot in every theatre of war, to a position in which Italy had been invaded and the Mediterranean freed to Allied shipping, Leningrad and Kiev liberated and major advances made in the Pacific. Elliott, however, an air vice-marshal since 1 December 1943, was not to remain a staff officer but was to revert to an operational role, initially as AOC Gibraltar.

From the commencement of hostilities, Gibraltar had been a vital cog in the British, and later the Allied, war machine. As had been the case for 240 years, it was an essential base for the Royal Navy, which established a powerful fleet there in 1940 in the shape of Force H, commanding the entrance from the Atlantic into the Mediterranean. For the RAF it was a key staging post for long distance aircraft en route to Egypt or West Africa and, with Royal Navy co-operation, for the re-supply of fighters to Malta. 200 (Coastal) Group RAF had been formed there at the end of the first week of the war to provide some protection from submarines, and the group became AHQ Gibraltar as part of Coastal Command in December 1941. A number of squadrons rotated through Gibraltar for short periods, but the main anti-submarine effort was carried out by 202 Squadron with Consolidated Catalinas and 179 Squadron with Leigh Light equipped Vickers Wellingtons, whilst 520 Squadron, with Handley Page Halifaxes and Supermarine Spitfires, was responsible for meteorological reconnaissance.

With France fully occupied by the Germans, the majority of the air movements to the Mediterranean theatre continued to take the long route via Gibraltar. There were thus frequent VIPs arriving and leaving on their way to North Africa or Italy, and Elliott had to greet them and see them off again. One of the strangest was 'Monty's Double'. It was known that German agents operating on both sides of the Spanish border kept the airfield under scrutiny. In order to persuade their masters that an invasion of North-West Europe was still some way away, it was decided to send Clifton James, a subaltern in the Royal Army Pay Corps with a striking resemblance to General Sir Bernard Montgomery, who was known to be leading the Allied land forces in the invasion, to North Africa via Gibraltar. He arrived in Churchill's personal aircraft on 27 May 1944, just over a week before the planned invasion date, was greeted by Elliott, who was privy to the deception, attended a reception in Government House and was seen off again very publicly by Elliott. It is not thought that the ruse made any difference to the Germans' dispositions!

At the beginning of June 1944 Elliott was summoned at short notice to Italy to form and then command the Balkan Air Force. The background to the BAF lay in the varying fortunes of the Allies in 1944. The initial invasion of Italy, after some tricky moments at Salerno, had gone to plan, and by the end of 1943 Eighth Army and US Fifth Army were on the Germans' Winter Line, running from the mouth of the River Garigliano to just north of that of the Sangro. Here, however, they stalled for nearly five months as successive assaults on the stronghold of Cassino failed. At the end of May

The Air Marshals 131

1944 a breakthrough was achieved, at both Cassino and other key points, and the Allied armies in Italy surged forward on both sides of the Apennines, supported by their tactical air forces. The latter had been engaged on many occasions in supporting Marshal Tito and his Partisans in Yugoslavia, but this was now seen as a diversion from the Italian campaign.

In late May 1944 the Germans mounted a major attack on Tito's HQ at Drvar, causing significant losses, and he himself was evacuated by air to Italy and later set up a new HQ on the Allied-held island of Vis off the Dalmatian coast. Tito had for some time maintained that in order to continue Partisan operations he must have both local air superiority and a secure supply line. With the Mediterranean Allied Tactical and Coastal Air Forces now wholly focused on operations on the Italian mainland and coastal waters, it was decided by the C-in-C Mediterranean Allied Air Forces, Lieutenant General Ira Eaker, and his Deputy C-in-C, Air Marshal Sir John **Slessor**, to set up the BAF specifically to support the Partisans and to carry out other operations in the Balkans and along the Dalmatian coast.

Elliott formed his HQ near Bari on 7 June and began to prepare for the arrival of the first squadrons in July. The largest contingent came from the RAF, nine squadrons in all; one of these was transferred in September 1944, but the others remained until VE-Day. They were equipped with a variety of aircraft, mostly Spitfires, Hurricanes and North American Mustang fighter-bombers, but with one squadron operating Beaufighters and subsequently Martin Marauder light bombers. Two of the RAF's squadrons were manned by Yugoslavs and these superimposed red stars on their aircrafts' roundels. Three squadrons were provided by the South African Air Force, two of Beaufighters and one of first Lockheed Ventura and then Marauders. A further three came from the Royal Hellenic Air Force, two equipped with Spitfires and one with Martin Baltimore light bombers. All the squadrons were grouped into fighter or bomber wings as appropriate, with squadrons switching between them as required for operations.

Seven squadron-sized units were provided by the Italian Co-Belligerent Air Force, one with Spitfires, two with Baltimores, two with Bell Airacobra fighter-bombers and one each with Macchi 202 Folgore and Macchi 205 Veltro fighters; the last two suffered from a lack of spare parts, which were manufactured in the area still under German occupation, and the aircraft were in due course replaced by Spitfires and Airacobras. The Italian units formed a Fighter Liaison Section rather than a RAF Group.

In addition to these largely offensive units, the BAF also took under command 334 Wing, the core of which comprised 148 and 624 (Special

Duties) Squadrons equipped with Halifax heavy bombers modified to drop both men and supplies to the Partisans, as was the Polish-manned 1586 Flight. The BAF also controlled one flight of 267 Squadron flying Douglas Dakotas and had operational, but not administrative, control over 60th Troop Carrier Group USAAF for any Dakota flights to the Balkans and over two transport squadrons of the Italian Co-Belligerent Air Force flying modified Cant 1007s and Savoia Marchetti SM 82s.

In September 1944 334 Wing was joined at Bari by a Red Air Force Group with twelve Dakotas, plus twelve Yak-9s as fighter protection. These remained until the end of the year. BAF had notional operational control over this small force, but in practice this was seldom observed.

In addition to commanding the BAF, Elliott was appointed to co-ordinate the activities of the British Army and the Royal Navy to the extent that they were involved in operations on the Balkan shores of the Adriatic, for which tactical air support was provided by the BAF. The Flag Officer Taranto was permanently represented by a Captain RN in Elliott's HQ at Bari. HQ Land Forces Adriatic was located alongside the BAF at Bari, but had an advanced HQ on Vis, from where commando operations were mounted in the Dalmatian islands, the first of which took place early in the BAF's existence, with a raid on Spilje in Albania. The Allied Mission to Marshal Tito, under Brigadier Fitzroy Maclean, also had a representative at HQ BAF.

One of the main tasks was to provide air support for ground operations, but the BAF also took every opportunity to destroy the enemy's military assets on land and at sea. In the first four months of its existence the BAF destroyed 211 railway locomotives, 643 motor vehicles, 114 ships and 63 aircraft. The greatest success was achieved during Operation RATWEEK, which was launched on 1 September 1944. By this time it had become apparent that the Germans were beginning to withdraw from Greece and Yugoslavia, so Brigadier Maclean drew up a plan for the BAF and Partisans to act in conjunction in order to inflict as much damage on their personnel and equipment as possible, with a view to paralyzing movement. Yugoslavia was divided into sectors, each of which was controlled by a Partisan commander, alongside a British Liaison Officer who could call in raids as required. In addition to convoys and trains, static targets were identified, including bridges, viaducts, tunnels, marshalling yards, barracks and other military installations. Some of these were attacked by heavy bombers from the Mediterranean Allied Strategic Air Force as well as by the BAF. RATWEEK produced a major setback for the Germans, although the BAF did not have it all their own way, incurring the most significant casualties from anti-aircraft fire of the whole campaign. In its aftermath, Tito was able to mount an advance on Belgrade, which was liberated on 20 October.

In late September, the BAF supported landings and subsequent ground actions in Albania, whilst the Germans on Corfu surrendered on 19 October. Earlier that month British troops, supported by the BAF, had landed on the mainland of Greece and taken the major airfield at Megara, 20 miles west of Athens. The BAF remained involved during the confused fighting against the Communist ELAS organization, which had attempted to seize power in the country, and in November the RHAF squadrons moved permanently to Greece.

In the meantime, 334 Wing continued to deliver supplies to the Yugoslav Partisans, whilst some 20,000 men, women and children were evacuated from areas of conflict to safety in Italy.

On 13 February 1945, with victory clearly in sight in the Balkans, Elliott was relieved by AVM George *Mills* and returned to the UK, where he took over the post of Assistant Chief Executive at the Ministry of Aircraft Production ('MAP'). The MAP had been created in early 1940 out of the Department of the Air Member for Development and Production, who at that time was Air Chief Marshal Sir Wilfrid **Freeman**. It was a civilian ministry, but with a strong RAF presence. The first Minister was Lord Beaverbrook, who had been appointed by the then new Prime Minister, Winston Churchill, to ginger up what he saw as deplorably slow progress. Freeman became the Chief Executive but he never got on well with Beaverbrook and was in any event appointed Vice-Chief of the Air Staff six months later. When he retired from the RAF in October 1942 he rejoined the MAP, this time as Chief Executive. On his retirement in March 1945 his successor was a civilian, Ernest (later Lord) Plowden, who it was felt should have a senior RAF officer as his immediate subordinate.

Elliott had little relevant experience for his new job, but Freeman had advised that the new Assistant Chief Executive should carry the confidence of the CAS and the RAF and have operational experience as a commander or as a staff officer, a specification which he matched perfectly. In any event, the MAP was rolled into a new Ministry of Supply in early 1946, following which Elliott joined the Air Ministry as Assistant Chief of the Air Staff (Policy). This was a job to which he was well suited, looking forward as it did to the future. His predecessor was AVM William **Dickson**, whom he had known well as his opposite number as AOC Desert Air Force for the first six months of his service in Italy.

134   Churchill's Eagles

Elliott was ACAS (Policy) for less than eighteen months before being appointed AOC-in-C Fighter Command in November 1947. This was already a very different command to the one which had fought in the war: 9, 10 and 13 Groups had disappeared into history, whilst 11 and 12 Groups, covering the South and North respectively, were severely truncated. Seven months before the Russians cut off Berlin from Western Germany, the threat of enemy activity appeared to be very slight and economy was the watchword. The piston-engined aircraft of the war years had gone, other than the Spitfires which equipped the part-time RAuxAF squadrons, six squadrons of Mosquitoes and four of long-range twin engined De Havilland Hornets, and were replaced by jet-powered Gloster Meteors and De Havilland Vampires. For the time being, at least, these were sufficient to counter any threat by the current generation of bombers.

In April 1949 Elliott was appointed Chief Staff Officer to the Minister of Defence, A. V. Alexander (later Viscount Alexander of Hillsborough), who had served in Churchill's wartime government as First Lord of the Admiralty, followed in 1950 by Emmanuel (later Lord) Shinwell. Elliott's term of appointment coincided with the beginning of the Korean War, although it was decided at an early date that, apart from three squadrons of Sunderland flying boats and the secondment of pilots to fly for the RAAF, the RAF would play no part in the conflict.

By then an air chief marshal, Elliott's last appointment, from 1951 to his retirement in April 1954, was as Head of the British Joint Services Mission in Washington DC and simultaneously the UK Representative on the NATO Standing Group, vitally important roles maintaining essential contacts with the United Kingdom's allies.

Elliott had proved to be outstanding in both command and staff roles. Much admired by both Churchill himself and by Ismay as the Prime Minister's chief of staff, he could probably, like both Hollis and Jacob, have remained at the centre of Great Britain's military affairs in Whitehall for the duration of the war. He was, however, reluctant to be divorced from operations and succeeded in having himself posted to appointments where he could engage more directly with the enemy. He was the ideal commander for the BAF, whose short history was action-packed!

Air Vice-Marshal (later Air Chief Marshal Sir) Basil Embry GCB, KBE, DSO***, DFC, AFC (1903–1977)

The Distinguished Service Order was founded by Queen Victoria on 6 December 1886. Intended to reward officers in the armed services of the British Empire for meritorious service in wartime, it became not only a recognition of such service, but also effectively the next highest award for gallantry after the Victoria Cross and the George Cross. Unlike other orders, but in the same way as military decorations such as the Military Cross and the Distinguished Flying Cross, it is open to multiple awards, known as bars, to the same person. First bars have been relatively common, but second bars are much rarer, whilst only sixteen third bars have been awarded since the establishment of the order. Only two of these have been won by RAF officers. One was to Wing Commander (later Group Captain) J. B. 'Willie' Tait, who carried out no fewer than 101 bombing sorties during the Second World War, latterly as Leonard Cheshire's successor in command of 617 Squadron, in which role he led the raid which sank the battleship *Tirpitz* in a Norwegian fjord in 1944. The other was to Basil **Embry**, in recognition of his sustained gallantry and exemplary leadership over a long period.

Embry, who had been too young to serve in the Great War, was determined from a young age to learn to fly. He was granted a short service commission by the RAF in 1921, accepted for flying training and, once qualified, was in theory posted to 4 Squadron in the spring of the following year, although in practice he spent the next three months on a course at the Armament and Gunnery School. Having requested and been given a posting overseas, he embarked on a troopship heading for the Middle East, but he and his fellow passengers found themselves diverted to Turkey, where the 'Chanak Crisis' had broken out as the Turks pushed occupying Greek forces out of their country. Embry was employed temporarily as a newspaper censor!

Following the arrival of British reinforcements in Turkey, Embry resumed the journey to his destination, which was RAF Hinaidi, the home of 45 Squadron near Baghdad in Iraq. Not long after his arrival a new squadron commander was appointed in the person of Arthur **Harris**, who impressed him very favourably, as did the squadron's two flight commanders, Ralph **Cochrane** and Robert *Saundby*, both of whom were to serve under Harris in Bomber Command in the war, the former as a group commander, the latter as Harris's deputy.

The primary role of 45 Squadron, flying lumbering twin-engined Vickers Vernon transport aircraft, was to operate the air mail service between

136   Churchill's Eagles

Baghdad and Cairo, carrying passengers and cargo as necessary. However, it was also employed in supporting the operations of British and Indian troops against tribes in the north of the country in rebellion against the Iraqi regime, by flying up supplies and evacuating casualties. Harris, moreover, obtained permission from the AOC, Air Marshal Sir John Salmond, who was in overall command of all British forces in the country, to turn his aircraft into bombers by cutting a hole in the nose of the Vernon and rigging up a bomb sight and a release mechanism for bombs carried under the wings. This proved to be highly effective against the rebellious tribesmen, both the weight and accuracy of the bombing demonstrating a significant improvement over the performance of the DH9a light bombers designed for the purpose. Embry took part in many bombing raids, interspersed between carrying the mail, cargoes and passengers on 45 Squadron's more mundane operations. In order to gain additional experience, after just over three years he was transferred to 30 Squadron flying the DH9a. For his work he was awarded the Air Force Cross in the New Year's Honours of 1926.

On his return to the UK in 1927 Embry was sent on the Instructors' Course at the Central Flying School, before being appointed a flight commander at 1 Flying Training School at RAF Netheravon. In May 1929, now recognized as a pilot of exceptional ability, he was posted back to the CFS, once again as a flight commander. His last appointment in a training role was as a staff officer at 23 Group, which controlled all the training units.

Embry attended the 1933 course at the Staff College before once again applying for an overseas posting. Early in the following year he and his wife sailed for India, where he was appointed to the staff of 1 (Indian) Wing, based at Kohat near Peshawar in the North-West Frontier Province. The wing was commanded by an old friend, Alan *Lees*, who had succeeded Cochrane as a flight commander in 45 Squadron at Hinaidi. The RAF was engaged at this time in supporting the Army in the Mohmand campaign of 1935, and Embry, although technically a staff officer, took every opportunity of flying on operations.

In March 1936 Embry moved to HQ RAF India, which was based in New Delhi, except during the summer months when it moved with the Government of India to Simla. His duties initially involved operational policy and intelligence, but he became concerned subsequently with reorganization, as the RAF began preparations for switching from bi-planes to monoplanes. In November 1937 he returned to Peshawar as the commander of 20 Squadron, flying Hawker Audaxes on operations in support of ground troops in Waziristan, in which region the squadron maintained

The Air Marshals   137

a flight based at a forward airfield at Miranshah. Although the RAF had been badly misused in India in the 1920s and early 1930s, by this time the junior service's army co-operation capabilities were well understood and much better employed. At the conclusion of his tour in late 1938, Embry was awarded the DSO.

After spending six months in the Deputy Directorate of Overseas Operations at the Air Ministry, Embry applied for an operational posting and was initially appointed commander of 21 Squadron at RAF Watton, where it formed part of 2 Group Bomber Command. Before taking up his new post, however, he was summoned to the Group HQ at Huntingdon, to be told that he was instead to take command of 107 Squadron at RAF Wattisham. Having attended a very short conversion course onto the Bristol Blenheim, he took over the squadron ten days after the declaration of war on Germany. On 25 September he carried out his first reconnaissance operation over the Ruhr Valley, during which he was attacked by German fighters, whose fire hit the Blenheim in a number of places, although he managed to bring it safely home. It was a foretaste of the future!

During the 'Phoney War', the only operations permitted were similar reconnaissance sorties, usually by single aircraft, and offensive sweeps against German ships by up to six aircraft. There was a single success for the squadron when one of its Blenheim sank a U-boat, and it suffered no losses. On 8 April 1940 the squadron was ordered to attack a small fleet of ships moving north from Wilhelmshaven. These were located and bombed, albeit without success. They turned out to be the force for the German landings at Trondheim and Narvik, escorted by the battle cruisers *Scharnhorst* and *Gneisenau* and the cruiser *Hipper*. Shortly afterwards, 107 Squadron was transferred from Wattisham to Lossiemouth, to support British and Norwegian forces in Norway. Attacks were mounted on enemy positions at Stavanger, but the squadron was sent back to Wattisham on 3 May.

Exactly a week later, the Germans invaded France, Belgium and the Netherlands and 2 Group was drawn in immediately, mounting multiple attacks on German columns and strategic targets such as bridges. Significant losses were incurred, both from German fighters and from flak. After a few days, Hurricane escorts were provided, which kept off the fighters but not the AA guns, and the squadron had to be taken out of operations for three days to repair and re-equip. On 26 May Embry was informed that he was to take over as station commander at West Raynham, but he agreed with his successor that he would lead one more operation on the following day before handing over. Attacking an enemy column near St Omer, his aircraft was

138   Churchill's Eagles

hit a number of times and Embry lost control. He and the navigator both managed to escape from the aircraft and deploy their parachutes, but the air gunner was too badly wounded to do so.

Embry was captured before very long and incarcerated in a temporary prisoner-of-war cage in a football stadium. Two days later, whilst marching in a column of prisoners towards Germany, he spotted a signpost to Embry, a village three kilometres off their route. Taking this as a good omen, he took the first opportunity to dive down a bank, where he remained hidden until the column was out of sight. He was then lucky enough to knock on a door which was opened by a friendly farmer, who hid him and then provided him with clothes to replace his uniform, and food for his onward journey. Despite being captured once again, he managed to break away and make for the Normandy coast, where he hoped to find British troops. By this time, however, they had all been evacuated or captured and there were no boats, so he headed instead for Paris. From there, helped by both the US Consulate and the Salvation Army, he set out for Bordeaux, hoping that it was still in Allied hands. The capitulation of the French on 23 June put paid to this idea as well and he made his way to Marseille, where he hoped to be able to find a ship. His attempt failed, so in company with a British Army NCO he walked along the coast and crossed the frontier into Spain, travelling thence to Gibraltar via Madrid and eventually arriving back at Plymouth on 2 August.

If anything demonstrated Embry's determination and ingenuity, it was his escape from France. He was welcomed back warmly, interviewed by the Chief of the Air Staff, Air Chief Marshal Sir Cyril **Newall** and invited to Buckingham Palace for a private audience with the King. He had been hoping for a posting to Fighter Command and was very disappointed to be sent instead as Senior Officer Administration to 6 (Training) Group within Bomber Command. The new CAS, Charles **Portal**, came to his rescue with a posting to command a night fighter wing in Fighter Command, based at a former flying club which had been a satellite airfield for RAF Hornchurch and now became RAF Southend. There was only one squadron there, 264, which was equipped with the Boulton Paul Defiant. This aircraft, with its armament in a turret behind the pilot, had been a thoroughly unsatisfactory day fighter and was only slightly better in the night-time role. A Hurricane squadron was also intended to be based there, but this did not happen. In any event, on 19 December 1940, just over a month later, Embry was posted as a sector commander, based at RAF Wittering, near Peterborough. He had between two and four squadrons based there and at two satellite airfields at

The Air Marshals   139

Collyweston and King's Cliffe, one of which, No. 25, operated the Bristol Beaufighter night fighter equipped with Airborne Interception radar.

Embry flew regularly with 25 Squadron and became over time an expert in night fighting. His navigator was Peter Clapham, who had been declared medically unfit for aircrew duties but volunteered for them nevertheless; he was to serve alongside Embry for the rest of the war. The Beaufighter was a heavy aircraft and the airfield at Wittering proved all too often to be of inadequate length for one whose brakes were defective. Embry decided that he would link up with the runway at nearby Collyweston, and, after negotiation with the landlord and tenant farmers and by providing the workforce himself, created one of the longest strips in the country, frequently used thereafter by damaged returning bombers.

Ten months after arriving at Wittering, Embry was ordered to accompany the VCAS, ACM Sir Wilfrid **Freeman**, to the Middle East at the request of the AOC-in-C Middle East, Arthur **Tedder**, in order to bring the Desert Air Force up to date on the latest tactics developed in the UK. He suggested that he would be more effective if he held a proper staff role, rather than an advisory one. This was agreed and he was appointed Senior Air Staff Officer to the DAF's AOC, AVM Arthur **Coningham**. The DAF at this time was structured into four fighter wings, equipped with Hurricanes and Curtis P-40 Tomahawks, and two light bomber wings with Blenheims and Martin Marylands, together with a number of independent squadrons, for transport, maritime reconnaissance and other duties. There were no formal wing leaders, however, unlike in Fighter Command, and Embry recommended that these be appointed from amongst the squadron commanders, a suggestion to which Coningham readily agreed. He also advised using a number of tactics which had been adopted in the UK and building up reserves of spares, notably propellers for the Tomahawks, which were in short supply.

Embry's tour of duty coincided with Operation CRUSADER, the offensive mounted by Eighth Army under Lieutenant General Sir Alan Cunningham to relieve Tobruk and push the Axis forces out of Cyrenaica. This appeared to start well, with the largely armoured XXX Corps pushing towards the main Axis airfield at Sidi Rezegh. General Erwin Rommel, the Axis commander, then threw in his own armoured forces, which created mayhem on the Allied side, to the extent that Cunningham proposed to withdraw to the Egyptian frontier. As a result, he was replaced by Lieutenant General Neil Ritchie, with the GOC-in-C, General Sir Claude Auchinleck, himself moving up to the front and taking all the critical decisions. Rommel

140   Churchill's Eagles

then attacked British and New Zealand divisions on the Egyptian frontier but was repelled and forced to retreat to Benghazi and then out of Cyrenaica. Tobruk was duly relieved.

The RAF had achieved local air superiority before the battle began and was highly effective in attacking the Axis airfields and supply route, but less so in direct support of Allied formations as the situation on the ground was so confused. The German Junkers 87 Stuka bombers, however, were destroyed in large numbers and withdrawn from the battle. The Axis advance to the frontier had caused all the RAF's forward airfields to be evacuated, but this took place without serious loss. Now they were able to reoccupy them and establish more in Cyrenaica.

Embry admired Coningham, but the two did not always think alike and the former did not really enjoy being the latter's chief of staff. Particularly as his role was originally intended to be only a temporary one, once the battle was over he requested that he should return to the UK, where his appointment as a sector commander at Wittering had been kept open for him. Tedder asked him to stop off in Malta to advise the AOC, Hugh **Lloyd**, on fighter tactics. He spent time visiting all the squadrons there and came up with a number of recommendations for their employment, for the installation of ground control radar and for the running of the operations room. He also confirmed that the Malta airfields would be perfectly suitable for Spitfires, which would have the performance necessary to combat recent marks of the Messerschmitt 109. The first batch arrived in Malta less than two months later.

Embry returned to his appointment at Wittering at the end of January 1942 and was there until mid-November, when he was transferred to HQ Fighter Command in charge of night fighter operations. Early in 1943 he was appointed SASO to AVM William **Dickson** at 10 Group. The group was responsible for the air defence of South-West England and Wales, and by this time was primarily concerned with 'tip-and-run' raids. These were largely carried out by Focke-Wulf FW 190 fighter bombers against British cathedral cities, following up on the 'Baedeker Raids' which had taken place in the first half of the previous year. They were dealt with by standing patrols out to sea by Hawker Typhoons, the only aircraft at the time with the speed to deal with the 190s.

On his arrival back from the Mediterranean early in 1943 Embry had asked to be considered for a transfer to Bomber Command, and, indeed, it was as AOC 2 Group, in which he had served as CO of 107 Squadron in 1939/40, that he found himself appointed on 1 June 1943. In mid-1942 he had apparently been considered for the command of the new Pathfinder Force and was the preferred candidate of the Directorate of Operations at the Air Ministry, but it was said that Arthur Harris, now AOC-in-C of Bomber Command, had thought him to be too like himself in temperament; in any event, Harris instead chose Donald **Bennett** for the job. This was just as well, since in his new role Embry was to prove the perfect fit. It was, however, not to Bomber Command that he was to report, but to an entirely new formation, the Second Tactical Air Force ('2TAF').

2TAF, initially commanded by Air Marshal John *D'Albiac*, Embry's predecessor at 2 Group, was formed out of Army Co-operation Command specifically to provide air support for the Allied ground forces, other than those of the USA, during and following the invasion of North-West Europe. It was to consist of 83 and 84 Groups, whose fighter-bombers would provide close support to the troops and 2 Group, which was to carry out tactical bombing operations. 2 Group had been for some time something of an oddity in Bomber Command,which, under Harris in particular, was heavily focused on the strategic bombing of Germany. It was already very different from the formation in which Embry had served in 107 Squadron in 1939 and 1940. The Blenheims which had equipped the whole group at that time had been phased out and, by early 1944, the group was to consist of twelve squadrons flying three different types of aircraft. The North American B-25 Mitchell, of which there were to be four squadrons, was a highly capable medium bomber with a crew of five; the Douglas A-20 Boston, which was to equip two squadrons, was a robust three-man light bomber; the most versatile of the aircraft was the two-man De Havilland Mosquito Mark VI fighter-bomber, with six squadrons in the group, whilst two more were to join by the end of the war. 2 Group was a multi-national force, with one squadron each manned by French, Dutch, Polish, Australian, New Zealand and Canadian aircrews.

It was also proposed that 2 Group should take on the US-manufactured Vultee Vengeance dive bomber. Embry took one up to test it, found it sluggish and very poorly armed for its defence and went immediately to see AM Sir Trafford **Leigh-Mallory**, the designated C-in-C of the Allied Expeditionary Air Force, who agreed that it should not be used and promised to substitute Mosquitoes in its place.

With Harris so focused on strategic bombing, 2 Group had not been particularly well employed whilst in Bomber Command, its most notable exploit having been the successful attack on the Philips factory in Eindhoven on 6 December 1942. The most common forms of operation were the

142   Churchill's Eagles

'Circus', which involved both fighters and light bomber engaged in general sweeps across France and the Low Countries, and the 'Ramrod', which was more tightly focused on individual objectives such as power stations and railway centres. Under Embry both 'Circuses' and 'Ramrods' continued, but they were much better focused than they had been in the past. Moreover, in October 1943, the Air Ministry became aware of the construction of launch sites for V-1 flying bombs in Northern France and these became the focus of attention, not only for 2TAF, but also for the US Eighth and Ninth Air Forces.

Embry immediately set an example by flying on operations himself, something which had been completely forbidden to group commanders in Bomber Command but which was sanctioned in 2TAF. He also insisted that all his station commanders should take part in operations, albeit not with the frequency required of their subordinates. In order to conceal his true identity in the event that he was brought down and captured by the Germans, he flew as 'Wing Commander Smith', with the appropriate rank badge and with his identity disc and clothes all carrying the same name.

In January 1944 D'Albiac was relieved as AOC-in-C of 2TAF by Coningham and, whilst Embry had not enjoyed working as his SASO, he was perfectly happy with him as his operational superior. Shortly afterwards, he was asked by Coningham if the Mosquitoes were capable of carrying out a pin-point low-level attack on Amiens Prison, where hundreds of French Resistance members were awaiting trial and almost certain death. The plan was to breach the walls with such force that not only would this create an escape route for the prisoners, but many of the cell doors would be forced open. Embry was deeply concerned that many of the Frenchmen would be killed in such an attack, but their compatriots in the UK assured him that such a sacrifice would be worthwhile if a good number were able to escape. Operation JERICHO, which was mounted on 18 February, was carried out with such accuracy that 258 prisoners escaped, although many were subsequently recaptured, whilst 102 were killed and 74 were wounded. This was hailed as a great success by the Resistance.

Some weeks later another pin-point attack was mounted, this time on a building in the Hague which held the identities of many members of the Dutch Resistance. Once again the operation was a success, with most of the records destroyed. This and JERICHO, as well as future similar operations, were aided immensely by the creation of a special unit within 2 Group which produced models of the target and surrounding buildings derived from low-level photo reconnaissance and were of the greatest value in the pre-raid briefings.

In May 1944 attacks on V-1 sites ceased in favour of raids on coastal batteries and bridges, not only in Normandy, but also, for deception purposes, in the Pas-de-Calais. On D-Day itself the Group was fully committed, with the Bostons laying a smokescreen over the landing craft, whilst the Mitchells bombed coastal batteries and the Mosquitoes focused on disrupting enemy movement by road and rail. In early August, Embry was on just such an operation when his aircraft was hit by flak. He managed to dive out of further trouble and make his way back across the Channel, but the aircraft's undercarriage collapsed on landing.

Such operations continued throughout the rest of the campaign in France, the Low Countries and Germany. As territory was occupied by the ground forces, the wings comprising the group were moved over to airfields on the continent, until only a support unit remained in the UK. In addition to the attacks on ground forces, communications and infrastructure, there were a number of occasions on which specific buildings were successfully targeted, including the Gestapo HQs in Aarhus, Copenhagen and Odense. The only major surprise came on 1 January 1945, when the Luftwaffe mounted attacks on numerous Allied airfields, including those of 2 Group; but whereas the Allied aircraft and pilots were quickly replaced, the Germans, who had suffered greatly themselves, had few reserves of men or machines.

By VE-Day Embry had enjoyed a highly distinguished war. To the DSO he had been awarded for his service in India were added two bars in 1940, one for his command of 107 Squadron, the other following his successful escape from the Germans. In June 1945 he was awarded a DFC for his participation in operations whilst leading 2 Group, whilst a third bar to the DSO was conferred on him a month later.

In a complete change of role, in October 1945 Embry was appointed Director-General of Training at the Air Ministry, where he had only served once before, and then briefly, in 1939. Since he had several months to wait before taking up the role, he took the opportunity, accompanied by Peter Clapham, to fly to all the overseas commands, except those in Hong Kong and Khartoum, in order to gain a picture of their training requirements. In 1946 the Air Staff in the Air Ministry was reorganized and he became the ACAS (Training). In this role he oversaw the re-opening of the RAF College at Cranwell, for the initial training of all permanent officers in the General Duties Branch of the RAF, and the founding of the RAF Flying College at Manby, in collaboration with Ralph Cochrane, now AOC-in-C Flying

144 Churchill's Eagles

Training Command. The latter institution was conceived as the practical flying equivalent of the RAF Staff College, focusing on developments in technology in an age in which jet propulsion was rapidly replacing piston engines, advanced navigational aids were being developed to follow those conceived during the war and new weapons were being introduced.

In April 1949 Embry was appointed AOC-in-C Fighter Command, which was much reduced from its heyday in 1945. The great majority of the regular squadrons were equipped with the RAF's first jet fighter, the Gloster Meteor, which had entered squadron service in the summer of 1944 and had proved its worth by bringing down large numbers of V-1 flying bombs. Night fighter variants were to follow during Embry's term of appointment. By the time that he arrived, the last Mosquitoes were shortly to be phased out of regular squadrons, whilst Spitfires were already only operated by RAuxAF squadrons, and even these were to be replaced by Meteors and the RAF's second jet fighter, the De Havilland Vampire, before very long. Two Groups remained, 11 and 12, the former now based in the South of England and Wales, the latter covering East Anglia, the North-East of England and the whole of Scotland.

Even before Embry arrived at Fighter Command, the security situation had deteriorated significantly. The UK was only modestly involved in the Korean War, but the decision by the Soviet Union in June 1948 to cut off land and water access to Berlin showed that the Cold War had begun and this halted any further moves to truncate the command, whilst it also provoked greater urgency in establishing early warning radar, although this came under the control of 90 Group in Signals Command. Embry put together a committee, whose recommendations in due course produced a more integrated capability within the whole apparatus of air defence.

In July 1952 the CAS, MRAF Sir John **Slessor**, asked Embry if he would accept a posting to NATO when his term at Fighter Command ended, either as the Air Deputy to the Supreme Allied Commander Europe or as the C-in-C Allied Air Forces Central Europe. For a number of reasons, Slessor advised accepting the latter role, which Embry agreed to do. By the time that his appointment was announced, however, the structure of NATO had changed and Embry found that he would now be subordinate to an overall C-in-C who would be Marshal Juin of France. He hesitated about accepting the position, as it no longer stood at the head of a clear chain of command, but nevertheless agreed to do so. As it happened, he and Juin got on very well.

From his HQ at Fontainebleau Embry began to get a grip on his widely disparate forces. He was deeply concerned that many of his subordinates, with the exception of the Americans, had not moved beyond 1945 and were not particularly well qualified to handle the threat of nuclear warfare. He took the initiative in setting up a Commanders' Council with his opposite numbers at NATO land and naval forces, but found the whole process of decision-making deeply frustrating. Although he enjoyed excellent relationships with both his immediate superior and his many colleagues, he found it impossible to push through the reforms which were necessary. On the conclusion of his posting he was retired from the RAF at the early age of fifty-one.

One organization with which Embry was very closely associated was the RAF Escaping Society, whose chairmanship he took on at the request of Portal not long after the end of the war. The Society's main objectives were to provide financial support to the widows and orphans of those who had died as a result of helping an escaping airman and to encourage reciprocal visits, contributing to the costs of those coming from the Continent. A large number of children were invited on free holidays in the UK and some were supported in their education, whilst medical expenses were also covered in some cases. Embry himself was delighted to visit the French couple who had first taken him in, hidden him and then helped him on his way.

Shortly after his retirement Embry emigrated, initially to New Zealand and then to Western Australia, where he became a sheep farmer.

An energetic, pugnacious and no-nonsense officer, Basil Embry was in his element in the RAF, particularly in wartime, and this was recognized by his superiors, who for the most part gave him appointments to which he was well suited. He was particularly happy in command of 2 Group for the last two years of the war, welding it into an outstandingly effective precision bombing formation, able to bring off the most remarkable feats. Trusted and admired by his aircrews, his leadership by example was exceeded by no other senior officer in the service.

Air Marshal (later Air Chief Marshal Sir) Sir Douglas Evill GBE, KCB, DSC, AFC (1892–1971)

The first Deputy Chief of the Air Staff was appointed in 1920, only two years after the formation of the RAF. For the next twenty years the DCAS was responsible directly to the Chief of the Air Staff for Operations, Intelligence, Operational Requirements and Training and sat on the Air Council alongside the Air Members for Personnel and for Supply and Organisation. In late 1940, however, with significant pressures placed on the

146   Churchill's Eagles

shoulders of the CAS following the capitulation of France to the Germans and the Battle of Britain, it was decided to create a new appointment, that of the Vice-Chief of the Air Staff. The VCAS was now to be responsible on the Air Council for all the air staff departments, with the DCAS reporting to him on these, but he would also be the CAS's chief confidant, would act for him when he was abroad and would, with his opposite numbers in the Royal Navy and British Army, form a committee to handle the growing number of inter-service issues. The post of VCAS from March 1943 to June 1946 was held by Air Marshal (later Air Chief Marshal) Sir Douglas **Evill**.

Evill, always known in the RAF as 'Strath' after his third name, Strathearn, was born in New South Wales, as was his first cousin, later Air Chief Marshal Sir Arthur **Longmore**, who encouraged him to learn to fly. Like Longmore, Evill opted to join the Royal Navy, passing out of the Britannia Naval College in Dartmouth in 1910 and joining his first ship, the new Dreadnought HMS *St Vincent*, shortly afterwards. He served on a number of other ships before attending a flying course at the Central Flying School in 1914. In February 1915 he was posted to 1 Squadron RNAS at St Pol near Dunkirk. Flying a variety of aircraft, he was frequently in action and, less than six months later, became a flight commander of the now renamed 1 Wing RNAS. He was awarded the Distinguished Service Cross in June 1916, the citation noting in particular his special ability in carrying out experiments in signalling and spotting. By the end of the year he had become the Officer Commanding 2 Squadron RNAS, flying Sopwith 1½ Strutters.

In the summer of 1917 Evill had a break from operations when he became station commander at Calshot and commander of the Seaplane Training School, going on to be appointed officer commanding all flying boat units and bases shortly after the end of the Great War. He received a permanent commission as a major, later squadron leader, in the newly formed RAF in August 1919 and, at much the same time, was decorated with the Air Force Cross. With his background it was unsurprising that he was appointed Chief Instructor of the School of Naval Co-operation and Aerial Navigation in early 1920.

In January 1921, Evill attended the third post-war course at the Army Staff College at Camberley, which had been closed for the duration of the Great War. The course lasted for a single year – it was extended to two years shortly afterwards – and, having passed out, he was appointed to the technical staff at HQ Coastal Area, carrying out work on the employment of aircraft carriers.

The Air Marshals 147

In October 1923, following a short refresher flying course at 4 Flying Training School at Abu Sueir in Egypt, he was posted to Iraq to command 70 Squadron, flying Vickers Vernon transport aircraft out of Hinaidi, near Baghdad. The aircraft were originally intended to fly the mail route between Cairo and Baghdad, carrying passengers and freight as well, and to support British and Indian ground forces fighting rebel tribesmen in the north of the country by carrying supplies and evacuating the wounded. However, Evill's opposite number at 45 Squadron, Arthur **Harris**, persuaded the AOC, Air Marshal Sir John Salmond, to convert his Vernons into bombers by cutting a hole in the nose and rigging up a bomb sight and a release mechanism for dropping under-wing bombs. 70 Squadron followed suit and saw action alongside its fellow unit, in which Harris was succeeded in October 1924 by Roderic **Hill**.

Evill returned to the UK in early 1925, in plenty of time to take up his new appointment as a member of the Directing Staff at the RAF Staff College in Andover. The college had been set up only three years earlier as one of the most important elements of Lord Trenchard's plan to establish the RAF as a third service which was both fully independent of and equal to the British Army and Royal Navy. The first Commandant, Robert Brooke-Popham, was still there, and on the Directing Staff were three men who would, many years later, all sit alongside Evill on the Air Council, Christopher *Courtney*, Bertine *Sutton* and, albeit very briefly, Guy **Garrod**. Many of the students were also to rise to high rank, including Ralph **Cochrane**, Hugh **Lloyd**, Trafford **Leigh-Mallory** and Charles *Medhurst*. Unlike the Army Staff College, which by this time had extended its course to two years, that of the RAF remained at one year and was focused heavily on staff work, unlike the wider curriculum at its sister institution.

After nearly four years at Andover, Evill was posted in January 1929 to another job which was focused on training, Assistant Commandant at the RAF College at Cranwell. This was another of Trenchard's creations and as vital to the service as the Staff College; indeed, such was its importance that it was ranked at this time as an independent command, with the Commandant as its AOC. It may or may not have been a coincidence that the Commandant for the majority of Evill's posting was his first cousin, Arthur Longmore! Ostensibly, the primary purpose of the college was to teach the cadets to fly, but in practice it went a long way beyond this, giving them a thorough overview of the RAF and a basic knowledge of navigation, air gunnery and engineering, whilst also encouraging participation in sport to

148   Churchill's Eagles

build teamwork and leadership. It was the primary source of officers joining the General Duties Branch of the RAF as fully qualified pilots.

Evill's term of appointment at Cranwell, during which he was promoted to group captain, was interrupted in April 1932 by his falling ill so severely that he was unable to carry out his duties. He became a 'Supernumerary' and was placed for a short period on the half-pay list. He recovered in time to join the Imperial Defence College course of 1933, which was at least not physically stretching, although it was intellectually demanding. Attendance at the College was regarded as something of an accolade by all three services, which each year nominated a small number of those whom they considered to be destined for higher rank. The students considered the military and political issues of the day alongside representatives of the other services and the Civil Service. Guy Garrod was a fellow student and Sholto **Douglas** was the RAF member of the Directing Staff.

Almost inevitably after the IDC course, Evill found himself posted to the Air Ministry for the first time in his career. His initial appointment was as Deputy Director of War Organisation, with a subsequent elevation to Director. The department was a new and relatively short-lived one, set up in the context of an increasingly worrying set of developments in Europe, notably Germany's withdrawal from both the Disarmament Conference and the League of Nations in October 1933. Germany was clearly now re-arming, so the notorious Ten Year Rule, the assumption that no major war would take place within ten years, came to an end and the first of many expansion plans was drawn up in July 1934. Other innovations were the appointment of an Air Member for Research and Development and a Director of Air Staff Duties. At the command level Air Defence of Great Britain ('ADGB') was abolished and replaced by Bomber, Fighter, Coastal and Training Commands in 1936.

It was to Bomber Command that Evill was posted in September 1936 as Senior Air Staff Officer to the newly arrived AOC-in-C, Sir John Steel. Like Evill, Steel had originally joined the Royal Navy. He had previously commanded both the Wessex Bombing Area and ADGB itself, so was completely familiar with the current generation of bombers, which had not moved on very far from the Vernons which Evill remembered from more than a decade earlier. The heavy bi-plane Handley Page Heyford had only entered service three years before and was not retired from the command until just before the war, whilst the Vickers Virginia, a relative of the Vernon, also equipped a number of squadrons, as did monoplanes with fixed undercarriages such as the Handley Page Harrow and Fairey Hendon. However, three new medium bombers with retracting undercarriages, the

Handley Page Hampden, the Armstrong Whitworth Whitley and the Vickers Wellington were on order, all of which would reach squadrons before Evill left the command, as would the new light bombers, the Bristol Blenheim and Fairey Battle, which replaced the reliable, but now seriously inadequate, Hawker Hart.

In the meantime, the various expansion plans agreed to by the government meant that large numbers of airfields were being constructed, most of those for Bomber Command being sited in Eastern England from Suffolk to Yorkshire, in the knowledge that Germany would be the most likely enemy in the future. There was thus a great deal of work for Evill, which increased in intensity when the relatively easy-going Steel was succeeded as AOC-in-C in September 1937 by Air Chief Marshal Sir Edgar **Ludlow-Hewitt**. The latter was a non-drinking, non-smoking Christian Scientist with an eye for detail and a passion for efficiency, who made it his business to know exactly what was going on in his command. Six months after Ludlow-Hewitt's arrival, Evill switched jobs within Bomber Command to become Air Officer Administration, which brought with it promotion from air commodore to air vice-marshal. The job was different but the purpose identical, to have the command made as ready for war as possible.

Evill was one of a small number of senior officers who accompanied Christopher Courtney, AOC-in-C Reserve Command, on a visit to the Luftwaffe in Germany. The realization that the country was far ahead of the UK in both the size and the capability of its air force was to provide a major spur to Evill's efforts to modernize Bomber Command. It may have been because of his knowledge of the enemy that, soon after war was declared on Germany, he was appointed a permanent member of the Anglo-French Supreme War Council. 'Staff Conversations' had been taking place between the two countries for some time and some measure of agreement had been reached, but in wartime the Council turned out to be a highly frustrating body. The French made it clear, inter alia, that they were unwilling to provoke the Germans into bombing Britain and France by themselves attacking industrial targets in Germany or dropping mines into the Rhine to destroy barges; at the same time they insisted that Bomber Command was to take the leading role in attacking enemy ground forces.

In January 1940 a new organization, British Air Forces in France, was set up, with Air Marshal Arthur **Barratt** as AOC-in-C and Evill as his SASO. It took under command both the Air Component of the British Expeditionary Force, whose Hurricanes, Blenheims, Gloster Gladiators and Westland Lysanders were to be employed in direct support of the ground troops, and

150   Churchill's Eagles

the Advanced Air Striking Force ('AASF'), whose Blenheims and Battles were originally intended to make pre-emptive strikes on the Germans. However, following discussions with General Maurice Gamelin, the French C-in-C, and General Joseph Vuillemin, the Chief of Staff of the French Air Force, it was clear that the French would not support such raids.

When the Germans launched their invasion of France, Belgium and the Netherlands on 9 May 1940, both the Air Component and the AASF were fully committed at once and suffered very heavy losses from the outset, as did the squadrons sent over by a highly reluctant Fighter Command and the Blenheims of 2 Group Bomber Command, which flew from stations in East Anglia. All efforts to stop the German advance proved to be fruitless and, thanks in large part to the arguments of Hugh **Dowding**, AOC-in-C of Fighter Command, all remaining British aircraft, other than those south of the Somme, were withdrawn by 20 May. With the failure to halt the Germans on the Somme, the remaining aircraft were also withdrawn and BAFF ceased to exist.

It was clear by this time that Evill was a staff officer of considerable ability and he did not have long to wait for his next appointment, which was as SASO to Dowding at Fighter Command. He and Dowding, whom he knew from his time at the Air Ministry in the mid-1930s but had never served under, got on together exceptionally well. Working in nearly adjacent offices, they saw each other every day and found that they shared standards of professional and personal behaviour. During the Battle of Britain, Evill was able to take much of the pressure off his superior, ensuring the smooth running of the HQ at Bentley Priory and allowing Dowding to focus on what really mattered, the destruction of the enemy.

When the 'Big Wing' controversy erupted between the AOCs of 11 and 12 Group, Leigh-Mallory and Keith **Park**, Evill took a more nuanced view than either of them or, for that matter, than Dowding, who leant towards Park on the subject. He was to say subsequently that he thought there were times when the participation of a 'Big Wing' might well have been appropriate to the circumstances of the individual battle.

Evill stayed on at Fighter Command after Dowding had been relieved by Sholto Douglas, whom he knew well from the IDC. During a period in which the attention of Fighter Command moved first to night fighters during the Blitz on London and other cities and then, in the spring and summer of 1941, to sweeps across Northern France, he continued to apply the same firm control over the running of the 'back office', allowing Douglas to concentrate on operations. He was especially admired for the way in which

The Air Marshals   151

he handled the news of the death of his son, a bomber pilot who was killed in a raid over Germany.

On 22 February 1942, just over two months after the declaration of war on Japan and Germany by the United States, Evill succeeded Harris as Head of the RAF Delegation in Washington, becoming thereby the RAF's standing representative in the United States on the Combined Chiefs of Staff (the American Joint Chiefs of Staff and the British Chiefs of Staff Committee, who in practice only met physically on rare occasions, usually at the major Allied Conferences). This was a position vital to the UK's conduct of the War, with the USA already a major supplier of aircraft to the RAF but also committed to deploying a very large air force of its own, not only in Europe, but also in the Pacific theatre. Evill's most important tasks were to establish and maintain close contact on behalf of Charles **Portal**, the Chief of the Air Staff, with Lieutenant General H. H. ('Hap') Arnold, Chief of the Army Air Forces and Head of the Air Board, in order to facilitate the movement of USAAF units to the UK and to ensure that Great Britain's voice was still being heard when it came to the supply of equipment to the RAF.

The first task, building a relationship with Arnold, proved to be difficult as the temperaments of the two men were very different. It did not help that the Americans proposed initially that the RAF should receive only enough aircraft to maintain squadrons already equipped with American types and subsequently that all US aircraft production should be allocated to the USAAF with the exception of light bombers, in which the RAF was not particularly interested. Field Marshal Sir John Dill, the highly respected Chief of the Joint Staff Mission in Washington, urged that Arnold and Admiral Towers, Head of the Naval Bureau of Aviation, should be invited to London to meet Portal, which they duly were, arriving in late May. They were accompanied by Evill and Colonel Hoyt S. Vandenberg, who was to remain in the UK to organize the build-up of the USAAF there. A compromise was reached in due course and the ACAS (Policy), Jack **Slessor**, was sent to Washington to tie up what became known as the ATP (Arnold-Towers-Portal) Agreement.

One aircraft which continued to be supplied to the RAF was the North American Mustang, powered by an Allison engine which produced good results at low and medium altitudes but not at high altitude. Tests with the new Rolls-Royce Merlin 61 replacing the Allison showed that the Mustang was, as a result, now highly effective at all altitudes. Evill was co-opted into the team trying to persuade the Americans that adoption of the Merlin would create a superb fighter. After some resistance from Arnold, the enthusiasm

152   Churchill's Eagles

of Lieutenant General Carl A. Spaatz, who was now in overall command of all US bombing operations in Europe and who wanted the best possible long-range fighter protection for his daylight raids, swung the argument in favour of the Merlin.

In October 1942 ACM Sir Wilfrid **Freeman** stood down as VCAS to join the Ministry of Aircraft Production as its Chief Executive. Freeman's successor was Charles *Medhurst*, a very much younger man who was at the time the ACAS (Intelligence) and had proved to be a consummate staff officer, but it was understood that his was a temporary appointment. Churchill expressed a preference for Sholto Douglas, at the time the AOC-in-C Fighter Command, but whilst Douglas was an outstanding operational commander he was not really cut out for the role of VCAS. Portal accordingly resisted this suggestion, strongly supported by Archibald Sinclair, the Secretary of State for Air, and, in March 1943 and after more than a year in Washington, it was Evill who was appointed to succeed Medhurst.

Evill proved to be an excellent foil for Portal. Both were inherently courteous men who achieved their goals by persuasion. Portal was quite content to leave more mundane staff matters to his Air Council colleagues whilst he dealt with affairs of state alongside his colleagues on the Chiefs of Staff Committee, and this also meant leaving most issues affecting the Air Staff to Evill and the DCAS, Norman **Bottomley**.

However, as well as having significant departmental responsibilities, Evill did play other roles apropos of Portal. In the first place, he became the CAS's most frequent confidant, helped perhaps by being seven months older than Portal, although the latter never relied on him as much as he had on Freeman. Secondly, he stood in the shoes of the CAS, including on the Chiefs of Staff Committee, whenever Portal was away, which he was on numerous occasions. Portal attended all the major Allied conferences other than those in Moscow in 1942 and 1944 and on each occasion was out of the UK for a long time. Moreover, he also carried out visits to RAF units in North Africa, Italy and North-West Europe, although he never went to the Far East. During such times, Evill was effectively in charge, although he had to refer to Portal on vitally important decisions

One example of these was the launch of the Dambusters Raid. The Admiralty, which was in the course of developing its own bouncing bomb, 'Highball', resisted the decision to go ahead for fear of compromising its own device for the future. Evill immediately signalled to Portal, who was in Washington and who persuaded Churchill and his fellow Chiefs of Staff that

Newall inspecting a Fairey Battle during the 'Phoney War'.

Barratt with French officers during the 'Phoney War'.

Longmore with General Wavell, C-in-C Middle East, and Anthony Eden, Secretary of State for War, in Palestine, October 1940.

Dowding escorts the King and Queen on a visit to HQ Fighter Command during the Battle of Britain.

Ludlow-Hewitt, AOC-in-C Bomber Command, with AVM John Baldwin.

Freeman as VCAS.

Churchill and Portal at Lyneham on their return from the Casablanca Conference.

Tedder (second from left) and others meeting Churchill, General Eisenhower, General Sir Henry Maitland Wilson and others in Carthage, Christmas Day 1943.

Harris and Cochrane at the Dams Raid debriefing.

Cochrane and Guy Gibson show the King a model of the Moehne Dam after the famous raid.

Bennett leaving Bentley Priory with his Navigation Officer, Group Captain Searby.

Tedder meeting Bowhill, C-in-C Transport Command, at Maison Blanc, Algeria.

Broadhurst meeting Montgomery, his Chief of Staff, Freddie de Guingand, and Generals Freyberg, Allfrey and Dempsey, prior to Monty's departure from Italy.

Garrod as Temporary Air C-in-C South-East Asia Command, talking to one of his pilots.

Douglas with Churchill and Alan Brooke, Chief of the Imperial General Staff, in Cairo.

Portal with Churchill and his fellow Chiefs of Staff, Field Marshal Sir Alan Brooke and Admiral of the Fleet Sir Andrew Cunningham, and Churchill's Staff Officers, Generals Ismay and Hollis, in the garden of 10 Downing Street, VE Day 1945.

The Air Marshals 153

the raid had to happen immediately, before the water levels in the dams fell too much. The raid was duly approved and went ahead.

The instances of disagreement on the Vice-Chiefs of Staff Committee were rare and Evill got on well with his fellow vice-chiefs, Lieutenant General Sir Archibald Nye and Vice-Admirals Sir Neville Syfret and later Sir Rhoderick McGrigor. Like the Chiefs of Staff, they held regular meetings, which were mostly to discuss inter-service matters of less importance than those debated by the Chiefs.

Evill remained at the heart of the RAF hierarchy until June 1946 and retired at the beginning of the following year. He served for the next two years as the Director-General of the English Speaking Union and took on some other non-executive roles, including as a member of the Council of the King Edward VII Hospital for Officers. Never a senior commander, but for much of his career a consummate staff officer, he had never sought a high profile but was always much admired by his colleagues and subordinates for his dedication and professionalism.

Air Chief Marshal Sir Wilfrid Freeman, Bt GCB, DSO, MC (1888–1953)

Just three and a half years before the declaration of war on Germany in September 1939, the RAF was in a parlous state as far as its aircraft were concerned. The most modern type of fighter in squadron service was the bi-plane Gloster Gladiator, with a top speed insufficient to intercept the new generation of German medium bombers, whilst Britain's own such aircraft, of which only the Vickers Wellington would prove to be an unqualified success, were yet to make an appearance. New types of fighters, bombers and other aircraft were on order, but the ability of politicians and civil servants on the one hand and aircraft manufacturers on the other to produce them for front-line service on a timely basis in the numbers required was highly questionable. On the Air Council the Air Member for Research and Development, Air Marshal Sir Hugh **Dowding**, was deeply frustrated, but he was shortly to become AOC-in-C Fighter Command, of whose deficiencies for these reasons he was only too well aware. It was his successor, Wilfrid **Freeman**, who would be largely responsible for the decisions and actions which would see into service in sufficient numbers not only the great British fighters, the Hawker Hurricane and the Supermarine Spitfire, and the new generation of heavy bombers, notably the Handley Page Halifax and the Avro Lancaster, but also an aircraft which would prove to be the most

154   Churchill's Eagles

versatile of them all, the De Havilland Mosquito, which in 1936 was not even a glint in anybody's eye.

Having attended the Royal Military College at Sandhurst, Freeman was commissioned into the Manchester Regiment in February 1908. As soon as the Royal Flying Corps was formed in 1912 he was determined to join it and in the following year he took leave from his regiment to learn to fly at the Farman School of Flying in France. Having passed out, he underwent further training at the Central Flying School and in April 1914 was posted to 2 Squadron in Montrose. Four months later the squadron was sent to France, equipped with BE2s. These carried out aerial reconnaissance for the British Army during the retreat from Mons and, on one occasion, flying in company with another pilot acting as observer, Freeman's aircraft was forced down by a mechanical problem behind the German lines and the two men had to swim across the River Aisne to escape, luckily undetected by the Germans.

That October, Freeman was posted to 9 Squadron, which was commanded at the time by Dowding. All the focus was now on artillery spotting. He was continuously in action throughout the winter and the following spring and for his work was awarded one of the first Military Crosses in the RFC. By way of a rest from active service he was then appointed an instructor at a new Flying Training School at Shoreham. In January 1916 he was posted to Egypt, where he took command of 14 Squadron, flying sorties against the Turks and their allies, the Senussi of the Western Desert.

In the summer of 1916 Freeman returned to the UK, initially to take command of first 4 and then 7 Training Wing, before returning to France at the end of the year to command 10 (Army) Wing, which comprised four squadrons with a variety of aircraft at a time when the German Albatros D.III was dominating the skies. Freeman took over 9 (HQ) Wing from Cyril **Newall** in October 1917, finding it equipped with two excellent aircraft, the Bristol Fighter and the De Havilland DH4, with which it supported the British ground forces in the Battle of Cambrai. In the following March all Freeman's squadrons were focused on the German offensive on the Somme. He then returned to the UK, initially to command a training group and then to attend the Royal Naval Staff College course at Greenwich as one of only two officers from the newly formed RAF.

Freeman went on to help with the establishment of the RAF Staff College and was an instructor on its first course in 1922. Robert Brooke-Popham was the Commandant and fellow instructors during his three years there included Guy **Garrod**, Philip **Joubert** and Bertine *Sutton*, whilst among the students were Norman **Bottomley**, Sholto **Douglas**, Roderick **Hill**, Leslie **Hollinghurst**, Keith **Park**, Charles **Portal** and Richard **Peirse**. In April 1925 Freeman was appointed Commandant of the Central Flying School, which moved during his term there from Upavon to Wittering.

In January 1927 Freeman was posted to the Air Ministry for the first time, as Director of Operations and Intelligence; Trenchard was still the CAS and the two men got on well together. In October of the following year Freeman became Station Commander at RAF Leuchars before being posted as the Chief Staff Officer at Inland Area. In October 1930 he was sent to the Middle East, initially as SASO to the AOC Iraq, Edgar **Ludlow-Hewitt**, and then as AOC Transjordan and Palestine. He was there for nearly three years, during which the tensions between the Arabs and the Jews were kept mostly under control, although trouble did flare up briefly from time to time.

Freeman returned to the UK at the end of 1933 to become Commandant of the Staff College, an appointment which he held for just over two years. In April 1936 he was appointed to the Air Council as Air Member for Research and Development ('AMRD') at the behest of the new Secretary of State for Air, Philip Cunliffe-Lister, shortly to become Viscount Swinton, who had been Secretary of State for the Colonies at the time that Freeman was AOC in Palestine. The two men had worked together well then, and Swinton now wanted someone he trusted completely to address the major issues confronting the RAF in its efforts to develop the new aircraft which it would need so badly in any war with Germany.

At the time of Freeman's appointment as AMRD the RAF was equipped with antiquated aircraft, including bi-plane fighters and bombers with fixed undercarriages; the former lacked firepower and the latter heavy bombloads, whilst the maximum speed of both types was very slow. There was thus an urgent need for all-metal monoplanes with retractable undercarriages and much more powerful engines. By this time the Expansion Scheme was well underway; indeed, shortly before Freeman's appointment Scheme F had been approved, calling for 8,000 aircraft to be in service in the spring of 1938. Freeman's task was to ensure that these were increasingly composed of advanced designs.

The Hurricane was already on order, as were the medium and light bombers, the Wellington, the Armstrong Whitworth Whitley, the Bristol Blenheim and the Fairey Battle, but it was Freeman who placed the first order for the Spitfire as well as for prototypes of the new generation of heavy bombers, the Short Stirling, Handley Page Halifax and Avro Manchester. Freeman was responsible for the choice of engines from the two largest

156   Churchill's Eagles

manufacturers, Rolls-Royce and Bristol, specifying the Merlin and Vulture from the former and the Mercury and Pegasus from the latter. He was also concerned with developments in radar. The Chain Home system had already been approved at the time of his appointment as AMRD, but he now insisted that its coverage be extended beyond what had previously been planned.

In August 1938 Freeman's remit was extended to aircraft manufacture and he became Air Member for Development and Production. He himself now focused on the production side, bringing in AVM Arthur **Tedder** as Director-General of Research and Development to handle his other responsibilities. One of Freeman's first moves was to insist that a great deal of the work on both air frames and engines should be sub-contracted so that there should be no order backlogs due to limited space at the main contractors' factories. He also succeeded in gaining approval for the procurement in the USA of the first non-UK manufactured aircraft to be employed since the early days of the Great War. This was the Lockheed Hudson, specifically designed for the RAF to equip the otherwise woefully deficient Coastal Command, whilst the North American Harvard, which was the best available single engine advanced trainer for would-be fighter pilots, was also ordered.

The aircraft whose name is most readily associated with Freeman was one whose concept he supported from the outset against the considerable scepticism of most his colleagues. In late 1939, with Freeman's encouragement, De Havilland began work on the prototype of the Mosquito, which was entirely different, both in structure and in its employment, to anything then in existence. For a start, it was substantially constructed of wood, at a time when the overwhelming majority of military aircraft were made of aluminium. Secondly, it was originally intended to be entirely unarmed, using its very high speed of 370 mph and its service ceiling of comfortably over 30,000ft to escape interception by enemy fighters when carrying out its originally intended purpose, photo reconnaissance. The Mosquito aroused strong opposition, not only from Ludlow-Hewitt, now GOC-in-C of Bomber Command, but also from the ACAS, Sholto **Douglas**, and even from Tedder, Freeman's immediate subordinate, and it was initially known as 'Freeman's Folly'! Nevertheless, Freeman persisted with his support and the prototype flew on 25 November 1940, exceeding its specifications in every respect. It was to be employed by Bomber Command as a pathfinder and target marker, as a bomber capable of carrying a 4,000lb 'Blockbuster' bomb to Berlin, and even as a fighter protecting the bomber streams. In Fighter Command it was an outstanding night fighter, in Coastal Command a rocket-firing U-Boat and surface vessel destroyer, and in the

Second Tactical Air Force a pinpoint bomber of strategic targets. Far from being a folly, it became known as the 'Wooden Wonder'.

The increase in aircraft production after war had been declared proved to be disappointingly slow. There were shortages of materials and the new factories were slow to be built, whilst their employees were initially insufficiently skilled for their tasks. The AMDP's department was evacuated to Harrogate, making communication with the Air Staff that much more difficult. Salvage and repair work, originally the AMDP's responsibility, was transferred to the Civilian Repair Organisation, under the leadership of Lord Nuffield, with responsibility at the Air Ministry being exercised by the Air Member for Supply and Organisation. In April 1940 a new Civil Member for Development and Production, Sir Charles Craven, the Chairman of Vickers, was appointed to sit alongside Freeman on the Air Council, taking over many of his industry-facing duties.

On 10 May 1940, the day Germany launched its offensive against France and the Low Countries, Churchill replaced Neville Chamberlain as Prime Minister. One of his first actions was to create out of Freeman's department the Ministry of Aircraft Production ('MAP'), the minister responsible being Lord Beaverbrook, with Freeman himself designated as Chief Executive whilst remaining AMDP and retaining his seat on the Air Council.

From the outset Beaverbrook, egged on by Churchill, concentrated on increasing aircraft production to the exclusion of everything else. This was focused on the 'Big Five' aircraft, the Spitfire, Hurricane, Wellington, Whitley and Blenheim. Whilst the priorities were certainly correct in respect of the first three aircraft, other delays ensuing from this policy were more damaging. Freeman managed to persuade the Air Staff to insist on certain other priorities, notably training aircraft, but the heavy bomber programme was significantly delayed.

Freeman saw that some of the deficiencies might be made up by sourcing more aircraft and engines from the United States, which at the time still had significant unused manufacturing capacity. He arranged for the British Purchasing Commission to order 320 of the new fighters now being built by North American Aviation, the P-51 Mustang, and also reached an agreement with Packard to make Merlin engines under licence. Freeman himself harboured serious doubts about Roll-Royce's Vulture engine, which was to power the Avro Manchester. However, in discussions with Avro's chief designer, Roy Chadwick, he learnt that it would be possible to extend the wing of the aircraft to install four Merlins. The first prototype was immediately authorized, followed by a second with a number of design

158   Churchill's Eagles

changes, most noticeably the reduction of three tail fins to two, and the first production Lancaster was flown in October 1941.

As the months went by, Freeman found Beaverbrook increasingly difficult to work with, not only because of the Minister's style of doing business, but also because considerable friction was generated between the MAP and the Air Ministry, which tested his loyalty to the utmost. He was therefore slightly more receptive than he might otherwise have been to the offer of a new job, that of Vice-Chief of the Air Staff in succession to Richard **Peirse**, who was moving on to become AOC-in-C of Bomber Command.

At the end of October 1940 Cyril **Newall**, the CAS, retired, to be succeeded by Charles Portal. The choice of Portal, aged only forty-eight and, as a temporary air marshal, quite a long way down in seniority on the Air List, came as a complete surprise to the man himself, but was not unexpected amongst his peers, to whom it had been apparent for some time that he was a star in the making. Portal was by no means confident about doing justice to the top job in the service and immediately turned to Freeman, as a man whose judgement he trusted implicitly, to help him as VCAS. The two men had formed a friendship at the Staff College in 1922, when Freeman had been an instructor and Portal a student, and had kept in touch subsequently. From February 1939 to April 1940 they had sat together on the Air Council, Portal as Air Member for Personnel.

Having said that, and in spite of his difficulty with Beaverbrook, Freeman's first instinct was that he could serve the RAF better by staying put. Moreover, becoming VCAS would be a step down for an officer of his seniority. Portal appealed to him to accept the new post, realizing that Freeman was uniquely suited to support him, possessing as he did a first-class brain and deep integrity, but also knowing that he would command universal respect within the RAF. The Secretary of State for Air, Archibald Sinclair, weighed in to support Portal and, a few days later, Freeman agreed to accept his appointment.

The Vice-Chief of the Air Staff was a completely new position in the RAF when Peirse took it on in April 1940. Since 1920 there had been a Deputy Chief of the Air Staff ('DCAS'), who was directly responsible on the Air Council for the Air Staff departments – Operations, Intelligence, Operational Requirements, Policy and Training – but who was also seen as the right-hand man of the CAS. The other service members of the Air Council, the Air Members for Personnel, for Supplies and Equipment and for Development and Production, joined by an Air Member for Training in July 1940, were all subordinate to the CAS, whose remit thus went way beyond air staff matters, but he rarely interfered with their work. The responsibilities of the DCAS had proliferated during the war and the appointment of a VCAS now allowed the appointee to spend all his time on these, whilst the VCAS himself concentrated on supporting the CAS. Moreover, whenever the CAS was away, the VCAS effectively stood in his shoes.

Portal was, as it happened, rarely away for long during the first year of Freeman's appointment as VCAS, but whenever he was, Freeman had to attend the Chiefs of Staff Committee meetings in his stead. There was also a standing Vice-Chiefs of Staff Committee, at which Freeman and his Army and Royal Navy opposite numbers had to address a number of the less important inter-service matters which the Chiefs passed down to them. Freeman got on particularly well with Vice-Admiral Sir Tom Phillips, the Vice-Chief of the Naval Staff, who was to go down with HMS *Prince of Wales* in December 1941, following the declaration of war by Japan. At the time Portal was away in Washington for the Arcadia Conference, the first to be held after the United States entered the war, and Freeman found that he was stretched to the utmost to get RAF reinforcements to Malaya, Burma and India, which had been accorded a very low priority in equipment thitherto.

As it happened, the *Prince of Wales* was the very ship on which the first inter-Allied conference had taken place in August 1941 in Placentia Bay, before the Americans had entered the war. On that occasion Portal did not attend and Freeman represented the RAF. He had met General 'Hap' Arnold, the head of the US Army Air Force in London a few months earlier and the two men got on exceptionally well, establishing a relationship which was vital to the success of the early Lend-Lease arrangements and then helping to secure the delivery of at least some American aircraft at a time when the USAAF was giving full priority to its own gigantic expansion after Pearl Harbor.

Within the Air Staff, Freeman briefly inherited Arthur **Harris** as DCAS, a man who was entirely confident of his own abilities and who gave Freeman little trouble. Harris was succeeded by Norman Bottomley, who was to see out the war in the same role but who initially required a lot more support. Freeman allowed Bottomley to chair the meetings of the Assistant Chiefs of Staff and their Directors, stepping in himself when the circumstances demanded it.

Although he had multiple duties, which included a reorganization of both the Air Sea Rescue Service and the Photo Reconnaissance Units at RAF Benson, Freeman's major task was to oversee the huge expansion of the RAF, which in the two years that he served as VCAS more than doubled in

160   Churchill's Eagles

size from fewer than half a million men and women to over a million. All the new recruits required training and then deployment, both within the UK and overseas. Freeman himself was, for the most part, stuck in London, but in October 1941 he was dispatched by Portal to Egypt to sort out a major problem which had developed there.

Churchill had long been critical of the RAF's performance in North Africa, believing that, over a year after the beginning of hostilities there by the Italians, it should have established air superiority over the Axis air forces. The fact that the command had been accorded a low priority in terms of its equipment – there were no Spitfires there at all, and the Hurricane and the American-built Curtis P-40 Kittyhawk were no match for the newer marks of Messerschmitt 109 – carried little weight with him. The AOC-in-C since April 1940, Air Chief Marshal Sir Arthur **Longmore**, lost the Prime Minister's confidence in the summer of the following year and was replaced by Tedder, who was his deputy. A new ground offensive was being planned to drive the Axis forces out of Cyrenaica, but Tedder cast doubt on the RAF's ability to achieve clear air superiority before it was launched. Churchill was furious and threatened to have Tedder replaced, so Portal suggested that Freeman should be sent out to assess the situation, to which the Prime Minister grudgingly agreed.

Freeman left the UK on 18 October, accompanied by Group Captain Basil **Embry**, who was tasked with bringing the Desert Air Force up to date on tactics developed in the UK. He met General Sir Claude Auchinleck, the GOC-in-C, and Oliver Lyttleton, the Minister Resident for the Middle East, both of whom expressed their full confidence in Tedder. Churchill had suggested, in a confidential letter to Auchinleck carried by Freeman, that Freeman himself might replace Tedder. Portal, however, had got wind of this and asked for Freeman's views. The answer was that his appointment would make no difference to the RAF's success in the theatre and that, if he was offered the post, he would reject it. Tedder's assessment of the relative strength of the Axis air forces and the RAF was amended sufficiently to mollify the Prime Minister, and Freeman returned home, but not before arranging for a modest number of Spitfires to be sent to the theatre.

It was only very rarely that Freeman intervened in operational matters, the most significant of which concerned Bomber Command. The Butt Report of August 1941 had concluded, amongst other things, that only one in three British bombers came within five miles of their target. This deficiency was resolved to some extent by new navigational aids, *Gee*, followed by *Oboe*, for locating the target and *H2S* as a ground facing radar installed in the aircraft. There was, however, also a demand by the Directorate of Bombing Operations for a specially trained target-finding force to deliver much improved results. Most of the running was made by the Deputy Director of Bombing Operations, Wing Commander Sydney *Bufton*, who canvassed station and squadron commanders and found them strongly supportive; he was also backed by his Director, Air Commodore John *Baker*, and by Bottomley, the DCAS. The proposal, however, was resisted equally strongly by Harris as AOC-in-C of Bomber Command and by almost all of his group commanders. Freeman threw his weight behind Bufton and convinced Portal, who had been out of the country, that its implementation was vital to the future success of the command. Portal overruled Harris and the Pathfinder Force was formed in August 1942 under the command of Donald **Bennett**.

Having been responsible for ordering the P-51 Mustang for the RAF in the first instance, even before the USAAF expressed an interest in the aircraft, in the summer of 1942 Freeman proposed replacing its Allison engine with the Rolls-Royce Merlin. The former had been disappointing at higher altitudes, thereby confining the aircraft to army co-operation duties, but tests conducted with Merlin-engined aircraft in the UK demonstrated both a dramatically improved performance at all altitudes and a significantly longer range than even the latest version of the Spitfire, the Mark IX. It would, however, be well into 1943 before the Americans accepted that this would be the ideal fighter escort for their daylight bombing raids on Germany.

In October 1942, with Portal now fully confident in his own abilities as CAS, Freeman was able to return to where he felt he truly belonged, in the MAP as its Chief Executive. Beaverbrook had gone as Minister, succeeded in May 1941 by John Moore-Brabazon, who was followed in his turn by Colonel John Llewellin, with whom Freeman had had a somewhat uncomfortable relationship as VCAS. He was much more comfortable with Stafford Cripps, appointed only a month after his return. Charles Craven was still there as Controller-General, but he was in poor health and his duties effectively devolved onto Freeman.

The focus of aircraft production was now increasingly on the three outstanding British aircraft of the war, the Spitfire, the Lancaster and the Mosquito, together with two more recent arrivals, the Hawker Tempest Mark V, which remedied the inability of the Typhoon to operate satisfactorily other than as a low level fight-bomber, and the Gloster Meteor, the first British operational jet fighter. The Stirling, the first of the British heavy bombers,

162   Churchill's Eagles

had proved to be a disappointment and was relegated to glider-towing, whilst the Halifax was provided with a better engine and continued to equip one and a half bomber groups. Engine development and production still took up much of Freeman's time and there were a number of disappointments, but the Merlin proved to be capable of being upgraded almost infinitely.

Freeman retired as Chief Executive of the MAP a few weeks before the end of the war and was honoured, most unusually, with a baronetcy in appreciation of his exceptional service. Much sought-after for his knowledge of industry, he was approached by a number of companies and became a director and later deputy chairman of Courtaulds and a non-executive director of Babcock & Wilcox. However, he suffered from increasingly poor health and died on 15 May 1953, aged only sixty-four.

Freeman was one of the most outstanding, but least recognized senior RAF officers of the war. His term as VCAS was an important one, giving Portal the confidence which he needed as a relatively young and junior officer to carry out to perfection the most important job in the service. However, it was in development and production that Freeman excelled, creating order out of chaos, improving productivity beyond recognition and prioritizing the projects which were to produce war-winning aircraft.

Air Marshal (later Air Chief Marshal) Sir Guy Garrod GBE, KCB, MC, DFC (1891–1965)

When war was declared on Germany on 3 September 1939, the strength of the RAF totalled just under 200,000, almost all of whom were men. Four years years later it amounted to just under one million, of whom some 180,000 were women, and the total peaked briefly at just over a million during 1944. This had enormous implications for the service, not least because relatively few of those recruited, other than the aircrew and ground crew of the Royal Auxiliary Air Force and the Royal Air Force Volunteer Reserve, came with any experience of the jobs which they had to perform. In the summer of 1940, following the disastrous campaigns in Norway and France, it was decided to accelerate recruitment, but all those who joined had to be trained before they could be of much use. Training Command was split into Flying Training Command and Technical Training Command, whilst the overall responsibility for training at the Air Ministry, hitherto part of the Air Staff Department under the Deputy Chief of the Air Staff, was vested in a new post on the Air Council, the Air Member for Training. The first incumbent was Guy **Garrod**, who would hold this key position for nearly three years, during which the RAF expanded to close to its peak in numbers.

Garrod was commissioned into the Leicestershire Regiment shortly after the British Empire's declaration of war on Germany and Austria-Hungary in August 1914. His battalion was sent almost immediately to join the British Expeditionary Force in France, where Garrod was seriously wounded during the First Battle of Ypres, earning a Military Cross in the process. He returned to duty in September 1915, not in his regiment but in the Royal Flying Corps, having qualified in the meantime as an observer. He joined a squadron for brief experience before becoming a staff officer at HQ RFC. After nearly another year he applied to train as a pilot and proved to be sufficiently adept to qualify as a flying instructor. Initially appointed to 34 Squadron, two weeks later he was transferred as a flight commander to 12 Squadron flying BE.2s, before being appointed commanding officer of 13 Squadron, flying RE.8s in a reconnaissance and artillery observation role. He finished the Great War as an acting lieutenant colonel commanding 81 Wing, having earned a Distinguished Flying Cross and been mentioned three times in despatches.

Persuaded by Hugh Trenchard personally to remain in the RAF, like many of his particularly capable brother officers, in October 1919 Garrod became a staff officer at 29 (Fleet) Group, part of Coastal Area and responsible for RAF units serving in shore stations and on British warships. It was appropriate, therefore, that when he was selected for staff training, it was at the Royal Naval Staff College at Greenwich. After graduating he spent nine months as a squadron commander attached to the School of Army Cooperation, before being appointed a member of the Directing Staff at the RAF Staff College. The college had opened only a year earlier under the command of AVM Robert *Brooke-Popham*, who was selected for the job by Trenchard as an integral part of the latter's campaign to establish the RAF as a service entirely independent of the Royal Navy and British Army. Brooke-Popham was succeeded by Air Commodore Edgar **Ludlow-Hewitt** in 1926. Garrod's four years at the college saw many of the senior RAF officers of the next war serving there, either on the Directing Staff – Douglas 'Strath' **Evill**, Wilfrid **Freeman** and Philip **Joubert** – or as students – Norman **Bottomley**, Ralph **Cochrane**, Roderic **Hill**, Leslie **Hollinghurst**, Trafford **Leigh-Mallory** and Hugh **Lloyd** among others – and the relationships formed during this period were to be highly valuable.

On leaving the staff college in early 1927, Garrod was posted as Commanding Officer of RAF North Weald. The station had been first

164   Churchill's Eagles

opened during the Great War but was closed at the end of 1919. It was Garrod's task to re-open it as a component of the Fighting Area of Air Defence of Great Britain, in time to receive 56 Squadron, equipped with Armstrong Whitworth Siskin fighters, followed by 29 Squadron with the same aircraft. In the following year he moved to become the Chief Flying Instructor at the Oxford University Air Squadron. In 1931 he was posted to Iraq as a senior officer on the staff of the AOC-in-C, who was Ludlow-Hewitt. The HQ was situated at RAF Hinaidi, south of Baghdad, which also housed three squadrons, Nos. 30 and 55 with Westland Wapitis and No.70 with Vickers Victorias. The country was relatively quiet compared to the early 1920s, but the squadrons found themselves more heavily occupied in the spring and summer of 1932, in operations against the rebellious Sheikh Ahmed Barzani in Kurdistan.

Now recognized as a staff officer of some quality, at the beginning of 1933 Garrod returned to the UK, having been selected to attend the course at the Imperial Defence College alongside officers of all three armed services and the civil service, with some students from other countries in the British Empire. The RAF Instructor was Sholto **Douglas** and Garrod's fellow students included his former fellow instructor at the staff college, 'Strath' Evill. On graduating Garrod was appointed Deputy Director of Organisation at the Air Ministry under AVM William *Welsh*, himself one of the immediate subordinates of the Air Member for Supply & Research, who was initially Hugh Dowding and then Cyril **Newall**, under whom 'Research' was renamed 'Organisation'. Welsh and Garrod were responsible for nothing less than the organization of the RAF in peace and war, with the first Expansion Scheme being adopted three months after the latter's arrival and new schemes thereafter succeeding each other with bewildering rapidity. Two years later he moved to become SASO at 23 Group in the newly created Training Command and in early 1937, now promoted to air commodore, he was appointed AOC Armament Group, which controlled the Air Armament School and the Air Training Camps. The Air Armament School was responsible for the training of Armament Officers, Air Gunners and Air Bombers and was based at RAF Manby, close to the bombing and gunnery ranges on the Wash.

In March 1938 Garrod moved back to the Air Ministry as Director of Equipment, becoming Director-General two years later, with particular responsibility for ordering equipment and spare parts. With the proliferation of new aircraft entering service at this time, it was essential that they were properly fitted out as soon as they had left the factories and that they were then able to rely on spare parts to avoid being grounded for longer than absolutely necessary.

By the late spring of 1940 it was clear that Great Britain was to be in the war for the long haul as the Germans overran much of Western Europe and were joined as an ally by Italy. Recruitment into the RAF was accelerated and this meant a huge expansion of training facilities. It was clear that the current system would be unable to cope, and two major decisions were taken. The first of these was to split up Training Command, which was divided into two on 27 May 1940. Flying Training Command was set up to train substantially all aircrew, primarily pilots but also, as bomber aircraft became larger, navigators, bomb aimers, wireless operators and air gunners. There was one exception, flight engineers, who were trained within the second new formation, Technical Training Command, as the knowledge and skills which they had to acquire were substantially the same as those demanded of the ground crew, notably fitters, riggers and armourers. The training of aircrew was carried out at the appropriate specialist schools, the crews only coming together at a late stage, when they joined Operational Training Units ('OTUs'). OTUs, however, were not run under the auspices of Flying Training Command, but under the fighting commands Bomber, Fighter and Coastal, in the UK as appropriate, and also in the Middle East and India.

To deal with such a multiplicity of training activities, the second major decision was to effect a change at the Air Ministry itself. Instead of continuing to be part of the Air Staff, those responsible for training would in future work in a separate department under a new member of the Air Council, the Air Member for Training ('AMT'), with Garrod becoming the first officer to occupy the position. The AMT's department consisted of the Directorate of Flying Training and the Directorate of Technical Training. In terms of the division of responsibility between the Air Ministry and the commands, the AMT, like his other service colleagues on the Air Council, was responsible for formulating policy and strategy, which was conveyed to the various commands by means of directives. The commands were responsible for undertaking activities in line with these directives, including, as far as the 'fighting' commands were concerned, operations against the enemy.

The new structure worked very well up to the end of 1946, when, with the RAF reducing rapidly in size, the responsibility for training on the Air Council returned to the Air Staff, in the person of either the VCAS or the DCAS. In the meantime, however, the Air Member for Training and his staff were exceptionally busy as the recruitment of both men and women continued at an enormous pace, new types of aircraft came into service and

166   Churchill's Eagles

technology advanced at high speed. As far as technology in particular was concerned, there was a high demand for specialist schools to instruct on new developments in navigation, signals and weaponry.

Within Flying Training Command, both new would-be pilots and other aircrew began by attending Initial Training Wings, which instilled discipline and improved standards of fitness. Those who passed for initial selection as pilots then moved to Elementary Flying Training Schools, for lessons on small aircraft such as the De Havilland Tiger Moth, and then on to Service Flying Training Schools, which saw those in Bomber and Coastal Commands converted onto twin-engined aircraft such as the Airspeed Oxford and Vickers Wellington, whilst those in Fighter Command learnt on advanced single-engined aircraft, including the North American Harvard and the Hawker Hurricane. They then moved on to Operational Training Units (OTUs), where, apart from those destined for single-engined aircraft, crews were formed. Those moving to groups operating four-engined aircraft of which they had no previous experience also had to spend time at Heavy Conversion Units before being allowed to go on operations.

It had been recognised well before the War began that Great Britain had two great disadvantages when it came to flying training. Firstly, the country was small in geographical area, particularly relative to Germany or France. There was insufficient room to create enough airfields to meet the demand for both operations and training, and the former naturally took precedence. Secondly, most of the country was susceptible to attack by the enemy from the air. In December 1939 representatives from Great Britain, Canada, Australia and New Zealand met in Ottawa to sign an agreement creating the British Commonwealth Air Training Plan, also known as the Empire Air Training Scheme, whereby much of the training of the air forces of the Commonwealth would take place in countries other than the United Kingdom, notably in Canada, which had the attraction of both large open spaces on which to build airfields and relatively easy access by sea from the UK. The first training facility was opened in Canada on 29 April 1940, just over two months before Garrod became AMT. The scheme was later extended not only to Australia and New Zealand, which were relatively inaccessible to British trainees but would come into their own when war was declared against Japan, but also to Southern Rhodesia, South Africa and even Bermuda, whilst flying training schools were also opened in India, the Middle East and the Bahamas. By the middle of 1943 there were some 333 flying training schools, of which over half were situated outside the United Kingdom.

The Commonwealth Air Training Plan was run on the ground by officers of the RCAF, RAAF, RNZAF and SAAF as appropriate, although the first commander in Canada was Air Vice-Marshal Robert *Leckie*, a Canadian by birth, but one who had transferred to the RAF in the inter-war years. He transferred back to the RCAF in 1942 and later became its Chief of the Air Staff. However, the RAF continued to have a say on the work of the Commonwealth Air Training Plan to the extent that it concerned its own pilots. Ralph Cochrane, from October 1940 to September 1942 one of Garrod's immediate subordinates as Director of Flying Training, considered that, as users of the product, it was essential that the Air Ministry in the UK should have its say on the training programme. When it was discovered, for instance, that a constant 50 per cent of would-be pilots and navigators were regularly being failed by their Canadian instructors, Cochrane had some of the failures sent down to flying schools in the USA for assessment there, during which the majority passed. The Canadians were, as a result, required to adopt more sophisticated measurements of ability, which increased the pass rate, vitally important to the RAF at a time of shortages of aircrew. Those who did fail were usually re-mustered as navigators, bomb aimers or air gunners. The opening of access to flying schools in the United States had been agreed between Jack **Slessor**, General 'Hap' Arnold of the USAAF and Admiral John Towers of the US Navy in April 1941. Whilst never part of the Commonwealth Air Training Plan, the USAAF was to train thousands of pilots for the RAF over the coming years.

Although control of the OTUs was exercised primarily by the operational commands and AHQ Middle East or India as appropriate, the Department of Training also had some oversight. One decision, which was said by Donald **Bennett** to have been taken by Garrod and Cochrane, was the elimination of the second pilot in the new four-engined bombers, in order to speed up the flow of pilots into bomber squadrons. Bennett attributed to this the high rate of losses among relatively inexperienced pilots. Although Garrod and Cochrane concurred with it, the decision was actually taken by Arthur **Harris** as AOC-in-C Bomber Command, not only because it speeded up the introduction of fully trained crews, but also because it allowed him to include a trained bomb aimer in each crew.

Although the peak in the RAF establishment was not reached until 1944, by the spring of 1943 it was nearly there, with the training machine running very smoothly and new recruits by then largely replacing casualties and retirements. It was time for Garrod to move on and in April 1943 he was appointed Deputy AOC-in-C RAF India.

168   Churchill's Eagles

The defence of Burma and India against attacks from the east had never been very high on the list of priorities for the three British Armed Forces, let alone British politicians. Their neglect had been all too obvious in December 1941 and the first half of 1942, when the Japanese overran first Malaya and Singapore and then Burma. The fighter aircraft available to the RAF at the time, Brewster Buffalos and, very belatedly, a few Hurricanes in Malaya and Curtis Tomahawks, Buffaloes and Hurricanes in Burma, were no match for the much larger force of Japanese Zeros and were mostly destroyed, although some in Burma were saved. Air Marshal Sir Richard **Peirse**, a former VCAS and C-in-C of Bomber Command, was dispatched to the theatre after the fall of Singapore, but he was too late to make much impression on the advance of the Japanese in Burma, which was only halted by the monsoon and the difficult nature of the country.

As AOC-in-C Air Forces in India, Peirse began to build up his force to support the British and Indian ground forces during the next phase of the War in Burma. His first step was to change the structure of his command, with AHQ Delhi situated in New Delhi and directly controlling 222 Group at Colombo in Ceylon, 223 Group at Peshawar on the North-West Frontier, 225 Group at Bangalore covering most of India itself, 226 Group devoted to supply and maintenance and 227 Group responsible for training. AHQ Bengal controlled 221 Group and 224 Group, responsible respectively for bomber/reconnaissance and fighter operations against the Japanese. The Air Ministry was unhappy at the size of the commitment and sent out Edgar Ludlow-Hewitt, by that time Inspector-General of the RAF, to review it, but he pronounced himself satisfied. Air Marshal John *Baldwin* was initially installed as Peirse's deputy, but in the spring of 1943 he was appointed to command the Third Tactical Air Force (3TAF), incorporating 221 and 224 Groups, and Garrod was sent out to relieve him as Deputy Air C-in-C of what was now called Air Command South-East Asia.

Post-monsoon campaigning on the ground in 1943 was substantially carried out by 14 Division in the Arakan, the region of Burma closest to India on the coast of the Bay of Bengal. It was a failure, but 224 Group was deemed to have done well in support of the troops; indeed, it had made a major contribution to their eventual withdrawal, whilst Vickers Wellingtons from 221 Group and Boeing B-17 Flying Fortresses of the USAAF wrought considerable damage on the Japanese supply lines and infrastructure. Moreover, the RAF had also been involved with the First Chindit Expedition, dropping supplies and, on one occasion, evacuating sick and wounded.

The Air Marshals   169

In the autumn of 1943, with the arrival of Lord Louis Mountbatten as Supreme Commander South-East Asia, a new command structure was set up which reflected, amongst other things, the growing American presence in the theatre. The groups under AHQ India were detached from any responsibility for engaging the enemy but continued to carry out their former roles, whilst two new groups were formed, covering transport (229 Group) and maintenance (230 Group). Eastern Air Command was set up as the offensive arm of Air Command South-East Asia under the leadership of an American officer, Major General George E. Stratemeyer, having under its own command the Strategic Air Force, comprising effectively all the heavy and medium bombers, under Major General Howard C. Davidson, and 3TAF, comprising the fighters and light bombers, under Baldwin. Baldwin co-located his HQ with that of Lieutenant General Bill Slim, the commander of Fourteenth Army.

Eastern Air Command provided support to Fourteenth Army in the Second Arakan Campaign, in the defensive battles of Imphal and Kohima and in the Second Chindit Expedition. Close air support, tactical and strategic bombing, glider landings, the air lifting of supplies and the evacuation of the wounded were all undertaken to great effect, the result being a comprehensive defeat of the Japanese invasion of India.

In the late autumn of 1944, Peirse was removed from his appointment as Air C-in-C for a most unusual reason. He had been carrying on an affair with the wife of the C-in-C India, General Sir Claude Auchinleck, news of which had gone back swiftly to the CAS, Charles **Portal**. Portal, who insisted on the highest standards of behaviour amongst his senior officers, had wanted to relieve Peirse immediately, but had been persuaded by Mountbatten to keep him in post. When the affair became more widely known, however, even Mountbatten was powerless to retain Peirse and a replacement was found in the shape of Trafford Leigh-Mallory. However, Leigh-Mallory was killed when his aircraft crashed on the way to India, and Garrod was appointed as Temporary Allied Air C-in-C on 26 November pending the appointment of a substitute. Stratemeyer and his American colleagues pressed for him to remain in the role, but the Air Ministry had someone else in mind. However, it was not until 25 February 1945 that the new C-in-C, Keith **Park**, was able to take up his appointment, and Garrod carried on in the meantime during a very active phase of military operations, which included the early stages of a three-pronged Allied advance in Burma, by Fourteenth Army from Imphal, supported by 221 Group, by XV Indian Corps in the Arakan, supported by 224 Group, and by the American-led but Chinese-manned Northern

170 Churchill's Eagles

Combat Area Command in the North around Myitkyina, supported by the USAAF.

Garrod's new appointment was as Deputy Air C-in-C Mediterranean Allied Air Forces ('MAAF') and simultaneously as C-in-C RAF Mediterranean and Middle East. As far as the first was concerned, he was the immediate subordinate to Lieutenant General John K. Cannon of the USAAF, with whom he worked well, helped by a favourable recommendation from Stratemeyer. MAAF by this time was a huge command, comprising the Mediterranean Allied Strategic, Tactical and Coastal Air Forces and the Balkan Air Force. The Allied Armies in Italy launched their final attack on 9 April, with the various air forces and their subordinate commands, which included the Desert Air Force, providing devastating fire power against the Germans in the Po Valley. Bologna was taken on 21 April and the British Eighth Army arrived in Trieste on 2 May, with the American Fifth Army by that time spread out all over Lombardy and Piedmont. The Germans surrendered on 4 May, four days before VE-Day.

As far as the RAF alone was concerned, Garrod's command included not only Malta and the Eastern Mediterranean, but also the Levant, Iraq, Persia, Aden and East Africa, so there was much to do as these commitments were being run down to a peacetime establishment. At the end of 1945 Garrod was appointed as Permanent RAF representative on the Military Staff Committee of the United Nations and then, simultaneously from the following March, by which time he had been promoted to air chief marshal, as Head of the RAF Delegation in Washington DC. Having been very much part of an Allied team in both South-East Asian Command and MAAF, he was ideally suited to the role. Garrod retired in October 1948, subsequently taking on a number of business and educational appointments and joining the advisory panel on the official military histories of the war.

Notwithstanding his subsequent very senior operational and staff appointments, Garrod should be remembered primarily for his role in masterminding the enormous, highly complex and immensely successful training programme for the RAF during the period of its greatest ever expansion. Ralph Cochrane, who like many others considered him to be exceptionally able, was later to say that, as long as they were doing their jobs properly, he also possessed the great virtue of letting his subordinates get on with them without interference.

Air Chief Marshal (later MRAF) Sir Arthur Harris, Bt. GCB, OBE, AFC (1892–1984)

The two senior RAF officers whose names still come most easily to those who were alive in the United Kingdom during the war, or born there in the twenty or so years after it had ended, are Hugh **Dowding** and Arthur **Harris**. Dowding, the leader of Fighter Command during the Battle of Britain, was generally accepted as having played the leading part in saving the United Kingdom from a German invasion in 1940. Harris, on the other hand, was recognized for taking the fight back to the enemy, pulverizing his cities from the sky. But whereas few of the post-war generation would have known Dowding's nickname – 'Stuffy' – most of them would immediately put one to Arthur **Harris**. His friends knew him as 'Bert', but Harris was more familiar to the generation which had lived through the War and to their children and possibly even to their grandchildren by the name which encapsulated his role in the defeat of Germany – 'Bomber'. However, his success was not seen as the simple triumph of good over evil, as was Dowding's. It was, instead, highly controversial.

August 1914 found Harris in Southern Rhodesia, whither he had travelled eight years earlier seeking a more adventurous life than the one he could expect in the UK. He immediately volunteered for military service and joined the Rhodesia Regiment, initially as a bugler. Having served in the short campaign in German South-West Africa and still seeking action, he set out for England, where he immediately applied to join the RFC, qualifying as a civilian pilot in November 1915 and passing out of the Central Flying School early in the New Year. He served for the next nine months in the UK in no fewer than four squadrons, always flying BE2s and always focused on bringing down Zeppelins, but never actually doing so. However, he was sufficiently highly regarded to be made commanding officer of the last of these squadrons, No.38.

In September 1916 Harris was posted to 70 Squadron in France as a flight commander, flying Sopwith 1½ Strutters, the first British aircraft with guns firing through its propellers; but good as it was when it entered service, it suffered against the Fokker Monoplane and then the Albatros D.1. On 1 October Harris crash-landed, injuring himself seriously enough to require hospitalization in England. He returned to service briefly with 51 Squadron in the UK and was then posted back to France in June 1917 as a flight commander in 45 Squadron, flying the Sopwith Camel, one of the best dog-fighters of the Great War, with which he saw some success. When his CO,

Pierre van Rijneveld, much later to become Chief of the General Staff in South Africa, was himself shot down, Harris took temporary command of the squadron.

Invalided back to England with a serious bout of flu, Harris returned to active service in command of 191 Squadron, a training unit in the UK, before moving once again to France to see the war out in command of 50 Squadron, once again flying Camels. Having subsequently been appointed to command the RAF station at Brooklands, he was surprised but delighted to be offered a permanent commission. He then attended a course at the Air Navigation School at Andover, where he specialized in night flying, before spending eight months commanding 3 Flying Training School at Scopwick.

At the beginning of 1921 Harris was posted to India to command 31 Squadron, flying Bristol Fighters on the North-West Frontier. He was not at all happy there, entirely because of the treatment accorded to the RAF by the Army in India, which regarded the junior service with contempt and accorded it no priority for supplies and equipment, notably spare parts; this meant that the squadron's aircraft were frequently not airworthy. A tour of inspection by Air Vice-Marshal Sir John Salmond laid this bare, leading in due course to some improvement. Before that happened, however, Harris was posted to Air HQ in Baghdad, where Salmond now commanded not only the RAF, but also the British Army units in the country, due to recognition by the British Government that any rebellion there could be dealt with far more cheaply and effectively by air power than by tens of thousands of troops.

Four months later, in November 1922, Harris was appointed to command 45 Squadron at RAF Hinaidi, south of Baghdad. No longer a fighter squadron, No.45 was now equipped with lumbering Vickers Vernons, employed to operate the mail service between Baghdad and Cairo and to carry both air cargo and, to a limited extent, passengers. His two flight commanders were Robert *Saundby* and Ralph **Cochrane**, both of whom were to be closely associated with him in the next war and in the intervening years, whilst Harris's successor, Roderic **Hill**, was another who would achieve senior air rank later, as would Basil **Embry**, one of the junior officers.

Harris quickly determined that the Vernon was capable of activities beyond transport. With the consent of Salmond he ordered a hole to be cut in the nose of one of his aircraft, in which was placed a bomb sight which, together with bombs slung under the wings and an ingenious release mechanism produced by his ground crew, turned the aircraft into a much more powerful and accurate bomber than the DH 9s already in the country.

Salmond was persuaded that it would be effective against insurgents in the north of Iraq, and the Vernons duly began a successful career as bombers.

After a very satisfactory tour of duty in Iraq, Harris was posted back to the UK to command 58 Squadron at RAF Worthy Down in the Wessex Bombing Area. The squadron was equipped with the Vickers Virginia, like the Vernon a derivative of the wartime Vickers Vimy, but one designed specifically for bombing rather than transport. Harris was convinced by this time that bombers would be highly vulnerable to fighters and would, as a result, have to carry out their operations against a determined enemy in the hours of darkness. He insisted on his crews training for night operations and was joined in this by the CO of 7 Squadron, the other Virginia unit at Worthy Down, who was Charles **Portal**. A friendly competition developed between the two squadrons, both of which reached a high state of efficiency in day and night bombing, whilst their commanding officers established a close personal relationship.

At the beginning of 1928 Harris was selected for a staff college course, but it was at the Army Staff College at Camberley rather than the RAF College. The former always reserved two places for the RAF, whilst places were similarly reserved for the Army at Andover. The Army course was for two years rather than one, so Harris was able to establish a large number of contacts within both the Directing Staff and the student body. One officer he particularly admired amongst the former was Lieutenant Colonel Bernard Montgomery who, like Harris, would become a household name fifteen and more years later, but there were many others who would reach very senior positions in the British and Indian Armies, including two more future Chiefs of the Imperial General Staff, John Harding and Gerald Templer. Outside the curriculum, Harris much enjoyed the opportunity to ride splendid horses with the Staff College Drag Hunt.

Almost inevitably, Harris's next appointment was to a staff role and it turned out to be on the Air Staff of AHQ Middle East as Deputy Senior Air Staff Officer in succession to Sholto **Douglas**. It was not an exciting posting, but Harris did succeed in persuading the AOC-in-C, Cyril **Newall**, to let him lead a flight of Fairey IIIFs to East Africa by way of showing the flag. After two and a half years he returned to the UK, first to attend a flying boat pilots course at RAF Calshot and then to take command of 201 Squadron, which flew Short Southampton flying boats out of Pembroke Dock. This he much enjoyed and he was very popular with his pilots, who included Donald **Bennett**, so he was not pleased when, after less than four months, he was summoned to the Air Ministry to become Deputy Director of Operations and Intelligence. In the following year he succeeded Portal as Deputy Director of Plans. The work was not entirely congenial to him, but he had good subordinates, including Cochrane, and particularly enjoyed attending the meetings of the Joint Planning Staff with his naval and army counterparts.

It was with some relief that Harris moved to Bomber Command to become AOC 4 Group in June 1937. However, it was also a period of frustration, as the new Armstrong Whitworth Whitley, the first of the 'modern' medium bombers with which the group was beginning to equip, replacing its obsolete Virginias and Handley Page Heyfords, experienced teething problems, and the group lacked a lot of essential equipment. One compensation was that he developed an excellent relationship with his AOC-in-C, Edgar **Ludlow-Hewitt**, whom he greatly admired. The appointment turned out to be a short one, as he was selected to become AOC Palestine and Transjordan in early 1938. Just as he was preparing to leave the UK, however, he was diverted by Newall, now the CAS, to lead an RAF mission to the USA to buy aircraft to fill perceived deficiencies in the service's capabilities. This was to result in the purchase of the Lockheed Hudson for maritime reconnaissance and anti-submarine work, and the North American Harvard for advanced single-engined training. Harris also took the opportunity to see as much of the US Army Air Corps as possible in the short time available. He was not greatly impressed by its aircraft but he made a number of valuable contacts amongst its senior officers, including 'Hap' Arnold, the Deputy Chief of Staff, who was shortly to succeed to the top position, which he would hold until after the end of the impending war.

On his arrival in Palestine in July 1938, Harris took over from Roderic Hill, once his successor at 45 Squadron. His posting took place in the closing stages of the Arab Revolt, which had erupted in 1936 with a general strike. However, although the strike was dealt with through a few concessions and some international diplomacy, it was followed by small-scale attacks on the British Army and Palestinian Police. Unlike in Iraq, however, there was little bombing by the RAF of villages, but instead frequent leafletting, instructing the inhabitants to stay at home until the Army arrived. Bands of insurgents were, however, successfully attacked in the countryside with bombs and machine-gun fire. Montgomery, with whom Harris was delighted to renew an acquaintance, commanded 8 Division in the north of the country, whilst another very capable soldier, Richard O'Connor, led 7 Division in the South. Harris developed an excellent working relationship with both of them and with their overall superior as GOC-in-C, Robert Haining. Montgomery, however, was taken ill and sent back to England by ship; and not very long afterwards, Harris followed him with a duodenal ulcer problem, arriving back in the UK a month before war was declared on Germany.

As he had not been expected to return to the UK so soon, there was no immediate appointment for Harris once he was fit again. He appealed to Portal, now the Air Member for Personnel, and heard shortly afterwards that Ludlow-Hewitt wanted him for the command of 5 Group in Bomber Command, which he took up on 11 September 1939 at its HQ in Grantham. The group, operating from airfields in Lincolnshire, consisted of ten squadrons, two of which were later detached to form an operational training unit. The squadrons were equipped with the Handley Page Hampden, one of three medium bombers in the command, the others being the Whitley and the Vickers Wellington. The Hampden was the fastest of the three but it was a strange-looking aircraft, consisting of a 'pod and boom' construction, the 'pod' housing the crew of four, up to 4,000lbs of bombs and the gun turrets. Harris was not impressed by either the turrets or the armour, and some changes were made to improve these. In the case of the guns, and without first consulting the Air Ministry, he went directly to a local engineering firm, which produced a new mounting that effectively doubled the firepower of the aircraft. The cost was quietly agreed later.

Eighteen aircraft of 5 Group had conducted its first operation on the day war was declared, but the ships which were the target were never located. It was only on 26 September that the first raid took place under Harris's control, once again without any result. The third operation, three days later, was a disaster, with five out of eleven aircraft failing to return, proving that they were highly vulnerable to enemy fighters in daylight. There was little further activity for the rest of the year, although on one occasion two Hampdens were shot down by mistake by Spitfires returning from a sweep. Operations continued at a very modest level until the German invasion of Norway on 9 April 1940, in the aftermath of which strikes were directed against shipping in the south of that country and losses began to mount. Following the German invasion of the Low Countries and France, activity increased significantly, with the emphasis now being on land, particularly against roads and railways, as well as against ports.

On the night of 11/12 August 1940 Flight Lieutenant Roderick Learoyd of 49 Squadron earned Bomber Command's first Victoria Cross for his attack on the Dortmund–Ems Canal, and this was followed by a second VC in the group, awarded to Sergeant John Hannah of 83 Squadron for his heroism whilst bombing invasion barges at Antwerp on 15 September. In spite of

176   Churchill's Eagles

some modest successes as a bomber, the Hampden, in Harris's opinion, was never satisfactory in the role, but he thought that it would make an excellent minelayer and, for his last few months as AOC, it was increasingly deployed as such.

On 25 November 1940 Harris was appointed Deputy Chief of the Air Staff. From 1920 onwards the DCAS had been responsible for all the departments at the Air Ministry other than those in the remit of the Air Member for Personnel, the Air Member for Supply and Organisation and the Air Member for Research and Development. He had a number of specific responsibilities, notably Operations, Intelligence, Training, Policy and Operational Requirements, and from the late 1930s these were each run under his control by Assistant Chiefs of the Air Staff. The DCAS had also been seen as the right-hand man of the CAS, but in 1940 this role became the responsibility of a newly created position, the Vice-Chief of the Air Staff. Following the brief tenure of Richard **Peirse**, Wilfrid **Freeman** had been appointed as VCAS a few weeks before Harris took up his own appointment. This could have been very confusing, but in fact worked well, particularly as Portal had become CAS in October 1940. Moreover, Training now had its own Air Member in the shape of Guy **Garrod**, which meant one less responsibility for the Air Staff.

Harris had a number of Directorates immediately subordinate to him, and one of his early decisions was to create another, the Directorate of Bombing Operations under Air Commodore John *Baker*. This was to come back to bite him in due course, but for the time being it seemed to fill a pressing need. In general, however, Harris thought that the Air Staff were bloated and set about reducing the numbers by 40 per cent, resulting in much higher efficiency and, to the surprise of most of the survivors, fewer hours of work. More generally, Harris queried amongst other things the 2:1 ratio of fighter to bomber production, and this led to a significant increase in the latter at the beginning of 1941. The new bombers, the Short Stirling, the Handley Page Halifax and the Avro Manchester, were starting to come into service, and Harris insisted that more new squadrons be formed to operate them. To his great annoyance, many of the aircraft were grounded by technical problems. He also called for, and got, a change in the types of bomb used by the command to those with lighter casings and more explosives. Freeman, the VCAS, was critical of some of Harris's proposals, but he was greatly impressed by his capacity for work.

In the event Harris was only at the Air Ministry for six months before being appointed Head of the RAF Delegation to the USA in May 1941. He renewed his contacts with leading USAAF officers and established new ones with aircraft manufacturers, whilst at the same time adopting a low profile personally, as the United States was still a neutral state. He and his staff were now responsible to the Air Ministry for monitoring closely the allocations of aircraft and spare parts from US production lines, which had been agreed in late 1940 by Jack **Slessor**, 'Hap' Arnold and Admiral John Towers of the US Navy. A scheme providing access to flying schools in the United States had also been concluded between them and Harris was closely involved in its implementation, working with the full support of Guy **Garrod**, the Air Member for Training. Although not part of the Commonwealth Air Training Plan, it was to train thousands of pilots for the RAF over the coming years.

The attack on Pearl Harbor allowed Harris and his colleagues to change from civilian clothes into uniform, but its immediate implications were potentially disastrous for the RAF, as first priority on everything was now accorded to the USAAF and the US Navy. By dint of patient negotiation, Harris was able to mitigate some of the initially proposed shortfalls. He was appointed to represent the RAF on the Joint Chiefs of Staff Committee in Washington, as part of the British component under Field Marshal Sir John Dill, but was told by Portal, who arrived with Churchill on 22 December for the first Allied wartime conference, that he was now wanted for another appointment, as AOC-in-C Bomber Command.

As Harris was only too aware, Bomber Command had experienced a torrid time between May 1940 and the end of 1941. The failings in its capabilities had been exposed by the Butt Report of August 1941, which had concluded, among other things, that only one in three aircraft had come within five miles of their target and that the figure dropped to one in ten over the heavily defended Ruhr. Its aircraft had proved, for the most part, to be disappointing. The Bristol Blenheim was completely unsuitable for long distance night bombing and was reduced to making daylight raids over Northern France and the Low Countries with a fighter escort. The Hampden, as Harris knew well, was ineffective by day or by night. The Whitley was fast approaching obsolescence as a bomber, although it would continue to provide good service in other roles. Of the aircraft which had begun the war, only the Wellington was continuing to perform satisfactorily. The Short Stirling, first into service of the four-engined bombers, had only begun to undertake bombing operations after Harris left 4 Group, but it had not lived up to expectations. Neither had the Avro Manchester, due to its unreliable Rolls-Royce Vulture engines. On a more positive note, however, the Handley Page Halifax had showed a distinct improvement in capability

178   Churchill's Eagles

over the other aircraft and more still was expected of the Manchester's replacement, the Avro Lancaster, powered by four tried and tested Merlin engines.

On the night of 7/8 November 1941 both the ineffectiveness and the vulnerability of Bomber Command were starkly illustrated by a raid on Berlin in which 21 of 169 aircraft were lost, a rate of 12.9 per cent. In this case it was not only enemy action that was the cause: the weather conditions were appalling and many aircraft were lost to icing. Damage to the enemy was shown to be very modest. In the light of this and other examples of poor performance, the AOC-in-C, Richard **Peirse**, was removed on 8 January 1942, to be succeeded on a temporary basis by John *Baldwin*, the AOC 3 Group. It was Baldwin's misfortune that during the term of his appointment the command's failings were demonstrated yet again when it and other British air and sea forces failed to stop the 'Channel Dash', the escape of the German battlecruisers *Scharnhorst* and *Gneisenau* on 12 February from Brest to Germany.

Unsurprisingly, when Harris took over from Baldwin at Bomber Command's HQ at High Wycombe ten days later he was very much perceived as a new broom, a role with which he felt entirely comfortable. He was delighted, in particular, to find his former flight commander at 45 Squadron, Robert Saundby, as his SASO, which position, and later that of Deputy AOC-in-C Saundby would occupy for the rest of the war. Harris's timing was impeccable as things were about to change, to Bomber Command's great benefit. Firstly, Harris enjoyed Portal's complete confidence, unlike Peirse, and was given a much freer hand as a result. Secondly, his arrival coincided with the first operational sorties by the Lancaster, the outstanding night bomber of the war. Thirdly, it also coincided with the first instalment in the command's aircraft of a new navigational device, *Gee*, which was, with others yet more capable, to make a dramatic difference to the ability of aircraft to find their targets. Results began to show very quickly, notably in a devastating raid on Lübeck on 28/29 March, although Harris's one attempt at a daylight operation, the Augsburg Raid of 17 April, resulted in heavy losses and was not repeated.

On the night of 30/31 May, Harris launched the first 'Thousand Bomber Raid' on Cologne. He was only able to scrape together just enough aircraft by including OTUs and a few aircraft from Flying Training Command as well as every serviceable aircraft in his five groups. The results were good, unlike those of the second such raid on Essen and the third on Bremen, and the three raids were a vigorous demonstration of intent, although they were never repeated.

If he won that battle, he lost the next one, which was with his own colleagues. The Butt Report still rankled with the Air Ministry, not least with the Directorate of Bombing Operations. The Deputy Director, Sidney *Bufton*, believed very strongly in the creation of a discrete target-finding force which could use *Gee* and other devices both to find and to mark the targets. In this he was supported by his Director, John Baker, and by the DCAS, Norman **Bottomley**, but was vigorously opposed by Harris, who believed that each group should develop its own such capability. Bufton canvassed station and squadron commanders, who were strongly supportive, but the group commanders were largely of Harris's opinion. The debate rumbled on until Bufton secured the backing of Freeman, the highly influential VCAS, who in turn persuaded Portal that it was necessary.

If Harris did not get his own way, at least he ensured that he would have control over the choice of commander of the new force. He selected Donald Bennett, once his subordinate in 201 Squadron, whom he had long admired for his navigational skills, largely developed after resigning his commission to become a commercial pilot. Bennett had rejoined the RAF in late 1941, had commanded two squadrons in Bomber Command and had escaped capture after being shot down. In addition to selecting its commander, Harris also chose the name of the new formation – the Pathfinder Force – later to become 8 (Pathfinder) Group.

Bomber Command experienced mixed fortunes in the second half of 1942 as the Pathfinders gradually developed their techniques and the quality of aircraft improved, with 5 Group completely re-equipping with Lancasters. In early 1943, moreover, further advances in technology led to the introduction of *Oboe*, an improvement on *Gee*, and its installation in high-altitude De Havilland Mosquitoes in 8 Group. Furthermore, the new H2S ground facing radar was installed in the command's aircraft. On the other hand, there was what was considered by Harris to be a pointless diversion on numerous occasions to attack the U-boat pens at Lorient and St Nazaire, as they lay beneath thick reinforced concrete roofs, impervious to the bombs available at the time.

Much as Harris initially opposed the creation of the Pathfinders, so he did the formation of a new squadron to attack the great dams of the Ruhr Valley with a new weapon, Barnes Wallis's 'bouncing bomb', which he believed would never work. Once again he was overruled by Portal. Ralph Cochrane, recently appointed AOC 5 Group, was ordered to set up 617 Squadron and

180   Churchill's Eagles

to plan the operation. In the event it took place on the night of 16/17 May 1943 and turned out to be highly successful, although it was incapable of being repeated. Harris, in the event, was highly impressed by the squadron's skill and determined to use it in the future for special operations. He also became a strong supporter of Wallis.

The Dams Raid was a very small part of a new offensive by Bomber Command, later called the Battle of the Ruhr. At the beginning of the year there had been a further increase in the command's strength when 6 (Canadian) Group became operational, and it was with over fifty squadrons, not including the medium bombers of 2 Group, which was in any event shortly to be transferred to the Second Tactical Air Force, that he pursued the campaign. By this time the Pathfinder techniques had improved considerably, leading to successful attacks on Dortmund, Düsseldorf, Essen, Krefeld and Wuppertal amongst other cities, as well as Cologne and other locations outside the Ruhr. Moreover, in four raids at the end of July and in early August Hamburg was effectively destroyed.

Buoyed up by success at Hamburg, the second-largest city in Germany, Harris now set his sights on the largest, Berlin. However, whereas Hamburg, a Hanseatic city with houses constructed mostly of wood, had suffered appallingly from incendiary bombs, the modern concrete buildings and broad avenues of Berlin were relatively impervious to them and the city was out of range for *Oboe*, so the campaign, from November 1943 to March 1944, proved to be a major disappointment to him and was regarded as a defeat by many others. Moreover, on the night of 30/31 March, Bomber Command suffered its greatest ever loss when ninety-five bombers, 11.9 per cent of the attacking force, were lost in a raid on Nuremberg.

Although Harris was opposed to what happened next, it proved to be just the breathing space which Bomber Command needed to recoup its losses. The command and the US Eighth Air Force were diverted from Germany to operations in preparation for the invasion of North-West Europe, largely over France and against the communications network. Once Harris had accepted that he had no alternative, he gave it his full support and was pleased by its relative success. He was also happy to mount operations in direct support of the troops on the ground commanded by his old friend Montgomery, especially during the fighting in and around Caen in Normandy.

In the meantime, not only 617 Squadron, but the whole of 5 Group, had developed a target-marking capability which was different to, but just as effective as that of the Pathfinders and, much to Bennett's dismay, three of his squadrons, including one of Mosquitoes, were detached to come under

Cochrane's command, allowing the group to operate substantially on its own, informally styled 'the Independent Air Force'. The group, and particularly 617 Squadron, was to have much success in the latter part of 1944 and in 1945, particularly when using Barnes Wallis's new 'earthquake' bombs, the *Tallboy* and the *Grand Slam*, its operations including the sinking of the German battleship *Tirpitz* and the successful destruction of the U-boat pens. From Harris's point of view, it was the one part of his command over which he had direct control, rather than being shackled by the Air Ministry.

In mid-August 1944 Harris and Lieutenant General 'Jimmy' Doolittle, commanding the US Eighth Air Force, were released to turn their attention back to Germany; but whereas Doolittle was carrying out precision daylight bombing against strategic targets, notably oil and the aircraft industry, Bomber Command remained focused on area bombing, Harris coining the term 'panacea targets' for anything more focused and continuing to believe that Germany's will to continue fighting would be broken by raids on its cities. By the spring of 1945 his strength had increased to a little under a hundred squadrons, thirteen of which formed 100 (Bomber Support) Group, which provided electronic counter-measures to combat German ground and airborne radar and included 'Serrate' intruder Mosquitoes to attack German night fighters.

The most devastating raid of all came on the night of 13/14 February 1945, when 796 Lancasters carried out an attack on Dresden, the number killed possibly exceeding 25,000. Dresden was a transport centre in the path of the advance of Soviet ground forces, but its strategic importance was later questioned. However, the raids on this and other cities in the area were put forward by the Air Ministry and specifically approved by Churchill, although it was Harris who was to attract the bulk of the subsequent criticism. Dresden has remained the most controversial raid of the whole bombing campaign and was to do serious damage to Harris's reputation, although he himself never doubted that it had been justified.

With the end of the war in Europe, Bomber Command was speedily run down. Some squadrons were nominated for service against Japan, but the Japanese surrender meant that none were actually deployed. Harris retired on 15 September and was promoted to marshal of the RAF on 1 January 1946, the same day as Sholto Douglas, the two of them becoming the only RAF officers of that rank not to have served as CAS. Unlike Douglas, however, Harris was not subsequently offered a peerage, possibly because this would have been a step too far for a Labour Government only too aware of the controversy associated with his involvement in area bombing. After

182   Churchill's Eagles

Churchill returned to power the offer was made, but Harris rejected it in favour of a baronetcy. In the intervening years he had enjoyed a career as managing director of a new shipping company, South African Marine Corporation, known as Safmarine. This took him back to Southern Africa, a part of the world which he had enjoyed as a young man prior to the Great War. After he returned permanently to the UK in 1952 he devoted much time, right into his nineties, to the veterans of Bomber Command and especially to those of 617 Squadron, to whose reunions he was inevitably invited, which he usually attended and amongst whom he remained hugely popular.

'Bomber' Harris has remained a controversial figure to this day, entirely because of his association with area bombing, a strategy in whose design and introduction he had no part, but whose execution he readily and brilliantly carried out. Although one has to take with a pinch of salt his frequent claims that Bomber Command had been the decisive instrument of victory in Europe, there can be no doubt that, under his leadership, it became a vitally important factor in that victory. The command had been the one way in which Great Britain could strike back at the Germans in their homeland between May 1940 and June 1944, but up until the time of his appointment as AOC-in-C its achievements had been very modest. After he arrived, it acquired new purpose and continued to grow in strength and capability right up to VE-Day, for which reason he can justifiably be remembered as one of the Great Men of the War.

Air Marshal (later Air Chief Marshal) Sir Roderick Hill KCB, MC, AFC* (1894–1954)

Few senior officers of the RAF during the Second World War could be said to have had an academic bent. Most were wholeheartedly practical men, albeit that theirs was possibly the most technical of the three armed services. Few had been to university or had even thought of doing so. An exception was Roderic Hill, who had been an undergraduate when war was declared on Germany in August 1914 and would return to a largely academic life when he retired. In the intervening years he had, in a number of appointments, been much concerned with technical development, but he also turned out to be a highly capable front-line pilot in the First World War and a skilled operational commander in the Second.

Hill was born into an academic family, his father being a professor of mathematics at University College, London, whilst his uncle, later Sir

George Francis Hill, had taken a First in Classics at Oxford and later became the Director of the British Museum. Hill himself went up to University College with a view to taking a fine arts degree and becoming an architect, but before he could complete his degree his course was interrupted by the declaration of war. Even before then he had become interested in flying and, with his brother Geoffrey, had built and flown a glider of their own design. Geoffrey was destined to become an aeronautical engineer, but Roderic decided to join the Army, initially as a private soldier in the Royal Fusiliers, although he was rapidly commissioned into the Northumberland Fusiliers.

Hill served on the Western Front and was wounded at the Battle of Loos. When he recovered he applied to join the RFC and, having undertaken a flying training course, was posted to France in the summer of 1916, flying Nieuport 17s in 60 Squadron, in which one of his fellow pilots was Albert Ball VC. Hill himself was awarded a Military Cross for bringing down an enemy balloon whilst under very heavy fire. He was promoted to flight commander at the end of the year, but in April 1917 was appointed to command the Experimental Flying Department at the Royal Aircraft Factory, Farnborough, where he carried out test flights on a number of new types of aircraft, for which he was awarded the Air Force Cross. He remained at Farnborough after the end of the war and in 1922 received a bar to his AFC and also won the R. M. Grove Prize for Aeronautical Research.

In 1923 Hill was selected to attend the second course at the RAF Staff College. Almost inevitably he received a staff posting immediately afterwards, in this case to HQ Inland Area, where he worked on Air Staff Duties, essentially engaged in organization. Inland Area had been formed in 1920 at Hillingdon House, Uxbridge out of Northern and Southern Areas and consisted of three groups, 1, 3 and 7, all of which were involved in training. Hill was there for less than five months, however, before being appointed to command 45 Squadron at RAF Hinaidi in Iraq. The squadron's aircraft were lumbering Vickers Vernons, a transport derivative of the wartime Vickers Vimy bomber, and its primary tasks alongside its fellow Vernon operator, 70 Squadron, were to carry the mail and a small number of passengers and other cargo between Cairo and Baghdad and to provide transport services to British forces in the country, involving the supply of stores and equipment and the evacuation of sick and wounded.

Although the mail flights between Hinaidi and RAF Heliopolis outside Cairo were for a peaceful purpose, they involved serious risk and each one of them was an adventure. The route was largely over the desert and it was often difficult to follow the track on the ground which had been created by

184   Churchill's Eagles

a plough. There were a number of overnight stops at primitive airfields, and the aircraft engines were far from entirely reliable and occasionally broke down completely. On one occasion it rained so much overnight at a particular landing ground that the Vernons became stuck in a flood on the next day. Rescuing stranded crews and passengers was a commonplace event.

The two Vernon squadrons had, however, also been involved in the past in more warlike activities, due to the initiative of Hill's predecessor, Arthur **Harris**. Harris had received the permission of Air Marshal Sir John Salmond, who commanded both the RAF and the Army in Iraq, to convert the Vernons into bombers by cutting a hole in the nose to fit a bomb sight and attaching bombs under the wings. This had proved so successful that the aircraft were used on a number of occasions to drop bombs on the villages of rebellious tribesmen, having first warned them that this was to take place. It proved to be a very effective method of air control. By the time that Hill arrived, however, the short campaign had ended, but the squadrons continued to practise their bombing.

In November 1925 Hill was posted to HQ RAF Middle East in Cairo, where he worked on the Technical Staff. He returned to the UK at the beginning of 1927 to join the Directing Staff at the RAF Staff College. The Commandant was Edgar **Ludlow-Hewitt** and the staff contained a number of future leaders of the RAF, including Arthur **Barratt**, Ralph **Cochrane**, Douglas **Evill** and Philip **Joubert**. After three years he was appointed Officer Commanding and Chief Flying Instructor at the Oxford University Air Squadron and whilst he was there was awarded a Master of Arts degree by decree of the university. In September 1932 Hill, by that time a group captain, received his first posting to the Air Ministry, as Deputy Director of Repair and Maintenance. The facilities for repairing and maintaining aircraft were still very primitive and Hill put forward a proposal to divert major works to civilian repair centres which would have facilities not available to the RAF, but this was turned down by the ministry.

After nearly four years Hill was appointed AOC Palestine and Transjordan in the rank of air commodore. His arrival came after the beginning of the Arab Revolt, which had begun with a general strike, initially paralyzing labour and transport and later developing into a full-scale uprising, in which attacks were made by the Arabs on infrastructure, on British Army personnel and facilities and on Jewish settlements. Hill's predecessor, Richard **Peirse**, had established a strategy of providing air cover over both trains and road convoys with some success, whilst armed bands were bombed and strafed. However, rather than bombing villages, as had happened in Iraq, albeit with advance warning to the inhabitants, leaflets were dropped, warning the inhabitants to stay indoors pending the arrival of the Army. Hill got on exceptionally well with his Army opposite numbers, initially Lieutenant General John Dill and then Lieutenant General Archibald Wavell, and was mentioned twice in despatches.

In July 1938 Hill handed over command to Harris, his predecessor at 45 Squadron, and returned to the UK to become Director of Technical Development. This was at a time when the advancement of technology was moving at a rapid pace, and Hill was required to ensure that it was incorporated whenever possible in the new aircraft emerging from the factories. Initially his department was in the Air Ministry, but in 1940 it was renamed the Directorate of Research and Development and was placed in the Ministry of Aircraft Production under Lord Beaverbrook. Unlike some of his colleagues, Hill managed to establish a good relationship with his new master, but he differed with him on a number of matters, one of which led to his insisting successfully on later marks of the Supermarine Spitfire being armed with a combination of cannon and machine guns, rather than just the latter.

In late 1941 Hill was sent to Washington as controller of technical services, ensuring that American–built aircraft incorporated all the features required by the RAF. He found that he got on well with his American counterparts, but in the summer following the entry of the US into the war, with technical differences between the two Allies largely resolved, he asked to be posted back to the UK. He was disappointed, however, that his next appointment, in September 1942, was as Commandant of the RAF Staff College. This institution had been closed on the declaration of war but was re-opened two months later with a very much shorter course, designed to turn out staff officers in a matter of a few months. It had been closed again in 1940, but then relocated from Andover to Bulstrode Park, Gerrard's Cross.

Hill was desperate to get back to a front-line role and was thus delighted in July 1943 to be asked for by Trafford **Leigh-Mallory**, AOC-in-C of Fighter Command, to take over 12 Group as AOC. Leigh-Mallory had commanded the group himself during the Battle of Britain, espousing the use of 'Big Wings'. Things had moved on considerably since then, and the command, particularly 11 Group in South-East England, had taken the offensive with fighter sweeps over France and the Low Countries. Since that time 12 Group, relieved from the duty of defending London, had shrunk from thirty squadrons to fifteen and was continuing with its original role, the protection of the East Coast of England and the industrial areas of

186   Churchill's Eagles

Yorkshire and the East and West Midlands, operating out of airfields in East Anglia, Lincolnshire and Yorkshire. In practice the Luftwaffe restricted its activities to bombing industrial targets by night, rarely reaching the major industrial centres other than those around the Humber, notably Hull, and carrying out hit-and-run raids by day. The group was equipped with a number of different types of aircraft, six of the squadrons flying Spitfires and three Hawker Typhoons, the latter proving to have serious limitations as a day fighter, although it came into its own subsequently in a ground attack role. 12 Group used both types to carry out daylight sweeps over the Continent, although their relatively limited range often required them to refuel at stations in 11 Group further south. Night interceptions, of raids on Hull and Grimsby in particular, were carried out by three squadrons of De Havilland Mosquitoes and one of Bristol Beaufighters, whilst there was also an air-sea rescue squadron equipped with the Avro Anson and the Supermarine Walrus flying boat. Finally, 288 Squadron employed a miscellaneous collection of aircraft for target-towing and attack simulations.

12 Group enjoyed a great deal of success, but even so it came as a surprise to Hill when he was appointed AOC-in-C Air Defence of Great Britain ('ADGB'), as Fighter Command was renamed in November 1943. Leigh-Mallory had stepped up to become C-in-C of the Allied Expeditionary Air Force, taking with him as its British component the new Second Tactical Air Force ('2TAF'), which comprised a number of former Fighter Command squadrons in two groups, 83 and 84, together with 2 Group of light bombers from Bomber Command. The remaining fighter aircraft were left with ADGB in 10, 11, 12 and 13 Groups – 9 Group was disbanded – whilst 70 Group, which was all that remained of Army Cooperation Command, now took on a training role.

Hill relocated to Bentley Priory, Hugh **Dowding's** HQ during the Battle of Britain, where he was given a new directive which made him responsible for the whole of the air defence of the United Kingdom, including operational control of AA Command, Balloon Command and the Royal Observer Corps. As far as the first of these was concerned, it had been commanded by General Sir Frederick Pile since July 1939 and would continue to be so until shortly before the end of the war in Europe. Pile was invariably highly co-operative and he and Hill worked well together from adjacent offices.

ADGB's responsibilities for defence were effectively split into two. Daytime operations consisted of standing patrols to attack any German incursions, an expensive system which never really worked, although there was no obvious alternative and the damage incurred by the intruders in any event was relatively modest. The raids reached seaside cities and towns and sometimes London, but rarely penetrated to the UK's industrial heartlands. Night-time operations were not much more damaging. Although airborne interception radar had become much more effective, the use by the Germans of light and fast aircraft such as the Focke-Wulf 190 A-3 and A-4 and the Messerschmitt Me 410 Hornet tested the defence to the utmost, but the destruction they caused with their light payloads was of greater nuisance than strategic value.

In addition, ADGB provided escorts to USAAF bombers on daylight raids, but, because of the short range of its aircraft, these only covered the bomber streams as far as the enemy coast, after which the American Republic P-47 Thunderbolts and North American P-51 Mustangs took over. Some of the Mosquitoes were equipped with *Serrate* radar, which allowed them to lock onto German fighters whilst escorting Bomber Command raids at night, but this role was taken over by 100 (Bomber Support) Group shortly after Hill arrived at ADGB towards the end of 1943.

From the beginning of 1944, ADGB was also heavily committed to providing support for the forthcoming invasion, with sweeps over the Continent increasing, particularly on enemy airfields, albeit that these were eclipsed in number by the equivalent operations conducted by 2TAF. These sorties were ramped up in April and May, and on D-Day itself ADGB provided air cover over the invasion fleet and the beaches. As the campaign on the ground developed, 2TAF gradually relocated to the Continent, leaving ADGB in a purely defensive role. As it happened, even before then ADGB had been put to the test in the night defence against the 'Baby Blitz', which lasted from January to June 1944, with the Luftwaffe's major focus being on London. It was executed on a much smaller scale than the Blitz of 1940/41 and, although the German aircraft were themselves more effective, they were more than matched by the Mosquitoes of ADGB, and the intruders suffered very heavy losses.

On 13 June 1944, exactly a week after the D-Day landings, the first V-1 flying bomb to be launched against the UK exploded on hitting the ground near Gravesend. The existence of these weapons had been known to the British for a long time through *Ultra* and other intelligence sources and steps had already been taken to counter them, notably the bombing of their launch sites, albeit that this was only partially successful. In the knowledge that the V-1 would be launched from the Pas-de-Calais and would be aimed primarily at London, the guns of AA Command were concentrated in mobile batteries in the Maidstone-Tonbridge area of Kent, with ADGB patrolling

188   Churchill's Eagles

over the country between there and the coast. The results were initially poor, especially for the guns. Between them Hill and Pile came up with a new strategy, which involved the guns being transferred to fixed sites near the coast and allowed priority from six miles out to sea to four miles inland in what was called the 'Diver Belt'. Fighters patrolled on either side and there was a balloon belt close to London. The Americans lent to AA Command both their new SCR 544 AA radar sets and VT 98 proximity fuses, which led to much improved results.

All this had happened very quickly, without any reference to Leigh-Mallory at the Allied Tactical Air Force or to the Air Ministry, and the latter was furious when it heard of this fait accompli. Hill was told in no uncertain terms that, even though the idea had originated with AA Command, because he had agreed to it so readily he had exceeded his powers and that, if the new strategy failed, it was likely to have a dire effect on his career prospects. In fact, after a somewhat stuttering start, it proved to be highly successful, with the guns taking the major share of the destruction of the V-1s, but AGDB was also put in a better position to intercept those flying bombs that escaped the 'Diver Belt'. The situation was improved by the arrival in ADGB of a few squadrons of Hawker Tempests which, with a top speed of 435mph at low altitude, were more than a match for their prey. Hill, who still enjoyed flying immensely, took up a Tempest himself to test its capabilities and managed to fire at, albeit not to destroy, one of the flying bombs. By early September, with the V-1 sites overrun by 21st Army Group, the initial crisis was over and the Air Ministry was good enough to congratulate Hill.

The V-1 threat, however, was by no means at an end. Although the South-East of England was no longer so vulnerable, the use of aircraft to carry flying bombs and launch them over the North Sea threatened London from the east and north-east, as well as the Midlands and the North of England. The guns from the 'Diver Belt' were uprooted and transferred to the 'Diver Box' on the Thames Estuary, the 'Diver Strip' along the coast of East Anglia and later to the 'Diver Fringe' even further north.

On 15 October 1944, ADGB became Fighter Command again. This was appropriate as more and more offensive operations took place over the Continent, attacking the launch sites of both the V-I and the V-2, the missiles of the latter being invulnerable in flight to both aircraft and guns, and escorting bombers both by day and by night, made easier by the introduction of Mustangs to squadrons in greater numbers. However, the command also continued to carry out its traditional role against the relatively infrequent Luftwaffe attacks on the UK.

Hill stepped down as AOC-in-C exactly a week after VE-Day, to be appointed Air Member for Training with a seat on the Air Council. Training had involved a vast commitment for the RAF throughout the war but now had to be scaled down very significantly. The Commonwealth Air Training Plan, which had trained the majority of aircrew for most of the war, was formally wound up in March 1945, by which time it was clear that there would be a surplus of aircrew, although a skeleton staff and some airfields were temporarily retained. The distinction between elementary and service flying training schools was abolished, with a return to the pre-war model of 'all-through' training. Training Command had been split into Flying Training Command and Technical Training Command in May 1940, and this structure, which had been most successful, was to remain in place for more than twenty years.

In addition to his duties as Air Member for Training, Hill served as the chairman of a committee on the technical branch of the RAF, a role for which his past service had made him particularly well suited. The committee concluded that the technical branch should be retained as a separate entity on a par with the operational and administrative branches and that this should be recognized by a new position on the Air Council, the Air Member for Technical Services. Once again, Hill's background made him a suitable candidate for this appointment, which he took up on 12 December 1946, with promotion to air chief marshal in the following month.

Hill retired from the RAF in July 1948 and was elected as Rector of the Imperial College of Science and Technology in the University of London. Coming into the academic world so late in life proved not to be a problem, as he had a deep practical understanding of technology and was able to contribute this to the purely academic side of the curriculum. He presided over the post-war expansion of the college with great success and in 1953 was elected Vice-Chancellor of the University of London. Sadly, his health failed him in the following year and he was compelled to step down, dying shortly afterwards.

Within the higher ranks of the RAF, Hill was one of the few genuine polymaths, whose understanding of complex technical issues was as great as his capacity for command and his aptitude in administration. A quiet, even shy man who never threw his weight around, whilst at the same time remaining highly determined, he was much liked and well respected both by his superiors, who were able to rely on him implicitly, and by his juniors, who knew that they would never be asked to do anything which he could not do himself.

190   Churchill's Eagles

Air Marshal (later Air Chief Marshal Sir) Leslie Hollinghurst GBE, KCB, DFC (1895–1957)

Although only a tiny minority of senior Allied airmen, including Arthur **Harris** and some of his American colleagues, believed that the war could be won by air bombardment alone, it was abundantly clear to all that air superiority was vital for the prosecution of a successful land campaign. This had been proved in North Africa and Italy, and by the summer of 1944 it was also true in North-West Europe. From 6 June onwards the Allied ground campaign in the latter theatre could always rely on effective support from the air, but this superiority also permitted the deployment of airborne forces who either parachuted onto the battlefield or landed there in gliders. The RAF senior officer who was most closely associated with the British element of airborne operations was Leslie **Hollinghurst**.

Hollinghurst enlisted in the Royal Engineers as a sapper shortly after the outbreak of the Great War and served as such in the Gallipoli campaign. Having been evacuated to Egypt in January 1916, he was commissioned into the Middlesex Regiment in time to embark for Salonika, where he was wounded in the thigh and shipped back to Egypt again. He was accepted for transfer to the RFC and learnt to fly there, returning by ship to the UK in the spring of 1917. After a brief course at the Central Flying School and a short period as a test pilot, in April 1918 he arrived in France, where in 87 Squadron he flew the highly effective Sopwith Dolphin and in which, after eleven confirmed victories, he was awarded a DFC.

Following the Armistice, Hollinghurst served as a flight commander in 79 Squadron in Germany as part of the Army of Occupation. He was then posted to 5 Squadron, flying Bristol Fighters on the North-West Frontier of India during a relatively peaceful period, and was awarded a permanent commission in December 1919. He returned to the UK and in the spring of 1922 was posted as Adjutant of the Boys' Wing at Cranwell. The purpose of the Boys' Wing was to train teenage mechanics to serve in the RAF's technical trades. It had originally been Lord Trenchard's intention that these apprentices should be taught at a dedicated facility at RAF Halton, but Halton was not ready to accept them for another two years.

Hollinghurst was selected to attend the RAF Staff College course at Andover in May 1924. Among his fellow students were Norman **Bottomley** and Jack **Slessor**, whilst Wilfrid **Freeman** and Guy **Garrod** were on the Directing Staff under Robert Brooke-Popham as Commandant. An inevitable spell as a staff officer, in his case at Inland Area, which was largely responsible for training, was followed by a posting in April 1927 to China as a flight commander in 2 Squadron, part of the Shanghai Defence Force. This came at a period of unrest in China, during which the British Concession in Hankow was briefly occupied by Nationalist forces. Hollinghurst was only there for a short while, returning to the UK and a posting as a flight commander in 26 Squadron, flying the Armstrong Whitworth Atlas in an army co-operation role.

In May 1929 Hollinghurst was promoted to squadron leader and initially given command of 1 Coast Defence Co-operation Flight, the part of the Armament and Gunnery School which provided the aircraft to tow targets for the gun batteries. He was then posted back to India, initially on the air staff at 1 (Indian) Group, based at Peshawar in the North-West Frontier Province. This was at the time of the Red Shirt Rebellion by the Afridi tribe, but the RAF contribution was relatively modest in a revolt which was largely put down by the establishment of a secure road system for the troops on the ground. In November 1932 Hollinghurst was appointed Commanding Officer of 20 Squadron, which was in the course of converting from the Bristol Fighter to the general purpose Westland Wapiti, a rugged and reliable aircraft with a bomb load of up to 520lbs. In July 1933 another tribe, the Mohmands, began to cause trouble and a strong column of troops was deployed against them, commanded by Brigadier C. J. E. (later Field Marshal Sir Claude) Auchinleck. 20 Squadron was the only unit of the RAF involved, providing valuable support from the air.

Hollinghurst returned to the UK in 1935 to take up an appointment on the Directing Staff of the RAF Staff College, where Philip **Joubert** was now the Commandant. He remained there until the end of 1937, following which he became a student at the Imperial Defence College, where the Commandant was Arthur **Longmore**. Having graduated, he took up his first ever appointment at the Air Ministry, as Deputy Director of Peace Organisation on 1 January 1939. Just over eight months later it became clear that his job was redundant and, having by that time evidently developed a particular talent, he became successively Deputy Director of Organisation, Director of Organisation and then Director-General of Organisation, reporting directly to Christopher *Courtenay*, the Air Member for Supply and Organisation. These were hugely important, but also very demanding appointments as the RAF both moved onto a war footing and expanded dramatically. Hollinghurst was highly valued for his administrative talent and might well have remained at the Air Ministry until the end of the war, as did Courtenay. However, he was determined to get an appointment to a

192   Churchill's Eagles

fighting formation and was rewarded in July 1943 when he became AOC 9 Group.

9 Group was the last to be formed in Fighter Command, in August 1940 when the Battle of Britain began in earnest. Its creation proved necessary once it became clear that the task allocated to 12 Group was simply too great, effectively the defence not only of London from the north-east, and indeed from the south and south-east in support of 11 Group, but also of the East and West Midlands and the industrial cities of Yorkshire and Lancashire. The western half of 12 Group's area was thus hived off into the new group, along with North Wales. By some way the most important city to be defended was Liverpool, a major target for the Luftwaffe as the main terminal for Atlantic convoys and the site of some of the largest docks in the UK. However, Birmingham, Manchester and the large industrial areas around them were also covered. The group was small in size, however, relative to 10, 11 and 12 Groups, and never comprised more than a dozen active fighter squadrons, which from the autumn of 1940 onwards included night fighter units equipped with Bristol Beaufighters. It did, however, also incorporate a number of other units. By the time of Hollinghurst's arrival these included all those Operational Training Units which had previously formed 81 Group, and it thus had a vitally important training function.

9 Group also included the Merchant Ship Fighter Unit, which provided the aircraft and crews to man the Catapult Aircraft Merchant Ships. Pending the introduction of escort aircraft carriers, these were a stop-gap response to the intrusions of high-flying Focke-Wulf FW200 Condors, which located convoys for the waiting U-boats. The CAMS were each provided with a catapult to launch a Hawker Hurricane to attack the Condor, although the fighters were subsequently forced to ditch in the sea, their pilots having to hope fervently that they would be picked up by a Royal Navy escort.

The AOC-in-C Fighter Command was Trafford **Leigh-Mallory**, with whom Hollinghurst built a good relationship. In November 1943 Leigh-Mallory moved to become C-in-C of the Allied Expeditionary Air Force (AEAF) in preparation for the invasion of North-West Europe. As he did so he selected Hollinghurst to become the AOC of a new formation, 38 Group, which would have a unique role in the overall order of battle. The group was placed for the time being under the direct control of AEAF. Although in January 1944 it would revert theoretically to Air Defence of Great Britain, as Fighter Command had been renamed, in practice it would always remain very separate.

38 Group had its origins in 38 Wing, which had been formed in January 1942 to provide air transport for the relatively newly formed Airborne Forces, which consisted at that time of 1 Parachute Brigade and 1 Airlanding Brigade Group. The first commander was Group Captain Sir Nigel Norman, a remarkable RAuxAF officer who had formed Airwork Services in the inter-war years and who owned Heston Aerodrome. Norman's association with the Airborne Forces went back to their inception, when he had commanded the Central Landing Establishment, which provided parachute training for the paratroopers. He had also distinguished himself as commander of the RAF element of the Bruneval Raid, in which parachutists had seized a new German radar from a site on the French coast and been successfully evacuated by sea. He was particularly close to Major General Frederick 'Boy' Browning, who commanded the Airborne Forces. In May 1943, however, he was killed in an air crash on his way to North Africa, and the command of 38 Wing had devolved temporarily on another officer prior to the wing's elevation to group status.

Although the Airborne Forces had not had the wholehearted support of the Army hierarchy, they did have the powerful backing of both General Sir Alan Brooke, the Chief of the Imperial General Staff, and of General Sir Bernard Montgomery, who would be nominated at the end of 1943 as the Allied Land Commander for the forthcoming invasion. Leigh-Mallory was also broadly supportive and was committed to fulfilling the RAF's role in their deployment on active service. 38 Group was thus initially composed of nine squadrons, one of Handley Page Halifaxes and four of Short Stirlings, both of which had served initially as heavy bombers but which were now also being used for other purposes, and four of Armstrong Whitworth Albemarles, twin-engined aircraft which had been designed as medium bombers but were now all employed as transports and glider tugs.

Hollinghurst established his HQ at RAF Netheravon, close both to the HQ of Major General Richard Gale, General Officer Commanding 6 Airborne Division, which would provide the Airborne Forces element in the forthcoming invasion, and to that part of Browning's HQ which was not situated in London. Alongside HQ 38 Group was also to be found the HQ of Brigadier G. J. S. Chatterton, Commander Glider Pilots. The glider pilots and their gliders were divided into two wings, with one glider crew for each tug aircraft. The airmen and the soldiers trained together throughout the summer and autumn of 1943, with numerous exercises taking place for each to familiarize themselves with and develop confidence in the other. This worked well, so much so that, in a exercise carried out by one of the Parachute

194   Churchill's Eagles

Brigades and fifteen Albemarles in front of an audience of several thousand soldiers, the brigadier in command, who was first out of the leading aircraft, landed right on top of the smoke candle acting as the marker for the drop!

In the spring of 1944 38 Group, with the arrival of one more Halifax unit, had increased in size to ten squadrons, based at stations in Oxfordshire, Gloucestershire, Wiltshire and Dorset. It was realized at a very early stage that the group alone would not be large enough to carry the whole of 6 Airborne Division into action in Normandy. In January 1944, therefore, 46 Group was formed within Transport Command to be available to carry out major airborne operations alongside 38 Group. It was composed of five squadrons of Douglas C-47 Dakotas and commanded by Air Commodore A. L. Fiddament. Whenever it was needed by Airborne Forces it would come under Hollinghurst's overall command, but otherwise it would continue to carry out its normal duties, which were air supply and casualty evacuation. It was located at stations in the same geographical area as 38 Group.

At 23.03 hours on 5 June 1944 two Albemarles carrying some of the first troops to land in France, the pathfinders of 22nd Independent Parachute Company, took off from RAF Harwell south of Oxford. With one of them carrying Hollinghurst as a passenger, they arrived over the designated drop zone precisely at 00.20 hours on D-Day. At the same time the three gliders carrying the *coup de main* party tasked to capture and hold what would become known as Pegasus Bridge came into land. It was the beginning of a day of mixed fortunes, not only for the British Airborne Forces, but for their comrades in 82 and 101 Airborne Divisions of the US Army and all those landing from the sea, but at its end the majority would be firmly established on French soil. Leigh-Mallory had been particularly nervous about the US element of the airborne assault and had tried to persuade Eisenhower and Montgomery to cancel it. He was overruled and, despite a very wide dispersion of the American paratroopers, most of their objectives were taken, as were those of 6 Airborne Division, whilst the seizure of Pegasus Bridge had been a textbook operation.

The next two months for 38 Group provided a combination of routine air supply and cancelled operations. The latter included the capture of St Malo to enable an advance into Brittany, the capture of the Quiberon Bay area, a landing in the Paris-Orleans Gap, the seizure of a bridgehead over the River Eure at Tournai and the blocking of the Aachen-Maastricht Gap. One by one they and others were overtaken by the rapid advance of the Allied armies following the destruction of the German forces in the Falaise Pocket. In early September, however, the Germans managed to create both a more stable defensive line along the Meuse-Escaut Canal and a strong defensive pocket on the south bank of the Scheldt, and Montgomery's 21st Army Group was brought to a halt.

Montgomery, supported by Browning, was convinced that the only way to end the war in 1944 was by a major airborne and ground attack by 21st Army Group, bolstered by US formations, through the Netherlands and across the Rhine into the North German plain. This plan was opposed by his American opposite number, General Bradley, but gained some support from the Supreme Allied Commander, General Eisenhower. Browning was given the command of 1 Airborne Corps, composed of 1 Airborne Division, 82 US Airborne Division, 101 US Airborne Division and the Polish Parachute Brigade, with 52 (Lowland) Division in reserve. The plan was to drop airborne forces along a corridor, taking all the canal and river bridges from the Meuse-Escaut Canal northwards. Three major rivers had to be crossed, the Maas at Wesel and the Waal at Nijmegen by the two American divisions and the Lower Rhine at Arnhem by 1 Airborne. 38 Group and 46 Group would fly in the last of these. During the operation Hollinghurst would be based alongside Major General Paul L. Williams of IX US Troop Carrier Command at the Troop Carrier Command Post, under the overall control of Lieutenant General Lewis H. Brereton, Commanding General of the First Allied Airborne Army.

The major difference between Operation MARKET GARDEN and its predecessors, notably the airborne landings in Normandy, was that the landings would take place in daylight. In order to carry in as many paratroopers and glider infantry as possible on the first day, Browning asked that there should be two lifts, one in the early hours of the morning, the other in the early evening. Hollinghurst was quite amenable to this, but Browning's request was turned down by Brereton on the advice of Williams, who believed both that the aircraft would need servicing and that their crews would be too tired. Hollinghurst was, however, opposed to another request by Browning, to drop 1 Airborne Division close to the south end of the Arnhem road bridge, which they would then take by surprise. Hollinghurst's decision was based on intelligence, later proved to be faulty, which identified strong AA positions in the area and also on Deelen airfield, over which the returning aircraft would have to turn. Moreover, the ground there was considered unsuitable for glider landings. He therefore insisted that the drops should take place on heathland some six to eight miles from the bridge.

The initial drops and glider landings of 1 Airborne Division on 16 September went very well, observed by Hollinghurst, who was flying as a passenger in a Stirling glider tug. One battalion of airborne troops penetrated into Arnhem itself and captured the north end of the road bridge. Thereafter flying conditions deteriorated, both because of the increasing German defences and because of the weather, which turned to fog in England. Both 38 and 46 Group continued to bring in reinforcements, notably the much-delayed Polish Parachute Brigade, and to supply the men on the ground, but the latter was made very difficult by the failure of almost all radio communication from 1 Airborne Division and by increasing German AA defences. The guns, in spite of the expert flying and gallantry of the aircrews, caused many losses of aircraft, including the Dakota piloted by Flight Lieutenant David Lord of 271 Squadron in 46 Group who was posthumously awarded the Victoria Cross.

With the bridge retaken by the Germans and the situation within 1 Airborne's shrinking perimeter at Oosterbeek desperate, the decision was taken to evacuate the remnants on the night of 25/26 September. Although the Allies continued to hold Nijmegen, they were effectively in a cul-de-sac, unable to cross the Lower Rhine. This would be the last major airborne operation for nearly six months, but by the end of the first week of November Hollinghurst was immersed in another appointment thousands of miles away.

Between the two world wars India and South-East Asia had been the poor relations of the RAF, sparsely equipped with obsolete or underperforming aircraft. The opening of hostilities by the Japanese in December 1941 came as a great shock, and the relatively few squadrons based in Singapore, Malaya and Burma proved to be no match for modern Japanese fighters. From such inauspicious beginnings, however, the air forces of both Great Britain and the USA had been vastly enlarged by the summer of 1944 and were able to provide excellent support to the ground forces during the attempted Japanese invasion of India via the Arakan and the towns of Imphal and Kohima.

Almost from the outset the Allied air forces in the region had been commanded by Air Chief Marshal Sir Richard **Peirse**, who became the AOC-in-C Air Forces in India in March 1942 and the C-in-C Air Command South-East Asia in November 1943. On 1 June 1944 all the formations and units in contact with the enemy were placed under Eastern Air Command, commanded by Major General George E. Stratemeyer of the USAAF. The subordinate formations consisted of the Strategic Air Force, bombing Japanese targets not only in Burma, but in China as well; the 3rd Tactical

Air Force, which provided direct fighter-bomber support to the ground forces; and Troop Carrier Command, which was responsible for transport and supply, not only within the immediate theatre, but also over 'the Hump' to Chungking, the capital of the unoccupied part of China.

In November 1943 Admiral Lord Louis Mountbatten was appointed Supreme Allied Commander South-East Asia. Initially his HQ was situated in New Delhi, but he found the atmosphere in the capital not conducive to the independent exercise of his command and, in April 1944, he moved it to Kandy in Ceylon. He insisted that his three service commanders-in-chief should follow him, but both Peirse and his army counterpart, Lieutenant General Sir Oliver Leese, considered that they would then be too far away from the action, Peirse initially sending his deputy, Guy **Garrod**, to represent him there, along with the large majority of the administrative staff under AVM Victor *Goddard*. In November 1944 Peirse was sent back to the UK on retirement as a result of his affair with the wife of the C-in-C India, General Sir Claude Auchinleck. Garrod was appointed Acting C-in-C and kept his base in Kandy, pending the appointment of a permanent replacement, Keith **Park**.

The relocation of the administrative element of Air HQ South-East Asia had thrown up a number of other problems, linked to the close relationships which it had established with the providers of many services in India, which was effectively the base on which the fighting formations heavily depended. Hollinghurst was appointed the Air Officer Commanding Base Area, South-East Asia, with his HQ in New Delhi and his remit covering all administrative activity in India and also training, as well as liaison with the Government of India, which effectively provided the extensive facilities in that country. The need for such a role was questioned in London, but a visit by Christopher Courtenay, Hollinghurst's former superior and still the AMSO, confirmed that it was vitally important.

It was actually Courtenay's job to which Hollinghurst succeeded shortly after the surrender of Japan in September 1945. It was an important role as the RAF was rapidly reduced in size. Three years later he was appointed Inspector-General RAF, responsible for the inspection of airfields and other establishments around the world, on which reports were written with the aim of maintaining the highest levels of efficiency. He returned to the Air Council in October 1949 as Air Member for Personnel, dealing with all aspects of employment from recruitment to discharge. He retired on 27 December 1952, by that time an air chief marshal.

198   Churchill's Eagles

Hollinghurst never married, but he had an active retirement, involving himself, amongst other things, with the Boy Scout movement. He was called upon twice to investigate and write reports on certain issues affecting the RAF, notably its administration. He died shortly after returning from attending the D-Day anniversary celebrations in 1971, twenty-seven years after he had accompanied the vanguard of the invading army to France.

Hollinghurst had a highly distinguished career in the RAF, albeit that it was, for the most part, one with a relatively low profile. His talent for organization and administration were widely recognized, but it was his association with the Airborne Forces, particularly in the run up to the invasion of North-West Europe and later in Operation MARKET GARDEN, for which he will be best remembered.

Air Chief Marshal Sir Philip Joubert de la Ferté KCB, CMG, DSO (1887–1965)

In the words of Winston Churchill, 'The only thing that ever really frightened me during the war was the U-boat menace.' The Battle of the Atlantic lasted throughout the conflict, although by 1945 the threat from German submarines had become relatively modest. The nadir of the Allies' fortunes in the Atlantic came in the early months of 1943, when shipping losses were being incurred at an appalling rate. The AOC-in-C of Coastal Command at the beginning of that year was Philip **Joubert** de la Ferté, serving in the role for the second time in his career and only too aware of the deficiencies of his own forces and their lack of success in dealing with the U-boats. In fact this proved to be the darkest hour of the command, as a number of technical developments and an increase in both the number and capabilities of the command's aircraft, combined with the introduction of escort carriers for convoys and the breaking of the German Navy codes, were to deliver what was effectively a great victory before the middle of the year. Although it was his successor who would reap the rewards, much of Coastal Command's new capabilities had actually been put in place by Joubert.

Joubert was commissioned into the Royal Engineers from the Royal Military Academy in Woolwich in 1907, but he volunteered to join the newly formed Royal Flying Corps in 1913, having learnt to fly at his own expense. A brief posting to 2 Squadron was followed by another to 3 Squadron, commanded by Robert *Brooke-Popham*, at Netheravon. Three days after the declaration of war on Germany and Austria he became a flight commander, serving on what was shortly to become the Western Front and flying a strange mixture of British and French aircraft. The operations were initially of a reconnaissance nature, but artillery spotting very quickly became an important feature.

In May 1915 Joubert, by now promoted to major, was given command of 15 Squadron in the UK, and three months later succeeded Geoffrey Salmond in command of 1 Squadron in France. Three months after that he fell ill and was invalided back to the UK: it was early in the New Year before he was fit to return to duty. In July 1916 he succeeded Salmond once again, but this time in Egypt with promotion to lieutenant colonel in command of 5 Wing, which carried out reconnaissance flights over the Turkish forces which the British were gradually pushing back in their advance towards Palestine. He returned to the UK in early 1917, initially to a training wing and then back to France in command of first 21 Wing and then 14 Wing.

At the end of 1917 14 Wing became the core component of 6 Group in what was to become the Royal Air Force on 1 April 1918. The group, of which Joubert was appointed in overall command as a temporary colonel, was formed to support the British ground force dispatched to North-East Italy to prop up the Italians, who had recently suffered a disaster at Caporetto. Fighting against German and Austrian pilots on the other side was intense but, now equipped with modern aircraft such as the Sopwith Camel, the RAF gradually prevailed and by the time of the Armistice on 11 November 1918 was in almost full control of the air.

Joubert emerged from the Great War with a CMG, a DSO and five mentions in despatches. He decided to remain in the RAF and in early 1920 was selected to attend the second post-war course at the Army Staff College in Camberley. It was doubtless on the strength of this that, after a year in command of a motor transport depot, he was appointed to the Directing Staff on the first course at the new RAF Staff College. This was a creation of the Chief of the Air Staff, Air Chief Marshal Sir Hugh Trenchard, who saw it as a key component of a service which was constantly under threat of absorption into either or both of the British Army and the Royal Navy. The Commandant was Brooke-Popham and Joubert's fellow instructors included Wilfred **Freeman** and Bertine *Sutton*.

To his dismay, Joubert was only at the Staff College for the year of its first course, being appointed in April 1923 to the position of Deputy Director of Personnel, and subsequently Deputy Director of Manning, at the Air Ministry. After going on half-pay at the end of 1925 and into 1926, he was appointed chief staff officer to Sir John Salmond at HQ Fighting Area, part of Air Defence of Great Britain, before being posted, initially much against

200   Churchill's Eagles

his wishes, as an instructor at the newly opened Imperial Defence College. The contacts which he made there, however, turned out to be invaluable. The Chief Instructor was a future field marshal, John Dill, and the students included another, Alan Brooke, as well as John Tovey, a future admiral of the fleet, and three future marshals of the RAF, Charles **Portal**, Arthur **Tedder** and Sholto **Douglas**. The instructors were joined on the 1928 course by another future admiral of the fleet, James Somerville.

Joubert was clearly valued as an instructor, since in September 1930, after a short spell as AOC 23 Group, itself focused entirely on training, he returned to Andover as Commandant of the RAF Staff College. Although he enjoyed his term of appointment, he feared that he was in danger of being typecast, so it was with some relief that he took up his next post in January 1934, once again at Fighting Area, but this time as its AOC. Having had a history of employment on fighters for much of the Great War, he was interested to see how this arm of the service had developed. He was disappointed to find that his HQ near Uxbridge was poorly ventilated, badly equipped and thus not fit for purpose: moreover, there was no direct communication with his squadrons. All contact, other than a physical visit, had to go through the Post Office telephone network, resulting in quite unacceptable delays. At the HQ itself there was no semblance of the plotting of aircraft movements. The first priority was therefore to acquire dedicated phone lines to each sector, the second to redesign the Operations Room, which was provided with a gallery from which the AOC could view the progress of battle on the table below. Similar arrangements were made for each of the sectors' HQs. With the help of a number of brilliant scientists led by Sir Henry Tizard, the first steps were also taken towards the development of radar as an early warning and tracking system.

The aircraft deployed by Fighting Area were still all bi-planes. These included the elegant Hawker Fury, with a top speed of just over 220mph, and the slightly faster Gloster Gauntlet, both of which entered service under Joubert, but it was already recognized that monoplanes would soon be the order of the day, with a much greater firepower than the two machine guns in the noses of the bi-planes and a significant increase in performance.

Towards the end of Joubert's tour at Fighting Area, ADGB was wound up and separate commands – Fighter, Bomber and Coastal – were created. Joubert served initially as AOC 11 Group, much the largest group in Fighter Command, with responsibility for the defence of London and the South-East. On 1 September 1936, however, after less than two months in the post, he was appointed AOC-in-C of Coastal Command, with his HQ at Lee-on-

Solent, close to Portsmouth, the largest British naval base. The command's two groups, 16 and 17, were also based there, although some squadrons were located close to the Royal Navy's other main bases, at Devonport and Chatham. Notwithstanding the fact that the Royal Navy was still agitating for operational and administrative control of both the Fleet Air Arm, a move which would be successful, and Coastal Command, one which which would not, Joubert developed very good relationships with his naval counterparts. In particular, he proposed a combined headquarters, which was agreed to by his opposite number and rapidly implemented.

Coastal Command was very much the Cinderella of the RAF's front-line formations in the UK, with priority for both aircraft and airfields going to Bomber and Fighter Commands. Anti-submarine warfare was given a very low priority due to the Navy's belief that it could handle this by itself, the focus instead being on the general protection of shipping, particularly in the North Sea, and the prevention of attacks on British ports. At the time of its formation Coastal Command deployed only five squadrons, four of which were equipped with flying boats and one with bi-plane torpedo bombers, and there was only a modest increment during Joubert's term as AOC-in-C. Joubert was also informed by the Air Ministry that the command's other, and possibly more significant, role would be to support Bomber Command in any strategic air offensive.

Joubert served at Coastal Command for a year, the most interesting part of which was a round trip by flying boat from Calshot via Bordeaux, Toulon, Malta, Gibraltar and Lisbon. In September 1937, however, he was appointed AOC Air Forces in India. If Coastal Command had been a Cinderella, then the RAF in India was an even poorer relation. Its aircraft were general purpose bi-planes such as the Westland Wapiti and Hawker Hart and its major purpose was to support operations by the Army against rebellious tribes on the North-West Frontier. During Joubert's tenure these were limited to a number of relatively minor actions in Waziristan involving eight squadrons.

It was recognized that resources in India were poor, not only for the RAF, but also for the very much larger Army in India, and a commission was dispatched from the UK under the chairmanship of Admiral of the Fleet Lord Chatfield, with Air Marshal Christopher *Courtenay* as the RAF member, to determine ways of addressing this. The commission took evidence from all the most senior service officers in the country, including Joubert, as well as from officials of the Government of India. Joubert then became a member of the team which travelled in the other direction to give

202   Churchill's Eagles

further evidence to a War Office Committee. The result was a significant additional grant to the Government of India, and in particular, the arrival of ninety-six Bristol Blenheims for the RAF, one of them flown from the UK by Joubert himself. He also travelled widely within India and to Malaya, Singapore and Thailand.

Joubert returned to the UK in early 1940 and was delighted to be told that he had been appointed to represent the RAF on all matters relating to the development of radar, a subject which had first captured his interest whilst AOC of the Fighting Area, but he was initially to discover that he had no real authority and that others at the Air Ministry were already deeply involved. In due course, however, it became clear that, whilst he had little say in technical development, he would be deeply concerned with practical implementation, working closely with Robert Watson-Watt, who had led the development of the Chain Home radar system which would be so vital to success in the Battle of Britain. Now given the title of Assistant Chief of the Air Staff (Radio), Joubert also became involved in the work taking place on airborne interception radar and on the development of new navigational systems, later named *Gee* and *Oboe*, for the RAF's bombers.

In June 1941 Joubert succeeded the man who had followed him at Coastal Command, Air Marshal Sir Frederick **Bowhill**. The command was in a very different position to the one which he had bequeathed to Bowhill. More effective aircraft had replaced most of those in service in 1937, notably the Bristol Beaufort as a torpedo bomber, the Armstrong Whitworth Whitley as a general reconnaissance bomber and the highly capable Vickers Wellington in the principal anti-submarine role, whilst newly built Short Sunderlands had replaced the last of old bi-plane flying boats. Moreover, a number of American aircraft had been introduced, notably the Lockheed Hudson, which had been designed to British specifications as a short-range anti-submarine patrol aircraft, and the Consolidated Catalina flying boat, which complemented the Sunderland in convoy protection and anti-submarine duties. The number of groups had increased, with 15 Group situated alongside the Naval C-in-C Western Approaches in Liverpool, 16 Group at Gillingham in Kent focused on the English Channel and the southern part of the North Sea, 17 Group responsible for all training and based in Edinburgh, 18 Group at Rosyth, looking after the northern part of the North Sea and the coast of Norway, and 19 Group in Plymouth with responsibility for the South-Western Approaches and the Bay of Biscay. There were also separate HQs in Iceland and Gibraltar.

By this time it was quite clear that the Royal Navy, which had initially been so certain that it would have the measure of the U-boats, was incapable of providing anything close to full protection to convoys on its own. This was not least because of the very limited number of escort vessels at this stage of the war, before the Americans joined the conflict. Coastal Command would thus play a major role in anti-submarine warfare for as long as the war lasted. The command was, however, itself still limited in its capabilities by the relatively short range of its aircraft, the tactics which it had adopted and the relatively poor performance of the first version of air to surface vessel radar ('ASV'). In particular, it proved impossible to deliver effective cover to the convoys whilst they traversed the 'Atlantic Gap', a huge area of sea midway between Newfoundland and Iceland. Almost all of the losses to convoys during Joubert's first six months in command were incurred there and in the Eastern Atlantic down as far as Sierra Leone in West Africa.

Whilst at the Air Ministry as ACIGS (Radio), Joubert had been responsible for choosing one of the two systems designed to be carried underneath an aircraft to light up the sea below at night. This system was called Turbinlight, and the reason for its selection was the intensity of the illumination it provided. However, it was deficient in other respects, and after re-joining Coastal Command, Joubert quickly realized that its competitor, the Leigh Light, was much more effective. He ordered a small number of Wellingtons to be equipped with this device, which exceeded even his own expectations. The impact came not only with sinkings as a result of the Leigh Light's operation, but also with the decision by the Germans that U-boats would now have to cross the Bay of Biscay under water, thereby reducing the time spent in their selected operational area.

The war against the U-boats was the most prominent of Coastal Command's activities, but there were others, most notably the offensive by torpedo- and bomb-carrying aircraft against German coastal shipping and ports. In addition, the command had two other responsibilities. The first was the Photographic Reconnaissance Unit based at RAF Benson which, together with the related Photographic Interpretation Unit, also served all the other home-based commands and most notably Bomber Command. Employing unarmed Spitfires and Mosquitoes, whose pilots used height and speed to avoid detection and interception, it carried out highly valuable work, particularly on reconnoitring target areas and assessing the damage done on raids, but also on reporting back on weather conditions in planned operational areas. The second was the Air-Sea Rescue Service, whose high-speed launches and aircraft, notably the Supermarine Walrus flying boat, picked up thousands of aircrew out of the sea, whilst other aircraft dropped supplies, life rafts and even lifeboats.

The end of 1941 and the first half of 1942 provided some respite to Coastal Command, following the declaration of war by Germany on the United States. Because the Americans had not fully appreciated the value of convoys, and because they had few ships specifically designed as escorts and had not imposed blackouts on their coastal cities, the U-boats were able to enjoy their second 'Happy Time', the first having been immediately after the Fall of France, when submarine bases were established on the French coast, providing easy access to the Atlantic. The submarines now created havoc on the Eastern Seaboard of the USA, where their targets were frequently silhouetted against brilliant illuminations, as well as in the Caribbean and off the east coast of South America. Moreover, unknown to the British, the Germans had cracked the Royal Navy's radio codes and were able to read their opponents' signals, whilst at the same time adding a fourth wheel to their own Enigma machine, which left the codebreakers at Bletchley Park completely blind.

It did not help Joubert that he had been denied long-range aircraft, notably the Consolidated Liberator, whilst Arthur Harris at Bomber Command remained adamant that all the British-made heavy bombers should go to Bomber Command and was strongly supported in this by the CAS, Charles **Portal**. The Air Ministry was overwhelmingly 'bomber-minded', believing that the progressive destruction of German cities was the quickest, if not the only route to winning the War. The Admiralty, supported strongly by Joubert, could point out as often as it liked that the sinking of shipping was in danger of increasing to such a rate that the loss of essential cargoes, including fuel for the bombers, would result in the war being lost, but this argument fell on deaf ears. All that Joubert could obtain were more Whitleys, lacking either the range or the bomb capacity which he required. In the meantime, ASV III, the latest radar system, was denied to Coastal Command in a quantity which would make a significant impact, not least because its magnetron component was the same as that fitted in the heavy bombers' H2S ground facing radar system.

All this was to change early in 1943, but only after Joubert had moved on to his next appointment. In the meantime, instead of handing over to his relief, John **Slessor**, in November 1942, he was to stay on at Coastal Command until 10 February 1943, as Slessor was required by Portal to go first to the United States to participate in the negotiations on Lend-Lease aircraft and then, with these successfully concluded, to attend the Casablanca

Conference. It was at Casablanca that the highest priority was accorded to the campaign against the U-boats, giving Slessor everything that Joubert had asked for and not received, in terms of both capable aircraft and new technology. Moreover, it was only a few months later that the German Navy Enigma code was cracked again with the breaking of the four-wheel key by the codebreakers at Bletchley Park, leading to hugely adverse consequences for the U-boats later that year, although they remained a threat until the end of the war.

Joubert's new appointment was as an Inspector-General RAF, one of two. The role had been created in 1935, with Brooke-Popham as the first incumbent, followed by other very senior officers who were close to retirement. Since April 1940 it had been held by Air Chief Marshal Sir Edgar **Ludlow-Hewitt**, but the demands of the job, which were to examine and report on the efficiency of the service at its sharp end in terms of both men and materiel, were such that an additional Inspector-General was appointed, Sir William *Mitchell* from May 1940 to June 1941, succeeded by Sir Arthur **Longmore** from then until he was relieved by Joubert. The Inspectors-General were granted access to any facility, particularly operational stations, and to any formation or unit which they selected, not only in the UK but also overseas, and they reported back to the Air Ministry accordingly.

Joubert had hoped to be able to observe the Allied invasion of Europe in his capacity as Inspector-General, but in September 1943 he was approached by Lord Louis Mountbatten, who had just been appointed Supreme Allied Commander South-East Asia and who asked him to join his staff in a role which at first sight seemed to be most unattractive. This was to be one of Mountbatten's Deputy Chiefs of Staff, responsible in Joubert's case specifically for Civil Affairs, Psychological Warfare, Public Relations and Information to the forces within South-East Asia Command. Mountbatten considered that these matters were sufficiently important to have a very senior officer dealing with them, notwithstanding that officer's lack of experience in any of these fields. Joubert was also put off, as were many other very senior officers, by Mountbatten's relative youth, which he felt might make for a difficult relationship. In the end, however, with winter on the way, he was swayed by thoughts of service in a warm climate.

The relationships between Joubert's various responsibilities were not immediately obvious, other than a tenuous connection between Public Relations on the one hand and information to those under Mountbatten's command on the other. The latter was achieved through the publication of a newspaper – '*SEAC*' – under Frank Owen, formerly the editor of the

206   Churchill's Eagles

Evening Standard, whilst the former involved dealing with the dissemination of news to the world at large, but most particularly to the press in the UK, the USA, China and other Allied nations. There was an even more tenuous link between Psychological Warfare, aimed directly at the Japanese and any of their Burmese or Indian supporters, and Civil Affairs, which would take initial responsibility for the government of formerly occupied territories.

SEAC was a great success, largely because Joubert and Owen insisted on its priority distribution to troops on the ground, including those on the front line, who greatly appreciated up-to-date news. Public Relations proved to be far more difficult, due in large part to scepticism and misinterpretation on the part of those, particularly in other countries, receiving information on the progress of the campaign. Civil Affairs was bedevilled by the fact that there was already a government-in-exile, which had been established in Simla after the Japanese invasion of Burma in 1942 and which attempted to set the agenda for the civil control of all Burmese territory which was liberated thereafter. As for Psychological Warfare, it was initially difficult to wage against an enemy who had his own codes of conduct and who was relatively immune to western ideas. However, it came into its own towards the end of the campaign, when the Japanese were demoralized by both their own defeats and news from other fronts, whilst it also played a major role in persuading members of the Indian National Army, soldiers from the Indian Army who had changed sides after their capture, that there was no alternative but surrender.

All of this made for a difficult job for Joubert, whose career had in no way prepared him for the decisions which needed to be taken in what became a fast-moving campaign, with implications for all his responsibilities. He nevertheless managed to discharge them to the best of his and his team's abilities. He remained in the Far East until shortly after the fall of Rangoon on 3 May 1945, when he returned to London for discussions with both the War Office and the Colonial Office. However, whilst he was there he became ill enough to be hospitalized and was unable to return. He retired from the RAF five months later.

Joubert is best known for his service as AOC-in-C of Coastal Command in 1941 and 1942, but it was his misfortune that the period of his appointment coincided with Air Staff's deep-seated commitment to the bombing campaign against Germany at the expense of all other priorities. Joubert had neither the most suitable aircraft nor the technology which enabled his successor, John Slessor, in conjunction with the Royal and United States Navies, to gain superiority over the U-boats within six months of his appointment, but he should certainly be given much of the credit for putting in place the initial building blocks for victory in the Battle of the Atlantic.

Air Chief Marshal Sir Trafford Leigh-Mallory KCB, DSO (1892–1944)

There can be few senior RAF officers who have aroused in others as strongly held opinions as Trafford **Leigh-Mallory**, both during his career and following his death in service. This is true, in particular, of the most contentious episode of his service, his leadership of 12 Group in Fighter Command during the Battle of Britain. However, he went on to attract, if not controversy, then at least sharply differing views over the remainder of his career, which was tragically cut short as he was about to take on an important command.

Leigh-Mallory volunteered to join the British Army early in the Great War, shortly after coming down from Cambridge, where he had read History and Law. He was commissioned initially into the King's Liverpool Regiment in October 1914, but was transferred almost immediately to the South Lancashire Regiment, in which he saw active service in France in the spring of 1915, before being wounded and evacuated back to England. At the beginning of 1916 he undertook pilot training at the No. 1 School of Aeronautics and, having passed out, was transferred to the RFC and posted to France, flying initially in 5 Squadron and, very shortly afterwards, in 6 Squadron. The latter was engaged in army co-operation, which would become Leigh-Mallory's speciality. He flew BE2s, engaged in reconnaissance and artillery spotting on the Western Front and, in November 1915, was made a flight commander. In May 1917 he was appointed to command 15 Squadron, which flew RE8s, and then to command 8 Squadron, this time flying Armstrong Whitworth FK8s, still very much in an army co-operation role.

In August 1919 Leigh-Mallory, by this time a squadron leader with a DSO to his name, was awarded a permanent commission in the RAF and at the end of the year was appointed as Inspector of Recruitment for the South-East Area. In February 1921 he became the Officer Commanding 2 Squadron at the School of Army Co-operation. Two years later he was posted for the first time to the Air Ministry, where he worked initially in the Directorate of Training and then the Directorate of Staff Duties. This was followed by a year at the RAF Staff College in Andover, where his instructors included Douglas **Evill** and Guy **Garrod**, with Ralph **Cochrane** and Hugh **Lloyd** among his fellow students. He was not a universally popular member of the

208   Churchill's Eagles

student body, Cochrane describing him as cocksure and tactless. On passing out he served for a year on the Air Staff at 22 (Army Co-operation) Group, before being appointed as Commandant at the School of Army Co-operation and then, in January 1930, as the RAF Instructor at the Army Staff College at Camberley.

Leigh-Mallory returned to the Air Ministry in the summer of 1931, spending most of his time there in the Department of Staff Duties, interrupted briefly in 1932 by a temporary appointment as an Air Adviser to the British delegation at the Disarmament Conference in Geneva. He then commanded 2 Flying Training School at Digby in Lincolnshire, before being posted as SASO to AVM William *Mitchell* at AHQ RAF Iraq. The RAF had been responsible for keeping the peace in that country since 1921, when Hugh Trenchard persuaded the British and Iraqi Governments that it was the most economical way of doing so. For Leigh-Mallory this might have provided the best possible practical experience of army co-operation in action, but, as it happened, for the whole of his term of appointment the country remained peaceful.

Given that Leigh-Mallory had established a reputation for himself in army co-operation, his next appointment, as AOC 12 Group in December 1937, must have come as a surprise to many, if not to himself. 12 Group formed part of Fighter Command, which was charged with the air defence of the United Kingdom, and Leigh-Mallory's experience of fighter operations was negligible. Luckily, due largely to the Munich Agreement of September 1938 and the Phoney War in 1939 and early 1940, he had adequate time to prepare. He was, moreover, always supremely self-confident.

12 Group was responsible for the defence of the industrial heartland of England, including the East and West Midlands and most of Yorkshire and Lancashire, thereby covering the most likely targets, Birmingham, Manchester, Liverpool and Leeds/Bradford. The HQ was initially at Hucknall in Nottinghamshire, with the sector stations, from south to north, at Duxford, Coltishall, Digby, Kirton-in-Lindsey and Church Fenton. To the north was 13 Group, responsible for the most northerly counties of England and the whole of Scotland and Northern Ireland. 12 Group's own distance from the Continent of Europe meant that it deployed only a small number of squadrons, unlike its neighbour in the South-East of England, 11 Group which, it was already recognized, was likely to bear the brunt of any bombing attacks on and around London.

Leigh-Mallory did not distinguish himself greatly during the pre-war air defence exercises, attracting some criticism from both the AOC-in-C of

Fighter Command, Air Chief Marshal Sir Hugh **Dowding**, and Dowding's SASO, Air Commodore Keith **Park**. Park in particular had much experience of fighters, both during the Great War and later, having notably served as Station Commander at Tangmere before becoming SASO to Dowding at his HQ near Stanmore, Bentley Priory. He was appointed AOC 11 Group in April 1940, his position as SASO Fighter Command being taken by Douglas **Evill**.

On 9 May 1940, the day before the German invasion of France and the Low Countries, 12 Group's HQ moved to Watnall, a few miles from Hucknall. For the time being there was no action over the UK, with the Luftwaffe focusing exclusively on operations over France and Belgium. However, there was a demand for aircraft from the Air Component of the British Expeditionary Force which could only be satisfied by transfers from Fighter Command, much to Downing's dismay. Both 11 and 12 Group's squadrons were directly employed over the evacuation of the BEF from Dunkirk, although most of the action was at such a height that the soldiers were unaware of it. In the immediate aftermath of the evacuation, the Luftwaffe did mount a small number of night-time operations against coastal towns in 12 Group's sector, but these were easily countered. In anticipation of heavier action ahead, Dowding decided to reduce 12 Group's area, with 13 Group taking over the most northerly sector, Church Fenton, and a new 9 Group taking over responsibility for a slice of country to the west, including Liverpool, as well as North Wales, which had thitherto been unallocated.

From early July to early August, German bombing attacks were focused on convoys and coastal targets, notably in the English Channel. Although the damage done was relatively modest, 11 Group, with responsibility for the area, suffered losses to German fighters. On 12 August, the Germans dive-bombed the radar stations on the coast, temporarily blinding 11 Group, and on the following day they began attacks on that group's airfields. The attacks widened, with an attempted assault on the north of England and south-east Scotland seen off by 13 Group, and one on the Yorkshire coast leading to the first substantive, and successful, action by 12 Group.

For the time being, however, it was 11 Group's airfields which bore the brunt of the Germans attacks, with near-crippling strikes on all of them. Park's strategy was to tackle the bombers before they were able to drop their loads. On 24 August he requested assistance from 12 Group, but none arrived in time. The reason for this was a change of tactics by the group, which was to have significant implications for the careers of not only Leigh-Mallory, but also Park and Dowding.

210   Churchill's Eagles

The squadrons in 12 Group, particularly those in the most southerly sectors, had been desperate to get into battle, and none more so than 242 Squadron at Duxford, which was right on the boundary between 11 and 12 Group. The CO was Douglas Bader, who was already a hero in the eyes of most people who knew of him, a man who, despite the loss of both his legs in a flying accident, had recovered sufficiently not only to fly again, but to do so expertly. Imbued with offensive spirit, in the early stages of the battle he seethed with frustration that his squadron and others were not being called upon. Moreover, he had developed a new concept of how the air battle should be conducted.

Bader believed that it should be possible to create havoc amongst the attackers by the use of a considerable force attacking the bombers from above, insisting that this would be more effective than throwing in squadrons one by one. He approached Leigh-Mallory, who expressed enthusiasm and sanctioned the new tactic. The 'Duxford Wing' was thus created, with Bader's own squadron augmented by 310 (Czech) Squadron, also from Duxford, and by 19 Squadron from nearby Fowlmere. The problem with this strategy, at least in Park's eyes, was that the new wing was slow to form and was only able to attack the German bombers after they had unloaded their bombs on his airfields and were on their way home. In answer to this, Bader maintained that it was better to destroy a lot of aircraft on their way back to France than a small number on their way in.

There were, however, occasions when the 'Big Wing' did work, not least at the climax of the Battle of Britain on 15 September, when the Germans launched a massive attack, requiring all Park's available squadrons to be deployed. Two days later, with no sign that the RAF was exhausted and with the weather likely to deteriorate going into autumn, the Germans postponed the invasion of the UK.

Leigh-Mallory, who despised Dowding and had no great opinion of Park, then used Bader's squadron adjutant, a Member of Parliament, to approach Churchill and to lobby, quite improperly in the eyes of Downing, for a change in tactics. Dowding and Park were summoned to a meeting at the Air Ministry on 17 October, hosted by the DCAS, Sholto **Douglas**. Cyril **Newall**, the CAS, was indisposed, but his imminent successor, Charles **Portal**, was present, although he took no part in the debate. To the astonishment of Dowding and Park, Bader was also present and, when asked to speak, gave his opinion that it was the man in the air who should make the decisions on tactics, not the controllers on the ground. There was nobody of Bader's rank and experience present from 11 Group to demolish this theory or his contention that he could get his wing into the air in six minutes, whereas it had in reality often taken three times as long, with more time spent forming up before setting off to attack the Germans.

This was the beginning of the end in Fighter Command for both Dowding and Park, notwithstanding that they had together achieved a great victory, with the support of AVM Sir Christopher Quintin *Brand*, AOC 10 Group in the South-West, who had always provided effective assistance to Park whenever asked to do so. Dowding was given a job for which he was fundamentally unsuited, whilst Park was sent to command a training group. Their successors were respectively Douglas and Leigh-Mallory, the latter delighted to be in the heart of the action at last. By this time, however, the Battle of Britain was effectively over, to be followed by the night-time Blitz on London and other major cities, notably Coventry.

The major requirement at this stage of the War in the air was for night fighters, but these were in short supply. The Boulton Paul Defiant, with a small turret behind the pilot for an air gunner, had proved itself to be a hopeless day fighter because of its low speed and lack of manoeuvrability, but provided with a primitive Airborne Interception radar it did enjoy modest success as a night fighter. The Bristol Blenheim Mark 1 was an improvement, but was phased out in early 1941 with the arrival of the much more capable Bristol Beaufighter. From early 1941 onwards the Beaufighters were joined by the American Douglas Havoc, whilst the spring of 1942 saw the introduction of the best of all the wartime night fighters, the De Havilland Mosquito.

The night fighters were essentially defensive, but Douglas and Leigh-Mallory decided to take the daytime battle to the enemy. From early 1941 onwards two types of operation took place. The first were fighter-only, codenamed *Rhubarb*, in which relatively small numbers of RAF fighters would cross the Channel at low level and beat up anything worthwhile, notably enemy airfields, but also light shipping and ports. Shortly afterwards the first *Circus* operations were mounted. These consisted not only of fighters, but also of light bombers, for the most part Blenheims, targeted on industrial installations such as power stations. The value of such operations was highly debatable in 1941, long before any possibility of mounting an invasion of Europe, and did nothing to prevent the Germans from sending fighters to Russia. More British fighters were lost than German ones, and they were mostly valuable Spitfires, denying these aircraft to the RAF in North Africa and on Malta, where the Hurricanes and Curtis Tomahawks were hard pushed to deal with the more recent marks of the Messerschmitt 109.

212   Churchill's Eagles

Leigh-Mallory remained as AOC 11 Group, his operations including air support for the Dieppe Raid, until November 1942, when he succeeded Douglas as AOC-in-C Fighter Command. One year later, having in the meantime briefly visited North Africa to see army/air co-operation in action, he was appointed Commander-in-Chief of the Allied Expeditionary Air Force ('AEAF'), which would provide air cover for the naval forces and ground troops during the invasion of Normandy and subsequent operations on the continent. This new formation comprised the Second Tactical Air Force (2TAF) under Arthur **Coningham**, the US Ninth Air Force under Lewis H. Brereton and, for the early part of operations on the Continent, Air Defence of Great Britain (ADGB), as Fighter Command, now under Roderic **Hill**, had been renamed. 2TAF was itself composed of 2 Group (Basil **Embry**), which had formerly been the medium and light bomber element of Bomber Command, 83 Group (Harry **Broadhurst**), which contained squadrons of both fighters and fighter-bombers, and the US Ninth Air Force.

Leigh-Mallory had expected that the AEAF would comprise not only the tactical air forces, but also the strategic air forces, Bomber Command for the RAF and the Eighth Air Force for the USAF. However, there was no way that Arthur **Harris**, AOC-in-C of the former, who did not rate Leigh-Mallory highly and was determined to retain as much independence as possible, or Carl Spaatz, Commanding General of the US Strategic Air Forces in Europe, would accept this. Instead, overall control of the Allied Air Forces, including the strategic element, for the invasion of Normandy and subsequent operations in North-West Europe, would effectively devolve onto Arthur **Tedder**, the Deputy Supreme Commander of the overall Allied Expeditionary Force under General Eisenhower.

As far as liaison with the ground forces was concerned, Leigh-Mallory developed a good relationship with General Sir Bernard Montgomery of 21st Army Group, which was to comprise all the Allied ground forces for the first part of the campaign. In theory the latter's opposite number was Coningham, but he and Montgomery had not enjoyed good relations since the period after the Battle of El Alamein when both Coningham and Tedder had criticised him for being too cautious and, in particular, for not securing airfields sufficiently quickly. Montgomery therefore dealt as much as possible with Leigh-Mallory. The relationship remained good other than on one occasion when Leigh-Mallory vetoed an airborne operation south of Caen, but this was only temporary.

On D-Day itself, the Allied Air Forces dominated the day, allowing both the British and American airborne operations and landings from the sea to take place without much Luftwaffe interference. This remained the case in the subsequent campaign. Whilst Coningham later fulminated against Montgomery once again for not securing German airfields, both Leigh-Mallory and Broadhurst, whose aircraft were to use them, were more understanding. In the meantime, the operations of both Embry's 2 Group and Bomber Command, having focused on radar installations and gun emplacements in advance of and during the landings, significantly frustrated the movement of German forces to the front, largely by concentrating on bridges and railways. The fighter-bombers of Broadhurst's 83 Group subsequently created mayhem amongst the German ground forces, both in their failed thrust towards Mortain and in the Falaise Pocket.

With the creation of the new US 12th Army Group, the Ninth Air Force reverted to exclusively US control whilst 2TAF conducted all operations in support of 21st Army Group. There was thus no ongoing role for the AEAF. Leigh-Mallory was therefore delighted to be told that he would be succeeding Air Chief Marshal Sir Richard **Peirse** in command of the Allied Air Forces in South-East Asia. After a period of leave, he and his wife boarded an Avro York on 14 November 1944 to fly out to India. Some hours later it crashed into a mountain near Grenoble with the loss of all on board.

Leigh-Mallory remains one of the most difficult senior RAF officers to assess objectively. On the one hand he was held in high regard by many of his senior colleagues, notably by Portal and hardly less so by Douglas. Without their support he would not have been appointed successively as AOC-in-C Fighter Command, C-in-C Allied Expeditionary Air Force and, although he did not live to take it up, Allied Air C-in-C South-East Asia. He was perhaps most effective in the AEAF role, in which his long experience of army co-operation was of direct relevance and, for the most part, was appreciated by Montgomery; on the other hand, his relationship with Coningham, one of his immediate subordinates as AOC 2TAF, was poor. Leigh-Mallory was much less effective, although he himself was too self-confident to realize it, in Fighter Command, where his enthusiasm for the 'Big Wing' tactic was criticised not only by Park at the time, but by many Battle of Britain pilots subsequently, whilst his *Rhubarb* and *Circus* sweeps over France caused many more losses to his own side than to the enemy. He was far from universally popular in the RAF itself, but he got on well, on the whole, with the Americans. This might have played well in South-East Asia, where the appointment of Park in his stead was the final irony.

214 Churchill's Eagles

Air Marshal (later Air Chief Marshal) Sir Hugh Lloyd GCB, KBE, MC, DFC (1894–1981)

There were two great sieges during the Second World War. Arguably the better known is that of Leningrad, which lasted for an astonishing 872 days. Of very much the same duration, rather depending on when it might be said to have been finally raised, was the siege of Malta. During that time the defence of Malta lay substantially in the hands of the RAF, although vital roles were also played by the Royal Navy and by the Army anti-aircraft gunners, the latter including many Maltese. Directing the RAF's operations at the height of the siege, from June 1941 to July 1942, was the AOC Malta, Air Vice-Marshal Hugh **Lloyd**.

Known familiarly by both his felicitously rhyming given names, Hugh Pughe Lloyd began his military career in the Army, signing up from university at the beginning of the Great War and transferring from the infantry to the Royal Engineers as a signaller and dispatch rider in the following year. Seriously wounded in early 1917, he was evacuated to England where, following his recovery, he applied to join the RFC as a pilot and underwent the necessary training. In due course he was commissioned and posted to 52 Squadron at the beginning of 1918, flying RE8s in an army co-operation and light bomber role. In spite of his first exposure to flying operations coming so late in the War, Lloyd managed to earn both an MC and a DFC before the Armistice, as well as a Croix de Guerre

Having secured a permanent commission, Lloyd was posted to India, initially in 114 Squadron, which was then renumbered as 28 Squadron, flying Bristol Fighters on the North-West Frontier. The squadron was engaged in supporting the Army on operations in Waziristan, but the role of the RAF was a relatively modest one at this time and it would be some years before it was employed independently of ground troops. Lloyd returned to the UK at the end of 1923, by which time he had been promoted to flight lieutenant, and was placed in command of a flight of Bristol Fighters in 16 Squadron, once again in an army co-operation role.

In 1925 Lloyd attended the RAF Staff College, where his fellow students included Ralph **Cochrane** and Trafford **Leigh-Mallory**, whilst there was a strong Directing Staff under Robert Brooke-Popham, including Christopher *Courtenay* and Bertine *Sutton*. Inevitably his next role was as a staff officer, on this occasion on the air staff at the newly formed 23 Group, which at the time controlled all training units in the UK. Promoted to squadron leader in January 1930, he was appointed Chief Flying Instructor at 2 Flying

The Air Marshals 215

Training School, flying a variety of aircraft, but primarily the Avro 504. At the beginning of 1933 Lloyd returned to India, initially to attend the Army Staff College course at Quetta for two years, prior to a posting to the air staff at HQ 1 (Indian) Group at Peshawar. The group, which controlled all the squadrons in India at the time, had been formed into two wings. As before, the focus was on supporting the Army on the North-West Frontier, but this was a relatively quiet period and only one squadron, No. 20, was actively involved. Armed with his experience of army/air co-operation, however, Lloyd returned to the UK in mid-1936 to become the RAF Instructor at the Army Staff College in Camberley.

His next appointment, at the beginning of 1939, was to RAF Honington in Bomber Command as commanding officer of 9 Squadron, which was in the course of re-equipping with the Vickers Wellington, the outstanding British medium bomber of the time, if not of the war. He was just in time to lead the squadron in its early raids on German naval installations, before being appointed to the command of RAF Marham in Norfolk, which housed 38 and 115 Squadrons, also flying Wellingtons. His posting there was also very brief, as he was transferred to HQ 3 Group, the parent formation of all the Wellington squadrons, as a staff officer before the end of the year.

In May 1940, Lloyd was posted to HQ 2 Group as the Senior Air Staff Officer to AVM James **Robb**, the AOC. Unlike the other three groups in Bomber Command at this time, which all operated medium bombers, the Wellington, the Armstrong Whitworth Whitley and the Handley Page Hampden, 2 Group was equipped with a light bomber, the Bristol Blenheim. When the Blenheim was conceived some years earlier, initially as a passenger aircraft, it was thought that its speed would enable it to outfly enemy fighters. This had already been disproved during its operations early in the war against German ports and coastal convoys, and the aircraft turned out to be highly vulnerable when the Germans invaded the Netherlands, Belgium and France two weeks before Lloyd took up his appointment. Losses from both fighters and flak were atrociously high, with one squadron, No. 82, being reduced to virtually no aircraft on two occasions.

2 Group continued its cross-Channel operations throughout the Battle of Britain. Lecturing the crews of 218 Squadron at Oakington on 13 September, Lloyd predicted that, if the invasion had not been launched by the end of the month, it would not come that year. So it turned out, but 2 Group's operations against enemy-occupied ports and coastal shipping routes continued for the rest of the year and into 1941, with high rates of attrition within the squadrons.

216 Churchill's Eagles

On 1 June 1941 Lloyd was appointed AOC Malta, following an interview with the CAS, Charles **Portal**, who emphasised the island's immense importance to the war in the Mediterranean and North Africa. He flew there immediately by way of Gibraltar. After being briefed by his SASO at his underground HQ in Valletta, his first priority was to inspect his airfields. These were Luqa, south of Valletta, and Hal Far on the south coast, with the small strip at Safi lying between them, together with Takali, to the west of the capital and close to the small city of Medina. There were only fifty-nine serviceable aircraft on the island at the time, twenty-nine of them Hawker Hurricanes, the others being Blenheims, Martin Marylands and Fairey Swordfish, the last of these torpedo bombers crewed by the Fleet Air Arm, but under Lloyd's operational control. These aircraft were heavily outnumbered and, to a significant extent, outclassed by Luftwaffe Messerschmitt Bf.109 fighters and Junkers 88 bombers operating from Sicily. The nearest Allied aircraft at this time were based 900 miles away to the east on the border between Egypt and Libya, whilst Gibraltar was 1,100 miles away to the west. Sicily, on the other hand, from which the Luftwaffe and the Regia Aeronautica operated against Malta, was just over 100 miles away to the north. Whilst it was possible to get some warning of most enemy attacks from there, radar cover at low level was minimal.

Lloyd was able to see that much had been done already to put the airfields into operational order, but he was still dismayed at the state of the dispersals and the lack of maintenance equipment, which was at a deplorable level compared to what he had been used to in the UK. As far as aircraft were concerned, they were to remain in low numbers relative to the enemy. It had been decided to rotate through Malta Blenheim squadrons from 2 Group, with the crews of many of which Lloyd was still very familiar. The first of these was No. 82, which had twice before shrunk to almost nothing. On this occasion, the squadron fared a little better and was followed in due course by 105, 107, 18 and 21 Squadrons.

Lloyd had been told by Portal that his primary task was to destroy enemy ships plying between Italy and ports in Libya, notably Benghazi and Tripoli; these were essential to the maintenance of the German-Italian ground forces facing the British in Egypt. Although Lloyd's light bombers were tasked with this job, it proved to be very difficult, not only due to the enemy's air superiority, but also because the convoys were routed as far as possible from Malta, either around the western tip of Sicily and along the Tunisian coast, or else hugging the coast of Greece. Nevertheless, during the summer and autumn of 1941 many successful operations were conducted, against both convoys and the Italian ports, with longer-range Wellingtons even mounting raids on Tripoli. The operations were made easier by an Allied offensive, Operation CRUSADER, which took Allied ground forces beyond Benghazi and made available to the Western Desert Air Force the airfields in the bulge of Cyrenaica. However, Rommel's counter-offensive in early 1942 pushed the British Eighth Army back to Gazala, resulting in a considerable reduction in air support from North Africa.

Lloyd soon realized that the key to the RAF's survival on Malta was effective dispersal around the airfields, where pens were constructed surrounded by stone and rock blast walls. It also proved possible to link up Luqa with Takali, so that an aircraft could taxi all the way from one to the other, as well as to Safi in between the two. An increase in the tempo of the Axis raids in early 1942 accelerated the need for effective protection, but a dispersal pen for a Wellington required no less than three and a half tons of rock and earth, not an easy task for men who were by that time living on very low rations.

Lloyd was highly critical of the attempt to unload the ships of a convoy which arrived from Egypt on 25 March. One of the three vessels had been seriously damaged and had to take shelter in an inlet, but two others entered Grand Harbour. Instead of being brought alongside quays, as he had strongly recommended, they were left in the middle of the harbour. The only cargo which was unloaded was that required by Lloyd for his aircraft; the rest remained on the ships, both of which were then bombed and set on fire. His criticism did not go down well with Lieutenant General Sir William Dobbie, the Governor, who suggested to Arthur **Tedder**, the AOC-in-C RAF Middle East Command, that he should be relieved. This Tedder refused to do, expressing full confidence in Lloyd. In the event, Dobbie himself was replaced by Lord Gort shortly afterwards.

As far as the air defence of Malta was concerned, the Hurricanes were no match for the more recent marks of the Bf.109. What the island needed was Spitfires, but at the time of Lloyd's arrival in Malta these were all allocated to Fighter Command, which by this time was largely employed in carrying out sweeps over the French countryside to very little effect. It was not until 7 March 1942 that the first fifteen Spitfires arrived on the island, having been flown off an American aircraft carrier. It was three days before they were able to participate in their first action over the island, but it was a successful one, demonstrating their superiority over the 109s. A further nine arrived on 21 March and seven more on 29 March. They were not, however, the complete answer to Malta's prayers. The Spitfires were not easy to service

218   Churchill's Eagles

without spare parts and maintenance equipment, which took much longer to arrive on the island than the aircraft themselves, whilst they were no more impervious than the Hurricanes to being bombed or shot up on the ground. Furthermore, whilst the wings of the Hurricanes could be easily detached from the fuselage, leaving the wheels in place for easy towing, the Spitfires had to be towed complete, which was not an easy task on some of the narrow taxiways.

A further forty-six Spitfires were flown in from the USS *Wasp* on 20 April, but the Germans mounted enormous raids by both fighters and bombers from Sicily, and within seventy-two hours not a single one was serviceable. By the time of the next aircraft delivery, however, the British were much better prepared. In particular, large work parties from the island's three infantry brigades were recruited to fill in holes in the runways and taxiways, rebuild destroyed dispersal pens and construct new ones. Soldiers were also assigned to each aircraft as it landed to ensure that it reached its designated parking area as quickly as possible, whilst fuel was delivered by hand in hundreds of tin cans. Pilots from the Malta squadrons were on the spot to take over each aircraft as soon as the bare minimum of servicing had been completed, and many of them were back in the air within minutes. However, although a greater number of enemy aircraft were destroyed than ever before, it was not enough.

Sixty more Spitfires arrived on 9 May and the fast minelayer HMS *Welshman* docked on the following morning carrying, among other things, essential spares for the aircraft. On that day the Spitfires enjoyed one of their most satisfactory victories, with twenty-three enemy aircraft confirmed as destroyed, together with seventeen 'probables' and twenty-four damaged, for the loss of one Spitfire.

May 1942 saw extensive battles between the attackers and defenders, but the Axis losses were considerable, as a result of which they turned to night operations. By this time, however, the RAF had been supplied with four Bristol Beaufighter night fighters which caused considerable losses to the attackers. Fighting in the air reached a crescendo in the first thirteen days of July 1942, during which nearly one hundred Axis aircraft were shot down, for the loss of twenty-five Spitfires. The immediate battle had been effectively won, but the siege was by no means over. The *Pedestal* convoy, of which only four merchant ships and the tanker *Ohio* arrived in mid–August out of the fourteen vessels which left the UK, brought just enough supplies of food and oil to sustain the island until November, when, with the Eighth Army advancing once again across Libya, air cover from there became available and another convoy arrived intact from Alexandria..

Lloyd himself had been relieved as AOC by Keith **Park** in mid-July and was appointed as SASO to Tedder at Air HQ Middle East in Cairo. This came at a time of great change for the British Army in North Africa, with Harold Alexander replacing Claude Auchinleck as C-in-C Middle East and Bernard Montgomery appointed GOC-in-C Eighth Army. One of Montgomery's first decisions was to locate his own Main HQ alongside Air HQ Western Desert, later renamed the Desert Air Force and commanded by Arthur **Coningham**. The resulting beneficial effect on the co-operation between the two services was significant, with a much improved response to requests for air strikes.

Although Tedder's responsibility extended to all RAF activities in the Western Mediterranean and the Middle East, including Iraq, Syria and East Africa, in practice it was the co-operation between the Desert Air Force and the Eighth Army which dominated his work and that of Lloyd for the next few months, which included the Battles of Alam Halfa and El Alamein and the advance to Benghazi.

In March 1943, with Eighth Army temporarily stuck on the Mareth Line, there was a major reorganization of the Allied air forces, which now included all the formations and units, including those of the USAAF, which had supported the Allied landings in Algeria and Morocco in early November 1942 and which subsequently participated in the campaign in Tunisia. Tedder was appointed to lead the Mediterranean Air Command, with Coningham taking over the Allied Tactical Air Force, which incorporated both the Desert Air Force and the US XII Air Support Command, and Lloyd becoming the AOC North-West African Coastal Air Force. Whilst the Tactical Air Force supported operations against the Axis forces on the ground, the Coastal Air Force was responsible for all operations over the sea, including the destruction of enemy warships, submarines, and other Axis vessels, and the protection of Allied shipping and maritime reconnaissance, including that of ports under Axis control. It was a multi-national force, including three fighter groups from the USAAF flying Spitfires, Beaufighters and P-39 Airacobras, and two Free French squadrons. The British element was largely composed of 242 Group, whose two wings operated a variety of aircraft, not only fighters, but also Beauforts, Beaufighters, Wellingtons and Martin Baltimores, whilst there were also four Fleet Air Arm squadrons flying Fairey Albacore torpedo bombers. Amongst other operations, the Coastal Air Force was heavily engaged in the destruction of German transport

220   Churchill's Eagles

aircraft bringing in supplies and reinforcements to Tunisia, prior to the Axis surrender in May 1943. It was also involved in Operation HUSKY, the Allied invasion of Sicily in July 1943, with Lloyd returning to Malta, where his HQ was based for the invasion.

Following a difficult but ultimately successful land campaign in Sicily, landings took place on the Italian mainland in September 1943, supported by Lloyd's aircraft. In December 1943, the name of the formation was changed to Mediterranean Allied Coastal Air Force. By this time its remit was a large one, covering both the Tyrrhenian and the Adriatic Seas, with the aim of dominating these whilst the Allied armies fought their way up the Italian mainland. In this it proved to be very successful, much reducing Axis shipping movements, not only on the shores of Italy, but also along the Dalmatian coast.

In November 1944, with ultimate victory in Europe coming ever closer, Lloyd was called back to the UK to take command of a new formation to be called the Very Long Range Bomber Force, or more familiarly, Tiger Force. This was to be the British contribution to the bombing of Japan, hitherto confined to B.29 Superfortresses of the USAAF operating out of Okinawa. The Americans were initially highly reluctant to allow this, but at the end of May 1945 confirmed that there would be room for ten squadrons. The RAF was proposing to use not only its own B.29s, but also the Avro Lincoln, a derivative of the Lancaster with an extended wingspan and fuselage and more powerful engines to achieve both longer range and higher altitude. Lloyd set up a planning group to oversee developments and arranged to spend time at 5 Group Bomber Command to learn what developments had taken place in bombing technology and tactics since he had served in the command early in the war. In the event, the atomic bomb brought an end to the war before Tiger Force could be deployed.

In December 1946 Lloyd joined the staff of the Imperial Defence College as the RAF Instructor and, after two years at the college, was appointed AOC-in-C Far East. His final appointment, in February 1950, was as AOC-in-C Bomber Command, where he oversaw the introduction of the UK's first jet bomber, the English Electric Canberra, and the planning for the V-Bombers, although he retired in June 1953, two years before the first one, the Vickers Valiant, entered service.

Lloyd's forte, initially developed during his appointments in 2 Group and subsequently in Malta, before being honed to perfection in command of the Allied Mediterranean Coastal Air Force, was operations against enemy shipping, either at sea or in harbour. He was a popular commander, not only with his subordinates, but also with his superiors, who knew that he could be trusted to get the best results from sometimes unpromising circumstances; indeed, it was his successful defence of Malta which defined him in the eyes of most. It may have come as a surprise to many that in retirement he did not take on significant appointments in 'Civvy Street' but instead began what became a successful career as a pig farmer!

Air Chief Marshal Sir Arthur Longmore GCB, DSO (1885–1976)

Over the last more than two hundred years, Great Britain has demonstrated a marked tendency to begin wars badly and to finish them well. This was certainly true of the Peninsular War, the Boer War and the Great War, whilst the Second World War was no exception, as the campaigns in France and Belgium in 1940 and in Malaya, Singapore and Burma in 1941/42 demonstrated only too painfully. In North and East Africa in 1940/41, however, this historical trend appeared to have been reversed, but it was the result of facing an opponent who, whilst highly belligerent, was also militarily weak, not so much in numbers as in strategy, tactics and leadership. However, the appearance of a much stronger enemy in the Western Desert exposed the flaws in Great Britain's own capabilities, not only on land and at sea, but also in the air. Although most of the blame for this lay with the British War Cabinet, the sacrificial lamb was Arthur **Longmore** who, after two years of fighting with inadequate resources, was relieved of his appointment as AOC-in-C Air HQ Middle East in the summer of 1942.

Longmore had begun his military career in the Royal Navy, being commissioned in 1901 as a midshipman after training in HMS *Britannia*. From 1906 onwards his speciality was torpedo boats and he commanded a number of these in succession. He was, however, very keen to learn how to fly, becoming one of the first four Royal Navy officers to be accepted for flying training. He proved to be a highly competent pilot, so much so that in 1912 he was selected to become a flying instructor at the Central Flying School. Having subsequently commanded two Naval Air Stations in succession, the second one at Calshot flying seaplanes, in 1914 he was appointed to command first 3 Squadron and then 1 Squadron RNAS, based in Dunkirk, from where he and his fellow pilots carried out bombing raids on the advancing German armies and then mounted operations against the Zeppelin airships. In June 1915, by this time holding the rank of squadron commander, he was appointed to command No.1 Wing RNAS.

222   Churchill's Eagles

In early 1916 Longmore was disappointed to have to return to sea-going duties on the battlecruiser HMS *Tiger*, but at least this enabled him to serve in the Battle of Jutland. In June 1916 he returned to flying duties as officer commanding first Killingholme and then Eastchurch Naval Air Stations, followed by a spell as Assistant Superintendent for Design in the Air Department at the Admiralty. In February 1918 he was posted to Malta, initially as SASO Mediterranean and then as Officer Commanding the Adriatic/Malta Group, which operated successfully against German and Austrian submarines. By this time he had opted to join the newly created RAF, and following the end of the Great War he was awarded the DSO.

Longmore continued to serve outside the UK immediately after the Great War, as Officer Commanding the Aeronautical Commission for Bulgaria, but in November 1920 he was brought back to command 3 Group, based at RAF Spittlegate as part of the newly created Inland Area. During 1922 he attended the Army Staff College, its course at the time being for a single year, following which he was sent out to join the Air Staff at Iraq Command under Air Marshal Sir John Salmond. At the Cairo Conference of March 1921 the then Air Marshal Sir Hugh Trenchard had persuaded Winston Churchill, Secretary of State for the Colonies, and King Abdullah of Iraq that it would be economic to keep the peace in that country by using the RAF, together with relatively modest army units, instead of the large formations which would otherwise have been required. Longmore's part in achieving this was recognized by his appointment as a Companion of the Bath shortly after his return to the UK towards the end of 1924.

A brief term as AOC 7 Group was followed by four years at the Air Ministry as Director of Equipment. He then enjoyed three very happy years as Commandant of the RAF College at Cranwell, with promotion to Air Vice-Marshal. In 1933 he became AOC Inland Area, responsible for all training in the UK, before being appointed AOC Coastal Area and then, following its renaming, AOC-in-C Coastal Command. This was very much the poor relation of the front-line commands, with a paucity of squadrons and a remit which extended to the general protection of British shipping and the prevention of attacks on the country's ports, but not to the sinking of submarines, which at that time was the responsibility of the Royal Navy. The aircraft deployed were substantially bi-plane flying boats and torpedo bombers stationed along the south coast of England.

It was probably with some relief that Longmore, by this time an air marshal with a KCB to his name, became Commandant of the Imperial Defence College in September 1936. The purpose of the college was to bring together senior officers of all three services and those of the Dominions, together with a number of civil servants, to study the major defence issues of the day. The RAF instructor was Charles **Portal**, who would later play a pivotal role in Longmore's career, and the students included Keith **Park** and Ralph *Sorley*.

In the summer of 1939 Longmore became briefly the AOC-in-C of Training Command, in which position he was directly involved in the setting up of the Commonwealth Air Training Plan, which resulted in the training of hundreds of thousands of air and ground crew in skies which were devoid of enemy aircraft. Most of the training schools were in Canada, but South Africa, Rhodesia, Australia and New Zealand were also involved, and Longmore visited the last two of these.

In April 1940 Longmore was appointed AOC-in-C Air HQ Middle East, the largest and most important RAF command outside the UK. He was based in Cairo, but his geographical remit was enormous, covering Egypt, the Sudan, British Somaliland, East Africa, Palestine, Jordan, Iraq, Aden and the Persian Gulf. The command comprised 29 squadrons, but they were full of aircraft which by this time were obsolete in the Home Commands. The bombers were Bristol Bombays, mostly used as transport aircraft, but with a bombing capability, and Blenheims, most of which were old Mark 1s, whilst in East Africa there were long outdated Vickers Wellesleys. The most modern fighter in the theatre was the bi-plane Gloster Gladiator, but there were also numerous Gauntlets, the Gladiator's predecessor, still in service, together with a variety of derivatives of the Hawker Hart. The most modern aircraft available was the Short Sunderland flying boat, of which there were a mere two squadrons.

With Italy declaring war on Great Britain on 10 June 1940 and France capitulating to Germany two weeks later, the passage through the Mediterranean from Gibraltar to Alexandria was effectively cut. Reinforcements of more modern aircraft initially had to come round the Cape of Good Hope and thence to Suez, a journey of some five weeks for fast convoys and longer for most cargo ships. The alternative was to fly the aircraft across Africa, to achieve which the West African Reinforcement Route was created. This began at Takoradi in Ghana, where the aircraft were unloaded from ships and re-assembled; they were then flown to Lagos in Nigeria and on to Kano, Maidaguri, Fort Lamy (in territory held by the Free French), Genina and Khartoum in the Sudan, whence they flew up the Nile to Egypt. The first flight consisted of a single Blenheim and six Hurricanes, after which there was a constant stream of aircraft. In the

224   Churchill's Eagles

meantime, longer-range aircraft, notably the Vickers Wellington, could fly to Egypt via Gibraltar and Malta.

Longmore may have had mostly antique aircraft, but so, for the most part, did the RAF's opponent, the Italian Regia Aeronautica. This was just as well as he had to fight it on two fronts, in the Western Desert and in East Africa. The latter campaign, after a stuttering start, was in due course successful. By early April 1941 Addis Ababa was in British hands, and the rest of the campaign was less demanding of air support. In the Western Desert the Italians entered Egypt but settled down in Sidi Barrani, a long way from Cairo and the Delta. In a stunning land campaign under the command of Lieutenant General Richard O'Connor, the Italians were pushed back to the border with Tripolitania by early February 1941, the RAF playing a significant role in their defeat.

Longmore, however, now found his command assailed on a number of sides. In October 1940 Italy attacked Greece and, under the terms of a guarantee given to the Greek Government, the British were obliged to come to its aid. Longmore duly dispatched three Blenheim and two Gladiator squadrons, with more to follow. These made a significant contribution to the halting and pushing back of the Italians, but when the Germans mounted their own invasion of Greece in April 1941, the RAF was both outnumbered and outclassed; little was salvaged from that campaign or from the subsequent fighting on Crete. On the other hand, the heroic performance of the pilots at 4 Flying School in Habbaniya in Iraq was instrumental in putting down a pro-Axis rebellion against the regime in that country.

As in Greece, so also in North Africa, the RAF found itself outclassed by the Germans when they struck back in Cyrenaica, driving the British ground forces back to the Egyptian frontier. By this time the RAF was able to deploy Hawker Hurricanes, which were certainly much more effective than the Gladiators and which blunted the impact of the German Messerschmitt Bf 110s and Junkers 87 Stukas, but the ground forces had been seriously weakened by both the demands of the Greek campaign and by complacency in the higher ranks of the British Army, and it was impossible to stop the enemy advancing to the Egyptian frontier.

By this time Longmore's stock in London had sunk to a low level. His constant demands for more and better aircraft, his complaints about the state in which they were delivered to him, often requiring many hours of maintenance before they were fit for action, and his enrolling of his fellow Commanders-in-Chief, Admiral Sir Andrew Cunningham and General Sir Archibald Wavell, in his support, proved highly irritating to Churchill, who could only see the number of aircraft in service. When Longmore complained about serviceability, this went down particularly badly in London, not only with the Prime Minister, but also with Portal, since October 1940 the Chief of the Air Staff. In May 1941 Longmore was called back to the UK for discussions and, soon after he had arrived there, was relieved of his command, to be succeeded in Cairo by his deputy, Arthur **Tedder**.

This was not, however, the end of his career. Longmore was immensely experienced and knew the RAF as well as anyone. He was thus appointed one of two Inspectors-General of the RAF in July 1941, the other being Sir Edgar **Ludlow-Hewitt**, who had taken on the role after stepping down as AOC-in-C Bomber Command in April 1940. By that time the enormous expansion of the service demanded that there be two Inspectors-General, with Air Chief Marshal Sir William *Mitchell* becoming the second one before handing over to Longmore. The role of the Inspectors-General was to examine and report back on the efficiency of the service. Their remit was very wide as to both establishments and geography, but it covered in particular individual RAF stations, of which there were, by this time, an enormous number. Station Commanders had little notice of their arrival and the visitors could see whatever they wished, with full and unrestricted access to all ground facilities and to the aircraft. Reports were written immediately afterwards and sent to the Air Ministry.

Longmore retired in March 1942 in order to contest a parliamentary by-election in Grantham, a constituency he knew well from his time as Commandant at the RAF College at Cranwell. He was defeated by an Independent candidate, who achieved a majority of 367 votes out of 23,149 cast. In August of the following year Longmore rejoined the RAF to lead a team engaged in post-hostilities planning, accepting a temporary reduction in rank to air vice-marshal in the process. As a keen sailor and member of the Royal Yacht Squadron, he was also instrumental in the formation of the Yachtsmen's Emergency Service, which provided water transport manned by volunteers to, from and between the ships in the Channel ports preparing for and then undertaking the invasion of France in the summer of 1944. In his later years he became a vice-chairman of the Imperial War Graves Commission.

Longmore was one of a number of senior officers of all three services who held high command early in a war for which Great Britain was woefully unprepared and who paid the price of failure. He himself had been deeply frustrated by what he saw as the lack of priority accorded to the RAF in the Middle East, with deliveries of inferior aircraft and not enough of them. It

226 Churchill's Eagles

was his misfortune that his demands rankled with a prime minister who was being pressed on many sides. Success against the Italians in East Africa and the Western Desert was outweighed by failure against the highly trained Luftwaffe with its modern equipment, whilst his appeals for reinforcements and better quality aircraft became too much for a prime minister whose understanding of the true situation was limited and of a chief of the air staff who became exasperated by his constant complaints.

Air Chief Marshal Sir Edgar Ludlow-Hewitt GCB, GBE, CMG, DSO, MC (1886–1973)

At the beginning of the Second World War there were few officers in the RAF who were held in such high regard by their colleagues as Edgar **Ludlow-Hewitt**. In spite of being a non-smoking, non-drinking Christian Scientist who apparently lacked a sense of humour, he more than compensated for this with determination, an acute brain and a deep understanding of the RAF. These attributes had enabled him to bring one of its key commands to a state of readiness which would have seemed impossible only a few years earlier, albeit that it was still a very long way from being an effective instrument of war. As a wartime commander, however, he proved to be a disappointment, although he remained in the service, doing highly valuable work until after the end of hostilities.

Ludlow-Hewitt had been commissioned into the Royal Irish Rifles in 1905 on passing out from the Royal Military College at Sandhurst. When the Great War broke out in August 1914 he was undergoing flying training at the Central Flying School and later that year he was posted to 1 Squadron of the RFC. However, it was not until March 1915 that the squadron was ordered to France, where it operated substantially in a reconnaissance role, flying frequent operations against the Germans in a variety of aircraft, but most frequently the French Morane Parasol. Ludlow-Hewitt returned to the UK three months later and, that September, was promoted to major and posted to 15 Squadron as its commander. He was there for only three months before being sent to France to take command of 3 Squadron, in which he saw a great deal of action and was awarded the MC. His promotion was rapid: by the beginning of 1916 he was a temporary lieutenant-colonel in command of 3 Wing, and by October 1917 a temporary brigadier-general and Inspector of Training at the headquarters of the Training Division, which he was then appointed to command. By the time of the Armistice he had become the Chief Staff Officer of the RAF in France, with a DSO to add to his MC and six mentions in despatches to his name.

With such a record, it was unsurprising that Ludlow-Hewitt was granted a permanent commission in 1919, albeit with a reduction in rank to Group Captain. In 1923, by which time he had become a trusted protégé of Sir Hugh Trenchard, he was appointed Air Secretary to the Secretary of State for Air, Frederick Guest, in which role he was close to many of the major decisions being taken at that time. He then served as President of the Aerodrome Board for two years from October 1923, before attending the Royal Naval Staff College and then being appointed Commandant of the RAF Staff College, an institution which was a key part of Trenchard's long campaign to maintain the independence of the RAF. He was very highly regarded both by his Directing Staff, who included Roderick **Hill** and Douglas **Evill**, and his students, amongst whom were Hugh **Lloyd**, William **Dickson** and Guy **Garrod**.

In October 1930 Ludlow-Hewitt, by this time an Air Vice-Marshal, was appointed AOC Iraq. During the Cairo Conference of 1921 Trenchard had persuaded not only Churchill, then Secretary of State for the Colonies, but also King Feisal of Iraq, that the country could be controlled by the RAF very much less expensively and more effectively than by relying exclusively on troops on the ground. Although a small army establishment remained in the country, the RAF kept the peace largely by persuading rebellious elements that the damage it could wreak on their properties and livelihoods would be considerable. In fact there was one minor uprising during Ludlow-Hewitt's tenure in the spring and early summer of 1932, but it was put down very quickly by three RAF squadrons.

Ludlow-Hewitt returned from Iraq in early 1933 to take up an appointment as Deputy Chief of the Air Staff, with particular responsibility for Operations and Intelligence. This came at the same time as the appointment of Air Chief Marshal Sir Edward Ellington as Chief of the Air Staff and the belated beginning of the RAF's Expansion Plan in the light of the rearmament of Germany, with a very substantial increase in the number of UK-based squadrons and airfields. Furthermore, specifications for the first truly modern fighters, the Hawker Hurricane and the Supermarine Spitfire, had been issued, whilst new medium bombers, notably the Vickers Wellington and the Armstrong Whitworth Whitley, were also on the drawing board.

Ludlow-Hewitt, however, was not to see the early test flights of these aircraft, as in March 1935 he was posted to India as AOC RAF. If the RAF had been *primus inter pares* in Iraq, it was emphatically the poor cousin of the Army in India. Its aircraft, largely Westland Wapitis and Hawker Harts, were effectively obsolete in the UK, whilst its participation in campaigns was very much as a back-up to the Army in time of need, rather than a front-line force. There were nine squadrons in the country, four of which were designated for army co-operation and four for bombing, whilst one squadron was equipped with Vickers Valentias and largely used in a transport capacity. The majority of the squadrons were based in the North-West Frontier Province, at Kohat, Peshawar and Risalpur, with one at Quetta in Baluchistan and small detachments elsewhere. It was at Quetta that a major earthquake occurred on 31 May 1935, destroying much of the RAF station and causing a large number of deaths and serious injuries amongst RAF personnel. Ludlow-Hewitt flew up to Quetta as soon as he could to ensure that all the steps necessary were being taken to evacuate casualties and wives and children as quickly as possible.

It was probably with some sense of relief that Ludlow-Hewitt left this backwater to return to the UK, where in September 1937 he took up the most important role of his career, as AOC-in-C Bomber Command. He was horrified at what he found: a formation which, in his opinion, was totally unprepared for the war which by this time seemed to be almost inevitable. Hitler's revelation in March 1935, just as Ludlow-Hewitt was leaving for India, that the Luftwaffe had achieved parity with the RAF had provoked a rapid re-evaluation of the RAF's Expansion Plan, which had subsequently been changed on many occasions. There had been much progress in building new stations, most of which, as far as Bomber Command was concerned, were as close as possible to Germany, on the eastern side of England from County Durham down to Suffolk. There had also been progress in the production of new aircraft, including medium bombers. However, in Ludlow-Hewitt's opinion, not only were there not enough of these, but there were major deficiencies in their manning and armament.

He immediately identified the heart of the problem, which was totally inadequate training. Flying Training *per se* was good, but there was not enough of it, one very major deficiency being in night flying, which in 1938 accounted for only 10 per cent of the total hours of training. In a branch of the service which was going to have to operate for the most part in the hours of darkness, this was totally inadequate, and Ludlow-Hewitt insisted, against the opposition of the Air Ministry, that it be increased. Perhaps even more important was the lack of adequate crew training. Whereas for fifteen years after the end of the Great War most of the air gunners had primarily been employed as ground crew, who, for a modest increase in wages, could volunteer to man the machine guns in open cockpits, they were now to be permanent members of the aircrew. The new aircraft coming off the production line, moreover, would have crews of anything from four to seven, with the gunners situated in mechanically operated turrets. In addition, in the larger aircraft such as the Whitley and the Wellington there was a demand for specialist navigators. Ludlow-Hewitt was totally passionate about training for every member of a crew, but it would not be until about the time he left Bomber Command that the first dedicated Operational Training Units were formed.

However, this was by no means the only problem which he encountered. First of all, the bombs with which he was provided were lightweight – the largest was a mere 500lbs and was very unreliable, very often failing to explode – whilst bomb sights were relatively primitive and required a straight and level approach to have any hope of hitting the target, during which the aircraft would be very vulnerable to fighters and anti-aircraft fire. The ability of any of Bomber Command's aircraft to hit a target reliably from a high altitude was minimal.

The capacity of the bombers to find their targets in the first place was equally negligible. There were no sophisticated navigational aids in existence, with finding the right course made possible in daylight only by observation of the ground below or by using the wireless to fix a position from a medium or high frequency direction-finding station, which was impossible over enemy territory. As it happened, when war broke out in September 1939, the strict instruction to Bomber Command, under a policy of 'restricted bombing', was not to drop its bombs on enemy territory inland, but to target ports and other naval facilities and ships by day and to drop leaflets over Germany by night. Luckily, the enemy's own defences were poor at the time, without radar-controlled anti-aircraft guns and night fighters, so casualties were relatively light and were mostly due to accidents.

At the outbreak of hostilities, Bomber Command numbered twenty-nine squadrons in four groups. The command's original 1 Group was withdrawn completely to become the British Expeditionary Force's Advanced Air Striking Force. Its Fairey Battles were totally unsuitable in any event for medium or long-distance operations over enemy territory, and when the group was later re-formed it was equipped with Wellingtons. 2 Group flew Bristol Blenheims, light bombers which were expected initially to be fast enough to outrun enemy fighters, but which proved to be highly vulnerable. 3 Group was lucky to be already equipped with Wellingtons, the best British medium bomber of the war, largely due to its robust construction. 4 Group

230   Churchill's Eagles

flew the Armstrong Whitworth Whitley, a capable aircraft in 1939 terms, with a greater bomb load than the Wellington, but totally outclassed and reduced to other duties within two years. 5 Group was equipped with Handley Page Hampdens, faster that either Whitleys or Wellingtons, but very uncomfortable for their crews and better suited to mine-laying than bombing.

Whilst in many ways an outstanding commander who made many vital changes to his force, Ludlow-Hewitt did have some weaknesses. Although his insistence on the formation of Operational Training Units proved to be a vital contribution to the later success of Bomber Command, he felt that the roles of the crew, other than the pilots, should be interchangeable; this would, had it been acted upon, have been a serious mistake. Perhaps more worrying was the deep distress he displayed about casualties. Even before the outbreak of war, whenever aircrew were killed or injured, he would demand details from the station commander and send personal messages of sympathy to the relatives. His ADC of that time, the future Marshal of the RAF Lord Elworthy, believed that it was the most crushing burden to him and felt that he was insufficiently ruthless as a result.

There were some subordinates who felt that Ludlow-Hewitt was insufficiently decisive when it came to operations. On the other hand, two other future marshals of the RAF, Arthur **Harris**, who was one of his group commanders, and John **Slessor**, who served under Ludlow-Hewitt in India and was in regular contact whilst serving at the Air Ministry in the early months of the war, rated him very highly indeed, Harris going so far as to regard him as the most brilliant officer he had met in any of the three services.

In any event, by the spring of 1940, before the end of the 'Phoney War', the Air Staff had had enough of his badgering them on the subject of operational training, and he was replaced as AOC-in-C by Charles **Portal**. He was not, however, lost to the service, as he was appointed as Inspector-General of the RAF. This was a role which had only existed since 1935, when Sir Robert Brooke-Popham was appointed, followed in 1937 by a former CAS, Marshal of the RAF Sir Edward Ellington. With the huge expansion of the RAF and the outbreak of war, it was decided that there should be two Inspectors-General, with Air Marshal Sir Charles *Burnett* and Air Marshal Sir Leslie *Gossage* each holding the position for a short time. In the immediate aftermath of Ludlow-Hewitt's appointment, Air Marshal Sir William *Mitchell* became the second Inspector-General, followed in July 1941 by Arthur **Longmore** and in February 1943 by Philip **Joubert**. When Joubert left to go to India in 1943, however, he was not replaced and Ludlow-Hewitt soldiered on alone.

The role of the Inspector-General RAF, an appointment no longer in existence, was to ensure that the highest standards of efficiency were maintained throughout the service. This entailed a great deal of travel, not only within the UK, but also to other theatres of war. In the former and to some extent in the latter, Ludlow-Hewitt flew himself whenever possible. Even before the war he had his own personal Hawker Hart and he later used more modern light aircraft. This meant that he could descend upon his target unit or formation without warning, although in most cases he did notify them in advance.

At the most basic level, the Inspectors-General visited RAF stations and looked at every aspect of their operation, in offices, workshops and dispersals and, most importantly, in their aircraft. Reports were then written and sent to the Air Ministry, which was responsible for ensuring that the recommendations were acted upon. The remit of the Inspector-General went wider than this, however, and they could inspect other units and headquarters throughout the service. They were not limited to the UK. Ludlow-Hewitt travelled to the Middle East in the summer of 1941 to look not only at the Air HQ, but also at formations and units through the entire geography of the command. He and the AOC-in-C, Arthur Tedder, saw eye to eye on all things, except that Ludlow-Hewitt considered that the RAF's role should be in support of the army, whilst Tedder strongly believed that it was the first line of defence.

Ludlow-Hewitt was back in the Middle East a year later, this time having visited Malta at the height of the siege of the island. A much longer trip was undertaken shortly afterwards, when he travelled to India in the aftermath of the Japanese invasion of Burma early in 1942, which resulted in British forces being driven out of that country. Air Chief Marshal Sir Richard **Peirse**, who only arrived in India as AOC-in-C shortly afterwards, was desperate to reorganize his command. A number of groups already existed, 222 in Colombo, 223 on the North-West Frontier and 225 in Bangalore, whilst 226 Group in Karachi handled supply and maintenance and 226 Group in Lahore was responsible for training. Peirse, however, also proposed to establish a new group, 224, to act alongside 221 Group, which had recently been evacuated from Burma and, in order to be as close as possible to the action, to move his advanced headquarters from New Delhi to Calcutta.

The Air Ministry objected, stating that the current organization was quite sufficient. At this, Peirse signalled that, if he could not dispose of his

232   Churchill's Eagles

forces in the manner which he believed to be appropriate to the situation, he should be relieved. The Air Ministry backtracked, proposing that Ludlow-Hewitt should look at the organization and adjudicate on the matter. This was accordingly done, Ludlow-Hewitt signalling London that Peirse's proposals for a new group and an advanced HQ were completely appropriate to the situation. He went further, carrying out a full inspection of Peirse's command and making some valuable recommendations, notably that it should be free to organize itself without undue interference from the Air Ministry!

Ludlow-Hewitt's encyclopaedic knowledge of the service and his formidable intellect meant that he was also frequently consulted on other matters, one example being the rationalization of Army Co-operation Command. He retired after the end of the war against Japan, having made, over more than five years of unremitting work, a significant contribution to the efficiency of the RAF. In retirement he became the Chairman of the College of Aeronautics.

Marshal of the RAF the Lord Newall GCB, OM, GCMG, AM (1886–1963)

The towering RAF figure during the war was Charles **Portal**, whose leadership of the service from the last two months of 1940 until the end of 1945 was exemplary. His immediate predecessor as Chief of the Air Staff has become almost a footnote to the wartime history of the RAF, yet Cyril **Newall**, who retired little more than a year after hostilities began, did make an important contribution to the readiness of Great Britain for war, albeit that his judgement was flawed in other respects.

Newall was commissioned out of Sandhurst into the Royal Warwickshire Regiment in 1905. Having travelled with the regiment to India, he transferred to the Indian Army as an officer in the 2nd Gurkha Rifles, in which he served on the North-West Frontier. Whilst on leave in England in 1911 he learnt to fly, subsequently returning to India as an instructor at the Indian Central Flying School at Sitapur. On the outbreak of war, however, he returned to the UK and transferred to the RFC, initially as a flight commander in 1 Squadron and then as CO of 12 Squadron, which he took to France in September 1915. The squadron, flying BE.2s, carried out its sorties in an army co-operation capacity, notably during the Battle of Loos, which began shortly after its arrival.

It was during this period that Newall performed an act of heroism which resulted in the award to him, on the recommendation of Hugh Trenchard, of the Albert Medal (First Class), the equivalent at that time of the George Cross. A fire broke out in a shed where bombs were stored and, totally disregarding his own safety, he led three NCOs, all of whom were to be awarded the Albert Medal (Second Class), to remove the bombs closest to the conflagration and then supervised the use of hoses to extinguish what remained.

In February 1916 Newall returned to the UK to take command of 6 Wing and then, in December 1916, moved back to France to lead 9 Wing, which specialized in long-distance reconnaissance and raids on targets far behind the enemy lines. In October 1917 he was appointed to command 41 Wing, which was set up with the specific objective of carrying out strategic bombing raids against targets in Germany itself, changing its designation to VIII Brigade in the process. This was a response to the continued bombing of London and other British cities by the Germans, who initially employed Zeppelin and other airships, followed, after their vulnerability had been exposed, by multi-engine bombers, notably the Zeppelin-Staaken R.VI and the Gotha G.V. In a rather belated response to this, Jan Smuts, a member of the Imperial War Cabinet, was appointed by the British Government to write a report on the feasibility of strategic bombing of targets in Germany itself. He concluded that it would be feasible, and Trenchard, who had recently been compelled to step down as CAS, was selected to command what became known as the Independent Bombing Force to carry out long-distance bombing raids. Trenchard was reluctant to accept the appointment, but in the absence of any better job offers agreed to do so. Newall was appointed as his deputy.

Equipped with the Handley Page 0/400 heavy bomber and a number of lighter aircraft, the Independent Bombing Force began operations in June 1918 against targets in Germany from its base some forty miles from Nancy in Lorraine. These targets were the substantially industrial areas in the Saar and along the Rhine. This was not popular with the French, who were opposed to strategic bombing, not least for fear of retaliation, or with the mainstream RAF, which resented not having any control over the new force, and it was only modestly successful in terms of results, although it did draw a large number of German fighters away from the rest of the front. Moreover, it offered a glimpse of the future.

Newall was awarded a permanent commission in August 1919 and appointed Deputy Director of Personnel at the Air Ministry. Three years later he was appointed Deputy Commandant of No. 1 School of Technical Training at Halton. The school was very much the brainchild of Trenchard,

234 Churchill's Eagles

who saw it as fundamental to the existence of an independent RAF, along with the Cadet College at Cranwell and the Staff College at Andover. Halton was formed to train apprentices as ground crew, and although they passed out as airmen, a sizeable percentage went on to be commissioned.

At the end of his time at Halton, Newall was appointed AOC Special Reserve and Auxiliary Air Force. Both the Royal Auxiliary Air Force and the RAF Reserve were also created by Trenchard, the former to attract young men who were keen to fly, willing to contribute something from their own pockets for the privilege and prepared to devote much of their spare time to it, the latter to ensure that those who left after serving in the RAF with a short-term commission would keep up their flying and be subject to recall in times of need.

Having served briefly at the League of Nations Disarmament Committee, which was eventually to spawn the unsuccessful Disarmament Conference, in April 1926 Newall returned to the Air Ministry as Director of Operations and Intelligence and Deputy Chief of the Air Staff, with a seat on the Air Council from January 1930 as an Additional Member, an indication that he was perceived as a senior officer of some promise. He then held two operational commands, the first briefly as AOC Wessex Bombing Area. The second was his first posting overseas, other than in France during the First World War, as AOC Middle East, with his HQ in Cairo and responsibility for Egypt, the Sudan, Palestine and Transjordan. With a relatively modest establishment under his control and little in the way of action, this was not a particularly demanding job. He did take time, however, at the behest of the Air Ministry, which appointed Ralph **Cochrane** to accompany him as a temporary staff officer, to undertake a survey of the requirement for an RAF presence in other British possessions in East Africa – Kenya, Uganda, Tanganyika and Northern and Southern Rhodesia; he concluded that there was no need for a permanent establishment.

In January 1935 Newall was appointed to the Air Staff as Air Member for Supply and Organisation, essentially dealing with the logistical requirements of the service. The portfolio of the AMSO changed at the same time, part of it being hived off into a new department headed by the Air Member for Research and Development, who was initially Hugh **Dowding** and then, from April 1936, Wilfrid **Freeman**. This came at a time when war with Germany seemed quite possible, albeit not inevitable, and every sinew was being stretched to increase the size of the RAF, firstly through a series of Expansion Schemes and secondly by the agreement of specifications for two new fighters, the Hawker Hurricane and the Supermarine Spitfire, and three new heavy bombers, the Short Stirling, Handley Page Halifax and Avro Manchester. Producing these was the responsibility of the AMRD, but getting them into service came under the AMSO, as did commissioning all the new RAF stations now being built. Portal, as the Director of Organisation, was instructed by Newall to set up a new Maintenance Command.

This had all been valuable experience for Newall when, on 1 September 1937, he was appointed Chief of the Air Staff. He had certainly been an obvious contender for the appointment, although there were many who would have preferred either Freeman or Edgar **Ludlow-Hewitt**, the latter going to Bomber Command as AOC-in-C at much the same time.

Over the course of the next two years, Newall devoted himself to preparing the RAF for war. He was a strong supporter of the expansion of Bomber Command, but also insisted that Dowding, who was overdue for retirement but in whom he reposed great confidence, should stay on at Fighter Command. Like Dowding, he was not enthusiastic about army co-operation, and he argued against the deployment of light bombers to France in support of the British Expeditionary Force. When the Germans invaded Belgium and France, Newall was supportive of Dowding's efforts not to see his squadrons reduced to satisfy the demands of the French and encouraged him in writing his famous letter of 16 May to the Under-Secretary of State for Air describing the dire consequences of doing so. Towards the end of the Battle of Britain, however, Newall was notably absent from the meeting at the Air Ministry when the 'Big Wing' issue was debated, thereby denying Dowding his support.

Newall had, well before that time, become far from popular in certain circles, notably with Lord Beaverbrook, the Minister of Aircraft Production and a close friend and confidant of Winston Churchill. The CAS's support within the RAF by this time was also not strong, with many senior officers and two influential former Chiefs, Hugh Trenchard and John Salmond, pressing for more incisive leadership of the service. A very damaging anonymous letter was sent to Archibald Sinclair, the Secretary of State for Air, enumerating Newall's supposed weaknesses, although a future CAS, John **Slessor**, found him very good for morale in a personal capacity and considered him to be the prime architect of the wartime RAF. The opposition, however, became overwhelming, and Portal was appointed CAS in October 1940.

Promoted to Marshal of the RAF, Newall became Governor-General of New Zealand in February 1941, a position which he held until April 1946 and in which he was highly regarded. Following his appointment to a barony shortly afterwards, he disappeared into quiet retirement. He had been an

236 Churchill's Eagles

important figure in the RAF and had made a considerable contribution to its readiness for war, but he was not the man to lead the service in its extraordinary development over the next five years. By no means unintelligent, he nevertheless lacked the incisive brain which enabled Portal not only to lead the service, but to make an outstanding contribution to the Allied central direction of the war though his position on the Combined Chiefs of Staff.

Air Marshal (later Air Chief Marshal) Sir Keith Park GCB, KBE, MC*, DFC (1892–1975)

It is not for nothing that the Battle of Britain Memorial Flight remains so popular. The Flight's Supermarine Spitfires and Hawker Hurricanes represent both a heroic stand against the odds and a victory which denied Germany a successful invasion of the British Isles in 1940 and, with it, total domination of Europe. The heroes of the battle are not only the pilots who fought so gallantly, but all those involved on the ground, from the AOC-in-C, High **Dowding**, to the fitters and armourers at the RAF airfields, the WAAFs in the control rooms, the volunteers of the Observer Corps, the AA gunners and many others. In command of 11 Group, in whose airspace the majority of the fighting took place, was Air Vice-Marshal Keith **Park**, to whom much of the credit for victory is due. However, within weeks of the climax of the battle, both he and Dowding were controversially removed from their posts. Park went on in due course to achieve very high rank and to hold other important appointments, but his reputation has always been associated with the events of the summer and autumn of 1940.

Park was born and educated in New Zealand. When the Great War broke out in 1914 he was working as a purser with the Union Steam Ship Company, but he volunteered immediately to join the New Zealand Expeditionary Force, in which he served as a gunner at Gallipoli before being commissioned in September 1915. He was wounded in the following month and was shipped to England, where he transferred to the RFC in December 1916. Having demonstrated some skill as a pilot, he was initially employed as an instructor. In September 1917 he was at last posted to France, where he joined 48 Squadron, the first to be equipped with the versatile Bristol Fighter. This aircraft, which was to stay in service for no less than fourteen years after the end of the Great War, mounted not only a .303 machine gun firing forward through the propeller, but also a second machine gun, operated by the observer, to see off attacks from the rear. The squadron was largely engaged in reconnaissance and in escorting bombers on long-range raids. In August 1917 Park was made a flight commander and in August 1918 he was appointed the commanding officer, an unusual progression within a single squadron. During his service in the squadron he was credited with fourteen victories and awarded a MC and bar and a DFC.

Park received a permanent commission in 1919. After serving as a squadron commander at the School of Technical Training, he was regarded highly enough to be selected in early 1922 for the first intake of twenty students at the newly formed RAF Staff College. His fellow students included two future marshals of the RAF, Charles **Portal** and Sholto **Douglas**, as well as an officer whom he would succeed in a major command in 1945, Richard **Peirse**. The directing staff under the first commandant, Robert Brooke-Popham, included Philip **Joubert** and Wilfrid **Freeman**. Following his graduation, Park was posted to Egypt, initially in a technical capacity and then on the operations staff at AHQ. Very little of moment happened during his posting there, other than a demonstration of force to put down a mutiny in the Egyptian Army in the Sudan, but he enjoyed his first experience of overseas peacetime service.

After three years in Cairo Park returned to the UK, where he initially joined the staff of Air Defence of Great Britain, which had recently been formed under Air Marshal Sir John Salmond. In February 1926 he was appointed to command 111 Squadron, initially at Duxford and then at Hornchurch, both stations being part of ADGB's Fighting Area. The squadron was equipped with the Armstrong Whitworth Siskin, the first all-metal-frame fighter in the service. Park remained in command of 111 Squadron, which he always thought of as the happiest appointment of his career, until March 1929, when he joined the Air Staff of the Fighting Area. This was followed by command of RAF Northolt and then an appointment as Chief Flying Instructor at the Oxford University Air Squadron at Abingdon.

In the autumn of 1934 Park and his wife travelled to Buenos Aires, where he had been appointed Air Attaché at the British Embassy. His wife, Dol, had some family history there, her father having been on the board of the Great Southern Railway, so they were warmly accepted into local society. Initially accredited to the governments of Argentina, Brazil, Chile and Uruguay, Park's remit was subsequently extended to all the independent states of South America, and he visited many of them. He was well received, but his efforts at promoting the sale of British aircraft and parts was not particularly successful, especially with the United States on the doorstep.

238   Churchill's Eagles

Park returned to the UK at the end of 1936 in time to join the next course at the Imperial Defence College early in the following year. At the same time, he was appointed as an Air Aide-de-Camp to the new King, George VI, whom he attended at a number of RAF-related events. With the college situated in Buckingham Gate, opposite Buckingham Palace, this was exceptionally convenient, especially as 1937 was the King's coronation year. At the end of the IDC course, Park was appointed to command RAF Tangmere, a fighter station operating two squadrons of Hawker Furies, the RAF's penultimate bi-plane fighter. He was there for a little over three months before being appointed Senior Air Staff Officer at Fighter Command

Fighter Command had been formed out of the Fighting Area of ADGB in July 1936, with Dowding as its AOC-in-C. Park had been on Dowding's staff at the Fighting Area nine years earlier and regarded him highly. The two men worked well together, but not everything went their way. By way of example, they were forced to accept into the group several squadrons of the Boulton Paul Defiant, a fighter whose sole armament was a turret with four .303 machine guns, supposedly giving the aircraft more destructive firepower. In fact, the combination of additional weight and a less powerful engine than it needed slowed it down so much that it became easy prey for German fighters. The tactics to be used by Fighter Command squadrons also became the subject of much debate, Dowding and Park preferring 'interception of the many' to the Air Ministry's 'annihilation of the few'. At three of Fighter Command's four groups the commanders responded readily to Dowding's and Park's instructions on tactics, but this was not always true of 12 Group, commanded by Trafford **Leigh-Mallory**.

On 20 April 1940 Park was appointed AOC 11 Group, succeeded as SASO at Fighter Command HQ by Douglas **Evill**. With its HQ at Uxbridge, 11 Group was responsible for the South-East of England, covering the approaches from the Continent to London, whilst 12 Group stood in the way of bombing attacks on the great industrial areas around Birmingham, Manchester, Liverpool and Leeds. Two other groups had also been formed, 10 Group responsible for the South-West of England and 13 Group covering the far North of England and the whole of Scotland. The number of squadrons allocated to each grew slowly, with 11 Group receiving the lion's share. With the German invasion of the Netherlands, Belgium and France in May 1940 came calls for fighter reinforcement on the Continent, not only from the British army commanders, but also from the French. 11 Group, like its fellows, was forced to give up a number of squadrons for service on the other side of the Channel, until Dowding effectively put a stop to it.

The group then became deeply involved in covering the embarkation of the British Expeditionary Force from France, losing aircraft and their pilots not only to German fighters, but also to indiscriminate anti-aircraft fire from British destroyers.

The next phase of the battle, the attacks by the Luftwaffe on British shipping in the English Channel, proved difficult to counter, as very little early warning could be provided, whilst losses mounted. The Battle of Britain itself began on 12 August with German attacks on radar stations, which initially blinded 11 Group. However, most of its aircraft were back in action very quickly, allowing a good response to a major raid on the following day. It became clear that the targets from now on were 11 Group's airfields, and Park requested help on a number of occasions from his two neighbouring groups. Sir Christopher Quintin *Brand*, AOC 10 Group, was invariably swift to react, giving excellent support whenever requested. 12 Group, on the other hand, was notably less quick, largely because it was adopting a new tactic.

Chafing at the bit at Coltishall in command of 42 Squadron in 12 Group was Douglas Bader, who had lost both legs in a crash before the war, but who had subsequently re-learnt to fly as well as any able-bodied pilot. Bader believed that the tactics adopted at 11 Group, whereby squadrons would usually operate alone or at most with one other due to the limited notice of attacks, would not provide the most effective defence. Instead, he proposed to form a grouping of at least three squadrons – later increased to five – in what became known as the 'Big Wing' or the Duxford Wing, from the airfield over which the fighters formed up. This formation would gain a height advantage in order to shoot down as many aircraft as possible. Because of the time taken to do this, the attack could usually only take place after the German aircraft had dropped their bombs and were on the way home, and on several occasions the Germans had escaped long before the Big Wing arrived. Leigh-Mallory was nevertheless convinced that the tactic worked, and he was supported by Sholto Douglas, the DCAS. Dowding and Park, however, continued to make protecting 11 Group's airfields their priority, which required the bombers to be shot down on the way to their targets. This policy drove Park's conduct of the battle, which by mid-September had been effectively won, although it was to drag on for another month, after which the Germans turned their attention from the airfields to the night-time Blitz on London and other cities.

The argument over the use of Big Wings reached its conclusion at a meeting at the Air Ministry on 17 October 1940. The meeting was chaired

240   Churchill's Eagles

by Douglas and was attended by Dowding, Park, Brand and Leigh-Mallory, with the newly designated CAS, Charles Portal, also present, although he took no part in the debate. To the surprise of Dowding and Park, who regarded the presence of such a junior officer as most improper, Bader was also at the meeting and allowed to speak, inevitably in support of the 'Big Wings'. When the minutes appeared, Park requested that they be amended to convey his recollections more accurately, as did both Dowding and Brand, but this was refused by the Air Ministry. For all of them it soured a stunning victory.

The corollary to this was the removal of both Dowding and Park from their posts just over a month later. In Dowding's case it came as no great surprise, as he had been due for retirement for a long time and had only stayed on in response to the Air Ministry's wishes. Park was posted to 23 Group as AOC at the end of the year. With its HQ at South Cerney in Gloucestershire, the group was part of Flying Training Command, responsible for all the Service Flying Training Schools in the West and South of England and the Cotswolds, as well as the Aerospace and Armament Experimental Establishment, the School of Air Navigation, the Central Flying School and the Empire Flying School. The SFTSs sat between the Elementary Flying Training Schools, in which would-be pilots learnt initially how to fly, usually in De Havilland Tiger Moths or similar aircraft, and the Operational Training Units, the last step before being posted to active squadrons. For pilots destined for Fighter Command's single-seater aircraft, the SFTS training took place on Hawker Harts and Miles Masters, whilst for those heading for either Bomber or Coastal Command's multi-engined aircraft, the trainer of choice was the Airspeed Oxford.

Park soon realized that the work he was doing was highly valuable and approached the job with considerable energy. He increased the number of flying instructors, extended the flying hours, improved the training equipment and made night flying a priority. Overall efficiency was much improved. He was, however, keen to get closer to the action and was delighted a year later to be posted to the Mediterranean as AOC Egypt.

Park sailed just before the end of 1941 to Freetown in Sierra Leone, from where he flew across Africa to Khartoum and then up the Nile to Cairo. The main weight of the RAF in North Africa was deployed by the Desert Air Force under a fellow New Zealander, Arthur **Coningham**, whose aircraft flew in support of Eighth Army. Park's task was to defend the Nile Delta against attack, for which he deployed relatively modest resources, which included both day and night fighters, anti-aircraft guns and radar, with all of which he was very familiar from his time at 11 Group. Both Park and Coningham were the immediate subordinates of Arthur **Tedder**, the AOC-in-C Middle East. Towards the end of 1941 the Army had taken Benghazi and advanced as far as the border between Cyrenaica and Tripolitania, only to be thrust back again to the Gazala Line by early February. The Desert Air Force was at that time still a long way away, deploying the majority of the RAF's aircraft. The overall military picture deteriorated significantly, however, when the Axis forces broke out from the Gazala Line, captured Tobruk and advanced to El Alamein, where a hastily constructed defence, supported by both the Desert Air Force and Park's aircraft, brought them to a halt.

At just this time Park was sent in another direction. The precipitate retreat of the Eighth Army, initially from El Agheila to Gazala and then from Gazala to El Alamein, had meant that no land-based air cover was available to convoys to Malta from the Eastern Mediterranean. This had left the island both badly exposed to air attack on its supply line and, in the meantime, seriously short of food and other essential supplies. The island had been under siege since the Italian entry into the war in June 1940, since when it had been under constant attack from the air. The AOC, Hugh **Lloyd**, had held his command since June 1941 and had made a tremendous impact on the situation, but after incessant action he was overdue for relief. Park, with an outstanding reputation for air defence against the odds, was the ideal man to take over, which he did on 15 June 1942.

In fact, although it may not have seemed like it at the time, the worst for Malta in terms of air bombardment was over, but there was still a great deal to do. On the plus side, there were now adequate numbers of aircraft at Park's disposal, and the fighters were Spitfires and in good numbers, in addition to which there were Bristol Beaufighters, Bristol Beaufort torpedo bombers and Vickers Wellington medium bombers. Park's orders were not only to defend the island but to carry out vigorous attacks on Axis convoys carrying supplies to Libya for the German/Italian Army at El Alamein, as well as the ports from which they sailed and the airfields in Sicily. Instead of standing back to see how the enemy attacks developed, the RAF now took the initiative. As far as Malta itself was concerned, the centre and east of the main island now formed one big airfield, with the original sites at Luqa and Hal Far having been joined by Ta'Qali, Safi and Q'rendi, the last of these whilst Park was in command. All of them were now well defended, with solidly constructed dispersal pens. Just over a month after his arrival, Park issued a 'Fighter Interception Plan', which relied on radar to allow

242 Churchill's Eagles

his aircraft to engage those of the Axis much earlier than hitherto. In the meantime, his Wellingtons would hit the ports and his Beauforts would attack the convoys.

The Governor of Malta, Lord Gort, whose relationship with Lloyd had been poor (and was not much better with Park), was deeply concerned about stocks of fuel. This, and a growing shortage of other vital supplies, was to be overcome by dispatching a large convoy from the UK, as the voyage from Egypt was now deemed to be too dangerous. Operation PEDESTAL comprised fourteen merchantmen, including one tanker, the *Ohio*, and a very substantial escort of Royal Navy warships, including two battleships and three aircraft carriers. Having passed Gibraltar on the night of 10/11 August, the convoy came under air and sea attack as soon as it passed south of Sardinia, shortly after which the heavy warships turned round as planned, leaving an escort of cruisers and destroyers. Enormous damage was caused to both the escort and the merchantmen, and only five vessels, now protected by aircraft from Malta, completed the journey. The last of them was the *Ohio*, which was towed into Grand Harbour on 5 August, by a happy coincidence the Feast of the Blessed Virgin Mary, the patron saint of Malta. The tanker was able to discharge its cargo, including aviation fuel, before settling on the bottom of the harbour.

Gort continued to resist the use of fuel except in defence, but he was overruled by London, and Park was able to continue his operations. The Axis air forces attempted one last major offensive in mid-October, which was satisfactorily dealt with, and following the British victory at El Alamein and a headlong retreat by the German/Italian Army to the border of Tripolitania, a convoy from Alexandria arrived intact on 20 November carrying, among other things, significant supplies of fuel. Malta now became a major cog in what would in due course become Mediterranean Allied Air Forces ('MAAF') under Tedder, continuing to attack Axis targets in both Africa and Southern Europe. In due course MAAF provided the air cover for the Allied landings in Sicily in July 1943, tactically controlled by Park's HQ.

In December 1943, with Malta now a relative backwater, Park was appointed AOC-in-C Middle East, with promotion to air marshal. His command still formed part of MAAF, but his responsibilities were spread over a very wide geographical area, including Egypt, the Eastern Mediterranean and Cyprus, the Levant, Iraq, Aden, the Sudan and East Africa. His major responsibilities were training and maintenance, although operations against German shipping in the Aegean were mounted from Egypt.

In late 1944 events took place in the Far East theatre which would shortly impinge on Park. The Air Commander South-East Asia, Air Chief Marshal Sir Richard Peirse, had been conducting an affair with the wife of General Sir Claude Auchinleck, the C-in-C India, which eventually led to her leaving her husband. Lord Louis Mountbatten, the Supreme Allied Commander South-East Asia, was left with no alternative but to replace Peirse, who was quietly retired. Mountbatten's choice to replace Peirse was Guy **Garrod**, Peirse's deputy, who was particularly popular with the Americans. The Air Ministry instead decided to appoint Leigh-Mallory, whose job as C-in-C of the Allied Expeditionary Air Force in North-West Europe had recently become redundant. Leigh-Mallory, however, was killed in an air crash on his way out to India and Park was posted there in his stead, with Garrod moving in the other direction as Deputy C-in-C MAAF. Park, delighted to have an operational appointment once again, took up his new appointment in February 1945.

He found that his command was both huge and widely dispersed. The strategic element was substantially American, equipped with B-24 Consolidated Liberators and flying sorties from bases in India to targets in China and South-East Asia. There was also 231 Group RAF, equipped with two squadrons of Liberators and two initially of Wellingtons, later converted to Liberators. The tactical element was substantially British and consisted of 221 Group supporting IV and XXXII Corps pushing down from the north through Mandalay towards Rangoon, and 224 Group providing similar support to XV Corps in the Arakan. The transport element was very large in the light of the very difficult conditions being experienced by troops on the ground and the severe limitations on supply by road. Dominated by the Americans, it consisted of the Combined Air Transport Organisation, which had overall control of air supply and determined the priorities, and the Combat Cargo Task Force, which actually operated the aircraft and whose RAF component was 232 Group.

There were also a large number of other RAF groups in India, engaged in administration, training, maintenance and the preparation for use in the tropics of aircraft arriving there from the UK or the USA. When Mountbatten's HQ and that of the Allied Air Commander relocated from New Delhi to Kandy in Ceylon in late 1944, it proved necessary to set up an additional organization in New Delhi, Base Air Forces South-East Asia, under the command of Leslie **Hollinghurst**, to look after all activities not directly connected with operations and to provide day-to-day liaison with the Government of India.

244   Churchill's Eagles

Park actually spent relatively little time in Kandy and a great deal travelling around his far-flung command, including visits to forward airfields. During the six months between his arrival in India and the Japanese surrender, Park developed a very good relationship with Lieutenant General Sir William Slim of Fourteenth Army but a relatively poor one with Slim's superior, Lieutenant General Sir Oliver Leese, who had refused to relocate to Kandy until after the defeat of the Japanese. Shortly afterwards Leese was replaced by Slim as C-in-C Allied Land Forces South-East Asia.

On 12 September 1945 Park was present in Singapore at the formal surrender of the Japanese in South-East Asia. Just over two months later, Mountbatten and his immediate subordinates moved their HQs to Singapore. Peacetime presented its own difficulties, notably unrest in the RAF, as well as in the other two services, about the slow speed of repatriation to the UK for demobilization. During his term in Singapore, Park was asked by Evill, now VCAS, to visit New Zealand to discuss the county's post-war plans for the RNZAF. He and his wife were very warmly welcomed and spent three weeks going round the country, also spending time in Australia on their way back. In February 1946, however, Park received a letter from Tedder, who had succeeded Portal as CAS, to say that he was being retired once he had completed his tour of duty and written his despatches. In the event, he left the RAF on 20 December 1946. In retirement Park represented Hawker Siddeley, first in Argentina, and then in New Zealand until 1960. He also became Chairman of the International Airport Committee, identifying and arranging for the building of a new airport outside Auckland, which was eventually opened in 1966 He was also elected to the Auckland Council. He died on 6 February 1956 and a memorial service was held seven months later at the RAF Church, St Clement Danes, at which the address was given by his old 'Big Wing' opponent, Douglas Bader. Bader, to his credit, ascribed to Park the lion's share of responsibility for victory over the Germans in the Battle of Britain.

During his long career in the RAF, Park showed himself to be a capable administrator, but he was, much more importantly, an outstanding leader in operations against the enemy. He excelled both in the Battle of Britain and in the final stages of the Siege of Malta, and also proved himself as a senior commander of a large multinational force in the Far East. He did, perhaps, lack the political skills which were to keep some of his contemporaries in employment long after he himself had retired, but it is his name, not theirs, which has been remembered by subsequent generations.

Air Chief Marshal Sir Richard Peirse KCB, DSO, AFC (1892–1970)

During the war, Richard **Peirse** held some of the most senior appointments in the RAF, notably Deputy Chief of the Air Staff and Vice-Chief of the Air Staff, both of which gave him a seat on the Air Council, and AOC-in-C Bomber Command. Moreover, following his appointment as AOC-in-C Air Forces in India in early 1942, towards the end of the following year he became C-in-C Air Command South-East Asia, responsible to the Allied Supreme Commander South-East Asia not only for all the RAF formations and units in the theatre, but also for those of the USAAF. By the end of 1944, however, he was on his way to a premature retirement, for entirely personal reasons.

Having completed his officer training on HMS *Conway*, Peirse was commissioned into the Royal Navy in November 1912. In the following year he volunteered for training as a pilot in the Royal Naval Air Service and joined his first squadron, No. 2, in September 1914. He rose rapidly in rank to flight commander and then squadron commander, serving in a number of squadrons and wings and flying mostly Sopwith 1½ Strutters operating from the Dunkirk area against the German bases in Zeebrugge and Ostend, for which he received the DSO. After a period in the UK away from the conflict, he returned to Northern France, rising in due course to the rank of wing commander. In June 1919, with the RNAS absorbed into the RAF, he became Officer Commanding Aircraft in Fighting Ships, part of 29 Group, and subsequently a staff officer in that group.

Peirse was sufficiently highly regarded to be selected as one of twenty officers on the first course at the newly opened RAF Staff College in Andover, a key element of 'Boom' Trenchard's strategy to ensure the independence of the RAF. Amongst his fellow students were Charles **Portal**, Sholto **Douglas**, Keith **Park** and John *Baldwin*, whilst the directing staff, under the Commandant, Robert Brooke-Popham, included Wilfrid **Freeman** and Philip **Joubert**. On graduating, Peirse was appointed Officer Commanding RAF Gosport, which took him back to his RNAS days, the occupants of the station being a number of independent Fleet Spotter, Fleet Torpedo and Fleet Fighter flights, operating the Westland Walrus reconnaissance fighter in conjunction with the Royal Navy.

Peirse's next posting, in September 1925, was to the Air Ministry in the Directorate of Staff Duties. In January 1927, he became once again a student at a newly opened seat of learning, this time the Imperial Defence College, which had been established to bring together the most promising middle-ranking officers of all three British and Dominion armed services, the Indian

246   Churchill's Eagles

Army and the Civil Service. Douglas was once again a fellow student, others including the future Field Marshals Viscount Alanbrooke and Sir Claude Auchinleck, whilst Joubert was once again on the Directing Staff. Peirse's inclusion was a clear indication that he was seen as one of the coming men of his generation in the RAF.

On the conclusion of his course, Peirse was posted to Egypt, initially on the staff at HQ RAF Middle East, followed by an appointment as the Officer Commanding RAF Heliopolis, the most important airfield in the country and situated on the outskirts of Cairo. He returned to the UK in mid-1930, spending a few months unemployed on half pay before taking up an appointment on the Air Staff as Deputy Director of Operations and Intelligence. Just over two years later, with promotion to air commodore, he was posted back to the Middle East, this time as AOC Palestine and Transjordan. When he arrived, Palestine was quiet, but the Arab Revolt erupted in early 1936, largely in protest against extensive Jewish immigration. A general strike declared in April of that year ended in October, but serious unrest, with fighting between Jews and Arabs, continued. Roads were coming under attack, causing Peirse to devise a system of air cover, with all vehicle convoys accompanied by wireless vans, whose signallers could call for assistance from the RAF when necessary. When armed bands were identified, these were bombed. Although the Arab villages were not usually subjected to air attack, they were leafleted to threaten this if necessary. Peirse's strategy was continued by his successors, Roderick **Hill** and Arthur **Harris**.

Peirse, who had been promoted by this time to air vice-marshal, returned to the UK in January 1937 to become Deputy Chief of the Air Staff and simultaneously Director of Operations and Intelligence. After war had been declared on Germany in September 1939, he was advanced in rank to air marshal and appointed an additional member of the Air Council. In April he became the first Vice-Chief of the Air Staff, a more senior role than the DCAS and the right-hand man of the CAS, at that time Air Chief Marshal Sir Cyril **Newall**. It was a role which Peirse was to hold through the summer and early autumn of 1940, during which the Battle of Britain was at its height. On 4 October of that year, however, he was appointed to another very senior role, AOC-in-C Bomber Command in succession to Charles Portal, who had succeeded Newall as CAS.

During Peirse's appointment as VCAS he had expressed concern about the bombing of targets in Germany itself, which he feared would bring repercussions against British cities, but by the time of his move to Bomber

Command the Luftwaffe had already carried out its first raids on London, providing full justification for retaliation. At this time the command consisted of five groups. No.1 had formed the Advanced Air Striking Force in France, where its Fairey Battles had been wiped out: the group was now re-equipping with the Vickers Wellington. No.2 was equipped with the Bristol Blenheim, No.3 with the Wellington, No. 4 with the Armstrong Whitworth Whitley and No.5 with the Handley Page Hampden. Other than the Wellington, none of the aircraft proved to be suitable for a sustained bombing campaign. The Blenheims were largely engaged on raiding German naval facilities and coastal shipping, their sorties being carried out mostly in daylight, thereby incurring very heavy casualties. 2 Group subsequently moved on to carry out bombing sweeps across Northern France, targeting airfields and industrial installations. Although it was supported by Fighter Command, its own losses were shown subsequently to have been greater than those of the Luftwaffe. As far as 4 and 5 Groups were concerned, neither the Whitley nor the Hampden could carry more than a very modest load of small bombs, although the latter did do good work as a mine-layer.

A new generation of heavy bombers had been long planned, however, and the first of these, the Short Stirling, entered service in 3 Group shortly before Peirse's appointment as AOC-in-C. It was followed a month later by both the Handley Page Halifax, which was to equip 4 Group, and the Avro Manchester, which equipped 5 Group. None of these aircraft proved very satisfactory, although the performance of the Halifax was considerably improved by a change of engine long after Peirse's term at Bomber Command had ended, whilst the Manchester would later be removed from service to make way for its derivative, the outstanding Lancaster.

In March 1941, with the Battle of the Atlantic going badly for the British, Perise was ordered to suspend attacks by his medium and heavy bombers on targets in Germany and focus instead on attacking enemy naval targets, notably Brest, where the two German battleships, the *Scharnhorst* and the *Gneisenau*, were based. They had taken shelter there after a very successful voyage from Germany which had resulted in the loss of a considerable tonnage of merchant ships. The two vessels were hit during bombing raids, but neither sustained significant damage. The other naval targets for Bomber Command were the major U-boat bases at Lorient and Bordeaux, whilst further maritime-related targets included the shipyards at Kiel, Hamburg and Bremen and the airfields housing the Focke-Wulf Condor long range reconnaissance aircraft at Stavanger in Norway and near Bordeaux.

248 Churchill's Eagles

In the late spring of 1941 Bomber Command returned to what it considered to be its main task, bombing industrial targets in Germany, with a focus on the Ruhr Valley. By this time, however, the German defences had dramatically improved, with the creation of the 'Kammhuber Line' of massed searchlights and increasingly effective radar stations. Moreover, German night fighter capabilities were improving fast. The evidence also began to mount that the accuracy of British bombing was being greatly exaggerated. Mr D. M. Butt of the Cabinet Office was instructed to prepare a detailed report on the subject, using not only the photos taken by the bombers themselves when their loads were released, but also those of the Photo Reconnaissance Unit. The Butt Report was published in August 1941, based on over 4,000 photos from the previous two months, and its findings were shocking. Only a third of all bombs had been dropped within five miles of the target; in the Ruhr it was one in ten; and on new-moon nights the proportion was just one in fifteen.

Unsurprisingly it was Peirse who paid the price, following a very difficult interview with Churchill in early November, the immediate result of which was the curtailing of bombing operations during the winter months. By the end of the year it was clear that the War Cabinet had lost confidence in Peirse and he was relieved of his command on 8 January 1942, with John Baldwin appointed on a temporary basis, pending the appointment of a permanent successor.

Peirse was not unemployed for long. He had retained the confidence of both Portal and Archibald Sinclair, the Secretary of State for Air, and was now sent to a new hotspot, South-East Asia, where the Japanese were in the ascendant. Peirse visited both Singapore and the Dutch East Indies before the Japanese overran them and was appalled by the low numbers and the poor quality of the aircraft being deployed by the RAF. As far as India itself was concerned, at the time the Japanese attacked Pearl Harbor there had only been seven RAF Squadrons and three from the Indian Air Force in the whole of the sub-continent, all of which were equipped with largely obsolete aircraft, so major reinforcements were called for. Peirse was formally appointed AOC-in-C Air Forces in India on 6 March 1942 and began the urgent work of improving both the numerical strength and the quality of his command.

By this time the British and their American-equipped Chinese allies were conducting a fighting retreat in Burma, where the best aircraft available were Hurricanes, hastily dispatched from the Middle East, and the Curtis Tomahawks of the American Volunteer Group. Much further south a large Japanese task force entered the Bay of Bengal, where it sank HMS *Hermes*, the only aircraft carrier in the theatre. Colombo was bombed before the Japanese withdrew. In India itself, now seemingly under threat, the RAF had always been the poor relation of the Army and its only really satisfactory airfields and infrastructure were in the North-West, where they had supported campaigns on the Frontier, but these were useless for the prosecution of war on the other side of the sub-continent.

The pace of change was slow, but at least the Japanese advance was effectively halted by the monsoon, allowing Peirse some breathing space. Gradually more and better aircraft arrived, whilst large numbers of new airfields were constructed. The major threat was perceived to be on the frontier between Burma and India, the former country being, by the summer of 1942, almost completely under Japanese control. Two groups were established, 221 in support of operations to the north around Imphal, and 224 based in the south where fighting was taking place in the Arakan. Peirse set up AHQ Bengal to exercise control over these, attracting criticism from the Air Ministry, which considered it inappropriate. ACM Sir Edgar **Ludlow-Hewitt**, the Inspector-General of the RAF, was sent to adjudicate and came down unreservedly in Peirse's favour. The overall Command HQ remained in New Delhi, but other groups were also set up elsewhere to control repairs and maintenance, storage, salvage, training and the preparation of aircraft arriving in India from the UK or the Middle East for operations under local conditions.

Peirse, General Sir Archibald Wavell, C-in-C India, and the latter's successor, General Sir Claude Auchinleck, were all determined to take the fight to the Japanese whenever possible, with air superiority as the goal. This was difficult initially, as both the number of aircraft and their quality were significantly less than Peirse considered necessary, but by the end of 1943 there were over fifty RAF squadrons in service under his command and the first Spitfires had arrived to replace most of the Hurricanes.

November 1943 saw the arrival of Admiral Lord Louis Mountbatten to be the Supreme Allied Commander South-East Asia, with Peirse reporting to him as Air C-in-C. Whilst he retained command of all air activity in India and Ceylon, Peirse's focus was on the formations supporting ground operations. These came under a new organization, Eastern Air Command, whose commander was Major General (later Lieutenant General) George E. Stratemeyer of the USAAF, which by now had considerable forces in the theatre. There had been resistance to the supremacy of the British on the part of some Americans but, the matter having been decided upon by the

250   Churchill's Eagles

Combined Chiefs of Staff in London and Washington, the structure was accepted.

Stratemeyer had three subordinate commands. The Strategic Air Force under Major General Howard C. Davidson contained all the heavy bombers, very largely Liberators. Most of the units were provided by the USAAF, which employed them not only on operations against the Japanese in Burma, but also further afield, notably in China, where Chiang Kai-shek's Kuomintang armies were fighting the Japanese. By way of contrast, Air Marshal Sir John Baldwin's Third Tactical Air Force, which was responsible for army co-operation, deployed two RAF Groups. 221 conducted operations initially around Imphal, where a major battle was fought in the spring of 1944 as the Japanese attempted to invade India. The group later supported the advance of IV and XXXIII Corps into Central Burma and thence to Rangoon. 224 Group provided the same service to XV Corps fighting in the Arakan. The third component of Eastern Air Command was Troop Carrier Command, later the Combat Carrier Task Force which, under Brigadier General William D. Old, controlled the cargo aircraft, very substantially Douglas C.47s, which were vitally important to the supply of troops on the ground, as road access was at best limited and in most cases non-existent.

One relatively small but briefly important formation was the Air Commando Force, which supported Major General Orde Wingate's Chindits and included fighters, bombers, transport aircraft, light aircraft and gliders. It did not fit easily into any of Stratemeyer's commands, but was in the end placed under Baldwin's overall supervision. Peirse was never very happy with the Air Commando Force and had it disbanded in May 1944, when control of the Chindits was handed over to Major General 'Vinegar Joe' Stilwell. The commander of the Air Commando Force, Colonel Phil Cochran, was deeply upset and criticised Peirse openly, although Stratemeyer remained on very good terms with him.

When Mountbatten relocated his HQ from New Delhi to Kandy in Ceylon, Peirse reluctantly did the same, which necessitated thousands of additional miles of flying whenever he wanted to visit his front-line units or his more senior commanders. It also removed him from the delights of New Delhi, which included an affair he was conducting with the wife of the C-in-C India, as Auchinleck had become when Wavell was elevated to become the Viceroy of India. The affair soon became common knowledge and Mountbatten, who had formed an excellent relationship with Peirse, was reluctantly obliged to have him replaced. Peirse's intended replacement, Trafford **Leigh-Mallory**, was killed in an air crash on his way out to India, but Mountbatten felt that Peirse should leave in any event, with his Deputy, Guy **Garrod**, taking over temporarily pending the appointment of the new Air C-in-C, Keith **Park**. On his return to the UK accompanied by Jessie Auchinleck, whom he later married after divorcing his own wife, Peirse was quietly retired. He took on no other significant appointments outside the RAF.

Peirse is not one of the easiest senior RAF officers to assess. Somehow his achievements, which were not inconsiderable, were overshadowed by others of his generation whose careers were more spectacular. He was unlucky to lead Bomber Command at the nadir of its fortunes, before it received outstanding aircraft such as the Lancaster and the De Havilland Mosquito, and also before it became the beneficiary of new aids to navigation such as *Gee*, *Oboe* and *H2S*, and specialized target-marking formations. The monument to his success was the creation of a powerful and effective air command in South-East Asia, but in much the same way as its ground and naval counterparts this became the 'Forgotten Air Force', completely overshadowed by the operations of the Allied Air Forces in the Mediterranean and North-West Europe. Peirse deserved better, but he might also have been more widely recognized after the war if he had not put his private life first.

Marshal of the RAF The Viscount Portal of Hungerford KG, GCB, OM, DSO*, MC (1893–1971)

The RAF produced many great operational commanders in the Second World War – Hugh **Dowding**, Arthur **Harris** and Arthur **Tedder,** to name but three – but its towering figure was not a wartime commander, other than during a relatively brief period, but a staff officer. Charles **Portal** – Peter to his close friends – became the Chief of the Air Staff in October 1940 and remained in post until February 1946, many months after victory had been achieved over both Germany and Japan. During that time, he established himself not only as the unquestioned leader of his own service, but also as one of the small group of men who guided the Allies to ultimate victory.

When the Great War broke out in 1914, Portal was at the end of the second of his intended three years as an undergraduate at Christ Church, Oxford, but he volunteered immediately to join the Royal Engineers as a dispatch rider. Commissioned soon after arriving in France, he found the work tedious and asked to be seconded to the Royal Flying Corps. As he had not learnt to fly, he initially became an observer in 3 Squadron in the summer of 1915, spotting for the artillery from a French-built Morane Parasol.

252   Churchill's Eagles

Tiring of this, he applied to become a pilot. He had his initial training in the UK at 5 (Reserve) Squadron, followed by more advanced training at 8 (Reserve) Squadron. It was April 1916 before he was awarded his wings, and he left for France in the following month as a pilot in 60 Squadron. He was in the squadron for a brief but very active few weeks before rejoining 3 Squadron as a flight commander.

Once again Portal found himself artillery spotting, as well as carrying out reconnaissance flights, both very much part of the squadron's army co-operation role; but on a number of occasions he had to engage enemy aircraft, one of which he managed to shoot down. For this and many more mundane but vitally important sorties he was awarded the Military Cross in January 1917, followed by the Distinguished Service Order five months later. His quality was further recognized by his promotion in June 1917 to acting major and command of 16 Squadron, flying the RE8, a new reconnaissance aircraft built by the Royal Aircraft Factory, an improvement on the Morane Parasols and Bi-planes, but still no match for the German fighters. During the spring and early summer of 1918 the squadron was intensively employed during the German offensive and the Allied counter-attack.

After months of action, Portal was promoted to lieutenant colonel in June 1918 and sent back to England to command 24 (Training) Wing at Grantham. Shortly afterwards came the announcement of a bar to his DSO. Now in possession of a permanent commission, he returned to France briefly in the early months of 1919 before becoming Chief Flying Instructor at RAF Cranwell on the opening of the Cadet College there that November. Just over two years later, by this time clearly highly regarded by his superiors, he was included in the first intake at the new RAF Staff College in Andover, like Cranwell one of the institutions which Hugh Trenchard set up to demonstrate the RAF's independence from the Army and Royal Navy. Robert Brooke-Popham was the Commandant, whilst Wilfrid **Freeman** and Philip **Joubert** were on the Directing Staff and Sholto **Douglas**, Richard **Peirse** and Keith **Park** were amongst Portal's fellow students.

On graduating from the Staff College, Portal was inevitably posted to a staff job, working in the Flying Operations (Home) section of the Directorate of Operations and Intelligence at the Air Ministry. This brought him into direct contact with Trenchard, who was still fighting to preserve the RAF's independence and who had seen in Portal a potential future leader. By way of ensuring that Portal understood more about the other services, Trenchard sent him on the Senior Officers' War Course at the Royal Naval College at Greenwich, where Portal found himself among naval officers who knew little about the RAF, on which he was delighted to enlighten them.

His next appointment was as CO of 7 Squadron, for a short time at RAF Bircham Newton in Norfolk and then at Kings Worthy in Hampshire. Together with 58 Squadron at the same station, both equipped with the Vickers Virginia, it accounted for half of the heavy element of the Bombing Area of Air Defence of Great Britain. 58 Squadron was commanded by Arthur **Harris,** and whilst there was a considerable rivalry between the squadrons, the two men became firm friends and enjoyed a mutual admiration. Like Harris, Portal placed a great deal of emphasis on night flying and, on one occasion, won a bet with an army officer who maintained that Portal would not be able to remain over him all night. When dawn broke, Portal was still there!

On leaving 7 Squadron at the end of 1928, Portal was nominated for the third course at the Imperial Defence College, where he found himself in the company of others regarded as some of the most promising officers of the UK and Commonwealth armed services and the Civil Service. One fellow student from the Royal Navy, Captain Andrew Cunningham, was to play a significant part in Portal's career at a much later date. On leaving the college, Portal was sent on a tour of the RAF in India, very much focused on the North-West Frontier, the traditional stamping ground of the Indian Army. It provided him with some excellent background for his next posting, as Deputy Director of Plans, part of the Department of Operations and Intelligence at the Air Ministry. As a result he was required to attend the meetings of the Joint Planning Sub-committee of the Committee of Imperial Defence, where two issues emerged as by far the most important, the Frontier and Singapore. It was the latter, however, which exercised him most and particularly the naval base which was being created there, largely because of the threat posed by an increasingly militaristic Japan. The Royal Navy insisted on the base's defence taking the shape of very heavy naval guns on the seaward side of the island. Trenchard and his successor as CAS, John Salmond, pressed the case for torpedo bombers, fighters and reconnaissance aircraft, which they considered to be both more effective and a great deal less expensive. Portal was responsible for arguing the issue at the Joint Planning Sub-committee, but in due course the Royal Navy had its way, with disastrous results many years later. Portal had two excellent subordinates, Ralph **Cochrane** and Gerald *Gibbs*, but he insisted on writing the most important papers himself. Cochrane particularly admired his ability to come into the office first thing in the morning, produce a paper in

254   Churchill's Eagles

longhand in a very short space of time, have it copy-typed and then placed before the CAS in the early afternoon.

In early 1934 Portal was posted to Southern Arabia as Officer Commanding Aden Command. This was an important appointment, not least because the incumbent was in control of all British military activity, not just the RAF, in the Aden Protectorate and the surrounding area. There was, for the most part, only one RAF squadron, No. 8, based there, but Portal's responsibilities also included sundry army units, mostly engineers, an RAF armoured car squadron and the Aden Protectorate Levies, over five hundred-strong and British-officered. This structure was the product of Trenchard's contention that it would be much cheaper to rely on controlling the tribes within the Protectorate by air than by ground forces. This proved itself to be true time and again, most notably in Portal's time when the Quteibi tribe caused trouble and had to be threatened with its villages being bombed, which brought it back into line, albeit not before a few bombs had been dropped to demonstrate that the authorities were serious.

Potentially much more serious was the threat posed to peace in the area by the Italian invasion of Abyssinia in 1935, which caused Aden to be heavily reinforced, not only by the arrival of three more RAF squadrons, but also by significant units of the Royal Navy. Portal's wife and children had joined him in Aden, but the situation was serious enough to cause him to send them back to the UK. In the event, there was no direct threat to British interests in Aden or elsewhere, but the League of Nations was unable to halt the invasion.

Portal had enjoyed much of his time in Aden, but he was pleased to return to England to become the RAF Instructor at the Imperial Defence College, where Arthur **Longmore** was the Commandant. Among the students were Keith Park, who had been a fellow student at the Staff College, and Ralph *Sorley*, who had been instrumental in ensuring that the number of guns in the new British fighters, the Hawker Hurricane and the Supermarine Spitfire, were increased from four to eight and who would later hold a vital position as Controller of Research and Development at the Ministry of Aircraft Production. In July 1937 Portal was appointed Director of Organisation at the Air Ministry, an immediate subordinate to the Air Member for Supply and Organisation, Air Marshal Sir William *Welsh*. This was a key position during the run-up to war, when the overriding objective for the RAF was its rapid expansion. A series of Expansion Schemes had begun in mid-1934 and, by the time of Portal's appointment, Scheme F was underway, with additions from Scheme H, although Scheme J was already on the drawing board. This was followed in quick succession by Schemes K, L and M, but Scheme F was, in the event, the only one to be actually implemented.

Expansion required new aircraft in considerable quantities, many more airfields and an enormous increase in personnel. The aircraft required not only aircrew to fly them and perform other functions, such as navigation and air gunnery, but also a much larger workforce on the ground to repair and maintain them, all of whom had to be trained. Sites for airfields had to be identified and built on, whilst their owners had to be properly compensated. Most of the early ones had substantial permanent buildings and infrastructure, but the later ones, particularly the satellite landing grounds, were much more modestly equipped.

Seventeen months after being appointed Director of Organisation, Portal became Air Member for Personnel, with a seat on the Air Council. His task was now focused on recruitment and training. As far as the first was concerned, he set up a Department of Manning to expedite recruitment and also established a new Technical Branch, separate from the General Duties Branch of the service. The provision of training was much more problematic, as there were just not enough facilities in the British Isles to provide for the numbers which the Expansion Schemes demanded. The solution was to have large numbers trained elsewhere in the British Commonwealth. Whilst Canada, Australia, New Zealand and South Africa would provide all initial flying training for their own nationals, the more advanced service flying training for all would be concentrated in Canada, which was relatively easily accessible from the UK in particular. After extensive negotiations, the Empire Air Training Scheme was signed by all the countries in Ottawa on 17 December 1939. Subsequently, more capacity for training was created in Rhodesia, India and the Middle East. The Scheme turned out to be immensely successful, operating until August 1945.

In April 1940 Portal succeeded Edgar **Ludlow-Hewitt** as C–in–C Bomber Command. The command had lost 1 Group to the Advanced Air Striking Force in France, so was composed of four groups, No.2 under James *Robb*, equipped with the Bristol Blenheim, No. 3 under John *Baldwin* with the Vickers Wellington, No. 4 under Arthur **Coningham** with the Armstrong Whitworth Whitley and No. 5 under Arthur Harris with the Handley Page Hampden. The overall number of squadrons fluctuated, but for the most part was less than thirty. Up to the second week of May 1940, operations were limited to attacks on German shipping and naval installations, especially after the German invasion of Norway. With the German attack on Belgium and North-West France, however, the focus switched to that campaign, with

256 Churchill's Eagles

2 Group particularly committed to bombing German troop concentrations and suffering heavy losses as a result. The other groups, for the first time, launched attacks on mainland Germany, with the first significant attack on the Ruhr taking place on the night of 15/16 May. These raids, mostly on a small scale, continued by night throughout the summer and autumn as the Battle of Britain was taking place elsewhere, but the results were very modest due to poor navigation and small bomb loads. On the other hand, losses of aircraft at night were equally modest as the German night fighters and anti-aircraft guns lacked radar.

On 23 October 1940, Portal succeeded Cyril **Newall** as CAS. Newall had himself only been in the position for three years, but he had presided over the RAF's preparations for war with some success. He was, however, not popular with certain influential people, notably Lord Beaverbrook, who had the ear of Churchill, and he was more widely perceived as not being the right man to take the RAF through what was clearly going to be a very difficult time. Portal, on the other hand, was highly regarded both inside and outside the service, and there was a warm welcome from both the Air Ministry and the several commands at home and overseas.

With Peirse taking Portal's place in Bomber Command, there was a vacancy for the role of VCAS and Portal immediately asked for Wilfrid Freeman. Freeman was five years older than Portal and senior to him on the Air Force List. He was already on the Air Council as Air Member for Development and Production, in which role he had been working hand-in-glove with the Ministry of Aircraft Production. Portal had known him since his days as a student at the Staff College and had actually worked under him when he was Director-General of Research and Development and he had come to admire him greatly. Freeman, promoted to air chief marshal before Portal, offered to step down in rank, but this was not considered necessary. He was to provide not only advice to his superior, but also close friendship. Freeman, supported by Portal, continued to be intimately involved with the RAF's expansion, which was still accelerating, with new aircraft coming into service, whilst others, notably the De Havilland Mosquito, which was very much Freeman's particular 'baby', were close to fruition.

One problem which emerged in the early months of 1941 was the position of Arthur Longmore, the AOC-in-C Middle East. Very much the poor relation compared to the Home Commands, the RAF in the Middle East suffered from being equipped with aircraft, notably the Hurricane and the American Curtis Tomahawk and its derivatives, which underperformed relative to their German fighter counterparts. Longmore wanted more aircraft and better ones, and his constant demands for these succeeded in irritating Churchill in particular. Portal, too, became increasingly frustrated by Longmore's demands, and the latter was recalled from Cairo and removed from his job, albeit that he was then appointed as one of two Inspectors-General of the RAF. Longmore's Deputy C-in-C, Tedder, whom Portal rated highly, also fell foul of the Prime Minister with his demands and Freeman was sent out to investigate. He suspected that this was a precursor to Tedder being dismissed, and he and Portal agreed that they would both resign if this happened. In the event Tedder was retained and grew in stature as the war progressed, becoming in due course the Deputy Supreme Commander to Eisenhower in North-West Europe, with responsibility for all matters concerning the Allied Air Forces in that campaign.

In addition to his manifold responsibilities as the head of the RAF, Portal had a major new role, for which he had no real preparation. This was nothing less than a very close involvement in the overall British direction of the war, as a result of his membership of the Chiefs of Staff Committee, the meetings of which took place very frequently, indeed daily at certain times. Churchill was a member himself, together with his own Personal Staff Officer, General Sir Hastings Ismay, with the Royal Navy represented by Admiral of the Fleet Sir Dudley Pound and, after Pound's death, by Admiral of the Fleet Sir Andrew Cunningham, and the British Army by Field Marshal Sir John Dill and later by Field Marshal Sir Alan Brooke. Portal was very much younger than any of these men, but held his own in their company; indeed, he became highly respected by them.

The situation was further complicated by the entry into the war of the United States. The first meeting of the Chiefs of Staff Committee with their American counterparts, the US Joint Chiefs of Staff, took place in August 1941 in Placentia Bay, Newfoundland aboard HMS *Prince of Wales*, but Portal was unable to attend and Freeman represented him. Portal did, however, attend the meeting in Washington in December 1941, following the Japanese attack on Pearl Harbor. He had already met General Henry H. 'Hap' Arnold, the Chief of Staff of the USAAF, in the UK earlier in the year and was now to forge a close relationship with him. Portal attended thereafter all the meetings of the Combined Chiefs of Staff, except those with their Russian counterparts in Moscow in August 1942 and October 1944 – he did, however, meet the Russians in Teheran in November 1943 – and he made a significant contribution to the Combined Chiefs' decisions, notably the one arrived at in Casablanca in January 1943 which determined

258   Churchill's Eagles

that the Allies should invade Sicily, and later mainland Italy, before North-West Europe.

Other than for the meetings of the Combined Chiefs, Portal found it relatively difficult to get away from the UK, but he did visit RAF establishments in North Africa and Malta following the Casablanca Conference in January 1943. He also visited RAF units in France in the aftermath of the Normandy landings in June 1944 and went to Italy two months later. For the most part, however, he was tied to the UK. He never went to the Far East; indeed, Christopher *Courtney*, the AMSO, was the only member of the Air Council to visit that theatre during the war.

When Freeman became Chief Executive of the Ministry of Aircraft Production in late 1942, in response to concerns about its effectiveness, Portal's first reaction was to have him replaced as VCAS by Tedder. However, General Eisenhower, now the Supreme Commander in the Mediterranean, pressed for Tedder to remain in that theatre as the overall Air Commander, to which Portal agreed. The position of VCAS was held temporarily by Charles *Medhurst*, and then taken over by Dougal **Evill**, brought back from Washington, who held it for the remainder of the war. Evill turned out to be an ideal man for the job, looking after most of the issues on the air staff side, whilst leaving Portal to concentrate on the bigger picture alongside his colleagues on the CCS. Evill, who was actually slightly older than Portal, also turned out to be a useful confidant. Tedder subsequently moved in with Eisenhower, serving as his Deputy at Supreme Headquarters Allied Expeditionary Force and becoming in the process the effective air commander for the campaign in North-West Europe.

As far as the commands in the UK were concerned, Fighter Command took up little of Portal's attention. Coastal Command, on the other hand, became a major issue shortly after his appointment as CAS, when the Admiralty demanded that it be taken over by the Royal Navy. This would have caused both significant disruption and a threat to morale within the RAF. A solution was, however, found very quickly, when operational control was ceded to the Admiralty, but administrative control was retained by the RAF. There was also an attempt by the Chief of the Imperial General Staff, Sir Alan Brooke, to create an army air arm. However, with the exceptions of Air Observation Post squadrons, whose Austers were piloted by members of Royal Artillery and used for spotting, but maintained by the RAF, this was seen off by Portal.

Portal did have a great deal to do with Bomber Command, the most controversial of all. He had, of course, had direct experience of the command as its AOC-in-C for nearly seven months in 1940, so knew a lot of the background, but the bombing campaign was to be both more effective and more controversial as time went by. Initially there was the question of command. Peirse, who had taken over from Portal himself, proved to be a disappointment and was relieved in early 1942. His successor, after the brief interregnum of John Baldwin, was Harris, Portal's fellow squadron commander at Kings Worthy in the late 1920s. There was a mutual admiration between the two men, Harris taking criticism from Portal in a way he would not from any other senior officer, whilst Portal recognized that Harris would be a thoroughly aggressive commander who would, at least up to a point, do what he was told. Two examples of Harris submitting to Portal's orders contrary to his own better judgement were the formation of the Pathfinders and the creation of 617 Squadron to drop the 'bouncing bomb' on the great dams of the Ruhr and elsewhere. In both cases Harris was to accept subsequently that Portal had been right. Portal, however, did not always get his own way. When he asked Harris to release Ralph **Cochrane** to become ACAS (Policy) at the Air Ministry, Harris refused point blank, and this time Portal accepted it.

Portal also allowed Harris to get away with a loose interpretation of the *Pointblank* Directive of June 1943, which defined the key German targets for both Bomber Command and the 8th US Air Force as submarine construction yards, the aircraft industry, transportation and oil plants. The USAAF followed the Directive and subsequent iterations to the letter, but, whilst Harris encouraged more accurate bombing in Cochrane's 5 Group and to some extent in 3 Group, Bomber Command continued what was, to all intents and purposes, area bombing, culminating in the destruction of Dresden in February 1945. Whilst Portal was, in general, widely admired by both the British and the Americans, his toleration of area bombing has come to be seen by some historians as something of a stain on his reputation.

At the end of the war in Europe, however, Portal's standing in the eyes not only of his own service but of many others was very high. Honours were bestowed on him not only by the United Kingdom in which he became a Knight of the Garter and, successively, a baron in August 1945 and a viscount in early 1946, but also by the USA and many other Allied countries. Portal retired from the RAF at the end of 1945, at the age of fifty-two still a comparatively young man. He became subsequently a director of a number of multi-national companies, including the British Aircraft Company, which brought under one roof a number of the major manufacturers, initially Bristol, English Electric and Vickers. Moreover, in 1950 the Prime Minister,

260 Churchill's Eagles

Clement Attlee, persuaded him to take an appointment as Controller of Atomic Energy. This he did somewhat reluctantly, but he went on to lead the development of what was then a completely new science for both warlike and pacific purposes.

Portal must be regarded as one of the 'Giants' of the RAF, becoming to its second generation what Trenchard had been to its first. He also made a very considerable contribution to the overall prosecution of the Second World War by the Allies, his voice carrying great weight on the British Chiefs of Staff Committee and, as far as the Americans were concerned, on the Combined Chiefs of Staff. Moreover, he was inevitably close to Churchill, closer in fact than any other RAF officer during the war. Not only was Portal in regular conference with the Prime Minister whilst Churchill was in London, but he also accompanied him on many of his journeys to conferences overseas, during which he was regarded by the Prime Minister as one of his closest advisers and not only on specifically air force matters. Regardless of the fact that they did not always agree on a particular subject, their mutual respect was such that they could always reach an accommodation. According to Lord Moran, Churchill's personal doctor and confidant, in the Prime Minister's opinion, 'Portal had everything'.**

Air Marshal (later Air Chief Marshal) Sir John Robb GCB, KBE, DSO, DFC, AFC (1895–1968)

The war in the west against Germany and Italy would not have been won in 1945 if it had not been for the welding together of an extraordinarily effective coalition between the British Empire and the United States of America. Both in the Mediterranean theatre and in North-West Europe, the Allied armies, navies and air forces were welded together to act as one, with remarkably little disharmony between them. This was achieved at the top not only by the appointment of excellent commanders, but also by unifying their staffs. One such RAF officer, who distinguished himself both as an Allied Air Commander in the Mediterranean and as a very senior staff officer at Supreme Headquarters Allied Expeditionary Force in North-West Europe, was James **Robb**.

Like hundreds of thousands of other young men, Robb volunteered shortly after the Great War began. Commissioned into the Northumberland

---

** Charles Moran, *Churchill: The Struggle for Survival* p.677

Fusiliers, he saw action in France, but applied in the summer of 1916 to transfer to the RFC. After training he was posted to 32 Squadron, where he flew the Airco DH2 pusher bi-plane fighter on the Western Front. One of his fellow pilots in the squadron was Arthur **Coningham**, who became a close friend. The DH2 was no match for the German fighters of the time, and in March 1917 Robb was wounded, in the thigh, seriously enough to be evacuated to England.

It was not until the first half of 1918 that Robb returned to active service, this time in 92 Squadron, which was commanded by Coningham and equipped with the very capable Royal Aircraft Factory SE5 which, in the right hands, was able to tackle any opponent. He became a flight commander and after the end of hostilities, by which time he had achieved seven confirmed victories, was awarded the DFC. Following a short course in Administration and Organisation, which Coningham also attended, he was awarded a permanent commission in the RAF and appointed a flight commander in the Air Council Inspection Squadron. The squadron was renumbered as No. 24 in early 1920 and was based at Kenley as a communication and training unit, flying a number of different types of aircraft.

In September 1922 Robb was posted to Mosul in Iraq, in which country Trenchard had persuaded Winston Churchill, then Secretary of State for the Colonies, that the RAF could keep the peace much more cheaply than a few divisions of troops. Initially, Robb became a flight commander in 24 Squadron, flying the excellent Bristol Fighter, and that Christmas he had a highly enjoyable reunion with Coningham, now commanding 55 Squadron in the same country. Robb achieved his own first squadron command in January 1924, when he was appointed to 30 Squadron, which flew DH9a – usually known as 'Ninaks' – which were robust light bombers, highly suited to the sort of action which 'air control' demanded, largely against the Kurds in the north of Iraq. In 1926 he was awarded the DSO for his leadership of the squadron.

Robb returned to the UK in the spring of 1926 and was posted to Upavon, where he took over command of 3 Squadron, which flew the Hawker Woodcock, one of only two RAF squadrons to do so. Originally intended to be a night fighter, the Woodcock threw up a number of problems with its design and needed to be extensively modified before being accepted for service. After this had been done it proved to be well-liked by its pilots, but it was in due course replaced by the Gloster Gamecock. Robb, however, was not to see this, as he had by that time been appointed Chief Flying Instructor at the Central Flying School at Wittering.

262   Churchill's Eagles

By the summer of 1930 Robb had been on flying duties for a remarkable fourteen years without interruption, other than during his recovery after being wounded and whilst he was at the short course at Halton. He was now appointed to his first staff job, in the department of the Superintendent of the RAF Reserve. The Royal Air Force Volunteer Reserve was not to be formed for another six years, but the Auxiliary Air Force had been set up in 1925, with its squadrons formed on a geographical basis. The first four squadrons, 600 (City of London), 601 (County of London), 602 (City of Glasgow) and 603 (City of Edinburgh) had been formed in 1925, and others were to follow, including some numbered 500 and upwards which formed a Special Reserve before being absorbed into the Auxiliary Air Force. The pilots in the AAF were required to obtain flying licences at their own expense, to devote a significant amount of their spare time to training and to attend annual camps. Most of the ground crew were also volunteers, but in each squadron there were a small number of regular officers and men, including the adjutant and his staff.

At the beginning of 1932 Robb became a student at the Royal Naval College at Greenwich. Whereas the British Army regarded a staff college qualification as an absolute requirement for promotion beyond the rank of lieutenant colonel, and staff college attendance was also tantamount to a *sine qua non* for RAF officers holding senior appointments, in the Royal Navy advancement was achieved more by extensive sea time and specialization in a particular aspect of naval warfare, such as navigation or gunnery. The course was, nevertheless, valuable training for Robb in staff duties, and in addition provided an insight into one of the other services. It was followed by his appointment as the Senior RAF officer aboard HMS *Eagle*, one of six aircraft carriers in the Royal Navy, on the China Station. The Royal Navy at this time had no aircraft of its own, these being provided by the RAF; it would be another six years before it obtained control of the Fleet Air Arm. At the end of his tour in Far East waters in early 1935, Robb cemented his connection with the Royal Navy by becoming Fleet Aviation Officer to the C-in-C Mediterranean, Admiral Sir William Fisher, who was followed in early 1936 by Admiral Sir Dudley Pound.

At the end of 1936 Robb was appointed Commandant of the Central Flying School at Wittering. This was highly appropriate, since his own flying skills were second to none. The purpose of the CFS was to train instructors for flying schools, an increasingly vital task during the years of the Expansion Plan, with the number of squadrons increasing fast and the requirement for flying training growing with it. Robb was there for three and a half years, but his most important contribution to the wartime growth of the RAF was his involvement in the discussions which took place in Canada concerning the training of pilots and other aircrew outside the UK, which could neither sustain the increase proposed nor provide an environment safe from German attack. Robb, with his considerable expertise in flying training, was a key member of the RAF negotiating team sent to Canada. The outcome, after some tough negotiations, was an agreement with Canada in particular, relatively easy to access from the UK and with wide open spaces for new airfields, and with Australia and New Zealand as far as their own citizens were concerned, to provide both Elementary and Service Flying Training Schools. The Empire Training Scheme, later called the Commonwealth Air Training Plan, was signed in Ottawa on 17 December 1939 by representatives of the four countries, which were later joined by South Africa and Southern Rhodesia, whilst schools were also set up in India, the Middle East and the Bahamas. The 333 flying training schools which were formed eventually trained over 300,000 aircrew.

On 17 April 1940 Robb was appointed AOC 2 Group in Bomber Command. The group, which contained all the RAF's Bristol Blenheims other than those which had either joined the Advanced Air Striking Force in support of the British Expeditionary Force in France or were overseas elsewhere or were used for training, had been operating against German ports and shipping since the outbreak of war, and especially following the German invasion of Norway. The seven remaining squadrons were situated on airfields in East Anglia, with Robb's HQ in Huntingdon. On 10 May the Germans invaded the Netherlands, Belgium and France and 2 Group was immediately deployed to bomb bridges and columns of troops and vehicles. The aircraft were highly vulnerable to German fighters in broad daylight and losses were atrocious, although in a number of cases the crew managed to get out and make their way back to the UK. Following the evacuation of the BEF at Dunkirk, the focus switched to industrial targets and also to invasion ports and barges as well as troop concentrations and airfields, with the casualties continuing to mount.

Following the Battle of Britain, the emphasis for the light bombers switched to airfields and other targets in the occupied countries, but in the spring of 1941 the focus changed again, this time to ports and German shipping. Robb remonstrated against what he saw as the futility of these operations and was promptly sacked by the AOC-in-C Bomber Command, Richard **Peirse**. The CAS, Charles **Portal**, still held Robb in high regard and he was posted as AOC to 15 Group in Coastal Command. The posting coincided with the move of the group HQ to Liverpool, where it was situated close to the Royal Navy's newly formed Western Naval Command, with which the group was to operate closely on operations against U-boats in the Western Approaches and the Irish Sea. Air to Surface Vessel radar was becoming more effective, but other technical aids were still some way in the future, whilst Very Long Range aircraft were not yet available, so the results, whilst not insignificant, were relatively modest.

It was possibly because of Robb's connections to the Royal Navy, both recently and in the mid-1930s, that he was selected to be Deputy Chief of Combined Operations under Lord Louis Mountbatten in early 1942. There was also a Vice-Chief from the Army, as well as an Assistant Chief from the Royal Navy, albeit that these titles were later changed to Military Chief, Air Chief and Naval Chief respectively. Mountbatten was exceptionally energetic and expected the same from his subordinates. Numerous projects were begun, most of which were broadly directed at getting a foothold for the Allies back on the Continent of Europe. Some raids were mounted, notably on Vaagso in Norway, but the major operation during the summer of 1942 was the Dieppe Raid. Conceived as a large raid, with no expectation of it becoming a permanent lodgement in France, it turned out to be a disaster, albeit one from which painful lessons could be learnt. If there was one part of the operation which went more or less to plan, other than a successful attack by Commandos on one of the flanks of the attacking force, it was the RAF's, the Luftwaffe being substantially prevented from harassing the landings.

Armed with this experience, Robb was appointed Air Adviser to the Allied Air Commander, General Spaatz, for the Operation TORCH landings in Algeria and Morocco in November 1942. Following success for the Allies in securing a permanent lodgement in North-West Africa, he remained in the Mediterranean theatre during 1943 and was recommended by Arthur **Tedder** for the position of Deputy Air Commander of the North-West African Air Force under Spaatz. After holding this appointment, which brought him once again into close contact with Coningham, who was AOC North-West African Tactical Air Force, he served as a very senior air staff officer at Allied Forces HQ, becoming particularly popular with his American counterparts. When Eisenhower was appointed as Supreme Allied Commander for North-West Europe, it came as no surprise that he asked for Robb to join him at Supreme Headquarters Allied Expeditionary Force as Deputy Chief of Staff (Air).

Robb's immediate superior was Walter Bedell Smith, Eisenhower's Chief of Staff, but he also had much to do with Arthur **Tedder**, the Deputy Supreme Commander, who was given responsibility for the whole of the air element of the campaign in North-West Europe, whether based in the UK or on the Continent. Numerous issues arose even before D-Day, notably the appointment of Trafford **Leigh-Mallory** to command the Allied Expeditionary Air Force, consisting of the British Second Tactical Air Force, under Coningham, and the American Ninth Air Force, but also the diversion of Bomber Command, under Arthur **Harris**, and the USAAF's Eighth Air Force, under Ira Eaker, to supporting the invasion, although they both believed that the strategic bombing campaign should continue.

On the whole, the air campaign went very well, with the tactical air forces and the RAF's Fighter Command supporting the ground troops highly successfully during both the landings themselves and the battles thereafter, particularly at Mortain and the Falaise Pocket. Following the break-out from Normandy, the British and American ground forces advanced in different directions and Leigh-Mallory's role became redundant. There was something of a set-back at the end of 1944, when the Germans attacked in the Ardennes in bad weather which kept the Allied Air Forces grounded, but when conditions improved, both the RAF and USAAF hit the Germans very heavily. The Luftwaffe's last throw of the dice came on New Year's Day 1945, when the Germans mounted a massive attack on Allied airfields with considerable success, but it proved to be a Pyrrhic victory as the Allies were able to replace their losses very quickly, whilst the Luftwaffe, due to a lack of both pilots and new aircraft, never posed a major threat again.

On 14 May 1945, shortly after the German surrender, Robb was appointed AOC-in-C Fighter Command. The command had been heavily committed in 1944, both in support of the invasion and in shooting down as many of the V-1 flying bombs as possible. When the Germans were pushed back beyond the range of the V-1s, they stepped up V-2 ballistic rocket attacks, but these were effectively invulnerable to the fighters. The command was run down quickly after the end of the war, with some 500 operational aircraft on its strength in mid-1946, compared to 2,000 in 1943. Robb was deeply unhappy about this, believing that other threats would emerge, but the reductions continued. At the same time, the process of re-equipping with jet fighters continued, both Gloster Meteors, which had first reached squadrons in mid-1944, and De Havilland Vampires, which entered service in late 1946. Robb himself, always a first-class pilot, learned to fly the Meteor. In 1947 he was appointed Vice-Chief of the Air Staff, serving under Tedder as CAS.

266 Churchill's Eagles

On 8 October 1948 Robb became C-in-C Air Forces in the Western Union Defence Organisation (WUDO), a military alliance between the United Kingdom, France, the Netherlands, Belgium and Luxembourg. As such he sat on the Commanders-in-Chief Committee, which was chaired by Field Marshal Montgomery. The WUDO was set up in response to the blockade of Berlin in June 1948 by the Russians, who were becoming increasingly belligerent. It was later effectively subsumed into NATO, and in February 1951 Robb became Inspector-General of the RAF, with a remit to report on the efficiency of the service. He was in the job for a mere eight months before retiring, due to ill health. In retirement he became the Bath King of Arms.

Robb was a very popular senior officer and was highly regarded by his superiors, but he was not one whose name ever came to the attention of the general public. However, his ability to get on well not only with the other British armed services, but also with the country's American and European allies, made him a natural choice for senior appointments in multinational organizations.

Air Chief Marshal (later Marshal of the RAF) Sir John Slessor GCB, DSO, MC (1897–1979)

Of all the RAF officers who were born in the last five years of the nineteenth century, the most distinguished was arguably John **Slessor**, known to his friends as Jack. Recognized as having a promising future by his inclusion as one of the youngest students in the third year of the RAF Staff College in 1924, he went on to hold a number of senior command and staff roles both before and during the war and he distinguished himself subsequently as his service's most senior officer.

Extraordinarily for a man who both reached the highest rank in the RAF and became Chief of the Air Staff, Slessor was lame in both legs as the result of contracting polio as a child. Indeed, this disability was so evident that, when the First World War broke out, he was declared by a medical board to be totally unfit for military service. However, although he invariably walked with the aid of a stick, his disability did not prevent him from flying an aircraft; indeed, he could do so as well as any able-bodied man and better than most. In any event, he managed to circumvent the decision of the medical board through nepotism, in his case a family connection with the officer responsible for the selection of RFC officers and, shortly after his eighteenth birthday in June 1915, he was ordered to report to Brooklands airfield for flying training.

After serving very briefly in 14 Squadron, Slessor was transferred to 23 Squadron for night-flying operations against Zeppelins; but although he managed to intercept one he came nowhere near shooting it down! Very shortly afterwards he was posted to 17 Squadron in Egypt, where he flew sorties against the Turks in Palestine and rebel tribesmen in the Sudan. He was back in England a year later, initially in 58 Squadron, which not much later had to be broken up to provide replacements for losses in France, one of which was Slessor.

After becoming a flight commander in 5 Squadron in April 1917, flying BE2s and RE8s in action for seven months and earning a Military Cross in the process, Slessor attended a course at the Artillery School. On passing out he was appointed as Artillery and Infantry Co-operation Officer at 28 Wing. Notwithstanding this office job, his flying skills had developed greatly, so much so that he was appointed OC A Squadron of the Central Flying School in July 1918, becoming Assistant Commandant of the school in the following month. A succession of training-related appointments was followed in February 1920 by Slessor's appointment as a flight commander at No. 1 Flying Training School at Netheravon. Whilst there he took part in the first ever RAF Display at Hendon.

Having been awarded a permanent commission at the end of 1920, in May 1921 Slessor was posted to India as a flight commander in 20 Squadron, based at Parachinar on the North-West Frontier and flying Bristol Fighters. Unlike in the rest of the British Empire, the RAF was not viewed by the military administration in India as a separate service and was, at this time, shamefully misused, with very little money being spent on equipment and spares, sometimes with dire results. It took a visit by AVM Sir John Salmond to produce a report which would eventually lead to better treatment and a more valuable contribution to military activities on the Frontier. By that time, however, Slessor was back in the UK, initially posted to the Air Ministry in the Directorate of Training and Staff Duties before attending the Staff College in Andover, with Norman **Bottomley** and Leslie **Hollinghurst** amongst others as fellow students and Wilfrid **Freeman** and Guy **Garrod** on the Directing Staff. On passing out, his first appointment was not to another staff job, as might have been expected, but to the command of 4 Squadron, flying Bristol Fighters in an Army Co-operation role, which he much enjoyed for three and a half years.

In October 1928 Slessor was posted to the Air Ministry in the Department of Operations and Intelligence for two useful but unexciting years. He was then sent to the Army Staff College at Camberley, for the first year as a

268 Churchill's Eagles

student and then for a further three years as a member of the Directing Staff. This provided him with, for an RAF officer, an invaluable list of contacts with the largest of the three British armed services, something which would prove valuable in the future.

Slessor's next posting, by way of a complete contrast, took him back to India as OC 3 (Indian) Wing at Quetta in Baluchistan. Since he had last served there, some fourteen years earlier, things had improved significantly for the RAF following Salmond's report and further representations to the Government of India. It was now looked upon as a useful adjunct to the Army in India, both to support ground forces on operations and to ease communications with outlying positions on the Frontier. Only two months after Slessor and his wife arrived, however, in the early hours of 31 May 1935, a great earthquake struck Quetta. It was highly selective. Among the worst hit areas were the old city and the adjacent Civil Lines, including the Residency and the Quetta Club. On the other hand, the very extensive army cantonment to the north of the city was only lightly affected, whilst those living in and around the Staff College to the north-west had hardly felt a thing. The RAF Lines and airfield to the west of the army cantonment were particularly badly damaged. A number of the bungalows occupied by officers and married senior NCOs collapsed, and the barracks housing the other ranks and locally recruited men were the site of a total disaster. Slessor's wife emerged unscathed, but he was trapped by rubble and sustained a large wound to the head. Once he had been extracted and given basic first aid, however, he immediately took charge.

In addition to the damage to infrastructure, most of the aircraft had been destroyed. Fifty-two British men and 166 Indians were killed in the RAF area alone, and many more were seriously injured. There was a barely sufficient area for take-offs and landings, but aircraft from other RAF stations arrived with doctors and nurses and evacuated wives and children. With Quetta out of operation and the wing temporarily disbanded, the AOC India, Edgar **Ludlow-Hewitt**, insisted that the Slessors should go home on leave to recuperate. On his return, Slessor was temporarily employed at Air HQ in New Delhi, following which a reconstituted 3 Wing provided aerial support to ground operations against the Fakir of Ipi in Waziristan in the winter of 1936/7. Following the end of his tour, Slessor was awarded the DSO.

Slessor returned to the UK and to the Air Ministry in May 1937, where he took over from Arthur **Harris** as Deputy Director of Plans. His promotion to Director of Plans nineteen months later came in the thick of the pre-war Expansion Schemes, the first of which, Scheme A in July 1934, had been a response to the unexpected news that the Luftwaffe was already as large as the RAF and was growing much faster. Scheme replaced scheme as it was realized how monumental the RAF's task would be to achieve parity, let alone dominance. Only Scheme F, conceived in 1935, was ever completed, and Slessor himself was directly concerned with Schemes J to M, which majored on the build-up of the bomber force. The new medium bombers, the Bristol Blenheim, the Handley Page Hampden, the Armstrong Whitworth Whitley and the Vickers Wellington, were either beginning to equip RAF squadrons or were shortly to do so, and the heavy bombers, the Short Stirling, the Handley Page Halifax and the Avro Manchester, were on order. The first modern fighter, the Hawker Hurricane, entered squadron service in December 1937, and the Supermarine Spitfire would follow in September 1938.

During his time as Director of Plans, Slessor was at the heart of the development of the RAF into an air force capable of competing with the Luftwaffe. He was also involved in discussions with officers of the USAAF and notably with a team led by Colonel Carl Spaatz in the summer of 1940 during the Battle of Britain. This was followed, in late 1940 and early 1941, by Slessor's own visit to the USA to provide the Americans with further information and to request material assistance by way of aircraft. During his visit he also participated in the first UK/US 'staff conversations' in Washington, which lasted through to March 1941 and laid down the basis both for mutual co-operation, without the USA declaring war on Germany, and for Lend-Lease, whereby the RAF and the Royal Navy, and to a lesser but still not inconsiderable extent, the British Army, were able to equip themselves much more adequately than would conceivably have been possible on their own.

Slessor returned to the UK to take up a command appointment, this time as AOC 5 Group in Bomber Command. His arrival there coincided with the beginning of a new offensive against any targets on land or at sea threatening British shipping, which had been suffering serious losses, not only in the wider Atlantic, but also in the English Channel and the North Sea. These targets were not only U-boats, in co-operation with Coastal Command, and surface warships, but also ports, docks, shipyards and those industrial cities which manufactured and assembled engines and components for the German Navy. The U-boats had been enjoying a successful campaign, whilst two German battlecruisers, *Scharnhorst* and *Gneisenau*, had carried out a foray into the Atlantic in early 1941, during which they sunk about

270   Churchill's Eagles

twenty ships before proceeding to ports in Brittany. They were joined there by the heavy cruiser *Prinz Eugen.*

5 Group's aircraft at the time of Slessor's arrival consisted entirely of the twin-engined Hampden, a strange-looking aircraft constructed on a 'pod and boom' design. The narrow fuselage was uncomfortable for the crew, whilst the rear gunner was provided with an inadequate gun. It made up for this to some extent by having a slightly higher speed than the Whitley and the Wellington and much greater manoeuvrability. Although it carried a reasonable bomb load, it was best employed in 'gardening', the term used by Bomber Command for minelaying.

The maritime offensive, and particularly the repeated attacks on Brest, produced very poor returns for Bomber Command, and its attention swung back to German cities, without much more success; effective navigational aids were non-existent at this time and relatively little damage was caused to German industry. Morale plummeted after the 'Channel Dash', the escape of *Scharnhorst, Gneisenau* and *Prinz Eugen* on 12 February 1942 up the English Channel and into German ports, having suffered what appeared to be little if any damage. Informed only late in the day by reconnaissance aircraft, due to poor visibility, all the bomber groups put aircraft up to bomb the ships, with no visible success, and Slessor later sent his crews off to lay mines in the approaches to German North Sea ports. As it happened, both the battlecruisers hit mines, which incapacitated them for a considerable time, but these may have been laid in earlier operations.

In the light of this fiasco, Slessor was more than happy to return to the Air Ministry in early April 1942 as Assistant Chief of the Air Staff (Policy). This came at a vitally important period of the war, with the United States barely four months into the conflict and still learning what it entailed. Two days after Slessor took up his appointment, General George Marshall, the Army Chief of Staff, arrived in London with President Roosevelt's influential adviser, Harry Hopkins. A policy of 'Germany first' had been agreed already, much to the displeasure of Admiral Ernest King, the US Navy's Chief of Staff, who would have much preferred a focus on Japan. The Americans came proposing landings in France early in 1943, a hopelessly over-optimistic prospect. It was, however, decided to proceed with Operation TORCH, landings in French North Africa, with a view to joining up with the British Eighth Army advancing from Egypt. Slessor took part in meetings on both sides of the Atlantic to thrash out both the strategy and its execution. There were many other issues to deal with on the British side alone, not least the demand by Alan Brooke, the Chief of the Imperial General Staff, for an

Army Co-operation Command, something which the RAF felt was quite unnecessary, pointing to the success of close co-operation between the Desert Air Force and the Eighth Army in North Africa.

Following the landings in French North Africa in Operation TORCH, which installed the Allies firmly in Morocco and Algeria, albeit not, for many more months, in Tunisia, one of most important Anglo-American conferences took place in Casablanca in January 1943. The British, with Slessor part of the delegation as a senior aide to Charles **Portal**, the CAS, arrived much better prepared than the Americans and succeeded in securing a commitment to the invasion of Sicily, with a view to securing the Western Mediterranean, at the same time putting back the invasion of North-West Europe to 1944. As far as air operations were concerned, the conference resulted in a significant directive to Bomber Command and the US Eighth Air Force on the bombing campaign against Germany.

With the Casablanca Conference at an end, Slessor returned to the UK and to a new appointment, as AOC-in-C of Coastal Command. At the time he took over his command at Northwood from Philip **Joubert**, the Battle of the Atlantic had reached a critical juncture, largely because of a breakdown in intelligence. Unbeknownst to the Allies, the Germans had cracked the Royal Navy signal codes, which they were reading freely. Even more significantly, they had introduced a fourth rotor to the German Navy's Enigma machines, leaving the Government Code & Cypher School at Bletchley Park completely blind, with no access at all to the signals to the U-boats which had hitherto been vital to their interception. Losses of ships in convoy were increasing dramatically.

Slessor took over some 850 aircraft from Joubert, comprising 60 squadrons in five groups and two, later three, new operational areas outside the UK. 15 Group was based in Liverpool alongside the HQ of the Commander-in-Chief Western Approaches, Admiral Sir Max Horton, its squadrons operating mainly from the west coast of Scotland and from Northern Ireland, with responsibility for protecting the convoys as they approached the UK. 16 Group was based at Gillingham in Kent, with the English Channel and the southern part of the North Sea as its area of operations. 17 Group, with its HQ in Edinburgh, was charged with all operational training in Coastal Command. 18 Group was also based in Scotland, at Rosyth, and was charged with offensive actions in the northern part of the North Sea and along the coast of Norway. 19 Group, with its HQ in Plymouth, was responsible for all operations in the Bay of Biscay, known to Coastal Command simply as 'the Bay'. In addition, a number of squadrons were

272 Churchill's Eagles

based in Iceland and Gibraltar under local commanders. Finally, when the Portuguese Government allowed operations to take place from the Azores, a new group, No. 247, was established there.

The main operating area for the U-boats was in 'the Gap', an area of ocean between Iceland and the east coast of Canada which was outside the range of Coastal Command's existing aircraft. In March 1943, a month after Slessor's arrival at Coastal Command, the enormity of the challenge he faced was demonstrated by the fate of two eastbound convoys in the Gap: HX 229 lost thirteen merchant ship and SC 122 lost nine, a total of 140,000 tons. A single U-boat was lost to the actions of the escort and others were damaged, but the German victory was unequivocal. This was, as it happened, the low point of the Battle of the Atlantic, following which the Allies' fortunes improved rapidly.

The change for the better was due to two factors, great success in code-breaking, following Bletchley Park's solving the conundrum of the fourth rotor on the German Naval Enigma machine, and the belated introduction of both much more effective aircraft and the tools which they were able to employ. The most important aircraft was the VLR (Very Long Range) Consolidated Liberator, which for the first time could cover the Gap. The tools were ASV (Air to Surface Vessel) Radar and the Leigh Light, which illuminated submarines on the surface in the dark. These, together with the greatly improved intelligence and more effective depth charges, were to boost the fortunes of Coastal Command significantly.

From the time of his appointment Slessor had believed that the best place to sink submarines was not on the convoy routes, but on their way out into the Atlantic across the Bay, during which they had to surface regularly to recharge their batteries. Whilst on the surface they were relatively fast but highly vulnerable. Proceeding underwater they were reduced to a speed of only 3 knots, albeit that they were hidden from view. Slessor's firm focus on the Gap, together with the much improved intelligence, resulted in a significant increase in the number of U-boats sunk before they could reach the convoys.

Whereas the task of 15 and 19 Groups was essentially defensive, protecting the convoys, that of 16 and 18 Groups was offensive. They were charged with attacking German shipping and naval installations along the coasts of Norway, Denmark, Germany and the Netherlands, employing fast and effective Bristol Beaufighters, some of which, called 'Torbeaus', carried torpedoes, whilst others acted as fighters and light bombers. Their operations, which were frequently supported by aircraft from Fighter

Command, together with the minelaying sorties of Bomber Command, proved to be a very effective obstacle to maritime traffic along the coast, whilst aircraft were also employed in sinking ships bringing strategic cargo from Japan.

Slessor was also in charge of the five squadrons of 106 Wing, based in Benson and handling photo-reconnaissance for all RAF formations operating out of the UK. By this time the most effective aircraft for this purpose were the reconnaissance versions of the Spitfire and the Mosquito, stripped of their guns and any armoured plate and provided with additional fuel tanks, as well as increasingly sophisticated cameras. These flew, mostly at very high altitude, for long distances from Benson over Occupied Europe and the sea, bringing back highly valuable intelligence on enemy activity.

Coastal Command was also responsible for all the RAF's UK-based meteorological work, once again employing Spitfires, but also large aircraft such as the Handley Page Halifax and even old Gloster Gladiators, which were highly effective at lower altitudes. Finally, it also had overall control of the Air-Sea Rescue Service, whose invaluable work was carried out not only by Supermarine Walrus flying boats, which could land close to men in the sea, but also by larger aircraft carrying airborne lifeboats, which could be dropped to them. The ASR Service also employed high-speed launches which rescued many downed airmen.

At the beginning of 1944 Slessor was nominated to succeed Arthur **Tedder**, who was returning to the UK from the Mediterranean to become General Eisenhower's deputy in preparation for the invasion of North-West Europe. Tedder had been not only C-in-C of the RAF in the Mediterranean and the Middle East, but also the Allied Air C-in-C in the same area. However, as Eisenhower himself was being succeeded by a British officer, General Sir Harold Alexander, Tedder's successor was to be an American, General Ira Eaker, with Slessor as his deputy, albeit also becoming the RAF C-in-C.

As far as the RAF was concerned there was little operational activity outside Italy, where most of its resources were devoted to supporting ground operations. The RAF in Egypt, the Eastern Mediterranean and Cyprus, the Levant, Iraq, Aden, the Sudan and East Africa had by this time effectively become a training and maintenance organization, which Slessor could confidently leave to Keith **Park**, the AOC-in-C. In the area of active operations, Slessor got on very well with Eaker and deputized for him effectively whenever necessary, even if being a deputy was a frustrating business. Slessor was involved in all the decisions on the battles to break

274   Churchill's Eagles

the Gustav Line, including the controversial bombing of the monastery at Monte Cassino, and the landings at Anzio and in the South of France, but it was not until the middle of 1944 that he could really get his teeth into something new, for which he was to assume the main responsibility.

On the far side of the Adriatic Sea in Yugoslavia, Marshal Tito's communist partisans were causing a huge problem to the Germans, who were simultaneously attempting both to hold the country down and to ensure free passage for their troops to and from Greece. Thoroughly exasperated, they mounted a major attack on Tito's HQ at the end of May 1944 which forced him to flee the country, arriving at Bari in Southern Italy, before re-establishing his HQ on the island of Vis. It was agreed that he should continue guerrilla operations in Yugoslavia and that these should in future receive dedicated support from the air, both in terms of supply and transport and in offensive actions against the Germans. Thus was born the Balkan Air Force, possibly the most cosmopolitan of all the Allied ground, sea or air formations.

Commanded in the first instance and for most of its history by Air Vice-Marshal William **Elliott** and based near Bari, the Balkan Air Force consisted of between seven and nine squadrons of the RAF (including two manned exclusively by Yugoslavs with red stars replacing the RAF's red disk in its roundel), three squadrons each from the South African Air Force and the Royal Hellenic Air Force and seven squadrons from the Italian Co-belligerent Air Force. The aircraft were even more varied than the nationalities, including Spitfire, Hurricane, Beaufighter and Mustang fighters and fighter-bombers as well as Martin Marauder and Baltimore medium bombers, Lockheed Ventura light bombers, Bell Airacobras and, for two of the Italian squadrons, Macchi 202 and 205 fighters. Added to this were, from time to time, the Douglas C-47 Dakotas of both the RAF and the USAAF and, for a period of four months, two squadrons of the Soviet Air Force, one of Dakotas and one of Yakovlev Yak-9 fighters.

The objectives of the BAF were to supply the Partisans, to evacuate them when they were seriously threatened and to harass the Germans at every opportunity, especially, in late 1944, when they began to withdraw their troops from Greece to avoid being cut off by the Soviet advance. Frequent raids were carried out on columns of troops and vehicles and, in September 1944, Operation RATWEEK was mounted to close down all transport links to the Germans and destroy railway rolling stock and road vehicles, enabling Tito to recapture Belgrade.

Slessor became involved in two other theatres of war in 1944. The first was Poland, where the Warsaw uprising took place in August in anticipation of the Russians, now closing in on the east of the city, assisting in its liberations. Nothing of the sort was to happen as the Red Army halted outside and let the Polish partisans be killed or captured. A number of bomber squadrons, initially just Polish and then British and South African, were sent to the city to drop supply containers.. They all suffered very heavy losses and the rest of the operation was cancelled.

The second area of activity was Greece, where civil war was breaking out between the returning government-in-exile and ELAS communist partisans. Slessor ordered the Balkan Air Force to deploy a number of aircraft to Athens, where they were able to support British ground troops to good effect; they included squadrons of the Royal Hellenic Air Force, which subsequently took over.

In April 1945, with the end of the war in sight, Slessor returned to the UK to join the Air Council as Air Member for Personnel. This was in some way the antithesis of the appointment he had held as Director of Plans in the run-up to and the first years of the war, when a major part of his work was devoted to the expansion of the RAF. Now he had to manage an urgent reduction in manpower, not least because Great Britain was effectively bankrupt, whilst at the same time retaining as many of the best people as possible to man the peacetime air force. He held the appointment for nearly three years of difficult decision-making.

Slessor's next appointment was almost certainly more congenial to him, as Commandant of the Imperial Defence College in succession to Field Marshal Sir William (later Viscount) Slim. The IDC had been closed for the duration of the war, but regained its position as the senior British military academy in its aftermath. In 1950 he became the Chief of the Air Staff in succession to Arthur **Tedder**. Tedder's own choice for the job was Ralph **Cochrane**, but the Prime Minister, Clement Attlee, preferred Slessor, and it was probably the right decision. Cochrane had had an excellent career, but one which was largely inward facing towards the RAF. Slessor, on the other hand, had had close contacts with Great Britain's major ally, the USA, both as Director of Plans and as ACIGS (Policy), to which could be added his service alongside the Americans in the last part of the war in the Mediterranean. Moreover, his relationships with the British Army, through his years at the Staff College in Camberley, and with the Royal Navy during his appointment at Coastal Command, were undoubtedly better than Cochrane's. In the event, Cochrane became VCAS and the two men worked harmoniously together until Cochrane's retirement in November 1952, one month before Slessor himself retired.

276   Churchill's Eagles

Slessor, who had been promoted to Marshal of the Royal Air Force in 1950, enjoyed an active retirement, taking on a number of company directorships, including one at Blackburn Aircraft, and writing, broadcasting and lecturing on military subjects. A highly competent senior officer, he was popular with superiors, contemporaries and subordinates in the RAF and with many in the other two services.

Air Chief Marshal Sir Arthur (later Marshal of the RAF the Lord) Tedder GCB, BA (1890–1967)

Few very senior officers in the RAF endured as difficult a relationship with Churchill as Arthur **Tedder** who, in spite of this handicap, has been recognized subsequently as one of the great British airmen of the Second World War and who, in due course, was awarded a barony and became the first post-war Chief of the Air Staff. That he did so was due very largely to the unwavering support of his immediate predecessor, Charles **Portal**, whose faith in him was handsomely repaid.

Tedder graduated from Cambridge with a modest degree. His original intention had been to join the Diplomatic Service, but he decided instead to become a cadet in the Colonial Service, his first posting being to Fiji. Not long afterwards Great Britain declared war on Germany and he immediately resigned, taking ship back to England to join the Army. Commissioned in January 1915 into the Dorsetshire Regiment, he suffered an injury to his knee shortly afterwards which threatened his career on active service. He lobbied doggedly in pursuit of a commission in the RFC, but it was nearly a year before he was accepted for flying training. It was only in June 1916 that he joined his first squadron, No. 25, on active service in France, flying the FE 2b in a fighter reconnaissance role on the Western Front during the Battle of the Somme and becoming a flight commander only two months later.

In January 1917 Tedder was promoted to major and appointed CO of 70 Squadron, this time flying the Sopwith 1½ Strutter. He was with the squadron for six months before being sent to Egypt, initially in command of the largely Australian-manned 67 Squadron, followed by a brief posting in the summer of 1918 as the Officer Commanding the School of Navigation and Bomb Dropping and then one as OC 38 (Training) Wing as a temporary lieutenant colonel. After the end of the Great War he reverted to his substantive rank and returned to England.

Unlike many of those who had served in action for some time, Tedder was never awarded a decoration for gallantry, although he had two mentions in despatches. He was nevertheless granted a permanent commission in the newly established RAF and appointed successively to the commands of two bomber squadrons at Burcham Newton, No. 274 flying the Handley Page V/1500 heavy bomber and No. 207 flying the DH9a light bomber, the latter being chosen by Trenchard as one of the three squadrons sent to Turkey in support of the British Army at the time of the Chanak Incident. It was almost certainly Trenchard himself who nominated Tedder to attend the course at the Royal Naval Staff College at Greenwich soon after his return. Immediately after graduating he was appointed to command No. 2 Flying Training School, which brought him to the favourable attention of Wilfrid **Freeman**, at that time the Commandant of the Central Flying School. This was followed by his first experience of the Air Ministry, a year as Deputy Director of Training.

In 1928 Tedder attended the Imperial Defence College, where Philip **Joubert** was on the Directing Staff, and this was followed by an appointment for three years as Deputy Commandant at the RAF Staff College, with Joubert as his superior for much of the time. In January 1932 he became the Officer Commanding the Air Armament School at Eastchurch, where he served for two years before returning to the Air Ministry as Director of Training. In November 1936 he was sent out to Singapore to become AOC Far East in a command which covered not only Singapore itself, Malaya and Borneo, but also Hong Kong and Burma. The Far East was the poor relation of the RAF, with a very low priority for modern aircraft and a small establishment of squadrons, notwithstanding what was already perceived as a threat from Japan. Tedder did at least modernize the internal organization, build more airfields and accelerate the training regime, but the low priority accorded to his command in terms of both the number and the quality of its aircraft was to continue after he left, with disastrous results in late 1941 and early 1942.

It was Freeman who brought Tedder back to the UK in the summer of 1938. Freeman himself had just been appointed to the Air Council as Air Member for Development and Production, having made it clear that he would refuse the job unless Tedder became Director-General of Research and Development. For the next two and a half years Freeman and Tedder effectively modernized the RAF in terms of its aircraft, working closely in conjunction with the leaders of the armaments industry, their designers and a host of sub-contractors. In the first instance there was a switch in priority from bombers to fighters, with a highly beneficial impact in due course on the Battle of Britain. Tedder, like most of his colleagues, was highly sceptical about the concept of the unarmed Mosquito bomber, which was championed by Freeman, but he came round to supporting it in due course. He was particularly pleased by the decision to boost the production of training aircraft, without which there would have been a serious deficiency of aircrew when it mattered most. When Lord Beaverbrook was appointed Minister for Aircraft Production, Tedder sided with Freeman and Philip **Joubert** against Beaverbrook's plan to halt the development of airborne interception radar, which was to prove to be vital for night fighters. Overall, he was dismayed by Beaverbrook's handling of the MAP, as he revealed in a sharply critical letter when he left.

In November 1940 Tedder was ordered to fly out to Egypt to become the Deputy to the AOC-in-C Middle East, Arthur **Longmore**, who had specifically asked for him. Tedder had not been the first choice for the job, due entirely to Churchill, who vetoed his appointment in favour of AVM Owen Boyd. The Prime Minister was possibly influenced by Tedder's antipathy to Beaverbrook, whom he himself regarded very highly. Boyd, however, crash-landed in Axis territory on his flight out to Egypt and was captured and incarcerated. Tedder had a more successful journey, which included experiencing the 'Reinforcement Route' across Africa from Takoradi to Khartoum and then up the Nile to Cairo. He arrived to a background of success in the Western Desert as British and Empire troops trapped most of the Italian Tenth Army in Cyrenaica. The good times were not to last, however. In North Africa, Axis forces under General Rommel mounted a successful counter-offensive, pushing the British back into Egypt and capturing a number of their generals, albeit failing to take Tobruk, which was instead besieged,

Things were going from bad to worse in the Mediterranean, with the Germans invading Greece, unimpeded to any great extent by the modest RAF presence in the country. Longmore argued forcefully that the aircraft at his disposal were inadequate for his command. They did not include Spitfires, for instance, and the Hurricanes and Curtis P.40 Tomahawks were greatly inferior to the Messerschmitt 109s now entering the theatre. Moreover, the aircraft of all types arriving in Egypt from the UK along the Reinforcement Route needed considerable attention before they could join the front line, leaving the numbers available for operations greatly reduced. Longmore was so persistent in his criticism of both the number and condition of new aircraft that not only Churchill, but also Portal, became totally exasperated with him. He was recalled to London for talks in May 1941 and soon afterwards relieved of his command.

In the knowledge that the overall quality and number of aircraft sent to the Middle East would continue to disappoint Tedder, Portal, who had persuaded Churchill that he should be appointed AOC-in-C, invited him to enter into a personal correspondence on any matters of concern which was to last throughout the war. This provided Tedder with considerable comfort and Portal with the inside story on future campaigns in a way which would normally have been impossible.

Tedder's promotion brought him into much closer contact with his fellow commanders-in-chief, Admiral Sir Andrew Cunningham for the Royal Navy and General Sir Archibald Wavell for the Army. The situation in the theatre continued to be very difficult. The brief Greek campaign was followed by the German invasion of Crete, with serious British losses on land and at sea. There was also a revolt against the pro-British regime in Iraq, put down with the RAF playing a major role, notwithstanding its antiquated aircraft. Subsequently the pro-Axis French in Syria were overcome in an unpleasant little campaign, but the main focus was always on the Western Desert. Wavell was himself relieved to be succeeded by General Sir Claude Auchinleck, with whom Tedder got on very well.

A visit by Edgar **Ludlow-Hewitt**, the Inspector-General RAF, in the summer of 1941, proved to be very useful, providing independent confirmation to Portal that Tedder was in complete control of his command. This was just as well, as the RAF was to play a significant role in Auchinleck's first major operation by the newly named Eighth Army in the Western Desert, Operation CRUSADER. This kicked off in November 1941 and, after a very difficult start, eventually achieved its objectives, relieving Tobruk, taking Benghazi and pushing the Axis forces out of Cyrenaica. All too quickly, however, a German counter-attack was mounted, sending the British back to a line running south from Gazala on the Mediterranean into the desert. This proved to be gravely prejudicial to the situation in Malta, where the AOC, Hugh **Lloyd**, was hard pressed keeping his squadrons up to strength without any cover from airfields in Cyrenaica. Churchill remained sharply critical of Tedder, and it took a visit to Egypt by Freeman, now the VCAS, to persuade the Prime Minister that the air side of the campaign was under tight control.

Things went from bad to worse on the ground in the Western Desert as the Germans attacked at Gazala, taking Tobruk and pushing Eighth Army back to the Alamein Line, where a series of inconclusive engagements, later called the First Battle of El Alamein, eventually resulted in stalemate. In August 1942 Churchill arrived in Egypt with the Chief of the Imperial General staff, General Sir Alan Brooke. Auchinleck was replaced as GOC-in-C Middle

280   Churchill's Eagles

East by General Sir Harold Alexander, whilst the command of Eighth Army devolved onto Lieutenant General (later Sir) Bernard Montgomery. Tedder was initially delighted by Montgomery's philosophy of war, which was that the HQs of Eighth Army and the Desert Air Force, the latter now commanded by AVM Arthur **Coningham**, should be co-located and that the air battle should be won before the ground battle commenced. Newer models of aircraft in much larger numbers, including Spitfires, were now arriving in Egypt and air superiority was indeed achieved, with excellent results at the battle of Alam Halfa, the final attempt by Rommel to break the Alamein Line.

The Second Battle of El Alamein was conducted in line with Montgomery's philosophy. The German-Italian Army proved to be hard to crack, but in due course there was a major breakthrough followed by an advance into Libya. From the RAF's perspective, however, this advance was unnecessarily cautious, and both Tedder and Coningham began to be much more critical of Eighth Army and its commander, not least because the valuable group of airfields around Benghazi, which could provide air cover to Malta, took a long time to be captured. Nevertheless, progress was inexorable and Tripoli was entered in late January 1943.

Shortly before this, Tedder handed over Middle East Command to Sholto **Douglas**, with a view to taking up an appointment in London as VCAS in due course. In the meantime, he stayed on in North Africa for the Casablanca Conference, attended by Churchill, President Roosevelt and the Combined Chiefs of Staff of Great Britain and the United States. The main outcome of the conference was an agreement to invade Sicily in the summer of 1943. As far as the RAF and USAAF were concerned, this required the creation of a Strategic Air Force under Major General Jimmy Doolittle, a Coastal Air Force under Lloyd and a Tactical Air Force, incorporating the Desert Air Force as well as American units, under Coningham. Instead of returning to London, Tedder was appointed overall AOC-in-C Mediterranean Air Command, whilst simultaneously becoming AOC-in-C RAF Middle East and Malta, the latter now under Keith **Park**. The structure of Mediterranean Air Command organization, with some relatively minor alterations, was to see out the war in the Mediterranean.

The Sicilian campaign proved to be more difficult than expected, with Tedder once again sharply critical of Montgomery's caution, which delayed capture of the Axis airfields, but the island was clear of Axis forces by mid-August. The campaign was followed in September by landings in Italy. Those in the toe and heel of the country went well, whilst those at Salerno encountered stiff resistance at first, not least because air cover was only possible for short lengths of time and the capture of the German airfields was delayed by fierce fighting. Nevertheless, by the end of the year the Allies were on the Gustav Line, having, among other things, captured the group of airfields around Foggia, which opened up a significant opportunity for the Strategic Air Force to bomb German-occupied territory from there as well as from the UK.

By that time, however, Tedder was no longer involved in the Mediterranean theatre of operations. Towards the end of 1943, on the insistence of his former critic, Churchill, he was appointed Deputy Supreme Allied Commander for the invasion of North-West Europe, responsible solely to the Supreme Allied Commander, General Dwight D. Eisenhower, and through him to the Combined Chiefs of Staff. It was agreed that, as well as being Eisenhower's overall deputy, Tedder would also exercise control not only over the Allied Expeditionary Air Force, commanded by Trafford Leigh-Mallory, which would be fully committed to supporting the ground forces during the invasion of North-West Europe and the subsequent campaign, but also over Bomber Command and the US Eighth Air Force whenever they were required to support such operations.

There was considerable debate as to the pre-invasion priorities for the air forces. Tedder and Eisenhower argued forcefully for the implementation of the Transportation Plan, destroying railway centres, goods yards and bridges, thereby causing a major impediment to the movement of German forces and their supplies towards the invasion beaches. At the tactical level, the Allied Expeditionary Air Force, comprising the British Second Tactical Air Force under Coningham and the US Ninth Air Force under Lieutenant General Lewis H. Brereton, was wholly committed to executing the Transportation Plan. At the strategic level, on the other hand, Arthur **Harris** of Bomber Command, Lieutenant General Jimmy Doolittle of the US Eighth Air Force and Carl Spaatz, now overall commander of the US Strategic Air Forces in Europe, wanted to continue with what they had been doing, in Harris's case the continuation of area bombing, in Doolittle's and Spaatz's a focus on crippling German fighter production in Operation POINTBLANK. The Combined Chiefs of Staff came down in favour of the Transportation Plan, placing the strategic bombing forces at the disposal of Tedder, acting on behalf of the Supreme Commander, in the run-up to the invasion, during the invasion itself and for an unspecified time thereafter.

This placed Tedder in a position of great responsibility. On the whole his relationships with the air commanders were excellent. The attacks in the run-up to the invasion were widely spread, with more focus on the Pas de Calais than on Normandy, so as to persuade the Germans that the landings would take place at the former site. Because of both this and the more general attrition wrought on the Luftwaffe by the Allied air forces, the Germans put up little opposition in the air during the early stages of the land campaign, and the Allied Air Forces retained their dominance thereafter.

Such problems as Tedder encountered did not lie with his air force colleagues, but with the Commander of 21st Army Group, Bernard Montgomery. The relationship of the two men, which had begun so well in Egypt in August 1942, had deteriorated during the North African and Sicilian campaigns and had not improved subsequently. Tedder had two major problems with Montgomery. The first was the latter's inability to capture German airfields in Normandy, notably the large one at Carpiquet, southeast of Caen. Nevertheless, a number of new airfields were constructed, and Harry Broadhurst, AOC 83 Group, the close support element of the Second Tactical Air Force, and Major General Pete Quesada, his USAAF opposite number, were still able to provide an excellent level of support to 21st Army Group. The second was also related to apparent promises not being delivered. This was the case in particular with Operation GOODWOOD in July 1944, which Montgomery launched with a view to rolling up the right wing of the German forces in Normandy. In this case Montgomery had persuaded Harris, with whom he was on excellent terms, to lay down a carpet of bombs to allow British ground forces to advance towards Falaise. Bomber Command did what was required of them, but the ground forces were pulled up at the Bouguebus Ridge, well short of what Tedder and his colleagues were expecting.

By the beginning of August 1944 the Allied Air Forces in Normandy were at the top of their game. A German attempt to cut off the advance of the US ground forces into Brittany and towards Paris was foiled at Mortain, whilst what remained of the German forces were substantially destroyed at Falaise, although once again Tedder was critical of Montgomery for his inability to cut off the enemy's retreat to the Seine more effectively.

Following the subsequent Allied advance into Northern France and Belgium, the autumn and winter of 1944/45 proved to be more difficult, as the British were defeated at Arnhem and thus unable to break out into the North German Plain, whilst Antwerp, the best port available to the Allies, took a very long time to open. The German counter-attack in the Ardennes took the Allies by surprise and, in its early stages, the Allied air forces were hampered by very poor weather; but when this improved, they made a major contribution to the elimination of 'the Bulge'. The last fling of the Luftwaffe in the west took place on New Year's Day 1945, when it attacked Allied airfields in great strength and destroyed a very large number of aircraft on the ground. However, the Allies could re-equip very quickly and lost very few pilots, whilst the Germans were unable to make up their losses.

With the Allied air forces supreme, Tedder was able to focus more on his other role, as Eisenhower's deputy. This was, in its way, no less demanding, dealing with strong characters like Montgomery on the British side and George Patton on the American, but the result of the campaign, and indeed of the wider war, was inevitable. Following the provisional signing of a surrender document at Eisenhower's HQ at Reims on 7 May 1945, it was Tedder who signed the formal document in Berlin on behalf of the Western Allies, with Marshal Zhukov signing for the Soviet Union.

Tedder succeeded Portal as CAS on 1 January 1946 and was created a baron on the same day. He now had to preside over the running-down of the RAF to a peacetime establishment, which proved to be a far from easy assignment, as the allocation of funds from the Treasury was inevitably less than he would have hoped for. He became the Chairman of the Chiefs of Staff Committee, with Montgomery and Admiral of the Fleet Sir John Cunningham as his fellow members. Tedder's relationship with the former had not improved and Montgomery took to sending his Vice-Chief to represent him at the Chiefs of Staff's meetings unless Tedder was absent. There was a great deal of hard but unglamorous work as the RAF began to modernize, with the first jet aircraft already in service and many more on the drawing board. Tedder stepped down exactly four years later; his own choice to succeed him was Ralph **Cochrane**, but the Prime Minister, Clement Attlee, chose John **Slessor**.

Although Tedder had wanted to retire, he was persuaded by Attlee to become Chairman of the British Joint Services Mission in Washington, with a view to providing a strong British input on the establishment of NATO as a bulwark against Soviet expansion. He was there for just a year before retiring fully, becoming Chancellor of Cambridge University and taking on many other appointments, notably as a Governor of the BBC.

Tedder must be numbered not only amongst the top leaders of the RAF, but also, along with Portal, Dowding and Harris, as one of the Great Men of the War. Not a man to beat his own drum very hard, he was recognized for his cool competence, his capability as a commander of ever larger formations and his excellent relationship with Great Britain's foremost ally. For reasons which have never been entirely clear, but probably had to do with his dislike of Beaverbrook, which was mutual, he got off to a rocky start with Churchill, but even the Prime Minister had to accept in the end that he was instrumental to ultimate victory.

Appendix

War and Post-war Careers of Other Air Officers Referred to in the Text

Air Marshal Sir Philip *Babington* KCB, MC, AFC
1936   Director of Postings
1940   Air Member for Personnel
1942   AOC-in-C Flying Training Command
1945   Retired

Air Chief Marshal Sir John *Baker* GCB, DSO, MC, DFC
1940   Deputy Director of Plans
1941   Director of Bomber Operations
1943   SASO Air Forces in India
1943   SASO Air Command South-East Asia
1945   AOC 12 Group
1946   Director-General of Personnel
1948   AOC-in-C Coastal Command
1950   C-in-C Middle East Air Force
1952   Deputy Chief of the Air Staff
1952   Vice-Chief of the Air Staff
1953   Controller of Aircraft, Ministry of Supply
1956   Retired

Air Marshal Sir John *Baldwin* KBE, CB, DSO
1939   AOC 3 Group
1942   Acting AOC-in-C Bomber Command
1942   Deputy AOC-in-C India
1943   AOC Tactical Air Force (Burma) – ACSEA
1943   AOC 3rd Tactical Air Force – ACSEA
1944   Retired

Air Vice-Marshal Sir Quintin *Brand* KBE, MC, DFC
1936   Director of Repair and Maintenance
1940   Director of Maintenance and Design

War and Post-war Careers of Other Air Officers Referred to in the Text   285

1940   AOC 10 Group
1941   AOC 20 Group
1943   Retired

Air Chief Marshal Sir Robert *Brooke-Popham* GCVO, KCB, CMG, DSO, AFC
1939   Head of RAF Training Mission, Canada
1940   Head of RAF Training Mission, South Africa
1940   C–in–C Far East Command
1942   Retired

Air Vice-Marshal Sir Leslie *Brown* KCB, CBE, DSC, AFC
1939   SASO HQ Egypt
1939   OC 253 Wing
1940   SASO 202 Group
1941   OC AHQ Cyrenaica
1941   OC Iraq Relief Force
1941   AOC HQ RAF Palestine and Trans-Jordan
1941   AHQ Levant
1943   AOC 84 Group
1944   Commandant, School of Land/Air Warfare
1949   Retired

Air Vice-Marshal S. O. *Bufton* CB, DFC
1940   Attended 10 OTU
1940   OC 10 Squadron
1941   OC 76 Sqn
1941   OC RAF Pocklington
1941   Deputy Director of Bomber Operations
1943   Director of Bomber Operations
1945   AOC AHQ Egypt
1946   Attended Imperial Defence College
1947   Commandant, Central Bomber Establishment
1948   Deputy Chief of Staff (Operations/Plans), Air HQ Western Europe
1951   Director of Weapons
1952   AOA Bomber Command
1953   AOC RAF Aden
1955   SASO Bomber Command
1958   Assistant Chief of Staff (Intelligence)
1958   Retired

286   Churchill's Eagles

Air Chief Marshal Sir Charles *Burnett* KCB, CBE, DSO
1939   Inspector-General of the RAF
1940   Chief of the Air Staff, Royal Australian Air Force
1942   Retired

Air Marshal Sir Roderick *Carr* KBE, CB, DFC, AFC
1939   Base Area Commander, Advanced Air Striking Force
1940   AOC 61 Group
1940   AOC, HQ RAF in Northern Ireland
1941   AOC 4 Group
1945   Deputy COS (Air), SHAEF
1945   Air Marshal Commanding, Base Air Forces South-East Asia
1946   AOC in C India
1947   Retired

Air Vice-Marshal R. *Collishaw* CB, DSO*, OBE, DSC, DFC
1939   AOC Egypt
1939   AOC 202 Group
1941   AOC 204 Group
1941   Air Staff HQ Fighter Command
1942   AOC 14 Group
1943   Retired

Air Chief Marshal Sir Alec *Coryton* KCB, KBE, MVO
1940   Director of Operations (Overseas)
1942   AOC 5 Group
1943   Air Staff, Air Ministry
1943   Assistant Chief of the Air Staff (Operations)
1944   Commander 3rd Tactical Air Force
1944   Commander RAF Bengal & Burma
1945   Air Marshal Commanding RAF Burma
1945   Air Marshal Commanding AHQ Burma
1945   Controller of Research and Development, Ministry of Aircraft
        Production
1946   Controller of Supplies (Air), Ministry of Supply
1950   Chief Executive Guided Weapons, Ministry of Supply
1951   Retired

War and Post-war Careers of Other Air Officers Referred to in the Text 287

Air Chief Marshal Sir Christopher *Courtney* GBE, KCB, DSO
1939   AOC in C Reserve Command
1940   Air Member for Supply and Organisation
1945   Retired

Air Marshal Sir John *D'Albiac* KCVO, KBE, CB, DSO
1939   AOC Palestine and Transjordan
1940   AOC British Air Forces in Greece
1941   AOC Palestine and Transjordan
1941   AOC Iraq
1942   AOC 222 Group
1942   AOC 2 Group
1943   AO, Tactical Air Force
1944   Deputy Commander Mediterranean Allied Tactical Air Force
1944   Attached to HQ Tactical Air Force Central Mediterranean Forces
1944   Director-General of Personnel (Permanent Commission Selection Board)
1947   Retired

Air Marshal Sir Thomas *Elmhurst* KBE, CB
1939   OC RAF Abingdon
1940   Deputy Director of Intelligence (3)
1940   Controller, HQ Fighter Command
1940   RAF Member, British Mission to Turkish General Staff
1941   AOC 202 Group
1942   AOA, HQ Desert Air Force
1942   AOC, AHQ Egypt
1943   AOA, HQ North-West Allied Tactical Air Forces
1943   AOA, HQ 2nd Tactical Air Force
1945   Assistant Chief of the Air Staff (Intelligence)
1947   Chief of Inter-Service Administration in India
1947   AOC, Royal Indian Air Force
1950   Retired

Air Marshal Sir Victor *Goddard* KCB, CBE
1939   SOA Air Component BEF
1939   SASO Air Component BEF
1940   Director of Military Co-operation
1941   CAS RNZAF Pacific

288   Churchill's Eagles

1943   AOA Air Forces in India
1944   AOA ACSEA
1946   Air Representative Washington DC
1948   Air Member for Technical Services
1951   Retired

Air Marshal Sir Leslie *Gossage* KCB, CVO, DSO, MC
1936   AOC 11 Group
1940   Inspector-General of the RAF
1940   Air Member for Personnel
1940   AOC in C Balloon Command
1944   Chief Commandant and Director-General, Air Training Corps
1946   Retired

Air Chief Marshal Sir Edmund *Hudlestone* GCB, CBE
1939   Instructor, Air Staff College, Turkey
1941   Air Staff, HQ Middle East Command
1943   Member, Joint Planning Staff for invasion of Sicily
1943   SASO, North African Tactical Air Force
1944   AOC 84 Group
1946   Attended Imperial Defence College
1948   Head of UK Delegation to Western Union Military Staff Committee
1950   AOC 1 Group
1951   Deputy Chief of Staff – Plans & Policy, HQ SHAPE
1953   AOC 3 Group
1956   RAF Instructor, Imperial Defence College
1956   Chief of Staff (Air) to C in C, Operation 'Musketeer' (Suez Crisis)
1957   Vice Chief of the Air Staff
1962   AOC-in-C Transport Command
1963   Commander, Allied Air Forces Central Europe
1964   Deputy C-in-C, Allied Forces Central Europe
1966   C-in-C, Allied Forces Central Europe
1967   Retired

Air Marshal Sir Alan *Lees* KCB, CBE, DSO, AFC
1939   Senior Staff Officer HQ Bomber Command
1941   AOC 2 Group
1942   AOC 222 Group India
1944   AOA ACSEA

War and Post-war Careers of Other Air Officers Referred to in the Text 289

1945 Planning Post-War RAFVR & RAuxAF
1946 AOC-in-C Reserve Command
1949 Retired

Air Vice-Marshal R *Leckie* CB, DSO, DSC, DFC
1938 AOC RAF Mediterranean
1940 Director of Training RCAF
1941 Air Member for Training RCAF
1943 Acting Chief of Staff RCAF
1944 Chief of Staff RCAF
1947 Retired

Air Chief Marshal Sir Charles *Medhurst* KCB, OBE, MC
1937 Air Attaché, Rome
1940 RAF Secretary, Supreme War Council
1940 Director of Allied Air Co-Operation
1940 Director of Plans
1941 Assistant Chief of the Air Staff (Intelligence)
1942 Temporary Vice-Chief of the Air Staff
1943 Assistant Chief of the Air Staff (Policy)
1943 Commandant RAF Staff College
1945 AOC-in-C RAF Middle East Command
1945 Air C-in-C Mediterranean and Middle East Command
1948 Head of British Joint Services Mission, Washington
1950 Retired

Air Chief Marshal Sir William *Mitchell* KCB, CBE, DSO, MC, AFC
1939 AOC-in-C, RAF Middle East
1940 Inspector-General of the RAF
1941 Retired

Air Marshal Sir Richard *Peck* KCB, OBE
1939 Director of Operations
1939 Director-General of Operations
1940 Assistant Chief of the Air Staff (General)
1946 Retired

Air Chief Marshal Sir George *Pirie* KCB, KBE, MC, DFC
1937 Air Attaché, Washington
1941 AOC Northern Ireland

290   Churchill's Eagles

1941   AOA Middle East Command
1943   Director of War Organisation
1943   Director-General of Organisation
1945   Deputy Air C-in-C, Air Command South-East Asia
1946   AOC-in C-Air Command South-East Asia
1946   AOC-in-C Air Command Far East
1948   Inspector-General of the RAF
1948   Air Member for Supply and Organisation
1950   Head of RAF Staff, British Joint Services Mission – Washington
1951   Retired

Air Marshal Sir Patrick *Playfair* KBE, CB, CVO, MC
1938   AOC 1 Group
1939   AOC Advanced Air Striking Force
1940   AOC-in-C Air Forces in India
1942   Retired

Air Vice-Marshal Richard *Saul* CB
1939   AOC 13 Group
1940   AOC 12 Group
1943   AOC Air Defences Eastern Mediterranean
1944   Retired

Air Marshal Sir Robert *Saundby* KCB, KBE, DFC, AFC
1938   Director of Operational Requirements
1940   Assistant Chief of the Air Staff (Operational Requirements and Tactics)
1940   SASO HQ Bomber Command
1943   Deputy AOC-in-C Bomber Command
1946   Retired

Air Marshal Sir Ralph *Sorley* KCB, OBE, DSC, DFC
1939   SASO 6 Group
1940   Commandant Aeroplane and Armament Experimental Establishment
1941   Assistant Chief of the Air Staff (Operational Requirements and Tactics)
1942   Assistant Chief of the Air Staff (Technical)
1943   Assistant Chief of the Air Staff (Technical Requirement)
1943   Controller of Research & Development, MAP

War and Post-war Careers of Other Air Officers Referred to in the Text 291

1943	(Additional Member of the Air Council)
1945	AOC-in-C Technical Training Command
1948	Retired

Air Marshal Sir Bertine *Sutton* KBE, CB, DSO, MC

1939	AOC 21 Group
1940	AOC 24 Group
1940	Attached to staff of C-in-C, Home Forces
1941	Commandant RAF Staff College
1942	Air Member for Personnel
1945	Retired

Air Marshal Sir William *Welsh* KCB, DSC, AFC

1937	Air Member for Supply and Organisation
1940	AOC 11 Group
1940	AOC-in-C Reserve Command
1940	AOC-in-C Technical Training Command
1941	AOC-in-C Flying Training Command
1942	Controller of Operations from Gibraltar for Operation 'Torch'
1942	AOC Eastern Air Command
1943	Head of RAF Delegation, Washington DC
1944	Retired

Air Marshal Sir Thomas *Williams* KCB, OBE, MC, DFC

1939	Air Staff 1 Group
1939	Air Staff Advanced Air Striking Force
1940	Air Staff 1 Group
1940	Officer Commanding RAF Watton
1941	SASO 2 Group
1941	Deputy SASO Bomber Command
1942	SASO to C-in-C Far East
1942	SASO Air Forces in India
1943	AOC AHQ Bengal
1943	Deputy Commander Eastern Air Command - ACSEA
1944	Assistant Chief of the Air Staff (Operations)
1947	Commandant RAF Staff College
1948	AOC-in-C British Air Forces of Occupation
1951	Inspector-General of the RAF
1953	Retired

Abbreviations

2TAF	Second Tactical Air Force
3TAF	Third Tactical Air Force
AA	Anti-Aircraft
AAF	Auxiliary Air Force
AASC	Army Air Support Control
AASF	Advanced Air Striking Force
ACAS	Assistant Chief of the Air Staff
ACIGS	Assistant Chief of the Imperial General Staff
ACM	Air Chief Marshal
ADGB	Air Defence of Great Britain
AEAF	Allied Expeditionary Air Force
AFC	Air Force Cross
AHQ	Air Headquarters
AM	Air Marshal
AM	Albert Medal
AMP	Air Member for Personnel
AMRD	Air Member for Research & Development
AMSO	Air Member for Supply & Organisation
AMT	Air Member for Training
AOA	Air Officer Administration
AOC	Air Officer Commanding
AOC-in-C	Air Officer Commanding-in-Chief
ASV	Air to Surface Vessel (Radar)
ATFERO	Atlantic Ferry Organization
AVM	Air Vice-Marshal
BA	Bachelor of Arts
BAF	Balkan Air Force
BAFF	British Air Forces in France
BEF	British Expeditionary Force
BOAC	British Overseas Airways Corporation
Bt	Baronet
CAMS	Catapult Aircraft Merchant Ships

Abbreviations 293

CAS	Chief of the Air Staff
CB	Companion of the Order of the Bath
CBE	Commander of the Order of the British Empire
CID	Committee of Imperial Defence
CIE	Companion of the Order of the Indian Empire
CIGS	Chief of the Imperial General Staff
CMG	Companion of the Order of St Michael & St George
CO	Commanding Officer
CSO	Chief Staff Officer
DAF	Desert Air Force
DCAS	Deputy Chief of the Air Staff
DFC	Distinguished Flying Cross
DL	Deputy Lieutenant
DSC	Distinguished Service Cross
DSO	Distinguished Service Order
EFTS	Elementary Flying Training School
ELAS	Greek People's Liberation Army
FTS	Flying Training School
GBE	Knight Grand Cross of the Order of the British Empire
GCB	Knight Grand Cross of the Order of the Bath
GCMG	Knight Grand Cross of the Order of St Michael & St George
GCVO	Knight Grand Cross of the Royal Victorian Order
GOC	General Officer Commanding
HCU	Heavy Conversion Unit
HMS	His Majesty's Ship
HQ	Headquarters
H2S	Ground Scanning Airborne Radar
IDC	Imperial Defence College
JPS	Joint Planning Staff
KBE	Knight Commander of the Order of the British Empire
KCB	Knight Commander of the Order of the Bath
KG	Knight of the Order of the Garter
MAAF	Mediterranean Allied Air Forces
MAP	Ministry of Aircraft Production
MC	Military Cross
MRAF	Marshal of the Royal Air Force
NATAF	North African Tactical Air Force
NATO	North Atlantic Treaty Organization
OAMCU	Overseas Air Movements Control Unit

OBE	Officer of the Order of the British Empire
OM	Order of Merit
OTU	Operational Training Unit
PFF	Pathfinder Force
RAF	Royal Air Force
RAAF	Royal Australian Air Force
RAFVR	Royal Air Force Volunteer Reserve
RAuxAF	Royal Auxiliary Air Force
RCAF	Royal Canadian Air Force
RFC	Royal Flying Corps
RN	Royal Navy
RNAS	Royal Naval Air Service
RNVR	Royal Navy Volunteer Reserve
SAAF	South African Air Force
SASO	Senior Air Staff Officer
SFTS	Service Flying Training School
TA	Territorial Army
TAF	Tactical Air Force
UK	United Kingdom
USA	United States of America
USAAF	United States Army Air Forces
USAF	United States Air Force
WAAF	Women's Auxiliary Air Force
WDAF	Western Desert Air Force
VCAS	Vice-Chief of the Air Staff

Bibliography

Beevor, Antony, *The Second World War*, London 2012

Bennett, Donald, *Pathfinder*, London 1958 & 1983

Bowyer, Chaz, and Turner, Michael, *Royal Air Force – The aircraft in service since 1918*, Feltham 1981

Bowyer, Michael J.F., *2 Group RAF – A Complete History, 1936–1945*, London 1974

Bramson, Alan, *Master Airman – A Biography of Air Vice-Marshal Donald Bennett*, Shrewsbury 1985

Brickhill, Paul, *The Dam Busters*, London 1951

Cheshire, Leonard, *Bomber Pilot*, London 1943

Cheshire, Leonard, *The Face of Victory*, London 1961

Churchill, Winston S, *The Second World War, Volumes I–VI*, London 1949–1954

Cole, Christopher & Grant, Roderick, *But Not In Anger – The RAF in the Transport Role*, Shepperton 1979

Delve, Ken, *Fighter Command 1936–1968, An Operational Historical Record*, Barnsley 2007

Douglas, Sholto, with Wright, Robert, *Years of Command*, London 1966

Embry, Basil, *Mission Completed*, London 1957

Evans, Bryn, *The Decisive Campaigns of the Desert Air Force 1942–1945*, Barnsley 2014

Falconer, Jonathan, *Bomber Command Handbook 1939–1945*, Stroud 1998

Furse, Anthony, *Wilfred Freeman – The Genius behind Allied survival and air supremacy 1939 to 1945*, Staplehurst 1999

Gunston, Bill, *Aircraft of World War II*, London 1985

Harris, Arthur, *Bomber Offensive*, London 1947

Hastings, Max, *Bomber Command*, London 1979

Hough, Richard and Richards, Dennis, *The Battle of Britain – The Jubilee History*, London 1989

Joubert de la Ferté, Philip, *The Fated Sky*, London 1952

Lawrence, W J, *No. 5 Bomber Group RAF*, London 1951

Lloyd, Hugh, *Briefed to Attack – Malta's part in African victory*, London 1949

Longmore, Arthur, *From Sea to Sky, 1910–1945*, Frome & London 1946

Mead, Richard, *Dambuster-in-Chief – The Life of Air Chief Marshal Sir Ralph Cochrane*, Barnsley 2020

Melinsky, Hugh, *Forming the Pathfinders – The Career of Air Vice-Marshal Sydney Bufton*, Stroud 2010

Messenger, Charles, *'Bomber' Harris and the Strategic Bombing Offensive, 1939–1945*, London 1984

Middlebrook, Martin & Everitt, Chris, *The Bomber Command War Diaries – An Operational Reference Book 1939–1945*, Harmondsworth 1985

Miller, Russell, *Boom – The Life of Viscount Trenchard, Father of the RAF*, London 2016

Mondey, David, *The Hamlyn Concise Guide to British Aircraft of World War II*, London 1994

Mondey, David, *The Hamlyn Concise Guide to American Aircraft of World War II*, London 1996

Mondey, David, *The Hamlyn Concise Guide to Axis Aircraft of World War II*, London 1996

Newton Dunn, Bill, *Big Wing – The biography of Air Chief Marshal Sir Trafford Leigh-Mallory*, Shrewsbury 1992

Orange, Vincent, *Coningham – A Biography of Air Marshal Sir Arthur Coningham*, London 1990

Orange, Vincent, *Sir Keith Park*, London 1984

Probert, Henry, *High Commanders of the Royal Air Force*, London 1991

Probert, Henry, *Bomber Harris – His Life and Times*, London 2001

Probert, Henry, *The Forgotten Air Force in the War Against Japan 1941–1945*, London 1995

Richards, Dennis, *Portal of Hungerford – The Life of MRAF Viscount Portal of Hungerford, KG, GCB, OM, DSO, MC*, London 1977

Saundby, Robert, *Air Bombardment – The Story of its Development*, London 1961

Saward, Dudley, *Bomber Harris: The Authorised Biography*, London 1984

Slessor, John, *The Central Blue – Recollections and Reflections*, London 1956

Sturtivant, Ray, with Hamlin, John, *Royal Air Force Flying Training and Support Units since 1912*, Staplefield 2012

Tedder, Arthur, *With Prejudice – War Memoirs*, London 1966

Terraine, John, *The Right of the Line – The Royal Air Force in the European War 1939–1945*, London 1945

Ward, Chris, *5 Group Bomber Command – An Operational Record*, Barnsley 2007

Ward, Chris & Smith, Steve, *3 Group Bomber Command – An Operational Record*, Barnsley 2008

Wright, Robert, *Dowding and the Battle of Britain*, London 1969

Wynn, Humphrey, *Forged in War – A History of Royal Air Force Transport Command 1943–1967*, London 1996